CW00707118

THAIL
ORACLE

Down-to-Earth Guide for Independent Travellers

Trains 769 pead
Bus 92 Beach
421 Bankok-Chiag mai
348 Surat → Bankok
92 bus chiang mai to chiang lai

by Jim Rickman

Published by Jim Rickman

THAILAND ORACLE

**Down-to-Earth Guide for
Independent Travellers**

by Jim Rickman

First Edition : January 2001

ISBN: 0-9539531-0-6

Copyright © 2001 by Jim Rickman

Printed in the U.K.

Published by Jim Rickman
Blaenwaun, Coedwig Hudol,
Lampeter SA48 8LS,
Wales, U.K.

Tel: +44 (0)7092-271324
Fax: +44 (0)7092-066001

Author's E-mail: travelbook@supanet.com
Author's Homepage: http://www.travelbook.supanet.com/home.html

Publishing E-mail: travelbook@bizland.com
Publishing Homepage: http://travelbook.bizland.com

Cover design and web pages: Matt Armitage http://www.misanthropy.com

PREFACE

The objective of this book is simply to be as helpful as possible to the independent traveller.

The author is also a traveller and knows that what one needs most upon arrival in a strange town is a map and an indication of where accommodation of an appropriate price and quality is to be found.

To be sure, there are often tourist offices offering without charge colourful maps of dimensions and quality greatly superior to anything which can be fitted into a book of this size. The problem is that without a map it is very difficult to locate those offices.

Accommodation of all prices has been included in this book, and in almost every case the hotels are marked on the maps so that they can be located easily. In general, the author has tried to refrain from making recommendations concerning accommodation because these matters change so quickly. A hotel recommended in a famous guide book (which this is not—yet—of course) quickly becomes overcrowded and often starts to be complacent, so that by the time you—or I—arrive, it may well be the worst place in the town to stay at, rather than the best. Anyway, making your own decisions, or acting on current tips from fellow travellers, is much more fun, just as long as you can locate that accommodation.

The next thing which the author requires from a book is information about transport, so this book has tried to be a true oracle in that respect. Details of virtually every long-distance and medium-distance train and bus service in the country are included, with journey times, frequencies and prices. In the case of the railways, precise timetables are provided, since train times do not change very often or very significantly in Thailand. Bus times tend to change more often, so the frequency of each service is given, rather than exact times. In many cases details of local short-distance transport are also given, especially to likely destinations.

Prices will change, of course, so be prepared to add an appropriate factor to compensate for inflation. Regard these rates as being accurate for the year 2001 and add 10% for each year thereafter.

The author has spent many years visiting Thailand from time to time. His first trip there was in 1975, when many services were still operated by steam train. For interest, here and there in the book excerpts from postcards written home at the time of such visits are included, in the hope that they will be entertaining and informative.

Please heed the author's advice (on page 2) to travel light, but one item not to forget to take with you is this book. Then, wherever you go you will always be able to consult the Oracle.

Happy Travelling!

CONTENTS

PART 1   INTRODUCTION

PART 2   BANGKOK

PART 3   THE EAST

PART 4   THE NORTH-EAST

PART 5   THE NORTH

PART 6   THE SOUTH

THANKS

Thanks are due to a number of people who have helped with the production of this book.

First to family who have tolerated my whims and survived the atmosphere of general panic whilst this was being written. My brother, 'Little Rickman', has been invaluable in supplying bits for a reluctant and idiosyncratic computer, coupled with his own special brand of humour, and tolerant belief that, come what may, it would all go wrong in the end.

Then to my Little Old Mother who has supplied endless cups of coffee, and survived my typing well into the night with a surprising tolerance, and now promises to pack up and dispatch books to whoever might request them (perhaps convinced that this will not be a demanding job!).

My cousin Adrian has supplied technical assistance, and, indeed, has provided the cantankerous computer on which this is being written, for which a considerable debt of gratitude is owed.

Chutima Tachibana has given help with the Thai language, and kindly typed all the words which appear in Thai script in the book. Thank you.

Finally, there are all those in Thailand who were so tolerant of my enquiries and told me, for example, where all the buses in the bus station were going, and how much they cost, even though they could not understand why I could possibly want to know such irrelevant details.

Thanks too to so many people who displayed their kindness to me by, for example, stopping and giving me a ride. They will surely do the same for you, the reader, so do not hesitate to go to this beautiful country before it moves too far into the modern world of speed and greed. Thailand is awaiting your visit.

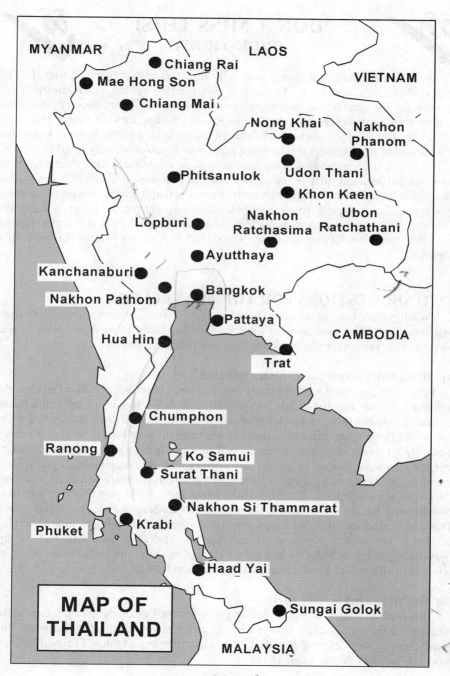

MYANMAR

LAOS

VIETNAM

● Chiang Rai

● Mae Hong Son

● Chiang Mai

Nong Khai ●

Nakhon
Phanom ●

● Phitsanulok

Udon Thani ●

Khon Kaen ●

Lopburi ●

Nakhon
Ratchasima ●

Ubon
Ratchathani ●

● Ayutthaya

Kanchanaburi ●

Nakhon Pathom ●

● Bangkok

Pattaya ●

CAMBODIA

Hua Hin ●

Trat ●

● Chumphon

Ranong ●

● Ko Samui

● Surat Thani

● Nakhon Si Thammarat

Phuket ● Krabi

Haad Yai ●

**MAP OF
THAILAND**

Sungai Golok ●

MALAYSIA

DON'T MISS THIS!
(RICK-TICKS)

Occasionally, here and there, you will find the above marks ('Rick-Ticks') sprinkled through this book. The author has tried to refrain from imposing his opinion on the reader too much and from making too many recommendations, finding from experience that people's likes and dislikes vary so much. However, when you see one of the above marks against the name of a place, you will know that it is the author's suggestion that here is a place which you absolutely should not miss.

When the mark appears against the name of an attraction, rather than a town or geographical location, that is the author's suggestion that, once having got to that place, you should be sure to see that particular attraction. In some instances the mark appears against a place of interest without appearing against the name of the town. This should be construed as meaning that the author does not think it essential to visit this town, but, once having got there, you should be sure not to miss this particular attraction.

TWO SUGGESTIONS FOR THE TRAVELLER

To tell people how to do their travelling is, of course, presumptuous. Each does best travelling in his own way, at his own speed, looking at what he wants to see. Nevertheless, the author would like to offer just two suggestions.

(i) Bring half of what you consider essential

People always travel with too many possessions. Therefore, decide on an absolute minimum — and then bring only half of that. The things to cut out are bulky items. Basically, you can bring as much underwear and as many pairs of socks as you wish, but do not bring spare pairs of trousers and several thick sweaters "in case it turns a bit chilly." Unnecessary encumbrances will turn out to be a real nuisance. Trousers and similar can be washed overnight and worn again the next morning. If you bring a sweater, you should make it a very light one. Moreover, the more you bring, the more likely you are to forget or lose something along the way. If you find that you have brought too much, try to leave the excess somewhere while you travel round Thailand. Remember that the happiest travellers are usually those who are carrying the least. The author recalls once meeting an Australian who had had all his possessions stolen in India. "I had only a change of shirt," he said. "I was never so relieved in all my life! I had a really good time from then on."

(ii) Get up and get moving early

This is always the best way, whether you are travelling or sightseeing. Get on the road before the masses do. It always helps to arrive at your destination early and find somewhere to stay before it gets dark. It is especially important in Thailand because most bus services stop at about 18:00.

PART 1   INTRODUCTION

WHY THAILAND?

What does Thailand have to offer the visitor which cannot be provided by any one of a multitude of other destinations? Basically, it offers beautiful scenery, a wealth of history, relative safety (the standard of driving is the main danger) and excellent cuisine, all at an affordable price.

'Beaches and Buddhas' is a description of the country which sticks in the memory. The author's only advice is that one should not regard these two as alternatives. Since Thailand has both history and recreational places in abundance, try to sample a little of each while you are there.

Does it have drawbacks too? Of course. Nowhere is Utopia. In Thailand, the hot humid climate is sometimes a discouragement. If you are going to lie on the beach all day, you may well enjoy it, but it will not encourage you to walk very far.

Also, the fact that the language is tonal and difficult to acquire easily is a slight problem. Moreover, Thai uses its own alphabet, so you cannot easily read anything either. However, these days more and more people are acquiring the ability to speak some English, so there will be no insuperable difficulties.

Go, therefore, and enjoy it, as you surely will, and do not forget to take this book with you to be your guide. Happy travelling!

PRICES AND TIMES

It is one of the disturbing practicalities of life that prices and times do change, and that prices always seem to go up and never down! The reader will naturally want to know how reliable the information contained in this book is. All information contained herein was gathered or checked during the period April to October 2000.

As for inflation, Thailand was badly hit by the currency crisis of 1997. Before that, there were 25 baht to the U.S. dollar. Following the crisis, the rate was 40 baht to the dollar. However, the level has not changed significantly since the crisis. Nevertheless, the Thai government tried to curtail inflation at the time, with the result that price increases from the crisis are still trickling through the system. In addition, transport has felt the effect of recent increases in oil prices, and these increases too are gradually being passed on. Therefore, one should allow for a certain inflationary factor.

It seems reasonable to suggest that the reader should regard the prices given in this book as being accurate in 2001 and should add 10% per year after that.

As for times of transport services, train times do not change much, so are likely to be reasonably accurate for some years to come. Bus and ferry times, on the other hand, are constantly changing, so in most cases frequencies of services have been stated, rather than exact times. Even so, these too often change. In particular, the reader is likely to notice a steady increase in air-conditioned bus services and a decrease in ordinary buses, as they gradually lose in popularity to their more comfortable and efficient rivals.

GETTING TO THAILAND

One of the reasons why Thailand is so popular as a holiday and travellers' destination is that it can be reached relatively cheaply from almost any place in the world and that it can be used as a free stop-over point on many inter-continental flights. In other words, if you are going somewhere in any case, you may well find that you can visit Thailand for only the additional cost of a 500 baht (U.S.$12) airport tax.

Examples of free stop-overs available in Thailand are flights between Europe and Australia or New Zealand and flights between Japan and Europe. Even when free stops are not available in Thailand, they may well be available in Malaysia or Singapore, and it is not so far from either of those to the southern tip of Thailand. In fact, one of the prime destinations, Phuket, is actually closer to Kuala Lumpur than to Bangkok.

If you want to visit only Thailand, these are examples of the lowest prices currently available for return tickets.

From London	£300
From Sydney/Melbourne	A$1,000
From Los Angeles	U.S.$800
From Tokyo	¥35,000

Of course, such comparatively cheap tickets have conditions and restrictions, but usually nothing too unreasonable.

If you need a ticket out of Thailand, Bangkok is one of the cheapest places in the world for air fares. Almost any place in the world can be reached for the equivalent of U.S.$300 one way.

VISAS AND FORMALITIES

Citizens of most western countries do not need a visa for Thailand. If you come without a visa, you will usually be granted a stay of thirty days upon arrival. This is extendable once only for a fee of Bt500. The extension will be for two weeks. If you stay over your time, you will usually be fined at the rate of Bt200 per day. You are not generally asked to produce an onward or return air ticket upon arrival, and you may enter by air and leave by land, or enter by land and leave by air or by land.

However, if you prefer, you may obtain a visa prior to arrival. The cost of this varies according to where it is obtained. If you enter with a visa, you will usually be granted a stay of sixty days. This too is extendable once for a fee of Bt500. The extension will be for thirty days.

There is nothing to prevent you from leaving Thailand and returning immediately and thus being granted a further period of stay, This can be achieved by land by making a visit to Malaysia, Laos, Myanmar or Cambodia. There are some points over which to exercise caution, however. One is that in some places you can choose whether to have a day trip to another country recorded in your passport (with greater bureaucracy) or not (with less bureaucracy). If you choose the latter option, there will be no record of the visit and you will be given no extra time. Also remember that if you have been granted a sixty day stay, by virtue of having a visa, and then you leave the country, your visa will have been used and so upon return you will be given only a thirty day stay. If you want to prevent this from happening, you must obtain a re-entry visa, for which there will be a fee, from the Immigration Office prior to departure. Also remember that when you leave the country without a re-entry visa, in any case, any unused portion of your original period of stay will be lost. In other words, you do not get an additional one month; you get a new one month to run from the date of your re-entry.

Surprisingly, the same principle applies to an extension. The new period is not usually added on to the old. It starts to run immediately, from the date on which you apply for it, so it is best to leave the application until fairly near the last minute.

HEALTH

There are no inoculation requirements for Thailand (at the time of writing). Occasionally one hears of cases of cholera in the region, so having an inoculation would do no harm, but the risk is not great.

Malaria exists in the hill regions in the north. Again the risk is not great in the towns, but if you plan to go trekking it would be a wise precaution to take anti-malaria tablets. Note that they have to be taken not only at the time of exposure to the infection, but for a period before and after. The period varies according to the tablet, but is usually at least two weeks either side, so plan well in advance.

There are enormous numbers of stray dogs in Thailand, and therefore there is a risk of rabies. Some people choose to have anti-rabies injections before coming, but the general thought is that it is sufficient to be aware of the risk and act immediately if one is unfortunate enough to get bitten, or even scratched. If that happens, you should go at once to the nearest hospital or consult a doctor.

There is also plenty of AIDS in Thailand, so be very careful. In fact, education on this point is generally good, so maybe Thailand, unlike some less educated nations, will manage to contain the spread of the disease. The problem is that prostitution is so accepted here that containment is not easy.

Hepatitis can be contracted through eating bad food or drinking contaminated water, but the disease is not prevalent. In fact, water in most large towns in Thailand is potable. Even though most visitors are wary, the author drinks tap water in all major places and suffers no ill effects.

As for food, sooner or later you are sure to eat something bad. Taking too many precautions will only spoil your holiday, and however much care you take it will probably happen anyway. The most likely result is diarrhœa for a day or two. The author's remedy in such circumstances is not to eat anything for at least twenty-four hours, but to drink plenty (to avoid dehydration).

These days, most common drugs, medications and health requirements are available in Thailand. Only prescription drugs or favoured brands need to be brought with you. Moreover, chemists nearly always speak English, as their training so requires. In fact the author finds that if I have any minor ailment the simplest thing to do is to go to a chemist and ask, "What should I do about this?" His advice is usually as good as any doctor's for everyday matters and he has the remedy at hand.

Other dangers include over-friendly snakes and scorpions. The author has found each of these in my room on one or more occasion, but has never had the misfortune to be bitten or stung. I have, however, been somewhere (Phuket) where somebody else was bitten by a snake. Although he was extremely worried, he survived to be living proof that not all snakes are poisonous. If you are unlucky enough to get bitten, try to kill the snake, if possible, or at least get a good description of it, because treatment with the correct antidote for that particular type of snake venom will greatly improve your chances of survival and minimise the discomfort to be endured.

If fact, though, to end this section by putting matters in perspective, it is appropriate to mention that the greatest risks to one's health in Thailand are the dangerous pastimes of being in or on a moving vehicle or of trying to cross the road in front of one. Those are the times to be really careful!

GEOGRAPHY

Thailand has a total area of 513,115 square kilometres, which makes it similar in size to France, or to the state of Texas in the U.S.A.

The country is shaped something like a frying pan with a long handle, the handle pointing south. Those with more poetic imaginations sometimes say that it looks like an elephant's head with the long trunk stretching down to Malaysia.

Much of the pan-handle is shared with Myanmar (Burma), Myanmar owning the western side and Thailand the eastern. At its narrowest point, just south of Prachuap Khiri Khan, Thailand is only twelve kilometres wide. Myanmar continues up the western side of the pan and across the top, where it meets Laos at the spot known as the Golden Triangle. At this location, one can stand in Thailand and look across the tip of Myanmar to Laos on the other side of the Mekong River. The Mekong continues to form a natural border between Thailand and Laos on the eastern side of the former, until, in the south-east, Cambodia is reached and takes a bite out of the frying pan surface.

Thailand is a surprisingly mountainous country. The peaks are not so high, but there are many of them. Not only is much of the mainland mountainous, but also many of the islands have a beautiful backdrop of hills. The highest point in Thailand is Doi (Mt.) Inthanon, near Chiang Mai, at 2,565 metres.

Thailand is usually divided into five areas, a division followed in this book. First there is Bangkok and the surrounding area. This is where some differences occur, because nobody seems quite sure where to draw the limits of this area. Often all the fertile plains are included, which seems geographically sensible. However, this book, as a guide book, has drawn the limit as the capital itself and places which can easily be visited as a day trip (and there are not many).

Next is the small area to the east and south-east of Bangkok (referred to in this book as 'The East'), between the capital and the border with Cambodia. For the visitor, this is an area of beaches. For Thailand, it is an area for the promotion of new industrial growth.

North of Cambodia lies the region traditionally known as I-san, the least developed and poorest part of the country, but a region with a long history and a depth of culture. This book refers to it simply as 'The North-East'.

Further to the west is the area which this book has called 'The North'. This is probably the most interesting part of the country for the visitor. It contains a great deal of the history of the country and is also an area of natural beauty.

Finally, 'The South' extends all the way down to the southern border with Malaysia, more than a thousand kilometres from Bangkok. For the visitor, it is another area of beaches. For Thais it is a region of relative prosperity, supported by such industries as fishing, rubber plantations and, of course, tourism.

CLIMATE

Thailand lies wholly within the tropics. Although there are seasons, as a basic guide it is hot and humid always and in all places.

The three seasons are the cool season, from November until February; the hot season, from March until May; and the rainy season, from June until October. The cool season is usually regarded as the ideal time to visit, although the word 'cool' should be regarded as being relative only. You will not be needing an overcoat. The author's opinion, however, is that you should just visit at any convenient time and not worry about the weather. Even the rainy season, the result of the monsoons which are prevalent at that time, is not a great inconvenience. It usually rains torrentially for an hour or so, and then clears up. If it remains cloudy, then at least you can walk around without getting exhausted by the heat. In fact, the author rather likes the rainy season. It seems to have character!

Places in the north of Thailand are slightly cooler than those in the south, mainly because they are at higher altitude. However, they are not very much cooler, unless you go to the tops of mountains.

The highest temperatures encountered in Thailand are around 38°C, but nearly always the humidity is high, so that it feels even hotter.

The country gets plenty of rain, so floods are not uncommon, even in Bangkok, a city which is slowly subsiding, to make the situation even worse. At some times of the year, a certain amount of paddling may be required.

As for clothing, short-sleeved shirts are generally all that will be needed, but it would be wise to bring one light pullover with you.

HISTORY

Thailand has, in fact, been an important area in the development of the human race. It is thought that the first agriculturists may have lived here and also that the Thai people may have been the first metalworkers. However, this is, to some extent, surmise and the recorded history of the region begins much later.

Indian Buddhist missionaries probably came to Thailand in the second or third century B.C., at which time the area was a loose collection of city states. In time this collection became known as Dvaravati. The Dvaravati Kingdom reached its peak in the sixth to eleventh centuries A.D. and its principal city was Nakhon Pathom, 56 kilometres west of modern-day Bangkok. This is probably the oldest city in Thailand, dating from the third century B.C., and it was a centre of art and culture.

In the eleventh century, the Dvaravati Kingdom suffered a rapid decline, succumbing to the might of the Khmer who invaded from the east (present day Cambodia). The Khmer established their headquarters at modern-day Lopburi, 133 kilometres north of Bangkok, Lopburi, then known as Lavo, having already become an important city during the Dvaravati period. Ruins from this period of Khmer dominance still remain, both in Lopburi, in the form of Phra Prang Sam Yot, and at the famous temples of Phimai and Phanom Rung. Phimai and Phanom Rung, in fact, may well have been the prototypes for the magnificent Angkor Wat complex in Cambodia, and every visitor to Thailand should place one of these two on his list of essential excursions. It was the Khmer who first referred to the Thais as *Syam* ('dark people'), because their skin was of a darker hue than theirs, and from this the name Siam derived.

In the middle of the thirteenth century, the Thais in Lopburi rebelled against their Khmer rulers and took control themselves. They have held power there ever since.

Meanwhile, the south of what is now Thailand was controlled by the Srivichaya Empire, which had its seat of power in Sumatra. Its capital in the Malay Peninsula was at Chaiya, 54 kilometres north of modern-day Surat Thani. Both there and at Nakhon Si Thammarat, south of Surat Thani, relics of this ancient Empire remain.

In the northern part of what is now Thailand, the unification of various small principalities led to the creation, in the thirteenth century, of the first real Thai state. In 1238, Sukhothai declared its independence, taking advantage of the decline in

Khmer influence in the east and the weakening of the Srivichaya Empire in the south. This is still regarded by most Thais as the Golden Age of the nation. The first king of Sukhothai was King Sri Indrathit, a capable leader who governed for forty years. In 1278 he was succeeded by his second son, who became King Ramkhamhaeng (1278 – 1317). It was King Ramkhamhaeng who laid the foundations of the Thai nation. Under his guidance, Sukhothai expanded peacefully until it stretched from Vientiane to the Bay of Bengal. Friendly relations were established with China and King Ramkhamhaeng made two visits there to meet the Emperor Kublai Khan. It was also King Ramkhamhaeng who was responsible for introducing in 1283 the Thai alphabet which is still in use today. He promoted Buddhism and believed in an enlightened form of government which would not overburden his citizens. Art and culture flourished and beautiful examples of religious art, in particular, were produced at this time. No wonder that even present-day Thais look back to this period with feelings of nostalgia for the time when their nation was an enlightened world leader. The ruins at Sukhothai, and at Sri Satchanalai nearby, are also sights which should not be missed by any visitor to Thailand interested in the history of the nation.

King Ramkhamhaeng was not alone in his enlightened form of government, though. Further north, the kingdom of Lanna Thai ('Northern Thailand') was being established almost contemporaneously. King Mengrai ascended the throne of Lanna Thai in 1259. He built his first capital at Chiang Saen on the Mekong, another fascinating place to visit. It is now only a small town, but one full of ruins from that era. Not satisfied with that headquarters, King Mengrai then moved to Chiang Rai on the Mae Kok River. Still expanding his territory, he then looked for a new capital further west and further south. He asked his friends King Ramkhamhaeng of Sukhothai and King Ngam Muang of Phayao to help him choose a site for the new city and together, on 14th April 1296, they chose the present location of Chiang Mai. Thus the people of Northern Thailand regard this same historical period as their own Golden Era. Moreover, King Ngam Muang's reign too was the climax of the Phayao Kingdom, so right across this northern part of Thailand a time of peace and prosperity was achieved which was never to be equalled.

This period ended with the rise of Ayutthaya. Ayutthaya, 76 kilometres north of modern-day Bangkok, was founded in 1350 by King U-Thong and gradually grew in power, until, in 1365, it had become strong enough to conquer the declining Sukhothai. It served as the capital of Thailand for 417 years, being ruled by 33 different kings, and became one of the most prosperous cities in Asia. The ruins here too should not be missed by any visitor to the country.

During this long period, conflicts with Burma became common and in 1767 Ayutthaya was finally captured during one of the Burmese incursions. The city was sacked and left in ruins, its opulence completely destroyed and everything of value transported back to Burma.

However, the Burmese did not have the power to hold on to their conquest. They were expelled by General Phraya Taksin, who established a new Thai capital at

Thonburi on the west bank of the Chao Phraya River, opposite modern-day Bangkok, and soon became King Taksin.

In 1782, General Chakri became king, assuming the title Rama I and founding the Chakri Dynasty which has reigned ever since. He immediately moved the capital across the river to its current location in Bangkok.

The Chakri Dynasty has produced some very able kings, of whom the most famous are King Mongkut (Rama IV, 1851 – 1868) and his son King Chulalongkorn (Rama V, 1868 – 1910). King Mongkut, the monarch featured in *Anna and the King of Siam* and *The King and I*, spent much of his life as a Buddhist monk and was a particularly well educated man. When he became king, therefore, he introduced an effective education system and also established diplomatic relations with several powerful European nations, whilst managing astutely to avoid colonisation.

King Chulalongkorn was the man who modernised Thailand. Railways were built, the legal system revised and a civil service established. Thailand became the only country in the region which was not a colony of a European power, although France managed to acquire a small amount of Thai territory to the east and Britain a small amount to the west. King Chulalongkorn's refined tastes in architecture can be experienced by a visit to his Summer Palace at Bang Pa In, eighteen kilometres south of Ayutthaya.

In 1932, a small group of military officers and civil servants staged a bloodless coup and demanded constitutional reform. King Rama VII agreed and the absolute monarchy was replaced by a constitutional monarchy. After a while, however, the King became disillusioned with these reforms and in 1935 he abdicated, leading to a lengthy period of political instability.

King Rama VIII, the nephew of Rama VII, was only ten years old when he thus had the throne thrust unexpectedly upon him. At the time he was studying in Switzerland and it was decided that he should remain there until he had completed his education. Power in Thailand was wielded by Phibul Songkram who had been one of the leaders in the 1932 revolution.

Within a short period war had come to the region. Phibul agreed to allow the Japanese to use Thai territory in return for not being annexed by that nation. He was also prepared to declare war on Britain and the U.S.A. himself, but was prevented mainly by the intervention of the Thai ambassador to the U.S.A., Seni Pramoj, who was to become Prime Minister at the end of the war.

In 1946 King Rama VIII returned to Thailand for a visit and suddenly died in the Grand Palace in mysterious circumstances. The throne came to his younger brother, King Bumiphol, who was only nineteen and had never had any expectations of being king.

A serious of military dictatorships ensued, punctuated by periodic coups d'état, some of them bloody. Through all of this turmoil, however, the monarchy survived and even proved to be a restraining influence, for the King has himself intervened on more than one occasion to prevent further bloodshed and is a genuinely respected figure.

In 1949, the name of the country was changed officially from Siam to Thailand.

In recent years, more stability has come to Thailand, although the military remains very influential in politics. However, the coups have ceased and the Bangkok curfew disappeared long ago. With stability came an increase in prosperity, as manufacturing nations, such as Japan in particular, started to move their production bases here, where cheap but reasonably skilled labour could be found. Although this new wealth is not well distributed, Thailand could no longer be accurately described as a poor country. One does not encounter desperate poverty in Thailand as one does in some other Asian nations and, although the 1997 currency crisis started here and hit Thailand hard, it had the resilience to recover.

Tourism too has flourished with the improvement in stability and continues to earn revenue for the country. Since Thailand already has a good basic education system, the future appears promising. Moreover, King Bumiphol (Rama IX) himself continues to contribute much to this aura of stability, for he is not only the longest ruling monarch in Thai history, but currently the longest ruling monarch in the world.

TRANSPORT

The options are the same as in most countries, except that it is not very practical to think of using your own vehicle in Thailand, unless you are planning to live here.

Railways

The State Railways of Thailand provides a very good and surprisingly efficient service and this is the author's first recommendation for any visitor. One of the great features of the railways is that if you want comfort, the trains are best and if you want economy, the trains are best again. They are not, however, the same trains.

First a few words about how the system works. If you are planning to travel immediately, you just go to a ticket window at the railway station and purchase a ticket. Tickets are sold from about half an hour before the train is due to depart. Your ticket entitles you to travel only on that train. If it is an ordinary train, you can sit in any seat. If it is a rapid or an express and you are boarding at the station of origin, you will be issued with a seat number and when you get to that seat you will find it already occupied, so you pick a nearby seat. If you are boarding further along the line, there will be no number and you will just have to search for a seat.

The rapid and express trains get crowded, by day and by night, so if you are boarding at the station of origin, go along early. If you are boarding along the way, remember that there are two sides to a train and that both have doors. Passengers will mostly get off on the station side. That makes access from the opposite side quicker in many cases.

As for the ordinary trains, they may get crowded temporarily, but people mostly travel relatively short distances, so passengers are getting on and off all the time and it will not be long before you get a seat. Usually everybody can sit down for most of the journey.

If you are reserving in advance, for first or second class accommodation, either seat or berth, there will be a special room at the station for that purpose, open for normal office hours, or a little longer. For first or second class travel, you will be given a seat or berth number and can expect to be able to travel in the specified seat or berth.

Fares are stated for ordinary trains and then supplementary charges are added according to the standard of train and of accommodation. Here is a list of supplements payable.

Rapid train	Bt40
Express train	Bt60
Special express train	Bt80
Air-conditioned seat	Bt200
Ordinary upper berth, 2nd class	Bt100*
Ordinary lower berth, 2nd class	Bt150†
Air-conditioned upper berth, 2nd class	Bt220*
Air-conditioned lower berth, 2nd class	Bt270†
Air-conditioned berth, 1st class	Bt520

* Bt30 extra in special express, † Bt50 extra in special express
Some trains also offer a catering service for a supplementary fee.

Third class basic fares are approximately Bt1 per five kilometres. In general, a second class ticket costs about double a third class ticket, and a first class ticket costs about double a second class one.

Reservations are always required for first or second class travel, for which reservations there is no extra charge. They may be made up to sixty days in advance. If you want to change a reservation, you may do so once on payment of a nominal fee, currently Bt10. If you want to cancel, you may do so and will lose a portion of the money paid, that portion depending on when the cancellation is made. If you cancel three days or more in advance, you will lose only 20%. The latest time that a cancellation can be accepted is three hours prior to the departure of the train.

The main disadvantage of trains is that there are many places where they do not go, so travel by train always has to be supplemented to some extent by travel by bus. You will see some maps with railway lines reaching distant points such as Chiang Rai, Mukdahan and Krabi, so it must be mentioned that such maps are illustrative only of the optimistic imagination of some railway planner. Plans for these lines clearly must exist, because they have been shown on railway maps for at least a quarter of a century. The problem is that there are, as yet, no tracks there. Actual railway lines are as shown on the railway map in this book. They cover the country reasonably well, but they do not reach all of the places where the visitor is likely to wish to go.

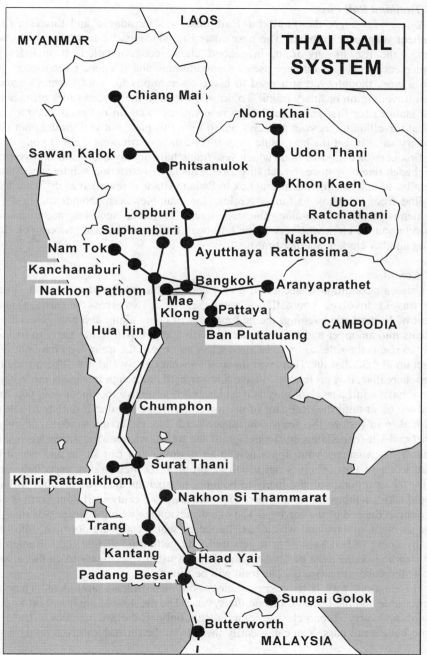

LAOS

MYANMAR

THAI RAIL SYSTEM

Chiang Mai

Nong Khai

Sawan Kalok

Udon Thani

Phitsanulok

Khon Kaen

Ubon Ratchathani

Lopburi

Suphanburi

Nam Tok

Ayutthaya

Nakhon Ratchasima

Kanchanaburi

Nakhon Pathom

Bangkok

Aranyaprathet

Mae Klong

Pattaya

CAMBODIA

Hua Hin

Ban Plutaluang

Chumphon

Surat Thani

Khiri Rattanikhom

Nakhon Si Thammarat

Trang

Kantang

Haad Yai

Padang Besar

Sungai Golok

Butterworth

MALAYSIA

(i)   *Thailand Rail Pass*

A few years ago, the **Thailand Rail Pass** was introduced and this is a truly excellent way to get around. The pass costs Bt2,000, is valid for three weeks and permits the use of any train, in second class accommodation. It includes all supplementary charges for expresses, air-conditioning and sleepers. Even though you have a pass, though, you still need to make reservations for your journeys, except when travelling on ordinary trains. To do so, you go to the special room provided at most stations for first and second class reservations. You do not need to do a great deal of travelling to get your money's worth from this pass, but you should plan your itinerary so as to get the best value from it. The only restrictions are that you cannot use first class accommodation (which few trains have in any case) and that you can travel each line only once in each direction. This latter restriction is interpreted fairly liberally, so that the line from Bangkok to Padang Besar is regarded as different from the line from Bangkok to Sungai Golok, for example, even though the first 945 kilometres of the two are along the same tracks. However, such interpretations will depend upon the clerk who serves you (although there is nothing to prevent you from trying another clerk at another time).

(ii)   *Comfort*

Using air-conditioned sleepers is a very comfortable way to travel around. If day-time travel is involved, you will have a wide seat (only two across the carriage) and a window. In the early evening, the bed-maker will come along and change each pair of seats into an upper and lower curtained berth and you will retire. Early to bed and early to rise is the rule, so try to be tired when you board the train. You may not wish to get up at 4:30, but the Thais will do so somewhat noisily and it will be difficult to sleep thereafter. It is preferable to have a lower berth, although that costs more if you do not have a rail pass. Not only is it wider, but if you have the upper one, you have nowhere to sit until the occupant of the lower berth decides that it is time to ask the bed-maker to restore the seats. The upper berth has either no window, or only a horizontal slit (depending on the design of the train), whereas the lower has a large window, so whatever your upper neighbour is doing you can sit up and watch the countryside go past. Theft is not usually a problem on these trains, especially since all the Thais around you are likely to be more prosperous than you are, but still you should take anything valuable to bed with you. Be more cautious if your berth is near the door at the end of the carriage. The one disadvantage with the sleepers is that you miss so much of Thailand which has slipped by while you were dormant. Minimise this by going to bed soon after it gets dark and getting up at first light. Remember that sleeping berths must be booked, and that it is usually necessary to do this at least two or three days in advance. The train will be full.

For daytime travel, the express air-conditioned railcars are ideal. They are comfortable and the fastest trains on the system. The most rapid are based on English designs and carry second class accommodation only. These are the ones to travel on if you have a rail pass. You can identify them from the timetables given on pages 73 to 74 since they are the only trains which carry nothing but second class. Ask for a window seat, but it will be a matter of chance whether that seat faces forwards or backwards. Again, you must book your seat in advance. The train will be full.

There are also expresses running during the day which carry an air-conditioned second class sitting carriage, which is suitable for rail pass holders. This is usually so air-conditioned that you are issued with a blanket and keep feeling your nose to make sure that it has not frozen off. Quite often there are seats available in this carriage even on the day of travel (possibly due to there being a shortage of eskimos in Thailand at the present time).

Where none of these luxuries is available, all rapid and express trains will carry a second class carriage with superior seating, usually reclinable. A few ordinary trains also have a second class carriage attached.

(iii) Economy

For those who want to be economical, rather than comfortable, the trains are still the best choice. Third class accommodation is quite acceptable on Thai trains and it is very cheap compared with any other option. As long as you are not in too much of a hurry, this is, as always, a good way to meet local people and see the country.

Third class seats are sometimes made of wood (older carriages) and sometimes slightly padded, but with upright backs. The windows open and are usually left open, except when it rains. There is also a metal or wooden sunblind, but that blots out all view. Before boarding a train, you need to consider whether to sit facing forwards or backwards, and on which side to sit. If you face forwards, you will have a view, but will get the wind and dust in your face all the way. Examine your shirt collar at the end of the day! You will also want to sit on the side which is going to be less exposed to the sun. You will never be hungry if you travel third class, because at each stop vendors board, or sell from the platform, so new delicacies are arriving all the time, and none of them very expensive.

Travelling third class is really quite fun by day, but by night it is much less so and not really recommended. There is also more of a danger of theft at night, if you manage to get a few winks of sleep. Thais are basically honest people, but there is always the one who is travelling by night with the purpose of relieving a sleeping traveller of his unnecessary possessions. Put your luggage on the rack a little in front of you. Then it is easier to keep it under observation.

(iv) Speed, Punctuality and Safety

One of the impressive points about the Thai railways is the punctuality of departures, at least from the station of origin. The trains may not be on time at the end of the line, but at least they are going to make the effort to start on time. Bells ring to warn of departure, whistles blow, and the train pulls out of the station punctual to the minute, or else there is a reason why.

There used to be a train leaving Thonburi station in Bangkok for Chumphon and Lang Suan every morning at 8:00. (This train now departs at 7:20.) Now, in Thailand a worn-out recording of the National Anthem is played through every loudspeaker in the nation at 8:00 and everybody stands to attention. One of the author's vivid memories is of being on the 8:00 train while intending passengers ran to catch it, but were then brought to attention as the National Anthem played – and, as they watched in horror, the train pulled calmly out of the station, right on time!

In fact, the trains try hard to adhere to their schedules. The problem is that, except for the line from Bangkok north to Ayutthaya and a little beyond, the whole system operates on a single-track basis. That means that once one train is late, it is likely to delay all the others in both directions. Priority is given to expresses, and, in general, they are fairly punctual. Ordinary trains are less reliable, but they are usually not very late.

If the Thai government had devoted to the rail system even a fraction of the attention which has been given to improving the roads, Thailand could have trains competitive in terms of speed with the buses. As it is, though, the trains have to run on an old, metre-gauge, single-track system which limits their potential, so travel by train is nearly always slower than travel by bus. Only the express railcars are really competitive in this respect. It is, though, a very much safer means of transport. The railways have an excellent record in this respect. Staff are visibly conscious of ensuring that proper and safe procedures are followed and accidents are rare indeed.

(v) Identification of Trains

At big stations, platform information is usually written in English. At smaller stations it is obvious which platform to use but, if not, one of the station clerks will help.

Each carriage of every train has its destination written on both sides, together with the number of the carriage if it is a rapid or express train. Such information has been in Roman script, as well as Thai, at least since the author first visited Thailand, and probably for a lot longer than that. Fortunately, that makes matters easy for the visitor.

Buses

There are various categories of buses, so first we need to distinguish the different types. Let us start at the most basic level.

(i) Ordinary Buses

Ordinary bus rides consist of a series of suicidal dashes interspersed with seemingly interminable delays. The buses usually operate with a crew of three for medium to long distance routes: a driver, a conductor and a mechanic/rounder-up of passengers. Short to medium distance routes may manage with a crew of only two. The principle which soon becomes evident is that the driver is the absolute master of this vessel and that the other members of the crew must humour him and pretend to agree with every whimsical decision which he makes.

Various strategies are used to attract passengers. You will probably not experience all of them on a single ride, but you are sure to get some of them. First the conductor and mechanic will tour the bus station shouting the name of their destination and trying to get a few potential passengers on board. After a while, the driver turns up and starts the engine to show that he means business. He then goes away for a cup of tea leaving the engine running to prove that departure is imminent. After ten minutes, he comes back and revs the engine a few times, then, after a while, engages reverse gear and starts to back the bus out, but changes his mind and lets it roll back to its original position a few times. Finally, with much shouting and directing of traffic by the conductor, he reverses right out and sets off. First he goes once round the bus station and comes back to where he started. At this point passengers start to think that he is in earnest and begin to materialise from the shadows to board. Finally the bus creeps out of the bus station and down the road. The conductor and mechanic lean out of their doors, one at the front and one at the rear, fingers pointing skywards, cajoling any moving being to board. A circuit of the town is performed and gradually the bus becomes full. Now we go to the bus company's depot and fill in necessary paper work and have a chat with the inspector. Passengers keep arriving until the bus is crammed to overflowing. We set off and go to the cheapest service station in order to refuel the bus. The driver gets out and goes to the toilet. These essentials performed, we proceed two kilometres along the main road, where the driver decides that he is going to stop for his lunch. He gets out, leaving the engine running, without giving any information to the passengers, who sit and sizzle in the hot sun. The other crew members get off and try to pretend that they are enjoying this unexpected delay. After twenty minutes the driver gets back in, slams the vehicle into gear and sets off at high speed. The crew run for their doors, cling onto the rails there, hanging out of the doorways, and we are away. The driver appears suicidal, overtaking everything on the road, ignoring all rules of safety, catapulting passengers out whenever they wish to alight, but never failing to pick up any who wish to board, however crowded the vehicle may become. And, after an hour or so of this, we reach the first major town on the route. We stop in the bus station, the driver climbs out and goes for a cup of tea, and the whole performance is repeated.

The result is that ordinary buses travel dangerously fast, but are still not very quick. They are, however, cheap, although not as cheap as the trains. One gets about three kilometres for Bt1. If you are issued with a ticket, incidentally, be sure to retain it, because that usually means that it will be inspected later – and if it is inspected once, do not assume that it will not be inspected again. Sometimes it is inspected three or four times along the journey.

(ii) 2nd Class Air-Conditioned Buses

Air-conditioned buses are increasing in popularity, which might not surprise anybody who has just read the section above referring to ordinary buses, and they have been divided, therefore, into two types. 2nd class air-conditioned buses have no toilet and will usually stop anywhere along their route to pick up and let off passengers. They are, however, altogether more civilised than the ordinary buses.

The times shown in this book for buses invariably indicate that air-conditioned buses are faster than ordinary ones. The reader may wonder why that should be. Do they have more powerful engines? Do they stop less frequently? Well, not the former. Maybe the latter to some degree, but the real difference lies in the more business-like manner in which the services are operated. 2nd class air-conditioned buses usually leave five minutes after their scheduled departure time, irrespective of the number of passengers on board, although they are none the less eager to find passengers at the bus station and along the way. They make only brief halts at each town and when the driver wants his dinner he tells the passengers the length of the halt so that they can have theirs too. Importantly, the vehicles are driven in a safer manner (although all is comparative). In addition, the vehicle is, of course, air-conditioned and generally more comfortable. The price for this degree of luxury is about a third more than for an ordinary bus. If you need to take a bus, this type, if available, usually represents the best value. The Thai people think so too, with the result that ordinary buses attract fewer and fewer passengers where there is a choice, so that their passenger-searching delays become longer and longer. On the other hand, as ordinary buses start to fade from the scene in some places, so 2nd class air-conditioned buses are starting to pick up some of their bad habits. Over the next few years 2nd class air-conditioned buses are likely to take over many routes, one feels, and ordinary buses may be left on only the shorter and more rural journeys.

(iii) *1st Class Air-Conditioned Buses*

1st class air-conditioned buses are another step up the bus scale. When you board such buses at the point of origin, you are usually allocated a specific seat. The bus carries a toilet (which one is often discouraged by bus crews from using) and makes only limited stops along its route. Sometimes a soft drink or cold water is provided for passengers. Such buses usually leave only a few minutes after their scheduled departure time and proceed with few interruptions or delays. They cost about a third more than 2nd class air-conditioned buses.

Times mentioned in this book for air-conditioned buses are for 1st class air-conditioned buses where they are available.

(iv) *V.I.P. Buses*

V.I.P. buses (or 'Tour Buses'), almost invariably travelling overnight, used to be operated by private companies outside the government system, and offered superior service at prices only a little higher than the official rates. Eventually they were persuaded to join the official system by carrying a route number and using the government bus stations. Also the government system started the operation of its own V.I.P. buses. These days it is difficult to know who is operating the bus, but the characteristics of a V.I.P. bus are that it will have fewer seats than usual, so that each has plenty of width and leg-room, that the seats will recline a long way, that the bus will be well air-conditioned, that a blanket will be supplied to each passenger and usually that a light meal, or at least a substantial snack, will be provided during the journey. V.I.P. buses generally carry passengers only from terminus to terminus, or almost, and make only a few stops along the way. They are generally quite expensive, although the relationship between their rates and those of other buses is not fixed. There are still a few operators of such vehicles remaining outside the system, and sometimes their services are surprisingly reasonable in price, particularly to popular destinations such as Chiang Mai and Phuket. Such services are still referred to sometimes as 'Tour Buses', but no tour is involved. The term merely denotes the standard of vehicle used.

(v) Minibuses

Recently, minibuses (or 'vans') have started to gain in popularity in certain areas, particularly in the south of the country. They generally run to fixed schedules, yet are reluctant to depart until they have a full complement of passengers, which means eleven to fourteen. Usually they convey passengers only between the towns of origin and destination. One feels rather cramped riding in these vehicles, and also rather vulnerable in case of accident, but they are fast and efficient. Fares are about the same as those charged by 1st class air-conditioned buses.

(vi) Speed, Punctuality and Safety

Buses are driven fast in Thailand. Drivers seem to believe, with justification, that if they are sufficiently aggressive, all other traffic will get out of their way. After all, who wants to collide head-on with a bus being driven at high speed? Just how fast these vehicles travel is not quite certain, though, since the speedometers are rarely in working order.

A few years ago, travelling the well used highway between Bangkok and Chiang Mai, one could see the wrecks of buses every few kilometres beside the road, a sight which had no obvious deterrent effect upon drivers. Now the highway is dual carriageway for much of its length, so the number of accidents has been greatly reduced. However, not all roads in the country have four lanes, so there are still plenty of accidents, and there will continue to be until the standard of driving improves, which is not in the foreseeable future. Many of these accidents occur at night, which is one good reason to avoid overnight travel, or to go by train.

However, if speed is what you want, at the expense of safety, buses are a good choice. On long distance journeys they can sometimes knock several hours off the travelling time by train, in addition to which they are comfortable and cool. In some cases they are the only choice, as you venture further from the frequented paths. It is just that one feels that the inevitable accident is going to happen sooner or later.

As for punctuality, that depends on whose figures you believe. When the bus company tells you how long the journey is going to take, that usually means that once, several years ago, in the middle of the night and without taking any breaks, their ace driver was recorded as having completed it in the time stated and that they are hoping that his record may be equalled by your bus. If you take the times from TAT (Tourism Authority of Thailand) information, for example, it depends on whether the officer compiling it merely wrote down what he was told by the bus company or whether he gave a suitable interpretation to such information.

The times given in this book are realistic assessments of how long journeys should take. It is reasonable to expect that you will arrive within the time stated, unless something serious goes wrong. They are not average times, but times within which about 80% of services will arrive. Of course, the author has not travelled every bus route in the country, but he has travelled quite a lot of them, so many of these timings are from actual experience, and the remainder are interpolations in knowledge of the distance and terrain involved.

(vii) Identification of Buses

Most buses do not have their destinations written in Roman script. However, they have a number painted on the side, for example '48-12'. The first part of this number (48) indicates the route of the bus. The second part (12) is the unique number of that particular bus, and can therefore be ignored for all practical purposes (unless you are thinking of leaving your umbrella behind on it). If you look in this book you will find the route numbers for almost every bus service mentioned. To find your bus just look at the number on the side of the bus. Thus, if your destination is Pattaya, you will be looking for this very no. 48. Towards the rear of the exterior of the bus you will also find the route painted and sometimes nowadays, especially in the case of buses serving Bangkok or serving a route where many visitors are encountered, this route is also in Roman script, but more often it is not so.

Where the route number is not mentioned in this book, it usually means that the bus does not bear one, but occasionally it just means that it could not be ascertained. Minibuses sometimes bear the route numbers of larger buses operating the same routes, sometimes have their own numbers, and sometimes do not carry a number.

Air

The national airline of Thailand is, of course, Thai Airways, and the company operates domestic routes to all major destinations in the country (see map opposite). To visitors planning their trips to Thailand, these services often seem quite cheap. To those who are here and are comparing with other methods of transport, they tend to seem rather expensive. Interestingly, though, flights in the north of the country seem to be better value than those in the south. If you travel to Thailand with Thai Airways, you may find that a domestic flight from Bangkok and one back to Bangkok (not necessarily from the same place) can be added at minimal cost.

There is a second airline, which is Bangkok Airways, operating smaller aircraft, mostly to popular destinations not served by Thai Airways, such as Pattaya, Ko Samui and Sukhothai. The airline also has international flights to Singapore, Phnom Penh and Siem Reap (for Angkor Wat).

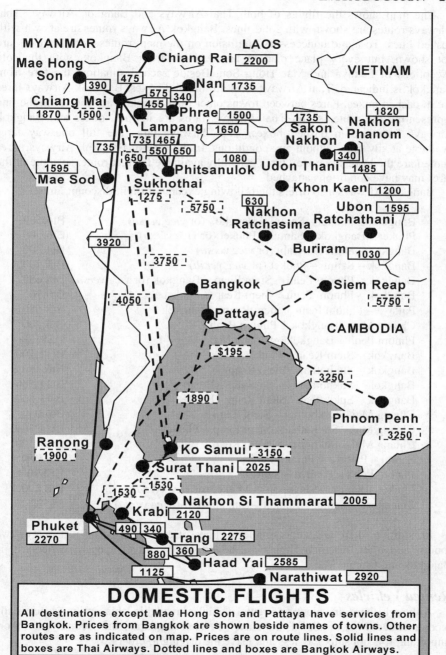

DOMESTIC FLIGHTS

All destinations except Mae Hong Son and Pattaya have services from Bangkok. Prices from Bangkok are shown beside names of towns. Other routes are as indicated on map. Prices are on route lines. Solid lines and boxes are Thai Airways. Dotted lines and boxes are Bangkok Airways.

The map shows the flights of both Thai Airways and Bangkok Airways. Thai Airways routes are shown with solid lines. Bangkok Airways routes are shown with dashed lines. To avoid unnecessary confusion on the map, routes from Bangkok are not shown, but every place marked has services from Bangkok, with the sole exceptions of Pattaya and Mae Hong Son. Beside each destination, the fare from Bangkok is indicated. Thai Airways fares are in solid boxes. Bangkok Airways fares are in dashed boxes. Fares between towns other than Bangkok are shown on the line representing the route. Again Thai Airways fares are in solid boxes and Bangkok Airways fares are in dashed boxes. Thai Airways fares are full one-way fares available at any time without any conditions. In the case of Bangkok Airways, fares quoted are the lowest one-way fares generally available for that route, so some of the fares may have conditions attached.

Bangkok Airways also offers the following excursion flight discount fares:

Bangkok – Phuket – Samui – Bangkok (or *vice versa*)	Bt6,500
Phuket – Bangkok – Samui – Phuket (or *vice versa*)	Bt6,500
Bangkok – Samui – Krabi (or *vice versa*)	Bt4,200
Bangkok – Samui – Phuket (or *vice versa*)	Bt4,200
Bangkok – Phnom Penh + Siem Reap – Bangkok (or *vice versa*)	Bt8,680
Bangkok – Phnom Penh + Siem Reap – Phuket	Bt9,765
Pattaya – Phnom Penh + Siem Reap – Bangkok	Bt8,680
Chiang Mai – Bangkok – Phnom Penh	Bt8,200
Phnom Penh – Bangkok – Chiang Mai	US$120
Bangkok – Siem Reap – Phuket	Bt11,500
Bangkok – Sukhothai – Siem Reap	Bt6,350
Bangkok – Sukhothai – Siem Reap – Bangkok	Bt11,500
Bangkok – Sukhothai – Siem Reap – Phuket	Bt11,500
Chiang Mai – Sukhothai – Siem Reap	Bt6,050
Chiang Mai – Sukhothai – Siem Reap – Phuket	Bt11,500
Chiang Mai – Sukhothai – Siem Reap – Bangkok	Bt11,500
Samui – Pattaya – Phnom Penh	Bt3,950
Phnom Penh – Pattaya – Samui	US$90
Phuket – Samui – Singapore – Phuket (or *vice versa*)	Bt8,890
Singapore – Samui – Phuket – Singapore (or *vice versa*)	S$522

In addition, there are some smaller airlines offering service on just one or two routes, and often discount flights are advertised by travel agents, particularly in Bangkok and Chiang Mai.

Rented Vehicles

Although there are plenty of rental vehicles available, this option is not really recommended. First of all, it is not cheap, by Thai standards, and secondly, and more important, it is not safe. Pay less and leave the driving to others.

Problems with renting include the likelihood that, as a foreigner, you will be presumed guilty should any mishap occur, and that it is difficult to know what is covered by the insurance, or even whether there is insurance at all, unless you use a well known and expensive company.

Despite these problems, visitors do use rental vehicles, particularly motor-cycles, in certain locations, especially the islands, where it is otherwise difficult or expensive to reach the attractions. As a result, there are numerous accidents and injuries, so take care. Remember that there is probably no insurance, and that if you remove the vehicle from the immediate locality you are likely to be in breach of the rental agreement in addition to having no insurance.

Local Transport

One of the strange aspects of Thailand is that, if you are not careful, you can sometimes spend more on a short trip from the bus or railway station to your hotel than on the long journey from the previous town to this one. Local transport can be quite expensive.

The most important point when taking any of the following forms of local transport is to ensure that the driver knows where you want to go. The problem is that very often he has no idea of your destination, but is eager to take you there anyway. He will then convey you to wherever he thinks that you ought to go – to the main tourist attraction in town, or the most expensive hotel, for example, and be quite put out when you are not satisfied with that. It is essential to ensure in advance that communication has taken place, and a question with a 'yes' or 'no' answer will not give such assurance. You need to have the driver repeat confidently the name of your destination before you board.

Also bear in mind that drivers of local transport are not usually well educated. If they were, they would not be doing that job. Even though he speaks a few words of English, your driver is unlikely to be able to understand a map, or to be able to read anything written in Roman script, and he may not be able to read anything written in Thai either.

You also need to determine clearly a price before getting into any local transport, and, if there is more than one person, to establish whether that is the total rate or the rate per person.

(i)   Songtaew

Most Asian countries have their own form of local transport, and Thailand's is the *songtaew*. These are like the *bemo* of Indonesia or the *jeepney* of the Philippines, for example – modified commercial vehicles which can hold about a dozen passengers in moderate discomfort, or about double that number in extreme discomfort. Most vehicles are small converted pick-ups with two benches in the back, each long enough for about six bottoms. Some, however, are larger trucks with longer benches and more bottoms. Most of these vehicles are open at the sides and rear, but have no vision, for the passenger, to the front. One cannot see much and feels rather cabined, cribbed and confined. Moreover, they are simply not comfortable for very long. The worst event is rain. Even though one closes every obvious aperture, it is futile. The driver in his perspex citadel speeds on oblivious, but in the rear it feels like sitting in the middle of Niagara Falls. Therefore, try to take this mode of transport for short journeys only. For up to an hour it can be endured. Beyond that, the novelty wears off.

Songtaew are not particularly cheap anyway, in addition to which drivers sometimes try to demand excessive fares, well above those authorised, so one needs to be cautious, especially in well touristed places. It is a good general principle to enquire the price in advance. This book tries to give indications as to when to be especially wary. On the positive side, *songtaew* drivers do feel an obligation to get their passengers to where they want to go, much as a taxi would do. They usually deliver around the town, stopping at exactly where you said that you wanted to go, or at least stopping at the nearest convenient point on their route.

In the best of circumstances, *songtaew* fares are about Bt1 per two kilometres, with a minimum of Bt4 or Bt5. At the other end of the scale, though, you may have to pay Bt2 per kilometre, or even more, but at that point maybe you should start considering some other form of transport.

(ii)   Taxis

Real taxis exist only in big cities like Bangkok. They have gained in popularity since introducing meters. It is no longer necessary to haggle, as a fair fare will be charged to all, assuming that the driver takes the most direct route. Be sure to take a taxi which does have a meter, as there are still a few without, and then check that the driver switches on the meter. Minimum fare in Bangkok is Bt35, which will take you a maximum of two kilometres. No tip is expected.

(iii)   Tuk-Tuks

Only a limited number of cities suffer from the tuk-tuk, those noisy little two-stroke taxi substitutes. Apart from the evil of the pollution which they create, tuk-tuks do not wear meters, so it is necessary to haggle over the price for every ride – and when you have finished, it is no cheaper than a taxi would have been. If it is cheap, there will be a catch – usually that you will have to call in on some merchant on the way. However, if you look at his wares without purchasing, probably all parties will be satisfied and the driver will get a small commission. It will just take time.

(iv)   Samlor

Since *samlor* means 'three-wheeler', it will be no surprise that these machines have three wheels. They may be human-propelled (rickshaws), or they may be motorised, with the front half of a motor-bike coupled to some sort of passenger box at the rear. Different towns have different designs. The human-propelled type tends to be more expensive, with most short journeys costing Bt20 and longer trips being

Bt30. In Thailand, the passengers sit in the rear, which is safer, and the pedaller sits up front. That feels less exposed than being in the front, as if one were in the shovel of a JCB, as in some other Asian nations.

The motorised *samlor* usually feel free to pick up other passengers along the way, so they often start at Bt10. If you can get to where you want to go for Bt10, they are probably worth while.

(v) Motor-Cycle Taxis

The motor-cycle taxi has been gaining in popularity recently, so now you can find this service at strategic points throughout all towns and at all major bus stops in the countryside. Drivers often wear some sort of identifying bib. There are so many of these vehicles and drivers around that one wonders how they can all make a living. Within town, a short journey of, say, two kilometres will cost only Bt10. A longer ride will be Bt20 or more. For anything other than a short trip, these vehicles are not very comfortable, and luggage is a problem, but they are sometimes useful for short distances. Protective headwear is not usually provided, although in Bangkok and other major cities occasionally it is.

Hitch-Hiking

Long-distance transport in Thailand is so reasonable in price that there does not seem much point in trying to hitch-hike. It is not, in any case, an accepted practice. However, you only need to try to walk somewhere out of town and you will soon discover the kindness and generosity of the Thai people, for you cannot get far before somebody stops and offers you a lift. Usually it is somebody on a motor-cycle, but occasionally it is a car. Thus even out-of-the-way attractions can be reached with a little determination, and luck, and without great expense.

ACCOMMODATION

All types of accommodation are available in major towns in Thailand, although in rural areas the choice becomes more limited.

If you are looking for first class hotels, you will find them in Bangkok and other big cities, at prices high by Thai standards, but reasonable by international criteria. You will also find such accommodation at major beach resorts such as Phuket, Pattaya and Ko Samui.

Most readers of this book, however, will be looking for either moderately-priced accommodation or cheaper hotels and guest houses. There is no shortage of such establishments.

So how much should you reckon to spend on your accommodation? If you want to be really comfortable, that is to have a pleasant air-conditioned room with attached bathroom every night, the most you should ever have to pay is Bt1,000, and the average is about Bt500 (U.S.$1 = Bt40). The price will be the same, or almost the same, for one person or for two.

If you are content with a lower standard, with a fan but no air-conditioning, and with an attached bathroom with shower, but no hot water, the price will be reduced to a maximum of Bt350 and an average of about Bt250.

At a lower level still, if a rather old and less than pristine hotel which may or may not offer attached bathrooms, with facilities barely in working order, or a guest house with dormitory accommodation, will do, you can sometimes get down to as low as Bt60, and about Bt150 per day will be sufficient to allow as an average.

The author's opinion is that the middle of the above three standards is a good one to aim for, with air-conditioning kept as an occasional luxury when the price is right. Hot water is not necessary without the air-conditioning, since the water, even when unheated, could hardly be described as cold.

This book has extensive lists of accommodation available and, in most cases, maps showing where each is. In a few locations, such as Bangkok and Pattaya, telephone numbers have been given, with the thought that readers might want to telephone ahead and reserve accommodation. In most places, however, this is unnecessary. Just go and find the hotel of your choice using the map.

In most cases, the author has refrained from making recommendations regarding hotels, because such matters change so quickly. If a guide book recommends an hotel, it quickly becomes overcrowded and standards start to deteriorate, so that soon, instead of being a good place at which to stay, it becomes the one place to avoid. Better to let readers make their own choices, or to obtain current recommendations from fellow travellers. The purpose of the information contained herein is to show the range available and allow you to be able to find almost any type of accommodation, rather than to make your choices for you.

FOOD

Food is one of Thailand's strong points and you will find eating here an interesting and enjoyable gastronomic experience, with a great range of dishes available. Some guide books recommend particular restaurants, but this book does not do so because there are places to eat everywhere in Thailand and what you eat and where you eat is simply a matter of personal preference. You will certainly never be at a loss as to where to get something to eat.

However, what people often do ask is, "What sort of establishment should I eat at? Should I stick to the expensive restaurants which I know to be hygienic, or can I risk eating at some of the street stalls?" To which the author replies without hesitation, "Go on. Risk it." If you are always afraid to eat, your sojourn in Thailand will not be much fun. And how do you know that the more expensive restaurants are hygienic? It is true that the really expensive ones, at first-class hotels, for example, will have high standards in order to protect the reputation of the establishment, but many others may suffer the problem that, because they are relatively expensive, the number of customers is limited, and therefore the food may not be sold as quickly as hoped. In reality some such restaurants, for all their immaculate appearance out front, may be just as risky as the street stalls operating in less than hygienic conditions but having a rapid turnover of ingredients.

The fact is that you are probably going to eat something suspect somewhere along the line and have a day or two of mild diarrhœa, so you might as well not worry about it and eat whatever you fancy. Actually, the street stalls are some of the tastiest and most exciting places to eat. Nearly every town in Thailand has a night food market. Often it is in an attractive location, such as beside the river. The ones at Chiang Saen and at That Phanom, beside the Mekong, come to mind as examples. Here you can walk along looking at the various delicacies available and choose either to eat a small meal at one stall or to nibble snacks from a variety. Either way, it will not be very expensive. Usually a single-dish meal costs Bt20 or Bt25. Moreover, language is not a problem. You just point and say, "This, please." In fact, much of the author's diet consists of "This, please."

If you want to cater for yourself (and miss many of the delights of Thai cuisine), there are supermarkets where you can purchase bread and tinned goods. There is also a chain of 'Seven-Eleven' stores with branches in every town, usually open twenty-four hours a day, where you can buy such items at only slightly higher prices than in the supermarket. Then there are markets, which usually close at dusk, where you can buy fruit and vegetables cheaply, but be sure to wash or peel your purchases before use.

DRINK

Can you drink the water? Most tourist literature advises visitors not to do so, but actually Bangkok water is potable, as is that in many other cities and towns. When the author first visited Thailand, the hotel where I stayed used to give each new arrival a bottle of cold water out of the refrigerator. When it was consumed, one took back the empty bottle and was issued with a new full one. I assumed that such water had been boiled, but one day, seeing the proprietor suspiciously adjacent to a wash basin with a collection of bottles, thought to ask, "How do you get the water?" "How do we get it? Out of the tap, of course. How else?" My myth shattered, I realised that if I had been drinking such water for several days without ill effects, it was probably all right.

If you prefer to play safe, you can buy plastic bottles of water for Bt5 per litre. This is not mineral water, just safe drinking water. Mineral water is also available, but costs a little more. The plastic bottles are convenient because they can be resealed. If you are going on a journey, buy water before you leave and take it with you. Bottles bought on a train or bus will probably cost Bt10. Similarly if you are going to an island or other remote location. Water bought there will probably cost Bt8, so you might as well take a bottle with you, rather than purchase one on arrival. When you arrive at an hotel, you may well be issued with one free bottle of water.

After that, the cost will probably be Bt10 per bottle, so pop outside and buy from the shop for Bt5. It may not seem like a big saving, but in a hot country like Thailand, you can consume quite a lot of water in a day – and a whole reservoir in a month's stay!

Soft drinks are readily available in cans and small bottles. Cans cost about Bt12, but bottles holding the same amount are usually Bt8 or Bt10. Why? Because you drink the contents and return the bottle for re-use, a much better system than buying a can which is not usually recycled, and certainly not re-used in the same form. If you want to take the bottled drink away, you can, but not in the bottle. It is poured into a plastic bag, with ice and a straw, and an elastic band deftly wound round the aperture with a hook left for hanging on the finger or any other suitable protrusion (like the window catch on the train, for example).

As for alcohol, beer is generally available and whether it is cheap or expensive depends upon what you buy, where you buy it and with what you compare it. In one sense, beer is cheap. You can go to the supermarket and purchase a bottle of the cheapest brand (*Chang* ('Elephant Brand') or *Leo*) for about Bt35, which is cheaper than it would be back home. On the other hand, compared with the general level of prices in Thailand, that is really quite expensive. Moreover, a superior brand will be Bt55, and if you buy it in an ordinary store it may be Bt65. In a restaurant or bar, even the cheap brand may cost Bt70 or more.

If you want stronger stuff, try the famous Thai *Mekong* 'whisky'. It does not taste too bad – not as bad as if it had come straight out of the river, as the name suggests! – but it is advisable to limit one's consumption of it – or be prepared to wake up with a terrible headache next morning! *Mekong* costs about Bt140 a bottle.

ADDRESSES

Thai addresses, even when Romanized, are not easy to understand. This section will not tell you exactly how to find a place from its address, but will give a few hints as to what the address means.

Thailand is divided into 76 provinces, each called by the name of its principal town. Therefore, the name at the end of an address does not indicate that a place is in that town, only that it is in that province.

Each province is divided into *amphoe* (districts). The central area of the main town in the province is called, almost invariably, *Amphoe Muang*. The other districts usually each bear the name of another town. Within the districts there may be *tambon* (sub-districts) and *muban* (villages).

When the name of a street is mentioned, it is often followed by the name or number of a *soi*. That means that the address is not actually in that street, but in a *soi* (lane) leading off it. Usually the *soi* are numbered, starting at one end, odd numbers often on one side and even numbers on the other. Similarly a *moo* is an area off a main street.

TELEPHONES

It is not too difficult to find public telephones in Thailand, and a few of them actually work. Those most likely to do so are the ones near the telephone office or the post office, or in places like airports and railway stations. There are two types: those which take coins and those which use cards. The card telephones are more likely to give results, but are you going to make sufficient calls while in the country to justify the purchase of a card? Local calls cost Bt1.

For international calls, the situation may well have changed by the time that this is read, but at present the cheapest way is to go to the Telephone Office (sometimes called 'Telecommunications Centre') to make the call. In some places you are asked to pay a deposit and your call is cut off at the end of the period for which you have paid. If you do not use the whole amount the change is refunded at the end of the call. In other places, you are trusted to pay when the call is finished. The opening hours of the Telephone Office will vary with the size of the town and amount of custom for the office. In Bangkok and Pattaya, for example, the office is open twenty-four hours a day. In small towns it is open from 8:30 until 16:30, Monday to Friday, only. In some places, it is also possible to make international telephone calls from the main post office. Rates are quite high, at around Bt35 per minute to most locations. There is a 10% discount after 21:00 and on Sundays (if the office is open at those times, of course).

It is also possible to make calls using a card, but not the same card as for domestic calls, and not from the same telephones. The most popular card is called a 'Lenso Card'. It costs Bt300 or Bt500 and can be used only in a special 'Lenso' yellow telephone. There will be only two or three such telephones in any big city (more in Bangkok) and there may be none out in the country. Rates are 10% higher than for going to the Telephone Office.

There is also a new card called a 'Thai Card' which allows the use of most telephones at reasonable rates. It seems logical to think that, in the face of competition, rates will be reduced gradually and other types of card will appear on the market, so the reader should investigate the current situation.

In addition to the above services, many private businesses, including guest houses, offer international telephone calls at high rates, in places where it is difficult to reach any other form of telephone service. Such calls typically cost about Bt60 per minute. Negotiation can sometimes reduce this to Bt50, but it is still expensive.

One stratagem which can be used to reduce telephone costs is to buy an international telephone card before departing from your home country and give it to whomever you want to call. Then book a one-minute call home from Thailand, during which you leave the number from which you are calling and ask the other party to ring you back. Most guest houses or private telephone service operators will accept this arrangement for a fee of about Bt100, including the one-minute call. The Telephone Office, of course, will not accept it.

Finally, only in Bangkok at present, but maybe the idea will soon spread, some Internet shops are offering international calls using Internet lines. The trouble with that is that the sound quality is only moderate and that there is a fearsome time lag, making you wonder whether the other party has gone off for lunch while you were speaking. The author is told that this is because the message travels via two different providers, one of which is in America. Judging by the length of the delay, the other might well be on the moon! However, the charge for this service is only Bt20 or Bt25 per minute. It works all right for a monologue, but not very well for a conversation. Maybe conditions will improve in the future.

E-MAIL

Contrary to what you might perhaps expect, there is no shortage of Internet shops in Thailand. What is surprising is the differences in the prices charged. Bangkok is a fairly standard location, with shops charging Bt1 per minute for you to collect your e-mail (or conduct any other business concerning Internet).

If you go to Hualampong, the principal railway station in Bangkok, though, you will find an Internet shop offering its services at a remarkable Bt4 per minute, with a small reduction if you use for a lengthy period. That is the record, as far as the author has seen, surpassing prices even on the islands such as Ko Samui and Ko Pha-Ngan. At the other end of the scale, there are shops at Bt20 per hour, Bt18 per hour and even Bt15 per hour. The problem with these is that it takes an eternity to receive or send any information. It is best to avoid the busiest time, which seems to be around 19:00 to 19:30. It is not just that these shops are busy, but that the providers seem to be very congested and slow.

Internet, incidentally, is effecting something of a revolution in Thailand, for it requires the use of English and suddenly young people are finding a practical purpose for the language and want to learn it and become good at it. Those operating the Internet shops are nearly always very proficient at English, as, indeed, they need to be.

The Telephone Offices mentioned in the previous section very often offer an Internet service too. It is not quite the cheapest, but it is very reasonably priced and it is the same price at all offices, irrespective of remoteness of location. One purchases a card for Bt100 (supposedly Bt300 too, but the author has never found an office with Bt300 cards) and scratches off a secret number on the back, then enters the number into the computer to be connected to the service. There is a Bt3 charge for connexion, after which the cost is Bt0.54 per minute. The card can be used at any Telephone Office, not merely at the one at which it was purchased.

BUSINESS HOURS

Government business hours are 8:30 until 16:30, Monday to Friday. Shops often open at 10:00 and stay open into the early evening. Nearly every town has a 'Seven-Eleven' store open twenty-four hours a day. Offices vary, but 8:30 or 9:00 until 17:00 or 17:30 is fairly standard. Post offices keep government business hours, but in major locations they open on Saturday and Sunday also from 9:00 until 12:00. The General Post Office (G.P.O.) in Bangkok opens at the same times as other offices, but stays open until 20:00 on weekdays and until 13:00 on Saturday and Sunday.

BANKS AND MONEY

The Thai unit of currency is the baht, abbreviated throughout this book to 'Bt'. There are 100 satang to one baht, but coins of less than one baht are no longer in common use. The only times that you are likely to meet them are in a supermarket or, at present, on the Bangkok buses. Soon they will probably disappear completely.

In approximate terms,

```
U.S.$1  =  Bt40
£1      =  Bt60
A$1     =  Bt25
```

Notes are in circulation in denominations of Bt10 (brown), Bt20 (green), Bt50 (blue), Bt100 (red), Bt500 (purple) and Bt1,000 (white).

Coins are in circulation in denominations of Bt10 (silver with gold centre), Bt5 and Bt1 (silver), 50 satang and 25 satang (copper). Of course, they are not actually composed of the metals stated, but the alloys are designed to give that impression.

Banking hours are 9:30 until 15:30, but in major cities currency exchange offices will be found which remain open until about 20:00. Exchange rates vary slightly from bank to bank, but not usually between branches of the same bank. The most advantageous rates are obtained for U.S. dollars, but all major currencies are acceptable. It is always wise to enquire about charges before changing money. Most banks make no charge for changing cash (but give an inferior rate) and charge Bt23 per cheque for changing travellers' cheques. To get the best value, you should bring your money in fairly large denominations of U.S. dollar travellers' cheques. The author suggests U.S.$500 denominations (although then you have the worry of carrying a fairly large amount of cash for a while).

Thai banks have reached the stage of having cash dispensers outside even in fairly small towns. If you have a bank card or credit card from your own country, the chances are that that card can be used to persuade such machines to give you some money. More and more people are using this method of obtaining cash. The exchange rate is usually the same as for travellers' cheques (but not always, so you

THAI PAPER CURRENCY

10 baht
(brown)

20 baht
(green)

50 baht
(blue)

100 baht
(red)

500 baht
(purple)

1,000 baht
(white)

need to enquire if obtaining a large amount of money, when differences in rates would be significant). However, there will be a charge, which will be determined by your own bank's policy, so check before you leave home. If you are not using a U. S. bank card, you may also suffer from the fact that the exchange rates are slightly unfavourable for other currencies compared with those for U.S. dollars.

The author's policy is to put Bt500 in my wallet every day for that day's expenses and carry the remainder in a money belt, or leave it in the hotel safe. If Bt500 seems too little for your budget, make it Bt1,000, but do not carry all of your cash round conspicuously. The Thai people are basically honest, but there is no need to challenge that basic honesty.

Also bear in mind that most people in Thailand cannot change large notes, so plan ahead and use the large denominations to pay your hotel bill, or use in the supermarket, or buy a bus ticket at the bus station (but not on the bus, if possible), keeping sufficient small money to pay those who are much less likely to be able to provide change. Tuk-tuk and taxi drivers, in particular, never have change, or so they hopefully claim.

POSTAL SERVICES

Thai postal services are fairly reliable but rather expensive. Domestic mail costs Bt3, but you are not likely to need that very much. A postcard sent internationally by airmail costs Bt12, or Bt15 if it is a large one. Letters start at Bt15.

If you need to send souvenirs home, you will find in Bangkok G.P.O. a good and inexpensive packing service. Postage is offered by surface mail, by S.A.L. (surface air lifted) or by airmail.

There is also a philatelic counter in Bangkok G.P.O., and in some other towns as well, but stamps must be purchased in complete sets.

There is a Poste Restante service, for which you need your passport. Items collected are charged at Bt1 each.

TOILETS

Toilets are an important consideration for the traveller. If you are travelling by train, there will always be a toilet available, even in a third class carriage on an ordinary train. It may even have water, if you are lucky.

Buses are different, however. Toilets are installed only on 1st class air-conditioned buses, and even on those their use is somewhat discouraged by the bus crews. Therefore, when you are travelling, the last thing to do before leaving your hotel is to use the toilet. Thereafter, control your liquid intake in the knowledge of when the next toilet opportunity might appear.

Bus stations and railway stations have toilets, although not free ones and not usually clean ones. The charge is generally Bt3. Many buses stop along the way for meal breaks. For this purpose they often choose roadside establishments well outside towns. The arrangement with these places is that free (but not clean) toilets will be provided in return for the patronage of the bus. Petrol stations too usually have free toilets, so when your bus stops to refuel, there will be another opportunity.

In towns, public toilets are available here and there. Again they are neither clean nor free. The usual charge is Bt3.

EMBASSIES AND CONSULATES

Here is a list of embassies and consulates in Bangkok, with telephone numbers.

Embassy/Consulate	Tel. No.	Embassy/Consulate	Tel. No.
Argentina	259-0401	Latvia	237-3585
Armenia	661-8477	Laos	539-6667
Australia	287-2680	Liberia	290-0125
Austria	287-3970	Luxembourg	260-4838
Bangladesh	391-8070	Madagascar	235-4113
Belgium	236-0150	Malaysia	679-2190
Benin	249-8633	Mali	254-1490
Bhutan	267-1722	Malta	235-9423
Brazil	679-8567	Mexico	285-0995
Brunei	204-1476	Monaco	662-3023
Bulgaria	391-6180	Mongolia	278-5792
Cambodia	254-6630	Morocco	260-6410
Canada	636-0541	Myanmar	233-2237
Chile	260-3870	Nepal	391-7240
China	245-7032	Netherlands	254-7701
Croatia	238-5112	New Zealand	254-2530
Cuba	381-2592	Nicaragua	262-0975
Cyprus	261-8408	Norway	261-0230
Czech Republic	255-3057	Oman	639-9380
Denmark	213-2021	Pakistan	237-9008
Djibouti	681-2222	Peru	260-6243
Dominican Republic	521-3445	Philippines	259-0139
Ecuador	295-1991	Poland	251-8891
Egypt	262-0236	Portugal	234-2123
European Commission	255-9100	Romania	279-7902
Finland	256-9306	Russia	268-1169
France	266-8250	Saudi Arabia	639-2999
Gabon	279-2800	Seychelles	619-0083
Gambia	224-0091	Singapore	286-2111
Germany	287-9000	Slovakia	285-0822
Greece	679-1462	Slovenia	234-2481
Honduras	231-0620	Solomon Islands	361-9111
Hungary	661-1150	South Africa	253-8473
Iceland	237-8010	Spain	252-6112
India	258-0300	Sri Lanka	261-1934
Indonesia	252-3135	Sweden	254-4954
Iran	259-0611	Taiwan (Trade Office)	251-9393
Iraq	278-5335	Tanzania	692-5071
Israel	204-9200	Turkey	274-7262
Italy	285-4090	United Arab Emirates	639-9820
Japan	252-6151	United Kingdom	253-0191
Jordan	391-7142	U.S.A.	205-4000
Kazakhstan	630-1800	Uruguay	225-3718
Kenya	391-8857	Uzbekistan	712-8883
Korea (North)	319-2686	Vatican	212-5853
Korea (South)	247-7537	Vietnam	251-5835
Kuwait	636-6600	Yemen	650-3301

THAI LANGUAGE

For most westerners, the Thai language is a difficult one because it is tonal. There are, in fact, five tones to struggle with, and for us it is difficult to hear the difference. For example, the Thai for rice is *khao*, the Thai for mountain is *khao* and the Thai for nine is *kao*. They all sound the same to the author, but to Thais these are three different words, so, in a restaurant once when I was trying to ask for more rice, my request was met with utter incomprehension and eventually a statement that unfortunately this restaurant did not serve mountains! To Thais these are completely different sounds and they do not readily comprehend why we foreigners cannot make such simple distinctions of tone.

In addition, of course, Thai uses its own script, so one cannot easily read anything. In these difficult circumstances, it seems best just to try to learn a very small amount of vocabulary in advance and to try to pick up whatever one can during one's visit.

Note that, in Thai, when speaking to somebody politely, one often adds the words *krab* or *kha* (sir/madam) to a phrase. For example, 'good morning/afternoon/evening' is *sawat dee krab/kha* and 'thank you' is *kob khun krab/kha*. Whether you add *krab* or *kha* depends upon your sex, not the sex of the person to whom you are speaking. Ladies say *kha* and men say *krab*.

Regarding spelling, there seem to be few fixed rules for transliterating the Thai script (or rather, there are rules, but nobody takes any notice of them). Therefore one sees the same word Romanized into many different spellings, some hardly recognisable as being the same word. The policy in this book has been simply to pick the most common spelling likely to give a comprehensible pronunciation, and to try to be consistent. (If any cases of inadvertent inconsistency have arisen, the author apologises for them.)

As for pronunciation, most transliterations are designed to follow basic English pronunciation. 'U' is invariably long, like 'oo'. 'H', though, is likely to be a problem. 'H' is generally not pronounced, as for example in the word 'Thai' itself. The pronunciation is 'Tai', almost as though the 'h' were not there. Maybe it would be a good idea to leave out these apparently unnecessary letters altogether, but since they are generally put in, for example in place names, the author felt that to omit them would only cause further confusion. However, note that for 'th' and 'ph', the 'h' is silent. Thus 'Thai' = 'Tai' and 'Phitsanulok' = 'Pitsanoolok' (*not* 'Fitsanoolok'). 'Ch', however, is pronounced as in English, so 'Chumphon' = 'Choompon'. How confusing!

In any language, essential vocabulary is "How much?" and the numbers, so start with those and then try to add a few more useful words if possible. There follows a brief list of suggested vocabulary, but even if you manage only to count, you will have achieved the most important element of basic communication.

A. NUMBERS

English	Thai (Roman script)	Thai (Thai script)	English	Thai (Roman script)	Thai (Thai script)
0	sun	๐	9	kao	๙
1	nung	๑	10	sib	๑๐
2	song	๒	11	sib-et	๑๑
3	sam	๓	12	sib-song	๑๒
4	see	๔	20	yee-sib (yib)	๒๐
5	ha	๕	30	sam-sib	๓๐
6	hok	๖	100	loi	๑๐๐
7	jed	๗	1,000	phan	๑๐๐๐
8	pad	๘			

B. USEFUL PHRASES AND VOCABULARY

English	Thai	English	Thai
Good morning/afternoon/evening	sawat dee, krab/kha	Train	rot fai
Thank you	kob khun, krab/kha	Bus	rot me
When?	meuarai	Car	rot yon
How much?	tao rai	Hotel	rang raem
Never mind	mai pen rai	Station	satha nii
Where are you going?	pai nai krab/kha	Post office	praisa nii
Today	wan nii	Bath/shower	ab nam
Tomorrow	prung nii	Market	talaat
Yesterday	meua waan	Beach	had
Too expensive	phaeng pai	Bay	ao
Cheap	thuk	Mountain	khao
A little	nit noi	Cave	tham
Food/rice	khao	Big	yai
Drink/water	nam	Small	lek
Bathroom	hong nam	No	mai
Room	hong	No, thank you	mai ao

C. FOOD

English	Thai	English	Thai
Water	nam	Duck	pet
Plain water	nam plao	Shrimps	kung
Boiled water	nam tom sook	Crab	poo
Ice	nam khaeng	Fish	plaa
Chinese tea	nam cha ciin	Egg	khai
Hot water	nam rawn	Hard-boiled egg	khai tom
Cold water	nam yen	Fried egg	khai dao
Iced tea, milk and sugar	cha yen	Omelette	khai jiaw
Black iced tea with sugar (Thai tea)	cha dam yen	Stuffed omelette	khai yat sai
Hot Thai tea	cha dam rawn	Spring rolls	paw pia
Coffee	kafe	Satay (barbecued meat)	sate
Milk	nom sod	Banana	kluay
Yoghurt	nom priaw	Watermelon	taeng moh
Beer	bia	Mangosteen	mang khut
Iced lime juice	nam manao	Rambutan	ngaw
Rice	khao	Pineapple	sapparot
Fried rice	khao pat	Mango	mamuang
Fried noodles	pat thai	Durian	durian
Beef	neua	Longan	lamyai
Pork	moo	Papaya	malakaw
Chicken	kai	Custard apple	noi naa

THINGS TO DO AND THINGS NOT TO DO

In general, Thais are quite tolerant of foreigners' lack of knowledge of social etiquette. However, familiarity with a few of the customs of the country will make one's stay more comfortable.

Greeting is done by putting one's hands into a prayer-like gesture and inclining the head. It is known, in Thai, as *wai*. It is not very important for foreigners to use this gesture themselves, but if a Thai gives one a *wai* greeting, one should reciprocate (usually dropping everything which one is carrying in the process).

Shoes should be removed before entering any private home. Some shops and hotels, particularly in more rural areas, also expect you to take off your shoes before going inside. Clues to whether this is expected or not are the state of the floor (clean or otherwise), the presence of a step suggesting the entering of a different level of privacy, and the presence of a line of shoes outside. It is particularly important to remove shoes before entering any temple, of course. This custom means that it is less embarrassing if you select for your trip to Thailand socks without too many holes.

The feet are regarded as the dirtiest part of the body and should be kept to oneself as much as possible. Try not to point the soles of your feet at anybody (for example, if sitting on the floor against a wall, or if feeling the temptation to put one's feet up on some piece of furniture).

Similarly, the head is regarded as the most sacred part of the body and you should be very careful not to touch anybody else's head. If you do so inadvertently, be sure to apologise. Do not, for instance, pat a child on the head.

Religion exerts a strong influence in Thailand. Except in the extreme south of the country (which is predominantly Islamic), nearly all Thais are Buddhists. Buddhism is a gentle type of religion, without unexpected or excessive rules, so all that is required of visitors to the country is ordinary common sense and respect for the beliefs of others. Do not, for instance, climb unnecessarily on religious monuments, particularly on Buddha statues. Remember that even though a temple is in ruins, that does not lessen its religious importance. This does not mean that one cannot climb up the steps of a ruined temple and walk inside it, of course. It is a question of respect. Do not do anything in a ruin (except keep footwear on) which would not be acceptable in a religious building in good condition. It is also inadvisable to enter into any discussions on religious topics, or to make any comments which could be regarded as being disrespectful of the Buddhist (or any other) faith.

You will see many monks in their conspicuous saffron robes. To these men you should also be respectful, bearing in mind particularly that their religious beliefs may preclude them from making any physical contact with women, or from accepting anything directly from the hand of a female. This is rather a nuisance on crowded public transport where it is sometimes difficult to avoid all-round human contact, so you may find one or two seats reserved specifically for monks. On buses, these are often the rear seats. Such seats can be used while no monks are aboard, but should be vacated if necessary, bearing in mind that the monk may not be able to sit next to a female.

The monarchy is a strong institution in Thailand and the monarch himself highly respected, so do not say or do anything which could be interpreted as being disrespectful of the royal family. At 8:00 and 18:00 every day, the National Anthem, reputedly composed by the King himself, is played distortedly from a worn-out recording through every public loudspeaker in the country and everybody within range rises wearily to his feet and stands stiffly to attention. It is polite to follow suit, although stiffness is not an absolute requirement.

Excessive exhibitions of affection in public are frowned upon, although the levels acceptable depend upon the location. As one would expect, the rural areas are more conservative, the cities and beach resorts more permissive.

PART 2

BANGKOK กรุงเทพฯ

One of the first surprises about Bangkok is that the city is not called Bangkok in the Thai language. It is called Krung Thep ('the City of the Angels') and the name Bangkok refers strictly to only a small part of the city. These days most Thais understand what foreigners mean when they say "Bangkok", but it is also useful for us to understand what Thais mean when they say "Krung Thep". For the majority of visitors, Bangkok, or, more specifically, Don Muang Airport, is the starting point for a visit, so let us begin by getting from the airport to our first night's lodging.

FROM THE AIRPORT

Don Muang Airport is on the northern edge of the city of Bangkok. As one arrives, one will find money changing facilities available and a Tourism Authority of Thailand (TAT) office waiting to offer advice and, in some cases, to book accommodation on request. Transport available to the city consists of three types of buses, an infrequent rail service, and taxis.

The first and most expensive type of bus is an airport bus. There are four routes.

Route A1 runs to Silom Road.

Route A2 goes to the Democracy Monument (near Khao San Road) and terminates at Sanam Luang.

Route A3 is to Sukhumvit Road, terminating at Thong Lor, just beyond the Eastern Bus Terminal.

Route A4 goes to the Hualampong Railway Station (the principal station in Bangkok).

Thus all common destinations for visitors to Bangkok are covered by the four routes. These buses cost Bt100 and leave every fifteen minutes from immediately outside the airport terminals. They run as expresses, using the new toll roads, and so are relatively quick. Even so, the journey into the city will take about one hour.

The other two types of buses are city buses, which run on the major road just in front of the terminal buildings. Walk down to the road and look for a bus stop on the near side of the road. The custom in Bangkok is to stand just upstream of the bus stop, as that is where the bus is most likely to stop. Those waiting gradually edge further and further up the road towards the on-coming buses. The most useful bus routes are the 29 and the 59 (both ordinary and air-conditioned buses operate on these routes), and the air-conditioned 4 and 13. These duplicate approximately the routes of the airport buses but at much lower cost.

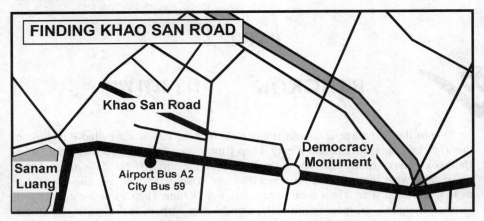

Route 29 runs to Hualampong Railway Station, where it terminates.

Route 59 runs to the popular Khao San Road area of Bangkok and terminates just a little further on by Sanam Luang, an open area next to the Grand Palace.

Air-conditioned 4 goes to the Silom Road area of night clubs and medium-priced to fairly expensive hotels, and then continues across the river to Thonburi.

Air-conditioned 13 runs down Sukhumvit Road past all the medium-priced hotels in that area.

From the airport to most places in the city, air-conditioned buses cost Bt16 if the bus is dark blue or Bt18 if the bus is orange or sky blue. The orange and sky blue buses are newer and slightly more comfortable. Fares are by distance, so it is necessary to state one's destination. The ordinary buses cost only Bt3.50 at the time of writing. It is a flat fare system, so not necessary to state destination. Bangkok traffic is chronically congested, a situation only slightly alleviated by the recent construction of expressways through the city. These journeys can, therefore, take a very long time. Allow at least 1½ hours. When boarding the bus, especially the ordinary bus, look for the destination sign in the front window. If it is blue, that is a healthy indication. If, however, it is red, that means that the bus is not operating for the entire length of the route and will probably not go as far as your intended destination. It may be better to allow such buses to pass by and wait for one with a blue notice. The 29 and 59 buses continue to operate all night, although not very frequently (Bt5 for the ordinary bus at night), and Bangkok, especially Khao San Road, stays awake all night, so, at whatever time you arrive, you can always get into the city and have a place to sleep. If you choose the popular Khao San Road option, the 59 will travel down a congested major road into the city for a long time and then turn right conspicuously. About ten minutes later, you will see the prominent Democracy Monument in the middle of the road, flanked by huge photographs of the King going about his daily duties. Get off at the next stop, cross this major road (if you can!) and Khao San Road is the next road parallel to that on which the bus was travelling (see map above).

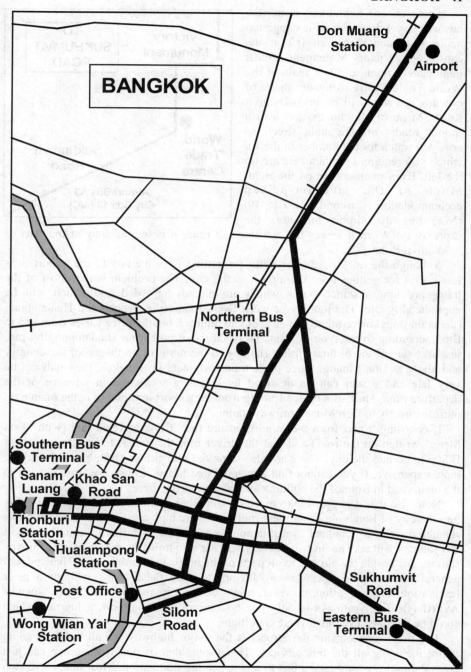

BANGKOK

Don Muang Station

Airport

Northern Bus Terminal

Southern Bus Terminal

Sanam Luang

Khao San Road

Thonburi Station

Hualampong Station

Post Office

Wong Wian Yai Station

Silom Road

Sukhumvit Road

Eastern Bus Terminal

If you choose Sukhumvit Road, the bus will travel down the same congested major road and then turn left at the conspicuous Victory Monument, almost immediately right, and left again at the World Trade Centre. Another couple of minutes and you will be in Sukhumvit Road. Most of the hotels are in *soi* (minor roads) off the main street, so now you watch for the number of the *soi* which you require. Odd numbers are on the left. Even numbers are on the right. Much of the medium-priced accommodation is around Soi 3 to 19. (Note that the airport bus uses the

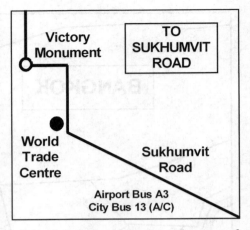

expressway. When it leaves the elevated toll road, it is immediately at the start of Sukhumvit Road.)

Although the railway can be useful for getting from the city to the airport, it is less useful for getting from the airport to the city. The problem is that most of the trains are long distance trains which are already crowded and which will be unpredictably late. The journey between Don Muang (the airport) and Hualampong (the main Bangkok terminus) takes about 50 minutes, but the price varies from Bt5 to Bt65 according to the type of train. To reach the airport from Hualampong by rail, just take one of the ordinary trains running to the north or north-east of the country and alight at Don Muang. Since these trains originate in Bangkok, they will not be very late and a seat can be obtained by boarding somewhat in advance of the departure time. There is a bridge leading from the airport terminal over the main road outside directly to Don Muang railway station.

If choosing a taxi from the airport, ensure that it is a metered taxi (with 'Taxi Meter' written on the roof) and that the driver uses the meter. Expect to pay about Bt300 to go into the city. There are also some flat rate airport taxis, but these will be more expensive. If you cannot find a metered taxi in the airport, just walk outside to the main road in front of the building and take one from there.

Note also that it is possible to reach certain other destinations without first going into the city of Bangkok. From the airport, there are high class air-conditioned buses running directly to Thailand's most famous beach resort at **Pattaya**. From the airport this journey will take about two hours. There are also trains from Don Muang railway station, just beside the airport, to all parts of the north and north-east of Thailand, but generally one would not want to attempt to take these trains without a prior reservation. The exception, however, might be for a journey to the historic town of **Ayutthaya**, for Ayatthaya is only one hour north of the airport, a journey which could be tolerated even in adverse conditions.

The main road outside the airport is the major highway for all traffic heading north, including all the bus services. That means that, if one wishes, one can just cross the highway and take a bus to any appealing destination. Most buses will stop here if they have seats available, but the problem is to know where any particular bus is going, for only a few have their destinations marked in Roman script (as used for English).

If in doubt, then, for which of the destinations in Bangkok should you head? It is a matter of price really.

Sukhumvit Road offers medium priced and high class accommodation.

Hualampong railway station area offers a little of everything, but only a little, and is, of course, most useful for those who have already decided that their preferred mode of transport is train. Within five minutes walk of the station is F.F. Guest House, where prices start at Bt150, for those who want economical accommodation. There is also the Station Hotel starting at Bt250, and Sri Krung Hotel, at Bt550, for those who want to be air-conditioned and comfortable at moderate price. For those requiring first class accommodation, there is the Bangkok Centre and, a little further away, the Mandarin Hotel (see map on page 71).

Khao San Road offers cheap to medium-priced accommodation, with prices starting at Bt100. If in doubt, head for Khao San Road for your first night. There is so much accommodation available that you should be able to find something to suit you, in addition to which there will be few language problems in this foreigners' ghetto. If you then decide that you do not enjoy this type of atmosphere, as many do not, you can visit other areas and find something more to your taste.

CITY TRANSPORT

Dirty, dusty, noisy, hot and humid, Bangkok is not a city which immediately exudes charm and appeal. It is, however, a metropolis which gradually grows on one and which contains a great deal of interest, if only one can tolerate the exhaust fumes and noise and can master the difficult art of getting around.

There is plenty of choice of means of transport. The city offers ordinary buses, minibuses, air-conditioned buses, microbuses, ferries, express boats, the Sky Train, taxis and tuk-tuks, roughly in ascending order of cost.

(i) Buses

Buses first. The buses go everywhere, but are slow, because of the chronic congestion, and somewhat difficult to get to know, because there are so many routes. However, the ordinary buses, which tend to be hot and overcrowded, are so cheap that making a few mistakes hardly matters in terms of cost. Moreover, if you find the buses difficult now, imagine the problems when the author first visited this city and the bus routes had no numbers, each service being identified by the buses being a different colour – and there were some fairly subtle distinctions of colour!

One of the priorities is to obtain a bus map. Such maps are sold by many shops in the travellers' areas, and by many hotels and guest houses. They cost Bt40 and are useful. They always say on the front 'Latest Edition', but then nobody prints a map saying 'Out of Date' on the cover and, whilst the map may once have been the latest edition, there is no knowing whether it still is. In any case, even if it is the latest, it will still contain many inaccuracies and uncertainties. Nevertheless, it helps and is almost essential for any visitor who wants to get anywhere in Bangkok. It also has a map of Thailand on the reverse which may later prove helpful. It is worth noting, however, that the TAT office also gives out a map which has bus numbers on it, and that that map is generally better, being more up to date, as well as free, of course.

Ordinary buses come in two principal hues. The predominantly red ones currently cost Bt3.50 per ride, a price which, despite the inflation resulting from the Asian currency crisis, has not changed for many years. The predominantly white ones cost Bt5. There are constant threats to raise the price to Bt5 for all buses, so, by the time this is read, that will probably be the rate. Night buses already cost Bt5. When catching a bus, look at the sign in the front window. If the sign is blue, the bus is operating over the entire route. If it is red, it is operating over only part of the route, so consider where you want to go and whether the bus is likely to go that far. If the sign is yellow, the bus is operating as an express over part of the route, usually by taking the elevated expressway, so there will be no hope of alighting during that part of the journey.

Some years ago, the buses became impossibly overcrowded, so that individual operators started to supplement the services by running illegal trucks on the same routes and, moreover, charging higher fares than the proper buses. This led to various confrontations with the authorities, but eventually the trucks were accepted into the system as a temporary measure, as long as they charged the same fares as the buses and operated in conjunction, rather than in conflict, with them. As the number of buses was gradually increased, support for the trucks declined, so they were replaced with more attractive proper minibuses which, in some cases, started to charge even lower fares than the larger buses. The current situation is that **minibuses** operate on some routes only. They are green and bear the same route numbers and charge the same fares as the larger buses, but tend to run more frequently. One point over which to exercise caution, however, is that they often operate over only part of the given bus route.

Air-conditioned buses are of two types. The older ones are predominantly dark blue and the newer ones are predominantly orange or sky blue. Both types charge by distance, so, unlike with the ordinary buses, it is necessary to know where you are going. The dark blue buses charge a minimum of Bt6 and a maximum of Bt22. The orange buses and the sky blue buses charge a minimum of Bt8 and a maximum of Bt24. When air-conditioned buses were first introduced, they were given their own set of numbers, but later many of the air-conditioned routes simply duplicated the ordinary routes and used the same numbering system. This anomaly has not been corrected, so some air-conditioned buses operate over completely different routes from ordinary buses with the same numbers. Be careful, therefore! For example, air-conditioned 4s travel to, from and via different places from ordinary 4s. It is possible to identify such deviants. Look at the route number. If the air-conditioned bus is travelling the same route as its ordinary counterpart, it will usually bear only the route number. If it has a different route, it will bear the route number preceded by two, and only two, Thai characters. Fortunately, though, when you want to travel from the airport to the city, you will find that air-conditioned 29s or 59s travel the same routes as ordinary 29s or 59s.

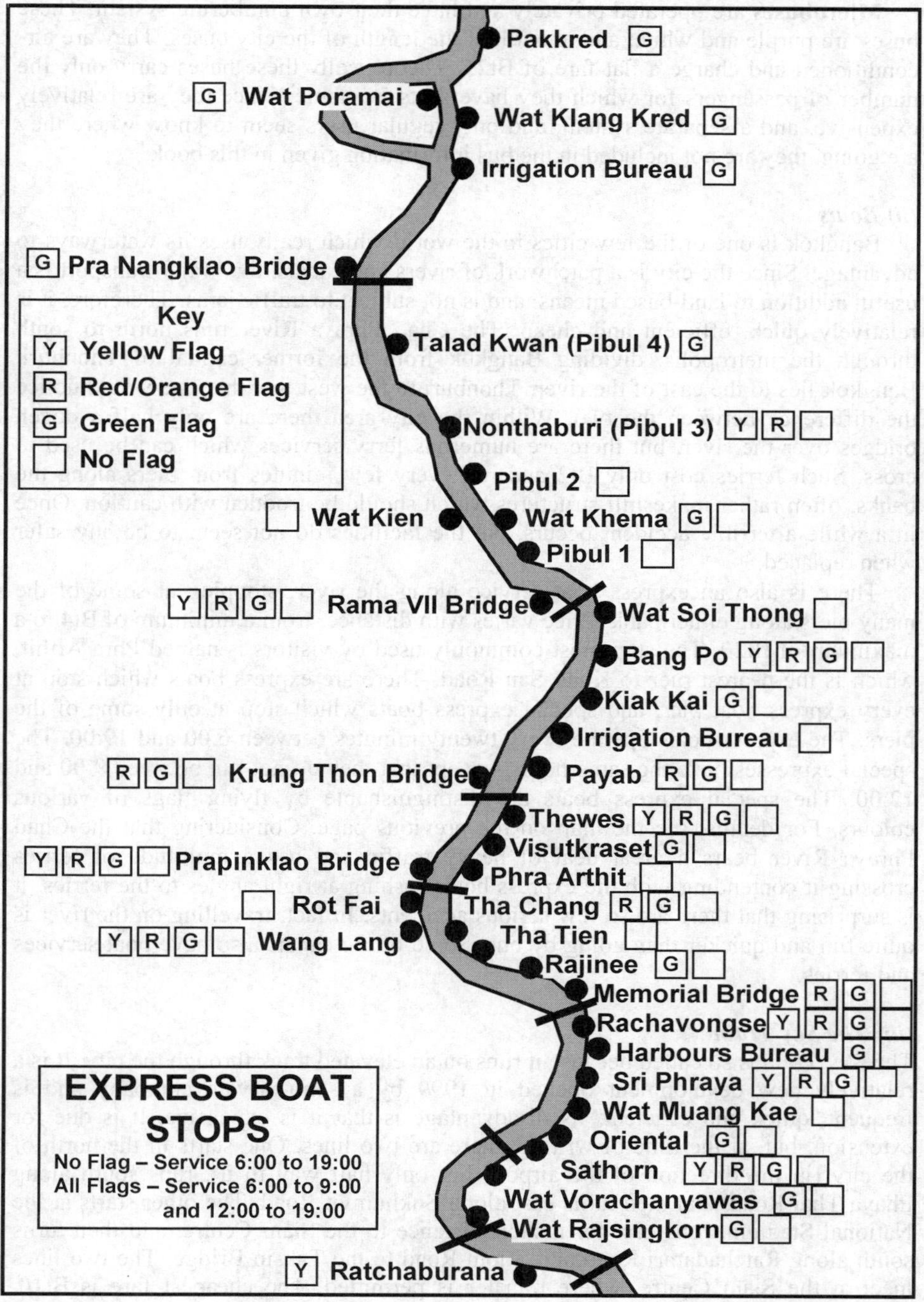

Pakkred [G]

[G] Wat Poramai

Wat Klang Kred [G]

Irrigation Bureau [G]

[G] Pra Nangklao Bridge

Talad Kwan (Pibul 4) [G]

Nonthaburi (Pibul 3) [Y] [R] [ ]

Pibul 2 [ ]

Wat Kien Wat Khema [G] [ ]

Pibul 1 [ ]

[Y] [R] [G] [ ] Rama VII Bridge

Wat Soi Thong [ ]

Bang Po [Y] [R] [G] [ ]

Kiak Kai [G] [ ]

Irrigation Bureau [ ]

[R] [G] [ ] Krung Thon Bridge Payab [R] [G] [ ]

Thewes [Y] [R] [G] [ ]

Visutkraset [G] [ ]

[Y] [R] [G] [ ] Prapinklao Bridge Phra Arthit [ ]

[ ] Rot Fai Tha Chang [R] [G] [ ]

[Y] [R] [G] [ ] Wang Lang Tha Tien [ ]

Rajinee [G] [ ]

Memorial Bridge [R] [G] [ ]

Rachavongse [Y] [R] [G] [ ]

Harbours Bureau [G] [ ]

Sri Phraya [Y] [R] [G] [ ]

Wat Muang Kae [ ]

Oriental [G] [ ]

Sathorn [Y] [R] [G] [ ]

Wat Vorachanyawas [G] [ ]

Wat Rajsingkorn [G] [ ]

[Y] Ratchaburana

Key

[Y]	Yellow Flag
[R]	Red/Orange Flag
[G]	Green Flag
[ ]	No Flag

EXPRESS BOAT STOPS

No Flag – Service 6:00 to 19:00
All Flags – Service 6:00 to 9:00
and 12:00 to 19:00

Microbuses are operated privately and have their own numbering system. These buses are purple and white, and about half the length of the city buses. They are air-conditioned and charge a flat fare of Bt25. Theoretically these buses carry only the number of passengers for which they have seats available. Since they are relatively expensive, and a separate system, and only regular users seem to know where they are going, they are not included in the bus information given in this book.

(ii) Boats

Bangkok is one of the few cities in the world which really uses its waterways to advantage. Since the city is a patchwork of rivers and canals, this water transport is a useful addition to land-based means, and is not subject to traffic jams. Therefore, it is relatively quick, efficient and cheap. The Chao Phraya River runs north to south through the metropolis, dividing Bangkok from the former capital of Thonburi. Bangkok lies to the east of the river, Thonburi to the west, not that one would notice the difference between the two. Within the city area there are only half a dozen bridges over the river, but there are numerous ferry services which can be used to cross. Such ferries cost only Bt2 and run every few minutes from piers along the banks, often rather makeshift structures which should be trodden with caution. Once in a while a terrible accident occurs, but the facilities do not seem to be any safer when replaced.

There is also an express boat service along the river, stopping at some of the many piers along either bank. Price varies with distance, from a minimum of Bt4 to a maximum of Bt20. The stop most commonly used by visitors is named Phra Arthit, which is the nearest pier to Khao San Road. There are express boats which stop at every express boat pier, and special express boats which stop at only some of the piers. The express boats operate every twenty minutes between 6:00 and 19:00. The special expresses have the same hours, except that they do not run between 9:00 and 12:00. The special express boats are distinguishable by flying flags of various colours. For details, see the map on the previous page. Considering that the Chao Phraya River bears a great deal of heavy traffic and has a multitude of ferries crossing it contending with the express boats rushing at right angles to the ferries, it is surprising that there are so few serious accidents. In fact, travelling on the river is quite fun and quicker than going by bus. Some of the canals also have boat services and ferries.

(iii) The Sky Train

The Sky Train is so called because it runs on an elevated track through the city. It is a relatively new development opened in 1999 by a semi-private company and is frequent, quick and efficient. Its disadvantage is that it is expensive. It is due for extension, but, at the time of writing, there are two lines. One starts in the north of the city (in the direction of the airport, but only half way to it), runs south along Phaya Thai Road, and then turns east along Sukhumvit Road. The other starts at the National Stadium, runs east for a short distance to the Siam Centre, and then turns south along Ratchadamri Road and Silom Road to the Taksin Bridge. The two lines meet at the Siam Centre, where transfer is permitted. The cheapest fare is Bt10, which will take one only a single station (walking distance). The most expensive ride costs Bt40. See the map below for further details of the system.

There are a few suburban train services on the conventional State Railways of Thailand tracks, but, except possibly for trains to the airport (mentioned above), they are not of practical use to the visitor.

Two underground lines are currently under construction.

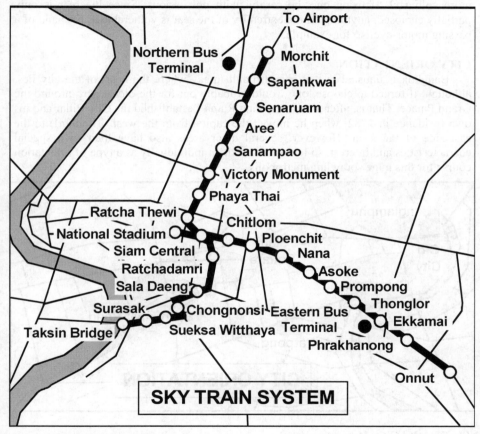

SKY TRAIN SYSTEM

(iv) Taxis and Tuk-Tuks

These days Bangkok taxis nearly all have meters, which is a great improvement. They bear the legend 'Taxi Meter' on the roof. The price starts at Bt35 for the first two kilometres, or waiting time (of which there is plenty) in lieu thereof. There are still a very few taxis without meters and these have just the word 'Taxi' on the roof, and are to be avoided. There is no need to tip.

Tuk-tuks are those charismatic little three-wheelers with a padded bench for two in the semi-open rear. They are two-stroke vehicles, named onomatopœically for the sound made by their engines, which belch out at high volume noxious fumes to pollute even further a city already swimming in carbon monoxide and pummelled by noise. Fares in tuk-tuks are negotiable, which is not to be misinterpreted as meaning that they are cheap. Since customers seem to prefer the comfort and fixed fares of metered taxis these days, it has become even harder to bargain for a reasonable price in a tuk-tuk. The shortest journeys will cost about Bt30, and that will cover only about two kilometres. In general they are no cheaper than metered taxis, although more colourful. If using one, be careful with possessions. Since the rear is only partially enclosed, anything on the extremity of the seat is vulnerable to the hand of a passing motor-cyclist, for example.

CITY ORIENTATION

Bangkok is unusual in that it is difficult to say where the heart of the city lies, although, if forced to choose, one would probably opt for the oldest part, around the Grand Palace. That is, after all, where King Rama I established the City Pillar and his own residence in 1782, when he moved the capital from the west (Thonburi) to the east side of the river. However, several other areas also have their own special characteristics and interest, so let us look at them individually as a type of orientation course for this huge sprawling metropolis.

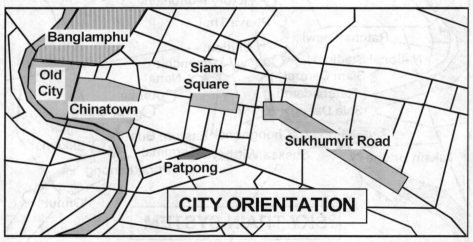

(i)   The Old City (Map opposite)

In fact, the old city is not so very old, especially in comparison with many other towns in Thailand, but it is full of temples, palaces and monuments, making it a most interesting place. The limits are easily defined, for King Rama I used the Chao Phraya River as the western boundary of Bangkok and then dug a canal to define the eastern boundary. Thus he had created an artificial island easily defensible if necessary. The atmosphere of this area is historic. It is not primarily a residential district. It is an area of temples, government offices and official institutions and an area containing the most important of the city's sights (see map opposite).

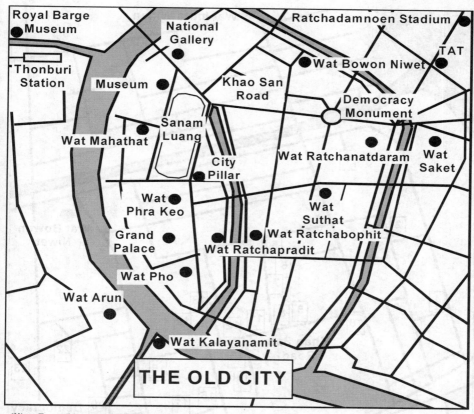

Royal Barge Museum

National Gallery

Ratchadamnoen Stadium

Thonburi Station

Wat Bowon Niwet

TAT

Museum

Khao San Road

Democracy Monument

Sanam Luang

Wat Mahathat

City Pillar

Wat Ratchanatdaram

Wat Saket

Wat Phra Keo

Wat Suthat

Grand Palace

Wat Ratchabophit

Wat Ratchapradit

Wat Pho

Wat Arun

Wat Kalayanamit

THE OLD CITY

(ii)   Banglamphu (Map on page 50)

Banglamphu (see map on next page) lies immediately to the north and north-east of the old city. Khao San Road, where so many travellers stay, is part of this area and lies just north of, but outside the limits of, the old city, but within a few minutes walk of many of the interesting sights. Banglamphu used to be simply a market district and, indeed, that is all that it was when the author first visited 25 years ago. Although the markets are still there, the character of this area has changed completely, for it has become virtually a foreign ghetto, with everything around Khao San Road catering to foreign tastes, and English almost the *lingua franca.* Here one can find cheap to medium priced accommodation of all types and qualities in a street of restaurants, travel agents, souvenir shops, taxi drivers and hawkers of fake student cards. Even if that sounds unappealing, it is not a bad place for a visitor to spend his first night in the country, for it is easy to start to acclimatise here. It is also a good place to look for onward tickets and for useful information. North of this area, incidentally, the old markets still exist, especially near the banks of the river. They have just been pushed back a little by the foreign influence.

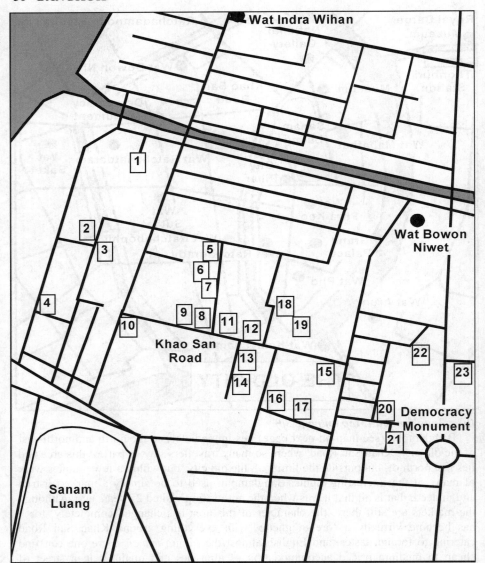

BANGLAMPHU

Showing accommodation around Khao San Road

(iii) Chinatown

To the south-east of the old city and west of Hualampong Station lies an extensive and interesting Chinatown full of crowded, narrow streets. Although it is an experience to wander around this area, the snarling traffic means that it is not a thoroughly enjoyable experience. In fact, the traffic moves so slowly in this warren of one-way streets that one can see Chinatown quite well and relatively painlessly from the window seat of an almost immobile bus. Many of the Chinese shops deal in gold and jewellery, but there are also fabric merchants, food stores, Chinese hotels and many other types of businesses.

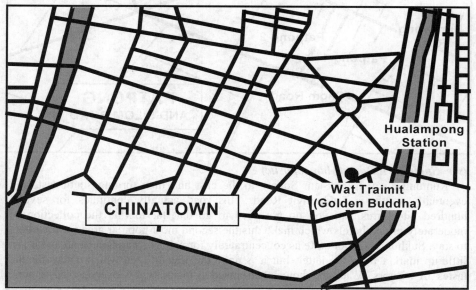

(iv) Patpong (Map on page 52)

Moving south-east again along Rama IV Road we come to a curious area named Patpong (see map on next page). This district is an odd mixture of night clubs and airline offices, but rather more famous (or infamous) for the former. Patpong is the name of two roads running the short distance between Surawong Road and Silom Road and these two roads are just packed with bars of dubious repute, which start to wake up in the early evening and continue all through the night. It is an interesting area to wander through in the evening.

(v) Siam Square (Map on Page 52)

North of Patpong is the Siam Square area. This is the high class district of Bangkok where many of the first class hotels can be found, together with expensive restaurants and department stores selling luxury imported goods. Everything here is modern and clean. It feels like Bangkok's answer to Singapore and you certainly need money to do more than browse here (map on next page).

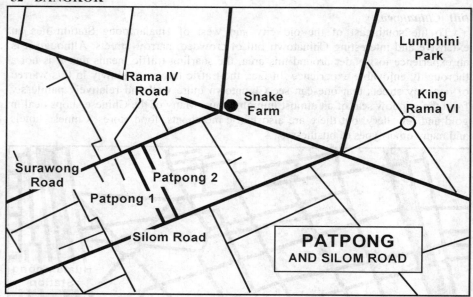

PATPONG
AND SILOM ROAD

(vi)   Sukhumvit Road (Map opposite)

Running away from Siam Square to the east and then turning south-east, and eventually south, is Sukhumvit Road. This road actually continues for several hundred kilometres, but you do not need to go that far to find the collection of moderately-priced hotels which make this the second most popular area for travellers to stay. Sukhumvit is not quite as concentratedly foreign as Khao San Road and it is a little up market from the latter, but it is none the less an area which caters for the tastes of visitors. With the hotels patronised principally by overseas customers,

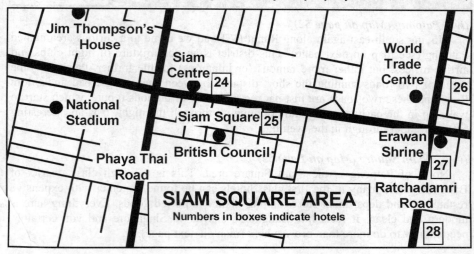

SIAM SQUARE AREA
Numbers in boxes indicate hotels

restaurants catering to foreign needs have sprung up, together with plenty of bars, frequented by plenty of bar girls. There are bookshops selling foreign language books and newspapers, together with numbers of travel agents, and altogether little doubt that the economy of this area too is greatly influenced by visitors from round the world.

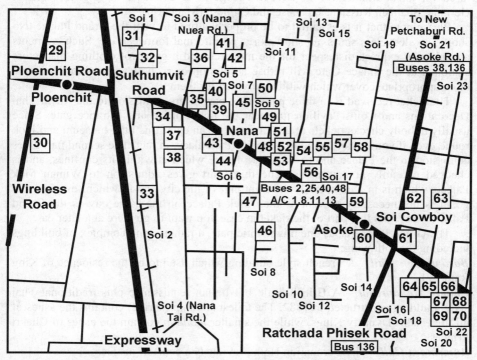

SUKHUMVIT ROAD
Numerals in boxes indicate hotels

MAJOR ATTRACTIONS

Bangkok is just full of interesting sites to visit, with some truly beautiful and memorable temples, for example. However, perhaps the first and most important place to see is the Grand Palace.

The Grand Palace (Old City, Map on page 49)

Right in the centre of the city, if Bangkok can really be said to have a centre, the Grand Palace is not where the king lives. He has a residence a little further north (Chitralada Palace). The Grand Palace is now just a tourist attraction used for a very few ceremonial occasions. It is a lucrative tourist attraction too, attracting thousands of visitors every day at the exorbitant price of Bt200 per foreign head (free for Thais, though). However, it is really not to be missed, so we had better pay up cheerfully and go inside. An audio guide can be hired for an additional fee of Bt100. The guide is available in English, French, German, Spanish, Russian, Japanese and Chinese (Mandarin).

Please note that it is essential to be properly attired to visit the Grand Palace. No shorts, no sleeveless shirts, no short skirts, no informal footwear, etc. Such garments are taken to express disrespect for the monarch and a group of clothing inspectors stationed at the Palace Gate will refuse admission or request wearers to don some more appropriate cover which will be provided for them.

The ticket received is in three parts. One part offers admission to the Royal Thai Decorations and Coins Pavilion just near the ticket office and entrance gate. Since usually nobody checks tickets at this point, you can enter this little museum and look round even if you do not intend to go inside the Palace, in fact. The second part gives admission to the Palace and to Wat Phra Kaeo, which is within its confines, and is checked carefully at a turnstile. The third part gives admission to Wiman Mek Palace, which is in a completely different part of the city and to which fewer people go. It is not necessary to visit Wiman Mek Palace on the same day as the Grand Palace. Just retain this part of the ticket in case you want to go there at a later date.

The Grand Palace is, as one might anticipate, a rather grand complex of buildings including the following:

Borombinan Hall – A French style building which used to be the residence of King Rama VI.

Chakri Mahaprasat – A British built, but Italian renaissance plus traditional Thai style, building constructed in 1882. The tallest *mondop* (shrine) contains the ashes of all the Chakri Dynasty Kings, while the smaller *mondop* contain the ashes of Chakri Princes.

Amarindra Hall – The Coronation Hall, previously a court of justice.

Dusit Hall – The Funeral Hall, originally a hall for royal audiences.

Wat Phra Kaeo – This is the most sacred temple in Thailand and it contains the **Emerald Buddha**, the most sacred Buddha statue in the country. The temple dates from 1782, the year when Bangkok became the capital of the country, and has been added to ever since, so that there are now more than a hundred separate buildings occupying a total area of 945,000 square metres.

The Emerald Buddha enshrined here was discovered in 1434 covered in stucco and lived first in a temple in Chiang Rai. He was moved to Lampang for a while, and then to Chiang Mai. From there, he was stolen by Lao invaders in the seventeenth century and taken to the Lao royal city of Luang Prabang, then later to the capital, Vientiane. He spent two centuries in Laos, before being recaptured when King Taksin fought a war against that country. General Chakri brought the statue back to Thonburi, which was, at the time, the nation's capital. General Chakri later became King Rama I, succeeding King Taksin and founding the Chakri Dynasty which has retained the throne ever since. He moved the capital to Bangkok and brought the

Emerald Buddha to this location in 1785. It is actually quite a small statue, only about 75cms high, and, since it can be viewed only from a distance, it is not really quite as impressive as one might expect. Moreover, it is not, in fact, made of emerald. It is a jade statue. King Rama I had two royal robes made for the Emerald Buddha, one for the hot season and one for the rainy season, and King Rama III added another, just in case it he should feel chilly during the cool season. The King himself changes these robes on the appropriate three dates every year. Note that no photographs of the Emerald Buddha are permitted.

Inside Wat Phra Kaeo you will also find a model of Angkor Wat, the famous Buddhist temple in Cambodia, a reminder that the ancient history of these two nations is closely intertwined.

The Grand Palace is open from 8:30 until 15:30, with a lunch break from 11:30 until 13:00, but during the lunch break one can still enter the outer (free) area of the palace grounds. When a ticket is purchased, a brochure is provided giving more details of the buildings.

Transport – The Grand Palace is within walking distance of Khao San Road. From Sukhumvit Road take bus no. 2, 25 or 48, or air-conditioned no. 1 or 8. From Hualampong Railway Station take bus no. 25 or 53 (the latter goes nearer), or air-conditioned no. 1 or 7.

Wiman Mek Palace (Maps on pages 57 and 72)

This palace is a little further north, near the King's current residence and behind the National Assembly. It is a traditionally constructed Thai teak building of three storeys, but with European architectural influence, and it was built in 1868 as a summer house and moved to its current location in 1901, where it was used as a favourite royal residence by King Rama V (King Chulalongkorn). It was disused from 1935 until 1982, when it was re-opened to mark the bi-centenary of the city as the national capital. There are 81 rooms, and it claims to be the world's largest building made exclusively of golden teak. No nails are used in its construction. It has Thailand's first indoor bathroom. Displays include the first Thai typewriter, old china, furniture and paintings. The Royal Carriage Museum, within the palace area, has a collection of imported turn-of-the-century European carriages and the Aphisek Dusit Throne Room has a collection of paintings. The Wiman Mek Palace is open from 9:30 until 16:00 and costs Bt50. However, if you have retained your ticket from the Grand Palace, admission will be free. The same rules regarding dress apply as for the Grand Palace.

Transport – The following buses pass Wiman Mek Palace: 9, 12, 18, 28, 56, 70, 72, 108 and 110, and air-conditioned buses 3, 9, 10 and 16. From Khao San Road take a 9, 12, 56 or 70. From Sukhumvit Road, take no. 2, or air-conditioned no. 11, and alight immediately after crossing the railway tracks, from where it is about 20 minutes walk. If that is too far, continue to the Democracy Monument and change to a 9, 12, 56 or 70. From Hualampong Station, take a no. 53 to its terminus, from where it is about 10 minutes walk.

Wat Pho (Old City, Map on page 49)

Wat Pho is famous for its huge Reclining Buddha and is the oldest temple in Bangkok. It dates from the sixteenth century, but was completely rebuilt in 1781. It is also the largest temple in the city. The Reclining Buddha is on a pedestal and is 46 metres long and 15 metres high, the largest Reclining Buddha in Thailand. He is covered in gold leaf and features mother-of-pearl inlaid soles to his feet. One can approach this Buddha closely, in fact so closely that taking his photograph is difficult because of his size. Wat Pho is also the centre for Thai traditional massage. One can obtain a massage here (about 200 baht for an hour) or learn massage techniques. Admission to the temple costs Bt20.

Transport – From Khao San Road, Wat Pho is within walking distance. From Sukhumvit Road, take bus no. 25 or 48, or air-conditioned no. 8. From Hualampong Station, take bus no. 1, 25 or 53.

Wat Benjamabophit (Maps on pages 57 and 72)

Wat Benjamabophit is often known as the **Marble Temple**. This beautiful piece of architecture is near Wiman Mek Palace. It is a relatively modern building constructed a century ago in white Carrana marble under the direction of King Chulalongkorn. Admission costs Bt20.

Transport – As for Wiman Mek Palace.

Wat Saket (Old City, Map on page 49)

Wat Saket is also known as the Temple of the Golden Mount. During the time of King Rama III, a *chedi* (pagoda) which was being built collapsed due to the soft nature of the earth. The pile of rubble was left for many years, but then King Rama IV ordered the construction of a small *chedi* on top. King Chulalongkorn (Rama V) enlarged the *chedi* and then the base was concreted this century. Now one can climb the steep steps to the top and obtain a good view of the city. One can climb to the top free, but to go inside one is invited to make a contribution of Bt10. In November there is a candle-lit procession up the steps.

Transport – From Khao San Road, again this is easy walking distance. From Sukhumvit Road, bus no. 2, or air-conditioned no. 11. From Hualampong Station, bus no. 35 (walk across the canal to catch it).

Wat Arun (Map on page 49)

Known as the Temple of the Dawn, Wat Arun is an impressive temple to view from a distance. It is on the 'wrong' side of the river, i.e. the Thonburi side, and is a seventeenth century temple named after Aruna, the Indian God of the Dawn. King Taksin made it a royal temple when Thonburi was the capital of the country, because it was the first temple to catch the rays of the rising sun. The Emerald Buddha was housed here at one time. The main Khmer-style *prang* (steeple) is 104 metres high and the terraces at its base can be climbed by means of steep steps. It is covered with porcelain previously used as ballast by ships visiting from China. Admission costs Bt20.

Ordinary Bus ▲
New Air-Conditioned Bus (Female!) ▼ 　**BANGKOK TRANSPORT** 　▲ **Skytrain**
▼ **Tuk-Tuk**

Songtaew ▲
Ordinary Train (Bottom)

TRANSPORT

▲ Motor-cycle Taxi
▼ Air-conditioned Express

Doi Suthep,
Chiang Mai

Sunset at Had Sai Ree, Ko Tao ▲

▼ Had Sai Nual, Ko Tao

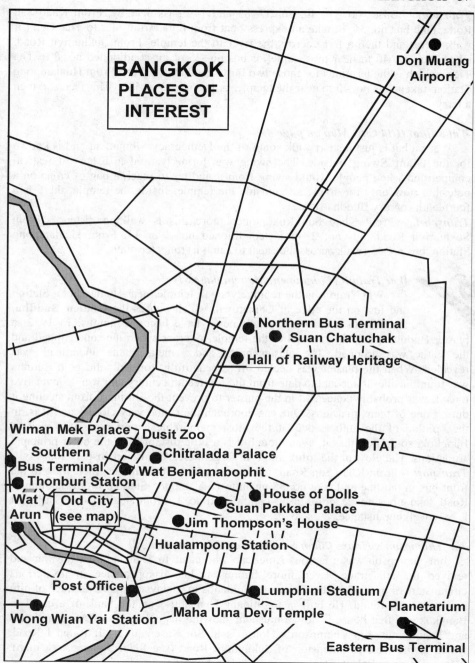

BANGKOK
PLACES OF
INTEREST

Don Muang Airport

Northern Bus Terminal
Suan Chatuchak
Hall of Railway Heritage

Wiman Mek Palace
Dusit Zoo
Southern Bus Terminal
Chitralada Palace
Wat Benjamabophit
Thonburi Station
TAT

Wat Arun
Old City (see map)
House of Dolls
Suan Pakkad Palace
Jim Thompson's House

Hualampong Station

Post Office
Lumphini Stadium
Wong Wian Yai Station
Maha Uma Devi Temple
Planetarium

Eastern Bus Terminal

Transport – Buses no. 19, 40, 56, 57, 83 and 149 pass near by. From Khao San Road, take bus no. 56, or take an express boat from Phra Arthit pier to Tha Tien (or walk there) and then a ferry across the river to the temple. From Sukhumvit Road, take a bus no. 40 to near the temple, or bus no. 25 or air-conditioned no. 8 to Tha Tien (which is the terminus for those two buses) and then a ferry. From Hualampong Station, take a bus no. 40 to near the temple, or bus no. 25 or 53 to Tha Tien and then a ferry.

Wat Suthat (Old City, Map on page 49)

Wat Suthat is just a short walk south of the Democracy Monument and is known for the **Giant Swing** outside. The swing was formerly used in a harvest festival competition when people would swing from it and try to reach a bag of coins on a pole, but now only the frame sits outside the temple. Inside the temple, there is a fourteenth century Buddha statue.

Transport – From Khao San Road, once more this is walking distance. From Sukhumvit Road, bus no. 2, or air-conditioned no. 8 or 11. From Hualampong Station, bus no. 35 (walk across the canal to catch it) to its terminus.

Wat Traimit (Chinatown, Map on page 51)

Wat Traimit is the relatively small temple, near Hualampong Station and just on the edge of Chinatown, which houses the **Golden Buddha**. But for an accident, it might never have become famous. In 1952, a plaster Buddha was being moved to the temple by crane when the rope slipped and the statue was dropped. The plaster broke and a metal statue underneath was revealed. When the plaster was peeled off, a beautifully formed solid gold Buddha was found inside. It appears to date from the fourteenth century and weighs over five tons. It was probably concealed in the plaster to prevent the Burmese from stealing it during one of their invasions. One can approach the statue very closely and it is, in the opinion of the author, one of the most memorable experiences of a visit to Bangkok, so do not miss it, even though it is a little distant from the other principal attractions. The glow of the solid gold is unforgettable. Admission costs Bt20.

Transport – From Khao San Road, take bus no. 35 to its terminus, then walk to the front bus in the line and take no. 35 again to Hualampong Station. From Sukhumvit Road, take a bus no. 25 or 40 or air-conditioned no. 1. From Hualampong Station, it is easy walking distance.

Jim Thompson's House (Siam Square Area, Map on page 52)

Jim Thompson was a famous American who came to Thailand after the war and revived the silk trade. Even more famous is his disappearance in mysterious circumstances in 1967 in the Cameron Highlands in Malaysia, where no trace of him has ever been found. He built a traditional Thai house on the bank of a canal in Bangkok and that house is now a museum showing his collection of Asian antiques and handicrafts. Jim Thompson's House is in Soi Kaseman 2, off Rama I Road, which is the western extension of Sukhumvit Road (see Siam Square Area map). Admission costs Bt100. The house is closed on Sundays.

Transport – From Khao San Road, take bus no. 15 or 47 to the National Stadium. From Sukhumvit Road, take bus no. 48, or air-conditioned no. 8. Alternatively, Sky Train to National Stadium (W1). From Hualampong Station, bus no. 73. No. 25, 29, 34, 40 and 113 also go very near. Alight at Siam Square.

SLIGHTLY LESSER ATTRACTIONS

The above are what one might define as major attractions of the city. By the time you have viewed all of them, you will probably be getting tired of temples and city buses. However, if you feel that you want a few more, try selecting from the following list.

Suan Pakkad Palace ('Cabbage Farm Palace') (Map on page 57)

This is a recent palace established in 1952 by the removal of some houses from Chiang Mai to Bangkok and the landscaping of what was originally a cabbage garden. The palace is now a museum of old statues, domestic items and Bronze Age discoveries from Ban Chiang, near Udon Thani in the north of the country. The gardens are also well known. Admission costs Bt150, but the palace is closed on Sundays.

Transport – The following buses pass near by: 14, 29, 34, 36, 38, 39, 54, 59, 63, 72, 74, 77, 201 and 204, and air-conditioned 2, 3, 4 and 13.

Chitralada Palace (Map on page 57)

This is where the king actually lives. Therefore, it cannot be entered, nor even viewed, except from a considerable distance. It is a little east of Wiman Mek Palace. If you are taking a long-distance train from Bangkok (Hualampong), you will see the palace on your left as you approach Samsen Station, the first stop, just five minutes along the line. You will also see the king's own special little station in front of the palace.

Transport – Nearby buses include 5, 8, 12, 18, 28, 50, 72 and 108, and air-conditioned 3, 10 and 16.

Wat Ratchanatdaram (Old City, Map on page 49)

Opposite Wat Saket is Wat Ratchanatdaram, built in 1846. It features unusual Burmese-influenced architecture consisting of a central spire 36 metres high with 37 surrounding lesser spires. It is also well known for its market of Buddhist amulets.

Transport – Buses 2, 5, 35, 39, 44, 56, 59, 60, 70, 79 and 201, and air-conditioned 3, 9, 11, 12 and 44 pass right outside and many others go near by.

Wat Bowon Niwet (Banglamphu, Map on page 50)

Just round the corner from Khao San Road, Wat Bowon Niwet's claim to fame is that many of the royal family enter the monastery for a while to serve as monks. The present King did so, for example. Although the temple was not founded until 1829, it houses an impressive Buddha statue dating from 1357. It also operates a Buddhist university (Mahamakut University), one of the two in Bangkok (Wat Mahathat houses the other – see below). Because of the temple's proximity to Khao San Road, no doubt, there is also an English language Buddhist bookshop across the street, and a Thai herbal medicine clinic.

Transport – Bus 56 and air-conditioned 11 go right past the gate, but any of those listed above for Wat Ratchanatdaram pass close.

Wat Mahathat (Old City, Map on page 49)

Just to the west of Sanam Luang, Wat Mahathat is an eighteenth century temple which features a fruit and vegetable market at weekends, a religious market of amulets just outside the grounds every day, and an impressive collection of pigeons. It also houses a Buddhist university (Mahathat Rajavidyalaya University) and offers Buddhist meditation instruction in English once per month, on the second Saturday.

Transport – Buses 2, 3, 6, 9, 15, 19, 30, 31, 32, 33, 39, 42, 43, 44, 47, 51, 53, 56, 59, 60, 64, 69, 70, 79, 80, 90, 91, 103, 201 and 203, and air-conditioned 3, 7, 9 and 11, but from Khao San Road it is easy walking distance.

Wat Ratchabophit (Old City, Map on page 49)

This temple is near Wat Pho and was constructed in 1869 by King Chulalongkorn. It offers some elaborate and unusual architecture, with European influence, a trait of that monarch. Especially notable is the mother-of-pearl decoration around the windows and doors.

Transport – Buses 1, 25 and 48 and air-conditioned 1, 7 and 8. Many others pass near by.

Wat Ratchapradit (Old City, Map on page 49)

Just across the canal from Wat Ratchabophit, this temple was established by King Rama IV and is known for its murals depicting the annual ceremonies performed by the monarch.

Transport – As for Wat Ratchabophit above.

Wat Kalayanamit (Map on page 49)

This is a mid nineteenth century temple on the Thonburi side of the river. It was built by King Rama III. It contains a particularly large Buddha statue and some fine murals. Outside is the biggest bronze bell in Thailand and an old Chinese stone pagoda.

Transport – Buses 4, 5, 6, 7, 8, 10, 12, 21, 25, 37, 52, 60, 73, 82 and 85, and air-conditioned 1, 6, 7, 8 and 12 to Pak Klong Talad Pier and then a ferry across the river to the temple. Alternatively, an express boat to Rajini and then ferry across the river.

Wat Indra Wihan (Banglamphu, Map on page 50)

This is another temple in the vicinity of Khao San Road. It is famous for its huge standing Buddha, 32 metres tall.

Transport – Buses 3, 6, 10, 12, 19, 30, 31, 32, 33, 43, 49, 53, 64 and 90, and air-conditioned 6.

San Lak Muang (City Pillar) (Old City, Map on page 49)

There is a shrine just opposite the southern (Grand Palace) end of Sanam Luang enclosing the wooden city pillar erected by King Rama I in 1782, when Bangkok became the capital of the country. King Chulalongkorn later added five more deities to the shrine. The spirit of the pillar is the guardian of the city, so many people come here to pray and it is usually crowded. This shrine has its own special atmosphere and is worth a visit, especially as it is so near to Khao San Road and to many of Bangkok's other major attractions. Sometimes classical Thai dance performances can be witnessed here.

Transport – Buses 2, 3, 6, 9, 15, 19, 30, 31, 32, 33, 39, 42, 43, 44, 47, 51, 53, 56, 59, 60, 64, 69, 70, 79, 80, 90, 91, 103, 201 and 203, and air-conditioned 3, 7, 9 and 11. From Khao San Road it is easy walking distance.

Erawan Shrine (Siam Square Area, Map on page 52)

This was a shrine connected with the Erawan Hotel, now demolished and replaced with the Grand Hyatt Erawan. (Erawan is Brahma's thirty-three-headed elephant.) It is famous for bringing good luck, so if you stand around for a while you will usually see some ceremony taking place, often classical Thai dancing to petition or thank the Gods for their mercy. The Erawan Shrine is on the corner of Ploenchit Road, which is an extension westwards of Sukhumvit Road.

Transport – Buses 2, 13, 14, 15, 17, 25, 40, 45, 48, 54, 73, 74, 77, 119 and 204, and air-conditioned 1, 4, 5, 8, 11 and 13, or Sky Train to Chitlom (E1).

Maha Uma Devi Temple (Map on page 57)

Maha Uma Devi is a Hindu temple, built in Silom Road, where many of the Tamil Indian population are concentrated, in the 1860s. As usual with such temples, it has an elaborately carved façade, featuring hundreds of Hindu gods.

Transport – Buses 15, 16, 17, 76, 77 and 115, and air-conditioned 2, 4 and 5, or Sky Train to Surasak (S5).

National Museum (Old City, Map on page 49)

Just to the west (river side) of Sanam Luang, the National Museum is only a short walk from Khao San Road. There are English language tours at 9:30 on Wednesdays and Thursdays (no extra charge) and in French on Wednesdays, Japanese on Wednesdays and German on Thursdays. The museum is closed on Mondays and Tuesdays. Admission costs Bt40.

Transport – Very many bus routes pass nearby, for example: 2, 3, 6, 9, 15, 19, 30, 31, 32, 33, 39, 42, 43, 44, 47, 51, 53, 56, 59, 60, 64, 69, 70, 79, 80, 90, 91, 103, 201 and 203, and air-conditioned 3, 7, 9 and 11.

Royal Barge Museum (Map on page 49)

The royal barges are used on ceremonial occasions and otherwise stored in a museum on the Thonburi side of the river not far from the National Museum. They are remarkable old style vessels up to fifty metres in length. The largest requires fifty oarsmen, seven parasol bearers, two helmsmen, two navigators, a flagman, a rhythm-beater and a chanter. Admission costs Bt30.

Transport – Buses 19 and 91 pass by the Royal Barge Museum. It is also possible to take a ferry or express boat to Thonburi Railway Station (Rot Fai), then walk along beside the railway until reaching a bridge over the canal on your right. The museum is just across the canal.

National Gallery (Old City, Map on page 49)

This is just opposite the National Museum and displays classical and contemporary Thai art, including paintings by the King. The gallery is closed on Mondays, Tuesdays and National Holidays. Admission costs Bt30.

Transport – As for the National Museum.

Museum of Sciences and Planetarium (Map on page 57)

These are next to the Eastern Bus Terminal (Ekkamai) on Sukhumvit Road. They are closed on Mondays and National Holidays and the planetarium has its last showing on other days at 14:30. Admission costs Bt30 for the museum and Bt30 for the planetarium.

Transport – Buses 2, 25, 38, 40, 48 and 72, and air-conditioned 1, 8, 11 and 13, or Sky Train to Ekkamai (E7).

House of Dolls (Map on page 57)

Dolls from all over the world, but especially from Bangkok. The address of this collection is Soi Ratchataphan, Soi Mor Leng, off Ratcha Prarop Road, so, as can be imagined, it is not so easy to locate. Closed on Sundays and National Holidays. Admission free.

Transport – These buses run along Ratcha Prarop Road, from where the House of Dolls is a 10 minute walk: 14, 38, 62, 74, 77 and 204, and air-conditioned 4 and 13.

Dusit Zoo (Map on page 72)

Located between Wiman Mek and the National Assembly on one side and the King's Chitralada Palace on the other, this is quite an old zoo, with a good range of animals and birds. Admission costs Bt30.

Transport – Buses 5, 18, 28, 70 and 108, and air-conditioned 10 and 16.

Snake Farm (Patpong Area, Map on page 52)

The Snake Farm is part of the Red Cross facilities on Rama IV Road. Snakes are milked of their venom in order to produce anti-snake serum. Milking demonstrations are held at 10:30 every day and at 14:00 on weekdays. At weekends, the Snake Farm opens only in the morning. Admission costs Bt70.

Transport – Buses 4, 16, 21, 46, 109, 119 and 141, and air-conditioned 2 and 7.

Lumphini Park (Patpong Area, Map on page 52)

This is a pleasant park, very popular with Thais, especially in the early mornings and at the weekend, situated on Rama IV Road and near Chulalongkorn University. It is named after the birthplace of Buddha, on the border of India and Nepal. The park contains a lake and wooded areas and, at the entrance on Rama IV, a statue of King Rama VI (which seems contradictory). There are food stalls within the park, and even fresh snake blood available, if you happen to fancy it!

Transport – Buses 4, 13, 14, 15, 17, 22, 45, 46, 47, 50, 62, 67, 74, 76, 77, 106, 109, 115, 116, 119, 141 and 149, and air-conditioned 2, 4, 5 and 7, or Sky Train to Ratchadamri (S1) or Sala Daeng (S2).

Suan Chatuchak Weekend Market (Map on page 57)

This area near the Northern Bus Terminal (Morchit) is open land during the week, but a vast market at the weekend. The prime commodity is clothing, but almost everything is sold there, and it is well worth a visit.

Transport – Buses 3, 8, 24, 26, 27, 28, 29, 34, 38, 39, 44, 52, 59, 63, 69, 77, 92, 96, 104, 107, 112, 122, 129, 134, 136, 138 and 145, and air-conditioned 2, 3, 4, 9, 10, 12, 13, 157 and 159, or Sky Train to Morchit (N8).

Hall of Railway Heritage (Map on page 57)

Just to the west of Suan Chatuchak, mentioned above, is this train museum displaying steam engines and model and miniature trains. The area adjoins the yards of the State Railways of Thailand and can be seen from the train on the right as one departs from Bang Sue station, fifteen minutes after leaving Bangkok (Hualampong). Unfortunately the museum is open only between 5:00 and noon on Sundays.

Transport – As for Suan Chatuchak above.

Thai Boxing

Thai Boxing includes the use of parts of the body other than the gloved hands for attack. Kicking, in particular, is common. Loud Thai music often accompanies boxing matches. There are two places to watch such bouts, viz.:

(i)   Ratchadamnoen Stadium (Map on page 49)

This stadium is just next to the TAT office on Ratchadamnoen Road and stages Thai Boxing on Mondays, Wednesdays, Thursdays and Sundays starting at 18:00.

Transport – Buses 10, 49, 53, 70 and 201, and air-conditioned 3, 9 and 32, but many other buses go near. From Khao San Road, it is walking distance.

(ii)   Lumphini Stadium (Map on page 57)

Lumphini Stadium is just beyond Lumphini Park and matches are held here on Tuesdays, Fridays and Saturdays, also at 18:00.

Transport – Buses 4, 13, 14, 22, 45, 46, 47, 74, 109, 115, 116, 141 and 149, and air-conditioned 7.

ONE-DAY TRIPS FROM BANGKOK
Floating Market

The most likely place for a one day trip is the Floating Market. There are, in fact, two floating markets, one at Klong Dao Kanong in Thonburi and one further out at **Damnoen Saduak** in Ratchaburi Province. It is generally agreed that the Thonburi

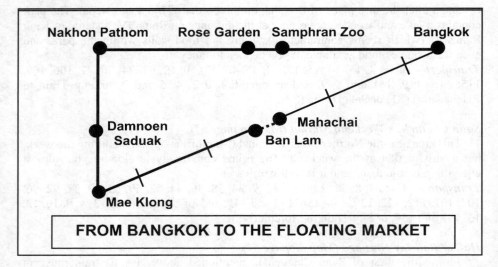

Nakhon Pathom   Rose Garden   Samphran Zoo   Bangkok

Damnoen
Saduak   Mahachai
                                  Ban Lam

Mae Klong

FROM BANGKOK TO THE FLOATING MARKET

market is disappointing because it has become primarily a tourist attraction, with more visitors than boats. Therefore, the expedition needs to be to Damnoen Saduak, which is a hundred kilometres from Bangkok, and one needs to go early.

There one will find hundreds of small boats, mostly operated by women, selling everything from meat to T-shirts. The purchasers are those living along the banks of the canal, those who come down to the waterside to buy, and also those in other boats. It is a colourful scene, although it too has become well touristed these days.

Transport – Buses leave from the Southern Bus Terminal in Bangkok. From Hualampong Station take a bus no. 40 or air-conditioned 7. From Sukhumvit Road take a no. 40 or air-conditioned 11. From Khao San Road, walk across to Sanam Luang and take no. 30 or 124, or, from Democracy Monument, take air-conditioned no. 3, 11 or 17. Early in the morning, as it will be, these journeys will be quite speedy.

From the Southern Bus Terminal, you want to take bus no. 78 or 996 (the number is written on the side) to Damnoen Saduak. It will take two hours and buses operate every 20 minutes starting at 6:00. The fare is Bt57 each way. You should try to go as early as possible, otherwise you will be too late for the best part of the market. After arrival at Damnoen Saduak, follow the map on the opposite page for the two kilometre walk to the site of the market.

If you want to go by train, see the section on Wong Wian Yai Station below on page 69. It will be quite an interesting journey, but you need to be at Wong Wian Yai Station by 6:00 at the latest, as there are only four trains every day from Ban Lam to Mae Klong and the one which you need to catch leaves at 7:30. Perhaps it would be safer to make the outward journey by bus and the return trip by train.

If you prefer to return by bus, however, one of the following stops can be added.

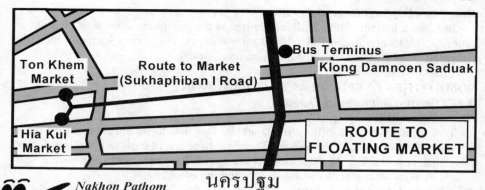

Nakhon Pathom นครปฐม

The major town on the way back from the Floating Market is Nakhon Pathom, which is probably the oldest town in Thailand, dating from the third century B.C. It was the principal city in the Dvaravati Kingdom in the sixth to eleventh centuries. Nowadays, however, it would be just an ordinary town but for the huge orange **Phra Pathom Chedi** which stands not far from the railway and bus stations and which dominates the landscape. It is the tallest single Buddhist monument in the world, rising to 127 metres. The original *chedi*, now hidden inside the current monument, was built in the early sixth century. In the eleventh century, the city was captured by the Khmer and a Brahman structure was constructed over the top, but then in 1057 the Burmese came and destroyed the city, leaving the monument in ruins until King Mongkut decided to restore it in 1860. It was he who built this gigantic *chedi* over the remains of the old ones.

This monument is really most impressive. Its sheer size is awe-inspiring and it should be visited. If you cannot manage to do so at the same time as going to the Floating Market, try to find another opportunity. It is on the way to Bangkok from the south, for example, or from Kanchanaburi, and the Phra Pathom Chedi is only ten minutes walk from the railway station and less from the bus station.

Transport – From Damnoen Saduak, bus no. 78 (but not no. 996) will pass Nakhon Pathom on its journey. From Bangkok, there are additional buses this far. The journey between Nakhon Pathom and Bangkok takes about 75 minutes. The 56 kilometre ride costs Bt32 for an air-conditioned bus. By train it costs only Bt14 third class.

The Rose Garden

Between Nakhon Pathom and Bangkok, 24 kilometres from the former and 32 kilometres from the latter, is the Rose Garden, which is another candidate for a stop. It has very pleasant gardens and a type of Instant Thailand show each afternoon at 14:45, in case you do not have time to explore the whole country yourself. The show includes Thai boxing, folk dancing, swordsmanship and an elephant display. It costs Bt300.

Samphran Elephant Ground and Zoo

Just one kilometre from the Rose Garden is the Samphran Zoo. It too has show times, at 12:45 and 14:20 (also 10:30 on holidays). The shows include crocodile wrestling, elephants and magic. Admission costs Bt300.

SOME OTHER USEFUL PLACES IN BANGKOK

TAT (Tourism Authority of Thailand)

(i) Airport (Map on page 57)

TAT actually has six offices in Bangkok. The first to be encountered by most arrivals is one of those at the airport. There are two, one at each terminal, so do not miss that opportunity. At least obtain a map of Bangkok, and, if possible, get information on other places which you are thinking of visiting.

(ii) Ratchadamnoen Nok Avenue (Map on page 49)

There is a TAT office in Ratchadamnoen Nok Avenue, an impressively wide tree-lined avenue close to Khao San Road. To walk there from the latter will take ten to fifteen minutes. Opening hours here and at all regional offices of TAT are 8:30 until 16:30 every day (including holidays).

Transport – Buses 10, 49, 70 and 201 and air-conditioned 3, 9 and 32 actually pass the office, but many other services run near by. From Khao San Road, one should walk. From Sukhumvit Road, take bus no. 2 or air-conditioned no. 11 and alight at the end of Ratchadamnoen Nok Avenue, just before the bus crosses the canal there. It is five minutes walk to the TAT office. From Hualampong Station, cross the canal and take bus no. 35, alighting at the end of Ratchadamnoen Nok Avenue, just as the bus turns left towards the Democracy Monument. It is six or seven minutes walk from there.

(iii) Head Office (Map on page 57)

The head office of TAT is in a somewhat inconvenient location on Ratchada Phisek Road in north-eastern Bangkok, on the 10th Floor of Le Concorde Building. This office is open from 8:30 until 16:30 on Mondays to Fridays only.

Transport – Buses 73, 136, 137 and 206, and air-conditioned 15, 18 and 22 run past. From Sukhumvit Road, take bus 136 or air-conditioned 22 from Soi 21. From Hualampong Station, take no. 73. From Khao San Road, there is no direct bus, so better to use the Ratchadamnoen Nok Avenue office which is only a short walk away.

(iv) Suan Chatuchak Weekend Market (Map on page 57)

There is an office behind the weekend market in the Market Office Building on Kamphaeng Phet 2 Road, but this is open only when the market is, i.e. at weekends.

Transport – Buses 3, 8, 24, 26, 27, 28, 29, 34, 38, 39, 44, 52, 59, 63, 69, 77, 92, 96, 104, 107, 112, 122, 129, 134, 136, 138 and 145, and air-conditioned 2, 3, 4, 9, 10, 12, 13, 157 and 159, or Sky Train to Morchit (N8).

(v) Khao San Road

There is a small office opposite the Chana Songkram Police Box at the western end of Khao San Road, but this office has very limited resources.

G.P.O. and Telecommunications Centre (including Internet) (Map on page 71)

These very useful and efficient institutions lie on a bend of the river south of Hualampong Station.

The **General Post Office** is open from 8:00 until 20:00 on weekdays and from 9:00 until 13:00 on Saturdays and Sundays. It is an old-fashioned, cool (without being air-conditioned) and spacious building, the type that makes you want to sit and read your mail in a relaxed manner while wondering why the world is in such a hurry. **Poste Restante** is located here and will keep your letters for two months. Show your passport, whereupon you are allowed to search the initial letters of both your given and your family name. You pay Bt1 for each item received. There is also a philatelic counter where you can purchase pretty stamps for your postcards home, but only in complete sets (i.e. you cannot buy one denomination in an issue without buying the same number of stamps of the other denominations also). Especially useful is the **packing service** offered in one corner of the office. Take your souvenirs there and they will be wrapped very professionally and effectively for a modest fee – an idea which many more post offices around the world might do well to imitate.

The **Telecommunications Centre** is just to the right of the G.P.O. and offers telephone calls and **Internet**. There are some other locations around Bangkok from which telephone calls can be made, but this is the only one which is open twenty-four hours a day. Telephone calls are made by direct dialling, but must be booked a few minutes beforehand, at which time a deposit is paid and any unused money is refunded later. Minimum charge is for one minute. The calls are relatively expensive.

Internet, however, is cheap. One purchases a card for Bt100, then reveals the secret number on the reverse and enters it into the computer. Take care, because I and 1, and also O and 0, look very similar (as indeed they do in this book). There is a Bt3 connexion fee, after which each minute of use costs Bt0.54. The same card may be used at any of the Telecommunications Centres in Thailand which has the Internet system.

Transport – From Hualampong Station, the G.P.O. is within walking distance. From Khao San Road, walk down to the river and take an express boat to Sri Phraya Pier. From Sukhumvit Road, take a bus no. 25 or 40 or air-conditioned no. 1 to Hualampong Station and walk from there.

Northern Bus Terminal (Morchit Mai) (Map on page 57)

Buses to the north, north-east and central parts of the country leave from here. This terminal has recently been moved. There is now more space, and a smart modern building, but it is not particularly easy to locate the right ticket window, as few destinations are written in Roman script. After that, locating the appropriate bus from the mass of vehicles lined up with throbbing engines is another challenging task.

Transport – The following buses actually go to the Northern Bus Terminal: 3, 26, 44, 49, 77, 96, 122, 134, 136, 138, 139 and 145, and air-conditioned 9, 12, 18, 23, 157 and 159. However, in some cases not all buses of these numbers actually go into the bus terminal and finish there. When they do not do so, they pass close. The following additional buses pass within reasonable walking distance: 8, 24, 27, 28, 29, 34, 38, 39, 52, 59, 63, 69, 92, 104, 107, 112 and 129, and air-conditioned 2, 3, 4, 10, and 13. Morchit Station (N8) on the Sky Train is also within walking distance.

Southern Bus Terminal (Sai Tai Mai) (Map on page 57)

This too has moved recently and expanded. Buses leave from here to everywhere west, south-west and south of the capital.

Transport – The following buses go to the Southern Bus Terminal: 19, 28, 30, 40, 57, 66, 123, 124, 127, 146 and 149, and air-conditioned 3, 7, 11, 17, 33 and 159. Nos. 28, 30 and 159 terminate here.

Eastern Bus Terminal (Ekkamai) (Map on page 57)

The Eastern Bus Terminal serves destinations east and south-east of Bangkok and is the smallest of the bus terminals. It is located along Sukhumvit Road by Soi 42 and Soi 63.

Transport – The following buses may be used to reach the Eastern Bus Terminal: 2, 25, 38, 40, 48 and 72, and air-conditioned 1, 8, 11 and 13. Alternatively, it is immediately outside Ekkamai Station (E7) on the Sky Train.

Bangkok (Hualampong) Railway Station (Map on page 51)

All of the express trains to destinations all over Thailand depart from Bangkok Railway Station in Hualampong. Most ordinary trains depart from here too, but a few leave from Thonburi Station (see under). Hualampong is an impressive domed station, constructed in 1910 and renovated within in 1998, with an atmosphere of coming and going, as all good stations should have. There are two types of procedure possible here. If you are catching a train departing immediately, line up at the appropriate window, buy a ticket and get on the train. For ordinary trains, that is the only way. If it is a rapid or express train, your ticket will bear a seat number. When you find that seat, there will probably be somebody sitting in it if it is a third class seat, but it is best to find a seat nearby if possible, just in case the rightful owner of that seat comes along and demands it, in which case you can start to demand your seat. If it is a second class seat or a sleeping berth, however, the procedure is to occupy the correct seat or berth.

The second type of procedure is to make an advance reservation. There is an office for the purpose at the rear of the concourse on the right. You enter, take a number and sit and wait until that number is called. If you want a sleeping berth, in particular, it is strongly advisable to make a reservation three or four days in advance.

It should be mentioned that Bangkok Railway Station is frequented by certain unscrupulous characters, so one should be cautious and alert, without being paranoid. Do not put anything down, as there may be somebody waiting to pick it up for you. There are also pickpockets operating here. Recently, also, visitors have started to find themselves approached by people who say that they work for the railways and are there to assist travellers. It appears that the purpose of this act is to lure travellers onto highly priced buses, by telling them that the buses are operated by the railways and are more convenient than the trains. It is a curious act, but bear in mind that the State Railways of Thailand does not employ anybody to offer assistance to passengers in this way. If you want help, you ask at the Information Desk.

Transport – The following buses pass or terminate at Hualampong Railway Station: 1, 4, 7, 21, 25, 29, 34, 35, 40, 53, 73, 109, 113 and 119, and air-conditioned 1, 7 and 159.

Thonburi Railway Station (Map on page 49)

The minor station at Thonburi has seven arrivals and seven departures every day. All services are by ordinary train and all are on the southern line: two to Chumphon and Lang Suan, one to Prachuap Kiri Khan, one to Ratchaburi, two to Kanchanaburi and Nam Tok, and one to Nakhon Pathom. It is not, therefore, a busy station. Just go there, buy your ticket and get on the train. In fact, this route, departing from the west side of the river, offers a short cut to the main line, which it joins at Thaling Chan Junction, about twelve kilometres out. Most travellers who use Thonburi Station do so for the Kanchanaburi trains which depart at 7:40 and 13:50.

Transport – The best way to reach Thonburi Railway Station is to take a ferry or express boat to Rot Fai Pier, which is immediately outside the station. From Sukhumvit Road take a bus no. 25 or an air-conditioned 8 to Tha Tien Pier, which is the terminus for both services, and then the express boat to Rot Fai. From Hualampong it is better to take the 53 to Phra Chan and then the ferry just across the river. Phra Chan Pier is also within walking distance of Khao San Road, if you prefer the ferry to an express boat.

Wong Wian Yai Station (Map on page 57)

Most people believe that there are two terminal stations in the Bangkok area. In fact, though, there are three. The line from Wong Wian Yai is little known, but fun. Wong Wian Yai Station has just a single platform, and you can pass right by it without even noticing that it is there. Trains depart approximately every twenty minutes for the journey of an hour to Mahachai Station in Samut Sakhon, west of Bangkok. There the line ends, but if you walk on a short distance and take a ferry across the river, then search to your right, you will find another station on the other side called Ban Lam. From here onwards, the service is operated by just a single train which shuttles back and forth four times per day. If you wish to return to Bangkok that day, the most useful services from here are at 7:30 and 10:10. The journey to Mae Klong in Samut Songkram takes a further hour. When the author went, the market, which covers the tracks, had to be moved out of the way to make room for the train. The reason why the line goes no further is immediately apparent. The buffers at the end are on the bank of another wide river (which is, in fact, the Kwai River which we shall meet again at Kanchanaburi), and again there is no bridge. We are now only 12 kilometres from the **Floating Market** at Damnoen Saduak, so if you feel like a little adventure, this is an alternative way to go or return. Trains leave for the return journey at 9:00 and 11:30, and there are two more departures in the afternoon.

Transport – The following buses pass or go very near Wong Wian Yai Station: 3, 4, 7, 9, 10, 21, 37, 42, 43, 57, 82, 84, 101 and 111, and air-conditioned 6 and 10. From Sukhumvit Road and Hualampong, the 40 goes near also, but for the return journey it is about ten minutes walk away.

ACCOMMODATION

Here follows a brief list of some of the accommodation which may be found in the most popular areas of Bangkok and maps showing these hotels and guest houses. In truth, though, these areas have so much choice to offer that it is probably best just to walk around until you find a place which appeals to you, or to act upon the recommendations of contemporary travellers, for these matters can change very quickly.

(i)   Khao San Road Area (Map on page 50)

Name	No. on Map	Rooms	Cheapest Price (Bt)	Name	No. on Map	Rooms	Cheapest Price (Bt)
Apple	1	15	100	Dior	13	30	100
Merry V	2	60	150	Bonny	14	9	150
My House	3	60	150	Sri	15	30	400
Peachy N.P.	4	50	150	160 Guest House	16	18	100
Green House	5	70	150	Seven Holder	17	28	120
J Guest House	6	33	120	Pro	18	6	100
Khao San Palace	7	40	200	Harn	19	17	100
Lek	8	20	150	C H II	20	18	120
Hello	9	16	150	Sweety	21	12	100
Ploy	10	24	150	Central	22	15	100
New Nith Charoen	11	24	300	Prasuri	23	24	200
Nut	12	10	150				

(ii)   Sukhumvit Road Area (Maps on pages 52 (nos. 24 - 28) and 53)

Name	No. on Map	Soi	Rms.	Price (Bt)	Name	No. on Map	Soi	Rms.	Price (Bt)
Siam Intercontinental	24		400	7,000	Grace	36	3	535	600
Novotel	25		429	5,000	Nana	37	4	334	900
Siam Orchid Inn	26		40	1,300	Rajah	38	4	420	600
Grand Hyatt Erawan	27		400	12,000	Amari Boulevard	39	5	315	3,500
Regent	28		356	10,000	Fortuna	40	5	100	900
Hilton International	29		338	9,000	Royal Benja	41	5	400	3,200
Holiday Mansion	30		95	1,600	Bel-aire Princess	42	5	160	3,000
Golden Palace	31	1	65	500	Landmark	43		415	1,200
Street One Lodge	32	1	30	500	Sukhumvit Crown	44	6	152	600
Atlanta	33	2	100	600	Park	45	7	139	2,200
J.W. Marriott	34	2	435	5,000	Royal Asia Lodge	46	8	40	900
Grand Inn	35	3	24	900	Promenade	47	8	42	1,000

(ii) Sukhumvit Road Area (continued)

Name	No. on Map	Soi	Rms.	Price (Bt)
City Lodge	48	9	28	900
World Inn	49	9	47	700
Federal	50	11	93	700
Swiss Park	51	11	108	1,500
A.W. Business Inn	52	11	10	600
Ambassador	53	11	750	2,500
Miami	54	13	123	500

Name	No. on Map	Soi	Rms.	Price (Bt)
Manhattan	55	15	203	1,500
Ruamchit Plaza	56	15	48	1,000
Somerset	57	15	76	2,500
Honey	58	19	75	700
Delta Grand Pacific	59	19	387	4,500
Sheraton Grande	60		445	10,000

(iii) Hualampong Railway Station Area

Name	No. on Map	Rooms	Cheapest Price (Bt)
Sri Krung	71	35	550
Sri Hualampong	72	40	250
Station Hotel	73	50	250
Bangkok Centre	74	246	1,500
F.F. Guest House	75	12	150
Mandarin	76	400	3,000

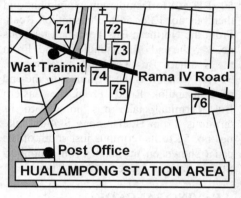

(iv) Silom Road Area

Name	Rooms	Cheapest Price (Bt)
Dusit Thani	530	12,000
Royal Orchid Sheraton	733	11,000
Sukhothai	224	11,000
Shangri-La	866	9,500
Oriental	396	8,000
Evergreen Laurel	160	5,500
Holiday Inn Crown Plaza	700	5,000
Pan Pacific	235	5,000
Monarch Lee Garden	454	4,500
Montien	475	4,500
Narai	500	3,500
Tawana Ramada	265	3,500
Tan Tawan Place	70	2,800

Name	Rooms	Cheapest Price (Bt)
Trinity	87	2,500
New Peninsula	102	2,200
Tower Inn	120	1,700
Silom City Inn	70	1,500
Manohra	230	1,300
Silom Plaza	200	1,300
Wall Street Inn	75	1,200
New Trocadaro	128	1,000
Rose	105	900
Surawong Tower Inn	80	700
Newrotel	45	500
Niagara	90	350

72 BANGKOK

There is also a **Youth Hostel** in Bangkok. It is located some fifteen minutes walk north of Khao San Road, in a *soi* (alley) just off Phitsanulok Road (see map opposite). It has air-conditioned dormitory accommodation for Bt120, air-conditioned single rooms for Bt280 or air-conditioned double rooms for Bt350.

To get there from the airport, take airport bus no. A2 (Bt100) or city bus no. 59 (Bt3.50) to Democracy Monument and then bus no. 12 or 56 to Phitsanulok Road. From the Northern Bus Terminal, take bus no. 3 to the end of Phitsanulok Road. From the Southern Bus Terminal, take bus no. 30 (for which it is the terminus) to the end of Phitsanulok Road. From the Eastern Bus Terminal, take bus no. 72 to its terminus. From Hualampong Station, take bus no. 52 to its terminus just south of the canal shown on the map. From Thonburi Station, take an express boat to Thewes.

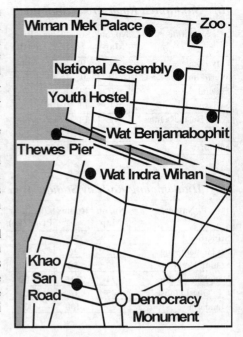

LEAVING BANGKOK

(i) By Train

Here are timetables for the various routes from Bangkok to other parts of Thailand, divided by area: North (Phitsanulok, Chiang Mai), North-East (Nakhon Ratchasima, Ubon Ratchathani, Udon Thani, Nong Khai), East (Aranyaprathet, Pattaya, Ban Plutaluang) and South (Kanchanaburi, Nam Tok, Surat Thani, Haad Yai, Padang Besar, Sungai Golok). Of course, times change, but generally they do not change very much with the State Railways of Thailand, so these will give a good guide. However, they should be checked before travelling. These are timetables only from Bangkok. Timetables to Bangkok appear in the sections for the towns of departure.

Key:
Type of Train: S.E. – Special Express
                        Exp. – Express
                        Rap. – Rapid
                        Ord. – Ordinary
                        Mix. – Mixed
                        * – Air-conditioned 2nd class available
                        † – 2nd class sleepers available

(a) To The North

Type of Train	Ord	Rap *	Exp *	Ord	Exp *	Rap *†	Exp *	S.E *†	Rap *	Exp *	S.E *†	Rap *†	Rap *†	Exp *	Ord
Classes	3	2,3	2	3	2	1,2,3	2	1,2	2,3	2	1,2	2,3	2,3	2	3
Bangkok	0705	0745	0825	0835	1055	1500	1635	1800	1810	1925	1940	2000	2200	2310	
Don Muang	0800	0846	0918	0932	1146	1556	1726	1852	1902	2016	2037	2056	2258	2400	
Bang Pa In	0839			1012				1938							
Ayutthaya	0852	0935		1025		1644		1945	1955			2123	2145	2346	
Lopburi	1004	1052	1041	1156		1756		2045	2055			2247	0047		
Phitsanulok	1510	1458	1337	1733	1645	2202	2220	0031	0103	0112		0314	0515	0532	1148
Ban Dalar	1632								0226					0646	1301
Sawan Kalok														0705	1345
Uttaradit	1707	1631	1452			2350		0158	0250	0226		0443	0713		
Sila At	1713	1645				0004		0204	0255		0345	0448	0728		
Den Chai	1810	1744	1548			0107		0258	0327		0442	0540	0625		
Lampang		2020	1753			0335		0510	0535			0700	1105		
Chiang Mai		2220	1935			0535		0710	0720			0905	1305		

Distances and Fares:	Distance (km)	2nd class (Bt)	3rd class (Bt)
Don Muang	22	11	5
Bang Pa In	58	28	12
Ayuttthaya	71	35	15
Lopburi	133	64	28
Phitsanulok	389	159	69
Chiang Mai	751	281	121

(plus supplements for sleepers, rapids and expresses, and air-conditioning)
For return timetable, see page 228..

(b) To The North-East

Type of Train	Ord	Exp *	Rap	Rap	Exp *	Exp *	Ord	Ord	Rap	Rap	Exp *†	Exp *	Exp *†	Exp *	Rap	Ord
Classes	3	2	2,3	2,3	2,3	2,3	3	3	2,3	2,3	1,2,3	2	1,2,3	2,3	2,3	3
Bangkok		0545	0615	0650	0820	1105	1145	1525	1845	1900	2030	2040	2100	2150	2245	2325
Don Muang		0634	0712	0748	0906	1158	1235	1621	1939	1954	2120	2130	2154	2237	2333	0017
Bang Pa In							1313	1659								0054
Ayutthaya		0718	0754	0833	0944	1242	1329	1712	2022	2040	2203	2213	2237		0015	0108
Nakhon Ratchasima	0615	1028		1222		1621	1819	2152	0030	0147	0226	0305			0501	0534
Buriram		1145		1420		1800	2024	0030	0215		0406		0455	0654		0806
Surin		1219		1507		1845	2125	0130	0304		0452		0545	0748		0921
Ubon Ratchathani		1405		1810				0445	0535		0720			1045		1230
Khon Kaen	0756		1510		1624					0402		0537			0434	
Udon Thani	1135		1707		1800					0616		0749			0625	
Nong Khai	1225		1800							0710		0840				

Distances and Fares:	Distance (km)	2nd class (Bt)	3rd class (Bt)
Don Muang	22	11	5
Ayuttthaya	71	35	15
Nakhon Ratchasima	264	115	50
Ubon Ratchathani	575	221	95
Udon Thani	569	219	95
Nong Khai	624	238	103

(plus supplements for sleepers, rapids and expresses, and air-conditioning)
For return timetables, see pages 121, 138 and 153.

74 BANGKOK

(c) To The East

Type of Train	Ord	Ord	Ord	Ord	Mix	Ord	Ord	Ord
Classes	3	3	3	3	3	3	3	3
Bangkok	0555	0655	0800	0940	1120	1305	1505	1725
Chachoengsao	0734	0848	0942	1130	1345	1440	1650	1905
Prachinburi	0903		1054	1245	1523	1552	1830	2020
Kabinburi	0950		1145		1635	1648	1855	
Aranyaprathet	1140					1830		
Pattaya		1037						
Ban Plutaluang		1110						

For return timetable, see page 116.

(d) To The South

Type of Train	Ord	Ord	Ord	Rap *†	Ord	Ord	S.E. *†	S.E. *†	Rap *†	Exp *†	Rap *†	Ord	Rap *†	Exp *†	Exp *	Exp *
Classes	3	3	3	1,2,3	3	3	1,2	1,2,3	1,2,3	1,2,3	1,2,3	3	1,2,3	1,2,3	2	2
Bangkok				‡1225			1420	1445	1550	1705	1735		1820	1915	2230	2250
Thonburi	0720	0740														
Nakhon Pathom	0853	0920	1104	1406	1419	1459	1547	1620	1730	1837	1910		1955	2049	2347	0001
Kanchanaburi		1100				1625										
River Kwai Bridge		1108				1642										
Nam Tok		1250				1840										
Cha-Am	1127		1324		1704				1944							
Hua Hin	1158		1345	1637	1728		1821	1853	2008	2107	2138		2230	2321	0146	0146
Prachuap Kiri Khan	1343			1755	1855			2016	2133		2309		2351	0041	0258	0332
Chumphon	1725			2047			2225	2305	0042	0117	0213		0304	0413	0513	0545
Lang Suan	1850			2218						0200	0321		0413	0520	0609	
Surat Thani				0037			0150	0218	0350	0442	0523		0625	0720	0735	0801
Trang	Exp *† 1,2									0835			1045			
Kantang													1125			
Nakhon Si Thammarat											0925	0955		1050		
Haad Yai	1510			0630			0705	0725	0945			1433				1217
Padang Besar #	1700						0850									
Butterworth #	2059						1255									
Kuala Lumpur #	0605															
Yala				0815				0913	1130				1705			1350
Sungai Golok				1000				1055								

‡ Train starts in Chachoengsao. Stops in Bangkok at Sam Sen (9:28) and Bang Sue (9:36) Stations.
# Malaysian Time (one hour ahead of Thai time).

Distances and Fares:	Distance (km)	2nd class (Bt)	3rd class (Bt)
Kanchanaburi	133		25
Nam Tok	210		41
Hua Hin	229	102	44
Chumphon	485	190	82
Surat Thani	651	248	107
Trang	845	311	135
Nakhon Si Thammarat	832	308	133
Haad Yai	945	345	149
Padang Besar	990	360	156
Sungai Golok	1,159	417	180

(plus supplements for sleepers, rapids and expresses, and air-conditioning)
For return timetable, see pages 265 and 369.

(ii) By Bus

Buses run from Bangkok to virtually every town in the country. Here is a list of bus routes arranged first by region, then alphabetically within the region, with journey times and prices for the different types of buses. It should be borne in mind that the nearer destinations will also be served by some buses travelling longer distances.

(a) To The North (from Northern Bus Terminal)

Destination	Route No.	Distance (km)	Price (Bt)				Journey Time (hrs)		Frequency	
			V.I.P.	A/C 1	A/C 2	Ord.	A/C	Ord.	A/C	Ord.
Chiang Kham	962	778		470		219	12	13	1/day	1/day
Chiang Khong	962	875		450	350	250	14	15	8/day	8/day
Chiang Mai	18	713	570	369	290	205	11	12	30 mins	5/day
Chiang Rai	909	805	640	412	321	229	12	13	8/day	9/day
Chiang Rai	90	844			337	241	13	14	3/day	10/day
Chiang Saen	3	910	730	470		261	13	14	1/day	1/day
Kampang Phet	94	358		189	147	105	6	6.5	4/day	4/day
Khao Khor	965	478		250			7.5		3/day	
Kuen Phumipol	93	482				140		8		1/day
Lampang	91	610	490	317	246	176	9.5	10	10/day	4/day
Lampun	924	685	550	355	276		10.5		4/day	
Mae Hong Son	961	928		509		292	17	18	1/day	1/day
Mae Sai	957	856	685	441	343	245	13	14	7/day	4/day
Mae Sod	956	520	420	272	211	151	8.5	9.5	7/day	2/day
Nakhon Sawan	95	237		128		71	3.5	4	Hourly	Frequent
Nan	910	677	545	351	273	195	11	12	6/day	1/day
Nan	96	747			300	214	11	12	1/day	1/day
Phayao	922	712	565	365	284	203	11	12	5/day	4/day
Phitsanulok	100/913	372	302	194	160	115	6	7	Hourly	Hourly
Phrae	923	559	445	288		160	8.5	9	2/day	2/day
Pichit	911	368		180	140	103	5.5	6	6/day	2/day
Sawan Kalok	925	478		250	195	139	8	8.5	8/day	4/day
Sukhothai	965	440		230	179	128	7.5	8	8/day	5/day
Sri Satchanalai	100	490		250			8.5		2/day	
Tak	93	420	345	221	172	123	7	8	4/day	3/day
Thaton	13	890		457			12		2/day	
Thaeng	91	803		414			12		2/day	
Thung Chang	47	766		394			12		3/day	
Uttaradit	912	481/546	390	252		140/158	9	10	10/day	8/day

(b) To The North-East (from Northern Bus Terminal)

Destination	Route No.	Distance (km)	Price (Bt)				Journey Time (hrs)		Frequency	
			V.I.P.	A/C 1	A/C 2	Ord.	A/C	Ord.	A/C	Ord.
Amnat Charoen	929	577		301		157	8.5	10	1/day	1/day
Bampheng	33	784			315	225	10	12	5/day	3/day
Bampheng	34	809			325	223	10	12	2/day	2/day
Bungkan	943	750		387		215	10	12	2/day	2/day
Buriram	32	402		205	168	120	5	6	14/day	1/day
Buriram	926	384				113		6		1/day
Chaiyaphum	28/9903	332		176	137	93	5	6	Frequent	1/day
Chiang Khan	29	609	490			176	10	11	1/day	2/day
Chumphae	29	432		227		126	6	7	Hourly	1/day

(b) To The North-East (from Northern Bus Terminal, continued)

Destination	Route No.	Distance (km)	Price (Bt)				Journey Time (hrs)		Frequency	
			V.I.P.	A/C 1	A/C 2	Ord.	A/C	Ord.	A/C	Ord.
Kalasin	30	513		268		149	8	9	4/day	2/day
Khemmarat	929	649		337		187	9.5	10.5	2/day	2/day
Khon Kaen	20	444	360	232	181	129	6.5	7.5	Frequent	7/day
Khong Chiam	955	707				203		11.5		1/day
Kuchinarai	927	603				175		10.5		1/day
Loei	29	560	450	292	227	162	9.5	11	Hourly	1/day
Loei (Khon Kaen)	938	653		338		188	10	12	4/day	3/day
Longnoktha	24	623				178		10.5		2/day
Maha Sarakham	932	469		245		136	7	8	7/day	2/day
Mukdahan (Ubon)	946	814		419				11.5		1/day
Mukdahan (Roi Et)	927	671	540	347		193	10.5	11.5	4/day	2/day
Mukdahan (Yasothon)	928	665		311		191	10.5	11	4/day	2/day
Nakhon Phanom	26	727	585	376	293	209	11	12	12/day	4/day
Nakhon Phanom	930	817		421	328	234	11	12.5	3/day	2/day
Nakhon Ratchasima	21	256		139		77	3.5	4.5	10 mins	Hourly
Nong Bua Lamphu	5	535		279	217	155	8	8.5	3/day	2/day
Nong Khai	23/935	614	495	319	263	177	9.5	10.5	6/day	7/day
Phang Khon	97	668		246			9.5		5/day	
Phanom Prai	941	527		275		153	8	10	2/day	2/day
Phayakka Phumisai	939	452		238		118	7.5	8.5	9/day	5/day
Phi Mai	944	322		170	130		5.5		4/day	
Phu Kheo	29	429				120		6.5		2/day
Rasisalai	945	555				160		10		1/day
Rattanaburi	944	491		256	199	142	6	7	Hourly	3/day
Renu Nakhon	27	722		372	290	207	11	12	5/day	1/day
Roi Et	24/927	509	410	266		148	7	8	11/day	3/day
Sakon Nakhon	26/27	647/633	505	325		182	9.5/10	10.5	6/day	3/day
Sisaket	926	547		284		165	8	9	2/day	4/day
Sisaket (Chakarat)	942	536			217	155	9	10	2/day	2/day
Somdet	30	553	445				8.5		1/day	
Sowdrin	31	428		229			6		4/day	
Sri Chiang Mai	5/933	646		335		186	10	11	5/day	1/day
Surin	31	451	355	225	183	131	7	8	Hourly	2/day
Surin	937	436			180	127	7	8	1/day	1/day
Suwanaphum	935	492		257		137	7.5	8.5	8/day	3/day
That Phanom	27/86	707	565	365		203	11	12	3/day	1/day
Ubon Ratchathani	98	679	520	337		193	10	11	Hourly	1/day
Ubon Ratchathani	931	624				180		10.5		2/day
Ubon R (Buriram)	947	601		311			9.5		4/day	
Udon Thani	22/23	561			292	162	8.5	9.5	18/day	13/day
Udon Thani (Roi Et)	24	673		351		195	8.5	9.5	2/day	2/day
Yasothon	968/929	522	420	272		151	9	10	3/day	2/day

(c) To Central Thailand (from Northern Bus Terminal)

Destination	Route No.	Distance (km)	Price (Bt)				Journey Time (hrs)		Frequency	
			V.I.P.	A/C 1	A/C 2	Ord.	A/C	Ord.	A/C	Ord.
Ang Thong	902/15	106/108		61	48/49		2.5		25 mins	
Aranyaprathet	60/921	299/269		160/144	125/112		5/4.5		30 mins	
Ayutthaya	901	75		43	34		2		10 mins	
Ayutthaya	17	97			45	32	2	2.5	30 mins	12/day

(c) To Central Thailand (from Northern Bus Terminal, continued)

Destination	Route No.	Distance (km)	Price (Bt)				Journey Time (hrs)		Frequency	
			V.I.P.	A/C 1	A/C 2	Ord.	A/C	Ord.	A/C	Ord.
Ban Mi	919	208		111			4		6/day	
Bang Pa In	16	78			35	25	2	2.5	20 mins	11/day
Chachoengsao	907/54	74/78			33/36	26	2	2.5	10 mins	10 mins
Chainat	906	194		106	83		3.5		12/day	
Chainat (Sanburi)	8	199		110	85	61	3.5	4	15/day	5/day
Chanthaburi	9907	236		135			4		Hourly	
Hankha	908	205		112	87		3		10/day	
Kamphaengsan	966	102			35		1.5		10/day	
Klong Lan	9	366		193	150		6.5		11/day	
Lom Sak	14	393		207	161	115	6.5	7	30 mins	Hourly
Lopburi	11/12	153		86	57		3		10 mins	
Nakhon Nayok	954/58	137		63/77	50		2		20 mins	
Pattaya	48/9905	138		79			2.5		30 mins	
Phra Chulchomklao	967	107			49	35	2	2.5	30 mins	6/day
Prachinburi	59/920	168/138		93/79	73		3/2.5		20 mins	
Rayong	57/9906	191		104	99	71	3.5	4	30 mins	40 mins
Samut Songkham	972	119			53	38	2	2.5	8/day	30 mins
Saraburi	904	108			49		2		Hourly	
Singburi	11/905	142		81	63		2.5		20 mins	
Suphanburi	974/951	102/155		59	45/67		2/2.5		20 mins	
Takli	919	199		110			4		Hourly	
Tha Chang	975	149/186		85/104			2/3		15/day	
Trat	9908	317		175			5.5		Hourly	
Uthai Thani	10/903	222/242		121	95/102		3.5		30 mins	
Wat Sing	19	226		117	95		4		30 mins	

(d) To The East (from Eastern Bus Terminal)

Destination	Route No.	Distance (km)	Price (Bt)				Journey Time (hrs)		Frequency	
			V.I.P.	A/C 1	A/C 2	Ord.	A/C	Ord.	A/C	Ord.
Ban Khai	915	217				66		5		Hourly
Ban Phe	915	196		108		60	3.5	4	Hourly	3/day
Banbung	51	94				31		2		4/day
Bang Khla	39/55	124		72	60	40	3.5	4	2/day	4/day
Bangsan	49	97		58			2		2 hrs	
Chachoengsao	40/53	100/87		55		33/26	2	2.5/2	30 mins	30 mins
Chanthaburi	914/42	239/309	151	130	101/129	72/92	4.5/5.5	5.5/6.5	30 mins	11/day
Chonburi	50/38	80/93		47	36	26/30	1.5	2	20 mins	20 mins
Jomtien	48	146			67	48	2.5	3	40 mins	40 mins
Klang	916	184/254		103		57/76	3	4/5	Hourly	Hourly
Laem Chabang	37	115		67			2.5		2 hrs	
Lam Mae Pim	916	201				97		4		4/day
Phanat Nikhom	52	104		61	47	34	2	2.5	50 mins	Hourly
Pattaya	48	136		77	62	43	2.5	3	20 mins	40 mins
Phanom Sarakam	56	122		70		39	2.5	3	2/day	3/day
Rayong	35/46	182/206		101	78/88	56/63	3.5/4.5	4/5	20 mins	Hourly
Samyan	916	215				103		4.5		4/day
Sattahip	36	161		90	70	50	3.5	4	50 mins	Hourly
Si Racha	37	104		61	47	34	2.5	3	30 mins	Hourly
Trat	917	317/387		169/197	132/158	101/113	5.5/6.5	7/8	Hourly	3/day

78 BANGKOK

(e) To The South (from Southern Bus Terminal)

Destination	Route No.	Distance (km)	Price (Bt)				Journey Time (hrs)		Frequency	
			V.I.P.	A/C 1	A/C 2	Ord.	A/C	Ord.	A/C	Ord.
Ban Pong	82	78		47			1.5		45 mins	
Bang Saphan	66	387		203	151	103	6	7	8/day	2/day
Betong	987	1,234		632			20		1/day	
Cha-Am	971	175		97			3.5		5/day	
Chumphon	990	468	286	245	190	136	8	10	10/day	2/day
Damnoen Saduak	78/996	97		57			2		20 mins	
Dan Chang	69/994	186		103			3		8/day	
Gaper	64	891		329			12		1/day	
Haad Yai	982	1,014	760	520	381	289	16	18	11/day	2/day
Haad Yai	992	954		490		272		18	3/day	1/day
Hua Hin	978	201/222		110	67/85		4		30 mins	
Kanchanaburi	81	119		68	59	41	2.5	3.5	15 mins	15 mins
Khanom	62	744	595	383	298		12		3/day	
Ko Samui	991	768	802	396	308		14		3/day	
Krabi	950/983	817	655	421	328	234	14	15	5/day	1/day
Lang Suan	89	540		281	218	156	9	10	7/day	1/day
Nakhon Pathom	83/997	56		32			1		20 mins	
Nakhon Si Thammarat	981	805	640	414	322	230	12	14	7/day	5/day
Narathiwat	986	1,200	950	614	477		19		3/day	
Padang Besar	992	1,020		530			17		1/day	
Pak Phanang	981	841		432			13		1/day	
Pattalung	989	888	680	457	356		14.5		4/day	
Pattani	986	1,100	875	563			17		4/day	
Phetchaburi	977/73	135/166		77	60/71		3		20 mins	
Phang-Nga	61	783/815	625	403/419	326		14		5/day	
Phuket	949/63	867/891	690	446/457	356	254	15	17	12/day	5/day
Potharam	77	85		50			1.5		Hourly	
Prachuap Kiri Khan	979	292		157	122	87	6	7	30 mins	Hourly
Pranburi	985	237		128			4.5		20 mins	
Ranong	64	583	470	302	235	168	10	12	9/day	1/day
Ratchaburi	76	109		63	50	35	2	2.5	20 mins	12 mins
Samut Sakhon	980/85	49		22			1		20 mins	
Samut Songkram	976	78		36			2		30 mins	
Satun	988	995	795	511	398		16		4/day	
Songkhla	973	1,004		514	400	286	16	18	5/day	1/day
Sungai Golok	986	1,266	1,005	646	503		20		3/day	
Suphanburi	88/952	102/156		59	71		3		30 mins	
Surat Thani	993	668	535	346	269	192	11	13	27/day	2/day
Takuapa	61	757		391			11		2/day	
Tha Chang	87/953	149		85			2.5		30 mins	
Thung Song	992	766		394			12		1/day	
Trang	984	862	685	443	344		15		5/day	
Yala	987	1,091	865	558			17		3/day	

PART 3   THE EAST

The area lying east and south-east of Bangkok is most famous for its beaches, many of which can be reached in only a few hours from the capital. Most famous of all is Pattaya, in the province of Chonburi, so let us start there.

PATTAYA   พัทยา

2 hrs 30 mins by bus from Eastern Bus Terminal
Until the Vietnam War, Pattaya was just a sleepy fishing village. It was developed by the influx of American military personnel on 'R and R' (Rest and Recreation) leave, the Sattahip Naval Base being only a few kilometres down the road. Gradually it has grown and grown and every time one comes back it seems more developed.

When the author first travelled in Thailand, I was advised to omit Pattaya from my itinerary as it was just an expensive uninteresting resort for the three-days-at-the-beach rich tourist. However, I went anyway and, maybe because I was forewarned, would not give the same advice to others. Pattaya is well worth seeing and, in fact, these days offers some of the best value in the country for good but moderately priced hotels and meals. From Bangkok, first find your way to the Eastern Bus Terminal (Ekkamai), from where air-conditioned buses depart every 20 minutes and ordinary buses every 40 minutes for the 147 kilometre journey. The bus number is 48. 1st class air-conditioned buses cost Bt77. 2nd class air-conditioned cost Bt62 and ordinary buses cost Bt43. The last bus leaves at 22:30 and the journey takes 2½ hours by air-conditioned bus and three hours by ordinary bus. There is some technique involved here. If you take a 1st class air-conditioned bus, it will terminate at the Pattaya air-conditioned bus station, which is a long way from the town and beyond reasonable walking distance. Then it will cost you almost as much again as your fare from Bangkok to get into the town. From the bus station, expect to pay Bt40 or 50 to your chosen hotel or to the town centre. However, if you take a 2nd class air-conditioned or an ordinary bus, it will usually continue to Jomtien (or Chomtien) Beach, just beyond the town of Pattaya. (Check that it does.) These buses used to pass right through the town of Pattaya, but that was too convenient, so now they merely continue along the main highway (Sukhumvit Road). Even so, they will reach a point at Central Pattaya Road (see map) where they are much closer to where most people want to go. Be alert, because it is not easy to spot the different landmarks when travelling along this major highway. There are traffic lights here and there is an overhead pedestrian bridge and a petrol station on your right. Some other passengers are sure to want to get off at this point. You are now two kilometres from the main part of the town, which is within walking distance. Just make your way down Central Pattaya Road. If you prefer not to walk, you will find *songtaew* lined up here and they will convey you the length of the road to the beach. Unfortunately, Pattaya is one of the worst places in Thailand for taking these small vehicles, as there is chronic over-supply and the drivers will overcharge in any way possible. The correct fare for this short journey is Bt5, but it is quite impossible to make it for that price. Even Thais are charged Bt10. Get on a vehicle which already has passengers and check the price first with the driver. Settle for Bt10 per head. If you want to go anywhere other than straight down Central Pattaya Road, it will probably be Bt20 per person.

To find the best value in accommodation, turn left when you reach Pattaya No. 2 Road (a one-way street) and walk along until you find something attractive. There are plenty of places here in the Bt250 to Bt500 range, with bathrooms, air-conditioning, satellite television, hot water and refrigerators. For example, try the Apex Hotel which starts at Bt350 for one person or Bt450 for two and also offers an eat-all-you-like breakfast until noon for Bt75 and a similar dinner for Bt130, or the Skaw Beach Hotel which has large air-conditioned rooms available from Bt390. If you want something cheaper, look in Soi 10, or keep going into the area south of South Pattaya Road.

There are also buses to Pattaya directly from Don Muang (Bangkok) Airport, so that you never have to go into the city at all there. These are privately operated luxury buses and they cost Bt200. There are only three buses per day.

Then there are buses from the Northern Bus Terminal (Morchit Mai) in Bangkok. The Northern Bus Terminal is not so far from the airport, so again you can avoid Bangkok if so wished when arriving by air or coming by bus from the north or north-east of the country. From the airport, take city bus no. 29 or 59 or air-conditioned 4, 10 or 13 to reach a point within walking distance of the Northern Bus Station. The fare from here to Pattaya by ordinary road is Bt79 and buses depart every 30 minutes until 19:00, but these are 1st class air-conditioned buses only, so you will arrive at the inconvenient air-conditioned bus terminal in Pattaya. There are also five buses per day which use the motorway and charge Bt83. These buses cover the distance in two hours, cutting about 30 minutes off the usual time. Bangkok air-conditioned city bus no. 13 runs from the airport to the Eastern Bus Terminal (Ekkamai), a journey of about 90 minutes, if you prefer to have a choice of bus types.

There is a Thai Airways 'limousine' (bus) service too from Don Muang Airport to Pattaya. It costs Bt200 and leaves at 9:00, 12:00 and 19:00. Journey time is two hours.

Finally, there is a train to Pattaya – just one. It leaves Bangkok (Hualampong) Station at 6:55 every morning and reaches Pattaya at 10:37. It is just an ordinary train with only third class accommodation and it travels first to Chachoengsao along the line to Aranyaprathet. Then it branches off south along a relatively new line going to

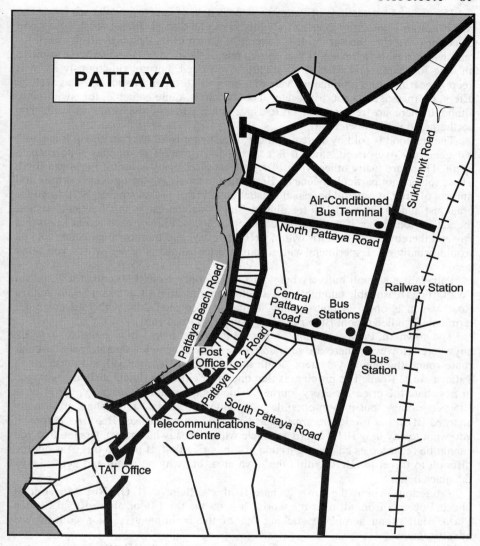

PATTAYA

Air-Conditioned Bus Terminal

Sukhumvit Road

North Pattaya Road

Pattaya Beach Road

Railway Station

Central Pattaya Road

Bus Stations

Post Office

Pattaya No. 2 Road

Bus Station

South Pattaya Road

Telecommunications Centre

TAT Office

Ban Plutaluang which is near (but not on) the main road between Sattahip and Rayong. This line is somewhat dusty, and Pattaya Station is a long way from the town, about a kilometre from the place where you should get off the bus to walk along Pattaya Central Road. Therefore, it is not really the ideal way to get to this resort. Its advantages are, though, that it is cheap, costing only Bt25, and unconventional.

The principal attractions of Pattaya are the beach, of course, and the sea food. The beach is four kilometres long and slightly crescent shaped, facing west, so a good place for observing the sunset. It is covered for most of its length by deck chairs for rent, with parasols for shade. If you do rent one of these, you will never have to move all day, for drinks and snacks, all slightly overpriced, but not ridiculously so, will keep appearing from ambulatory vendors. So will all types of souvenirs, as well as offers of massages, boat trips, etc. The beach is quite suitable for swimming, although there are recreational craft using some parts of the water as well. The northern end is the quieter part.

The sea food is sold by a great number of restaurants all over the town. It is good, but generally overpriced, since it is catering for a market on holiday with cash to spare. There are many other types of restaurant also, many offering European food. These too are not particularly cheap. Best value in meals are the buffet breakfasts and dinners offered by several hotels and restaurants. Prices are all similar, Bt70 to 80 for breakfast and Bt120 to Bt150 for dinner. Since one can eat as much as one wishes, the author found that if he took breakfast at 11:30, he did not need to eat again that day and thereby could feed for within Bt100 per day, and moreover eat better than he would usually do. Experiment with different establishments to see which you think best.

Pattaya has a small but very busy post office, open from 8:30 until 16:30, in Soi Post Office (reasonable enough!) and a Telecommunications Centre on South Pattaya Road which is open 24 hours a day. E-mail is also available, with four computer terminals installed (about Bt35 per hour, using a pre-paid card).

The town of Pattaya is not so big. Within the town, it is possible to walk anywhere. However, there are also *songtaew*. These vehicles operate on a circular route round the one-way system, south along Pattaya Beach Road and north along Pattaya No. 2 Road. The problem is that one must either be ridiculously overcharged or negotiate the price for every journey, which is a nuisance. Officially, the price is Bt5 per journey, but it is impossible to go anywhere at that rate. Thais are usually charged Bt10, but foreigners are frequently asked to pay at least Bt20. As before, if you want to pay only Bt10, board a vehicle which already has passengers (so that you cannot be regarded as chartering it) and ask the price first. If you do this, it is not too difficult to travel for Bt10 within the town area, but why not walk and get to know the place better?

Attractions within the town include **Ripley's Believe It Or Not Museum** of unusual objects from all over the world. It is on the third floor of the Royal Garden Plaza. Half of an aeroplane sticking out of the building gives it a conspicuous advertisement.

On the edge of the town just off Sukhumvit Road is the **Bottle Museum**. It is near Central Pattaya Road. This is an impressive one-man exhibition of models in bottles. The address is 79/15 Moo 9, Sukhumvit Road.

You will also find in Pattaya an amazing number of bars, and at the bars an amazing number of cajoling girls. Most of the girls work for the bars and are there to attract customers, but some are freelance. The bars vary greatly in price, but generally one can judge prices from looks, and, in any case, nearly always the prices are displayed. If you just fancy a quiet beer, of course, the best thing to do is to go to the supermarket, buy a bottle and take it home, but then you will not have the atmosphere of one of these bars. For a traveller, they seem expensive, but for a short-term visitor enjoying a week at the beach, they probably seem rather reasonable in price. The cheapest offer a draught beer for Bt40 at certain times.

Another discovery in Pattaya may be a number of pretty boys, for it is a popular place for 'lady boys' (transvestites). In reality, it is sometimes difficult to distinguish the sex of some of the people by whom you may be propositioned in Pattaya – quite an interesting town. Take care not to make any embarrassing mistakes. Fortunately, most of the hotels will discourage males from pursuing any of the offers which they may receive by imposing a substantial surcharge for any visitors.

Pattaya has a **TAT office**. It used to be very conveniently situated, right in the middle of the town. However, the problem was that the staff used to get bothered by a lot of tourists calling in, so now the office has been moved to the hill which lies between Pattaya and Jomtien. Few people make the journey there, so it is much more peaceful now. If you do struggle up the hill, you will find useful maps and information available, but if you think beforehand, you can obtain much of this material in Bangkok.

Nearby Attractions
Ko Lan

This island is eight kilometres from Pattaya, with boats departing every morning from Pattaya and returning in the late afternoon. The island has several beaches and has boats for viewing coral. There is also accommodation available. Fares from Pattaya are Bt100 to Bt150. The journey takes an hour.

Ko Krok

Ko Krok is a much smaller rocky island a similar distance away. There is one beach. Boat trips can be arranged, but prices usually depend on numbers. There is no accommodation.

Ko Sak

This is a small island near Ko Lan. Boats to Ko Lan can often be persuaded to call here. It has two beaches and diving is possible. There is no accommodation.

Ko Phai

Ko Phai is the largest of a group of islands 13 kilometres from Pattaya. There is no regular service, but boats can be chartered. The journey takes about two hours and the cost is a minimum of Bt1,000 (but usually more) per boat for the return trip. Boats can accommodate at least ten passengers. There is a lighthouse, but no accommodation.

Accommodation

There is a wide range of accommodation in Pattaya. Here is a list of the places which you will find marked on the diagrammatic maps. Numbers indicate the block or area in which each hotel can be found.

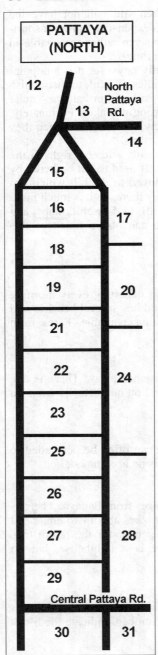

PATTAYA (NORTH)

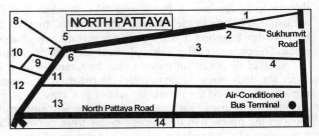

(i) Higher Class Hotels (Bt1,000 and above)

Name	No. on Map	Tel. No. (038-)	Rooms	Cheapest Price (Bt)
A.A. Villa	8	225515	51	2,800
A-1 The Royal Cruise	19	424242	196	2,200
Amari Orchid Resort	15	428323	234	2,400
Baiyok Pattaya	59	423300	136	1,500
Beverley Plaza	55	421278	200	1,400
Caesar Palace	31	428607	220	1,200
Central Wong Amat	12	426990	178	1,600
Day Night	52	427621	346	1,300
Dusit Resort	12	425611	474	4,000
Furama Beach	30	428580	51	1,000
Grand Sole	28	427551	253	1,500
Merlin Pattaya	29	421670	360	2,000
Montien Pattaya	29	428155	300	3,000
Pattaya Garden	12	426775	424	1,000
Pattaya Lodge	8	225464	35	2,200
Pattaya Palace	23	423025	261	1,800
Regent Marina	15	429298	220	2,000
Royal Garden Resort	45	428126	300	2,800
Royal Palace	46	426262	350	1,200
Royal Twins Palace	46	420260	380	1,500
Siam Bay Shore	58	428678	272	1,800
Siam Bay View	35	423871	270	1,800
Sunbeam	33	427120	270	1,200
Thai Garden Resort	13	426009	170	1,400
Town in Town	28	426350	360	1,800
Tropicana	26	428645	186	1,700
V.C. Pattaya	55	424504	100	1,050
Welcome Plaza	46	424765	269	1,000
Woodlands Resort	12	421707	80	2,000

(ii) Moderately Priced Hotels (Bt350 to Bt950)

Name	No. on Map	Tel. No. (038-)	Rooms	Cheapest Price (Bt)
Apex	38	428281	109	350
Astoria Resort	12	427061	60	900
Beach View	18	422660	110	600
Best Inn	40	422248	49	350

(ii) Moderately Priced Hotels (Bt350 to Bt950, contd.)

Name	No. on Map	Tel. No. (038-)	Rooms	Cheapest Price (Bt)
Bua Khao	40	425093	23	350
C.K. Pattaya	49	422487	78	450
Carlton Pattaya	23	421556	76	400
Central Pattaya	60	250051	150	700
Champ	59	422451	105	500
Charming Inn	21	428895	65	450
Classic Inn	54	424159	15	500
Corner Inn	41	425496	26	400
Cottage	17	425660	72	450
Diamond Beach	53	429885	138	350
Diana Inn	38	429675	144	500
Down Town	55	429728	88	400
East Sea Resort	12	426524	90	650
Flipper Lodge	35	426401	126	800
Florida	36	426527	30	400
Garden Lodge	12	429109	58	500
Garden Square	8	225373	400	600
Golden Beach	36	720355	339	900
Green	34	410039	50	500
Gulf Siam	14	426622	52	700
Holiday Corner	53	426072	39	600
Homex Inn	12	429039	35	500
Honey Lodge	48	429133	52	400
KK Palace	54	421498	27	350
Lek	41	425550	76	600
Lido Beach	48	422858	49	500
Little Duck	31	428104	180	750
Loma	12	426027	120	950
M.N. Bungalow	9	255300	10	350
Ma Belle	57	424456	94	500
Marina Inn	5	225134	70	450
Marina Inn Plaza	62	429232	70	400
Marine Plaza	56	424817	160	400
Midtown Inn	61	429744	60	350
Mike Hotel	48	422222	87	600
Moonlight on Sea	8	225252	42	700
Nautical Inn	39	428110	80	700
Nice	62	420771	63	350
North Pattaya View Resort	12	428093	90	700
O.D.	59	423612	74	350
Oasis	61	428754	143	450
Pacific Prince	28	420301	240	800
Palm Garden	15	429188	115	500
Palm Lodge	29	428779	75	600
Palm Villa	43	428153	69	400
Paradise Inn	55	426410	136	400
President Inn	40	426410	162	350
Queen Pattaya	30	428234	118	550
Rattanasuk Inn	6	420585	60	400
Romeo Palace	12	429022	79	500

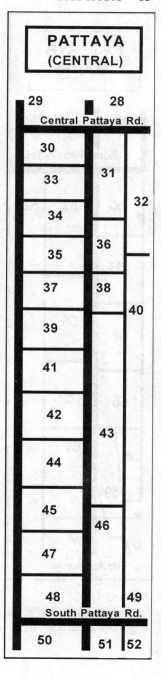

PATTAYA (CENTRAL)

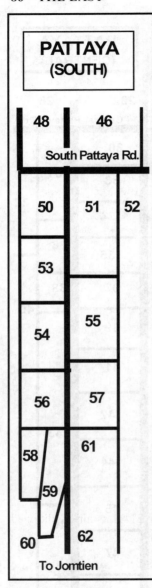

PATTAYA
(SOUTH)

48   46

South Pattaya Rd.

50   51   52

53

55
54

56   57

61
58

59

60   62

To Jomtien

(ii) Moderately Priced Hotels (Bt350 to Bt950, contd.)

Name	No. on Map	Tel. No. (038-)	Rooms	Cheapest Price (Bt)
Royal Night	23	428038	35	400
Sang Kaew	58	428085	54	350
Sawasdee Place	12	225651	60	600
Sea View Resort	12	424825	157	700
Skaw Beach	36	420802	60	600
Sunshine	34	429247	79	500
Sunshine Garden	12	421300	78	500
Sureena B&B	44	423211	25	350
Thai Palace	21	423062	40	450
Top Thai	56	422631	60	450
Villa Colonia	3	424295	7	400
Weekender	20	428720	202	600
Windmill Resort	13	425930	86	400
Windy Inn	59	428385	32	350

(iii) Budget Accommodation (below Bt350)

Name	No. on Map	Tel. No. (038-)	Rooms	Cheapest Price (Bt)
B.R. Inn	42	426449	14	250
Chez Wim	16	421450	27	300
Crystal Garden	58	421211	40	300
Drop Inn	42	249803	13	200
High Five	33	427118	24	250
Honey Inn	36	421543	68	300
Jiraporn	2	428569	46	200
Lucky Inn	59	429767	24	250
Meridian	44	429008	42	250
P 72	56	420301	27	300
Pattaya Inn 2	37	422781	34	300
Pattaya Plaza	6	428345	39	250
Petch Pattaya Inn	7	225202	79	300
Riviera Beach	12	429623	15	200
Robin Hood Villa	40	429030	10	200
Sawasdee Court	38	720201	60	250
Sawasdee Mansion	38	720560	60	250
SS Pattaya	28	429938	54	300
Sugar Inn	60	250687	31	200
Sun and Sand	47	421713	10	300
Verlanda Inn	53	429841	50	300
Viking	49	429841	30	300
White Rose 2	54	424643	68	300
World Resort	49	250476	40	300

Moving On

From Pattaya, there are three choices really – back to Bangkok, further on round the coast, or directly to the north of the country.

To Bangkok

The easy way to return to Bangkok is to walk up to Sukhumvit Road, the main road to Bangkok, or to take a *songtaew* there. Then you can take any bus at all with a number in the 40s or 50s. It will be going to the city. Such buses pass every few minutes, so you will not wait long. The one bus not to take is any type of 1631. Whatever the conductor may tell you in order to obtain your custom, such buses do not go as far as Bangkok.

If you want a 1st class air-conditioned bus, you can pick one of those up here too if seats are available. Alternatively, you can go to the air-conditioned bus terminal at the northern end of the town, which will be an expensive journey, and take a bus originating in Pattaya. Last service to the Eastern Bus Terminal departs at 21:00 and to the Northern Bus Terminal at 19:00.

There are private buses to Bangkok Airport at 9:00, 13:00 and 17:00 and Thai Airways 'limousines' at 6:30, 14:00 and 18:30. Cost is Bt200, but if pre-booked these services will pick up at certain points in the town.

The daily train departs from the Railway Station, about three kilometres from the centre of Pattaya, at 14:50, arriving in Bangkok's Hualampong Station at 18:35.

Further Down the Coast

The procedure for travelling away from Bangkok by bus is the same as for travelling towards the city. Make your way to Sukhumvit Road and wait on the other side of the highway this time. Look at the list of bus numbers on page XXX and wait until a bus for your destination comes along. There are plenty of buses and any except a no. 48 (destination Jomtien) will take you somewhere further along the coast.

To The North

There are now three different companies operating buses from Pattaya to the north and north-east of Thailand. These buses do not pass through Bangkok. They all go through Nakhon Ratchasima. The three companies all use different termini, so make sure that you get the right one. First, there is Service 589 to Ubon Ratchathani from a small bus station half way along Central Pattaya Road towards Sukhumvit. There are 1st class air-conditioned buses at 9:00, 17:00, 19:00, 20:00 and 20:30, 2nd class air-conditioned buses at 7:30 and 18:00 and ordinary buses at 19:30 and 21:00. Fares are Bt355 by 1st class air-conditioned bus, Bt275 by 2nd class air-conditioned and Bt200 by ordinary bus. The journey takes 10 hours by air-conditioned bus and 12 hours by ordinary bus.

If you continue walking to where Central Pattaya Road meets Sukhumvit, just to the right, on Sukhumvit Road, you will see another small bus station with Service 588, also to Ubon Ratchathani, Service 659 to Chiang Mai and Service 660 to Chiang Rai and Mae Sai. There are four V.I.P. air-conditioned buses to Ubon Ratchathani in the evening, at 17:00, 18:20, 20:00 and 20:30 (Bt400). 1st class air-conditioned buses leave at 7:45 and 17:45 (Bt355) and ordinary buses depart at 16:45, 18:00 and 18:45

(Bt200). Again journey time is 10 hours by air-conditioned bus and 12 hours by ordinary bus. To Chiang Mai, there are V.I.P. buses at 14:30, 17:25, 18:30 and 19:00 (Bt550), a 1st class air-conditioned bus at 18:30 (Bt470) and ordinary buses at 6:30 and 16:15 (Bt 260). Journey time is 14 hours by air-conditioned bus and 15 hours by ordinary bus. To Chiang Rai and Mae Sai, there are V.I.P. buses at 15:00 and 17:00 (Bt600), a 1st class air-conditioned bus at 15:30 (Bt540) and an ordinary bus at 12:30 (Bt300). Journey time is 16 hours by air-conditioned bus and 17 hours by ordinary bus. Some of the buses to Ubon Ratchathani and Chiang Mai start in Rayong.

The third company operates from a point on the near side of Sukhumvit just to the left as you approach from Central Pattaya Road. There is a petrol station there and the booking office is at the near side of it. This company's buses all start in Rayong and merely pass through this Pattaya bus station. There is one route, Service 590 to Nong Khai. 1st class air-conditioned buses leave at 8:15, 17:15, 18:30, 19:00, 19:45, 20:20, 20:45 and 21:30 (Bt360), while ordinary buses depart at 7:15, 14:15, 16:00, 17:00, 18:00, 20:00 and 21:30 (Bt200). There are additional air-conditioned services which terminate at Khon Kaen, leaving at 8:00 and 21:00 (Bt275). To Nong Khai takes 12 hours by air-conditioned bus and 14 hours by ordinary bus, To Udon Thani is one hour less and to Khon Kaen is 9 hours by air-conditioned bus and 11 hours by ordinary bus. Here is a summary of all these services.

Destination	Route No.	Price (Bt)				Journey Time (hrs)		Frequency	
		V.I.P.	A/C 1	A/C 2	Ord	A/C	Ord	A/C	Ord
Bangkok	48	200	77	62	43	2.5	3	20 mins	40 mins
Ubon Ratchathani	588	400	355		200	10	12	6/day	3/day
Ubon Ratchathani	589		355	275	200	10	12	7/day	2/day
Chiang Mai	659	550	470		260	14	15	5 /day	2/day
Mae Sai	660	600	540		300	16	17	3/day	1/day
Nong Khai	590		360		200	12	14	8/day	7/day

JOMTIEN   จอมเทียน

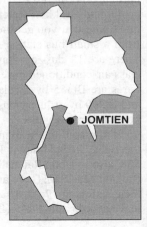

2 hrs 30 mins by bus from Eastern Bus Terminal
When Pattaya overflowed, it spilled into Jomtien (sometimes spelt Chomtien). There is a hill separating the two towns. It is possible to walk between the two, but it is a tiring walk. *Songtaew* operate for about Bt20. (Discuss the price in advance.) The journey takes ten minutes. Jomtien is similar to Pattaya but without the excitement. It is currently being developed by the construction of many towering blocks of condominiums. The beach here is straight and stretches for about six kilometres.

The 2nd class air-conditioned and ordinary buses (no. 48) from Bangkok terminate at the southern end of

Jomtien, so if you prefer Jomtien to Pattaya, you can come directly here. Note, however, that 1st class air-conditioned buses usually terminate at the air-conditioned bus station at the northern end of Pattaya.

Accommodation
Jomtien

Name	No. on Map	Tel. No. (038-)	Rooms	Cheapest Price (Bt)
A.A. Guest House	18	231812	10	250
Aqua Marine Cabana	41	231290	29	700
Asia Pattaya	8	250602	314	2,400
Chorntalay	42	231070	49	1,200
Coral Inn	38	231283	36	950
Cosy Beach	3	250800	160	1,800
D.D. House	30	231901	9	300
Dongtarn Villa	16	231049	23	1,700
Furama Jomtien Beach	37	231869	32	650
Golden Cliff House	9	250810	50	2,800
Hill Side Resort	6	250009	76	450
Island View	5	250813	209	1,300
J.B. Guest House	20	231581	12	300
Jomtien Bay View	10	251889	55	400
Jomtien Cosy Inn	33	231925	24	600
Jomtien Garden	25	231003	105	1,500
Jomtien Hotel	14	251606	124	1,400
Jomtien Lodge	26	232101	36	250
Jomtien Orchid	13	251634	122	400
Knight Inn	32	231475	40	600
Marine Beach	36	231129	60	600
Mermaids Beach Resort	22	232210	81	850
Mountain Beach	4	306051	320	1,400
Natural Park Beach Resort	39	231561	122	1,800
On Hill Luxury House	11	251844	25	600
Rio Beach	15	231876	160	600
Royal Cliff Beach Resort	1	250421	1,129	4,000
Sea Breeze	28	231056	105	800
Sigma Resort	40	231226	214	2,300
Silver Sand Villa	24	231288	107	650
Sugar Hut	12	251686	33	2,400
Sugar Palm Beach	17	231386	41	700
Summer Beach Inn	34	231777	22	600
Sunlight	19	429108	14	400
Surf House	21	231025	55	600
Swan Beach Resort	35	232464	126	1,500
Thanaporn	7	250012	46	500
Ubon Lodge	27	232114	42	200
Villa Navin	29	231066	25	2,600
Welcome Jomtien Beach	31	232701	382	2,100
White House Resort	23	232996	116	1,400
Wonder Land	2	250366	50	600

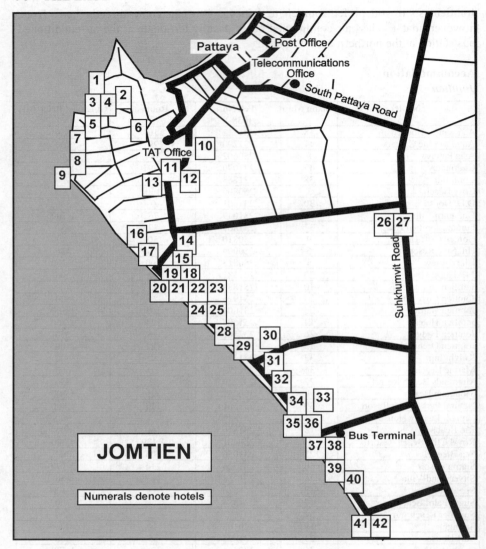

Moving On

There are frequent 2nd class air-conditioned and ordinary buses to Bangkok from the southern end of Jomtien. To go to other places, make your way to Sukhumvit and follow the same procedure as for Pattaya.

RAYONG   ระยอง

3 hrs 30 mins by bus from Eastern Bus Terminal

Rayong, a city of 500,000 inhabitants, lies further along the coast from Pattaya and is much less touristed than its neighbour. Whereas Pattaya faces west, Rayong faces south. Although the city administration seems to believe that its main claim to fame is the Maptaphut Industrial Estate, to the west of the city, in fact many visitors go to Rayong not for that scenic attraction but for the beaches.

There are two bus routes to Rayong. One is along the old road following the coast, via Pattaya and the naval and port area of Sattahip (although buses do not go through the towns themselves), that is to say travelling south and then turning east. The other route is to follow the new road which cuts the corner by travelling south-east from Chonburi. The new route reduces the distance from Bangkok by 24 kilometres, from 206km to 182km. However, the time required is reduced by a whole hour because this new road is much less populated and congested than the old one. If you take an air-conditioned bus from the Eastern Bus Terminal in Bangkok, you can reach Rayong in 3½ hours at a cost of Bt78 or 101, depending on the class of bus. Ordinary buses cost Bt56 and take half an hour longer. The service is frequent. There are also 1st class air-conditioned buses from the Northern Bus Terminal costing Bt104. The 2nd class air-conditioned and ordinary buses from the Northern Bus Terminal run via the old road and take longer. Fortunately, the bus station in Rayong is in the town itself and there are cheap to medium-priced hotels nearby on and just off Sukhumvit Road.

Sights of the town include the **King Taksin Shrine** at Wat Lum Mahachai Chumphon. It celebrates the King's organization of freedom fighters to counter the Burmese invasion and is particularly popular with those of Chinese ancestry.

Wat Pa Pradu is only five minutes walk from the bus terminal and has a Reclining Buddha twelve metres long.

Behind the Town Hall, which is on an island in the river, is **Phra Phut Angkirot**, with a Buddha statue in a pavilion. This Buddha is unusual in reclining on his right instead of his left.

On another island in the river is **Phra Chedi Klang Nam**, a pagoda of uncertain antiquity standing about ten metres tall. It is four kilometres from the town, but near Saeng Chan Beach.

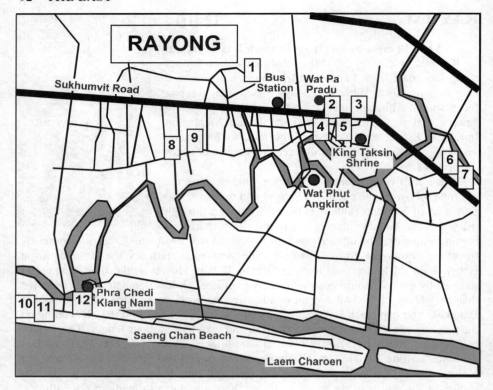

There is a **TAT office** at Rayong. You will not be surprised to hear that it is not actually in the town, but several kilometres east. It is, in fact, where the short cut from Bangkok joins the old highway (Sukhumvit Road) and where the road to Mae Ramphung Beach branches off. The large blue *songtaew* to Ban Phe will go right past (Bt10 to here), but it is not always easy to see the scenery from inside a *songtaew*. The TAT office is on the left and there is a large fruit and vegetable market, also on the left, just before it. The journey from Rayong takes ten minutes. You can also take the *songtaew* for Mae Ramphung and alight when it turns right. Then walk along Sukhumvit Road for about 500 metres. The staff will be very pleased to see you, as they get few visitors in such a location.

Accommodation

Here is a list of city accommodation, including some near to the city beaches. For locations, see map. Most visitors stay not in the town itself, but at one of the beaches.

Rayong City

Name	No. on Map	Rooms	Cheapest Price (Bt)	Name	No. on Map	Rooms	Cheapest Price (Bt)
P.M.Y.	11	115	2,800	Rayong Villa	7	70	300
Dee Pratap Chit	10	42	1,400	Otany	4	117	200
Star	1	240	850	Rayong	5	51	200
Rayong Seaview	12	26	850	R.M.	9	28	200
Melody House	8	15	450	Asia	2	60	150
Rose Inn	6	60	300	Tawan-oka	3	53	150

Beaches

It is the beaches for which most visitors come. There are various beaches around the city which can be reached by *songtaew* and which have accommodation available. Starting from the west, there are **Phala Beach, Payun Beach, Namrin Beach** and **Takron Beach**. From just outside the bus station, take a red *songtaew* to Ban Chang (Bt15) which is close to these beaches. Phala Beach, with shady trees, is probably the most attractive of this group. A bus along the old route from Bangkok will also pass Ban Chang. Accommodation starts at Bt200.

Almost in the town are **Saeng Chan Beach** and **Laem Charoen Beach** on a sand spit at the mouth of the Rayong River. Take a blue *songtaew* for the 5km journey (Bt10) to Laem Charoen.

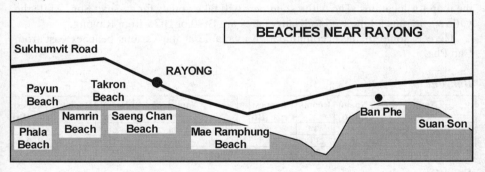

The most impressive beach, however, is **Mae Ramphung** which starts 12km east of the city of Rayong and stretches for some ten kilometres. Take a sky blue *songtaew* (Bt15). This is a beach which is relatively undeveloped at present, but which is seeing more construction, mostly of towering condominiums, day by day. Go now, while it is still tranquil and worth seeing. For those on a budget, there is a pleasant Youth Hostel three-quarters of the way along the beach and there are guest houses at the eastern end with moderate prices. Here is a list of some of the accommodation available. See map for locations.

Mae Ramphung Beach

Name	No. on Map	Rooms	Cheapest Price (Bt)	Name	No. on Map	Rooms	Cheapest Price (Bt)
Rayong Resort	16	168	4,500	Pram Vadee Seaview	6	26	900
Laemya Resort	10	16	2,200	Near Seaside	3	20	800
P.M.	14	13	1,700	Panachon	8	20	700
Song Ruen Villa	13	21	1,700	Ban Nori	9	14	600
Chonnikarn	4	18	1,400	S.M.	1	28	500
Yok Talay House	11	11	1,200	M.M. Villa	15	7	500
Ban Prom Pong	2	62	900	Ploy Pallin Hut	12	45	400
Ban Hin Kao	5	27	900	Ban Kon Ao Y. H.	7	6	150

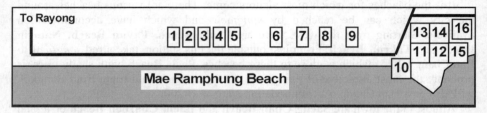

If you continue east from Rayong, you reach first the town of Ban Phe, from where ferries leave for Ko Samet, and then more beaches with accommodation. See the map for locations. The white *songtaew* will take you as far as Suan Son, while the yellow one runs all the way to Klang. Fares are Bt20 or Bt25 from Rayong.

Here is some of the accommodation available at the various beaches east from Ban Phe.

Ban Phe

Name	No. on Map	Rooms	Cheapest Price (Bt)	Name	No. on Map	Rooms	Cheapest Price (Bt)
Pine Beach	4	114	1,600	Suan Son Villa	6	29	350
N. S. Land	5	33	600	Queen	1	25	200
Ko Kaew Bungalow	3	30	350	Nuan Tip	2	15	200

Suan Son

Name	No. on Map	Rooms	Cheapest Price (Bt)	Name	No. on Map	Rooms	Cheapest Price (Bt)
Young Thong Villa	7	70	450	Jirawan Resort	9	35	450
Marina Hut	8	23	450	Camp Son Resort	10	40	450

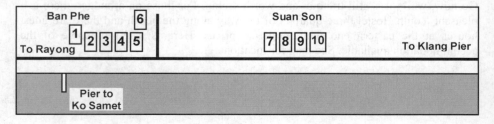

Klang Pier

Name	No. on Map	Rooms	Cheapest Price (Bt)
Ban Phe Villa	6	16	2,750
Ban Phe Cabana	1	25	2,500
Talay Ngam Resort	2	20	1,700

Name	No. on Map	Rooms	Cheapest Price (Bt)
Suan Rang See	5	16	900
Ban Tiew Son Resort	3	22	800
Ban Sin Samut	4	32	600

Wang Kaew

Name	No. on Map	Rooms	Cheapest Price (Bt)
Novotel	11	189	4,000
Amon Phan Villa	10	45	3,200
Hin Suay Nam Sai	13	174	2,800
Rayong Chalet	8	52	2,000
Ban Sang Resort	14	18	1,700
Tap Samet Village	16	10	1,700

Name	No. on Map	Rooms	Cheapest Price (Bt)
Palm Malee	17	65	1,600
Rung Napa Lodge	9	58	1,400
Bang Bai Resort	12	40	900
Pat Lodge	15	28	450
Ban Pak Chao Lay	7	18	350

Laem Mae Phim

Name	No. on Map	Rooms	Cheapest Price (Bt)
Phimnipa Villa	21	24	850
Sin Siam Resort	19	65	700

Name	No. on Map	Rooms	Cheapest Price (Bt)
Pen Pat	18	6	600
Porn Phim	20	54	600

Klang

Name	No. on Map	Rooms	Cheapest Price (Bt)
Rock Garden Beach	22	80	1,000

Name	No. on Map	Rooms	Cheapest Price (Bt)
Dam Rong Cheap Inn	23	30	400

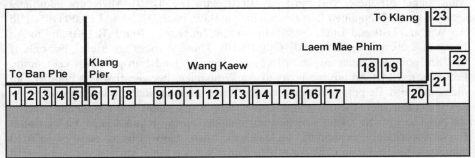

Moving On

To return to Bangkok, take a *songtaew* from any of the beaches to Rayong and from there a bus by the new route back to the capital.

To go further round the coast, it is necessary only to reach a major point along Sukhumvit Road and find a suitable bus heading east.

From Rayong, there are also buses to the north of the country, specifically to Nakhon Ratchasima (24 buses a day), Nong Khai (16 buses a day), Ubon Ratchathani (9 buses a day) and Chiang Mai (7 buses a day).

KO SAMET

เกาะเสม็ด

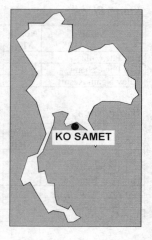

KO SAMET

**3 hrs 30 mins by bus from Eastern Bus Terminal.
Then 30 mins by ferry**

Ko Samet is a pleasant little island off the coast near Rayong. Like most of the places in this area, its main attraction is beaches. If one wishes to go to Ko Samet, it is not necessary to go to Rayong first. Indeed, it is better not to do so. There are direct buses to the ferry terminal at Ban Phe from the Eastern Bus Terminal in Bangkok. These buses are all 1st class air-conditioned buses. They take the new route, with its short cut, and cover the 196 kilometres in 3½ hours at a cost of Bt108 (including a drink and a cake). It is all very comfortable and efficient and the bus terminates right at the ferry pier. The service operates every hour.

However, if you need to go from Rayong, take the large blue *songtaew* from just outside the bus station at a cost of Bt15. The service operates every ten minutes and the journey takes half an hour.

The principal ferry service operates hourly, weather permitting, and takes half an hour to cover the six kilometres to Ko Samet. It is a small vessel, so subject to the vagaries of the climate to some extent. The destination is Nadan Pier and the fare Bt40. Do not be persuaded to purchase a return ticket. There is no saving and you may wish to take a different boat for the return.

This same ferry calls sometimes at Ao Noi Na (Noi Na Bay) en route, but if you want to get off there, you must pay Bt10 extra (i.e. Bt50). There are additional services to Ao Wongduen four times a day, at 9:00, noon, 13:30 and 17:00 (Bt50), to Ao Wai at 11:30 and 14:00 (Bt80), to Ao Kiu Na Nok at 10:00 (Bt100) and to Ao Phrao at 8:00, 11:00, 13:30 and 16:00 (Bt80). These services are useful, but only if you are going to those places, of course, because land transport will cost more. Probably most useful are the boats to Ao Wongduen, because that is a popular and pleasant beach. Be prepared to get wet feet since these destinations have no piers.

At **Nadan Pier**, there is a small town, with a few shops and restaurants. This is the only part of the island which is not included in the **Khao Laem Ya National Park**. Accordingly, as soon as one leaves the town, one will be asked to pay a Bt20 admission fee to the park. There is a *songtaew* service to the various beaches – Bt10 to Sai Kaew Beach, Bt20 to Ao Pudsa, Bt30 to Ao Nual, Bt40 to Ao Wongduen and even more to more distant beaches. In fact, however, it is no hardship to walk as far as Ao Tubtim, and even to Ao Wongduen is quite manageable. There is a pleasant highway running through the centre of this pear-shaped island, without too much fast traffic! (Walk along it and you will see.) Walking to Sai Kaew takes only about ten minutes. To Ao Wongduen in a leisurely manner would take about an hour. The beach accommodation generally gets cheaper the further south one goes on the

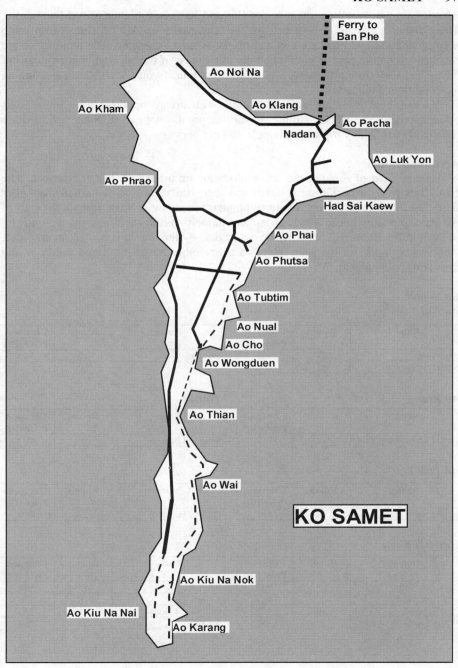

Ferry to
Ban Phe

Ao Noi Na

Ao Kham

Ao Klang

Ao Pacha

Nadan

Ao Luk Yon

Ao Phrao

Had Sai Kaew

Ao Phai

Ao Phutsa

Ao Tubtim

Ao Nual

Ao Cho

Ao Wongduen

Ao Thian

Ao Wai

KO SAMET

Ao Kiu Na Nok

Ao Kiu Na Nai

Ao Karang

island, although Ao Wongduen is popular and has some higher priced bungalows. The southern end of this beach is the cheaper too. All beaches offer some accommodation and nowhere could really be termed expensive. The majority of the beaches are on the east. It should be noted that most of the accommodation does not have electricity during the day, a point to ask about if you are considering using an air-conditioned bungalow.

Various boat rides are available, some with diving opportunities. Some boats circumnavigate the island, calling at various points of interest. Some go to other nearby islands. A day trip costs about Bt400 per person.

Accommodation

Here is a list of some of the accommodation on the island, beach by beach. The best strategy is to decide on a beach and then walk along to see what takes your fancy. At the time of writing, the most popular bungalow is Naga, right at the start of Ao Phai, probably because it is cheap and homely, but these things change quickly, so such information will probably be out of date by the time this is read. In any case, who wants to stay in the same place as every other traveller? Be adventurous and trust your own judgement.

Ko Samet
Ao Noi

Name	Rooms	Cheapest Price (Bt)
Samet Hut	21	600
Samet Resort	13	400

Name	Rooms	Cheapest Price (Bt)
Popeye	12	350

Ao Klang

Name	Rooms	Cheapest Price (Bt)
Prakai Kaew Bungalow	14	150

Nadan

Name	Rooms	Cheapest Price (Bt)
First and Best	10	400

Ao Luk Yon

Name	Rooms	Cheapest Price (Bt)
Pineapple	24	450

Name	Rooms	Cheapest Price (Bt)
Banana Beach	29	250

Had Sai Kaew

Name	Rooms	Cheapest Price (Bt)
Sai Kaew Villa	85	600
Toy Bungalow	5	450
Ploy Thalay	30	350
White Sands Bungalow	50	350

Name	Rooms	Cheapest Price (Bt)
Sea View	12	300
Kamol Villa	10	250
C.P. Guest House	15	250
Ya Kha	8	250

Ao Phai

Name	Rooms	Cheapest Price (Bt)
Ao Phai Hut	60	600
Samet Villa	28	400
Sea Breeze	50	180

Name	Rooms	Cheapest Price (Bt)
Silver Sand	35	180
Naga Bungalow	25	150
Odd's Little Hut	35	120

Ao Tubtim

Name	Rooms	Cheapest Price (Bt)
Tubtim Bungalow	73	450

Name	Rooms	Cheapest Price (Bt)
Ao Pudsa Bungalow	25	300

Ao Nual

Name	Rooms	Cheapest Price (Bt)
Ao Nual Bungalow	9	300

Ao Cho

Name	Rooms	Cheapest Price (Bt)
Tantawan	27	350

Name	Rooms	Cheapest Price (Bt)
Wonderland	65	100

Ao Wongduen

Name	Rooms	Cheapest Price (Bt)
Malibu Garden Resort	60	900
Wongduen Resort	54	900
Wongduen Villa	54	750

Name	Rooms	Cheapest Price (Bt)
Sea Horse	30	450
Samet Cabana	15	350

Ao Thian

Name	Rooms	Cheapest Price (Bt)
Candlelight Beach	20	750

Name	Rooms	Cheapest Price (Bt)
Lung Dum	38	350

Ao Wai

Name	Rooms	Cheapest Price (Bt)
Samet Villa	66	1,000

Ao Kiu Na Nok

Name	Rooms	Cheapest Price (Bt)
Ao Kiu Coral Beach	20	350

Ao Karang

Name	Rooms	Cheapest Price (Bt)
Ao Pa Karang Bungalow	12	250

Ao Phrao

Name	Rooms	Cheapest Price (Bt)	Name	Rooms	Cheapest Price (Bt)
Ao Phrao Resort	22	2,200	S.K. Hut	12	450
Dome Bungalow	22	1,200			

Moving On

Ferries run from Nadan Pier back to Ban Phe every hour starting at 8:00, and at 7:30 there is an additional boat operated by a different company. From Wongduen, departures are at 8:30, noon and 15:30; from Ao Wai only at 14:00; from Ao Kui Na Nok at 8:00 and noon; and from Ao Phrao at 10:00, 12:30, 15:00 and 17:00.

Buses go back to Bangkok from Ban Phe hourly. If you want to go further round the coast, take the big blue *songtaew* either to Rayong or just to Sukhumvit and pick up a bus there. However, the higher class buses may be reluctant to stop along Sukhumvit. To go to the north of the country, you must go to Rayong first, and most services north run either early in the morning or in the late afternoon and evening.

There is also a minibus service from Ban Phe to Pattaya, but, at Bt100, it is expensive.

CHANTHABURI   จันทบรี

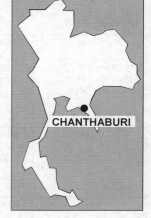

CHANTHABURI

4 hrs 30 mins by bus from Eastern Bus Terminal
Chanthaburi is a pleasant and interesting town of medium size, the centre of a province containing half a million people. Mountains form a pretty backdrop to the town, with the highest peak in Eastern Thailand, **Khao Soi Dao**, located nearby and the Chanthaburi River flowing through the town.

Using another short cut from Chonburi, buses can cover the 239 kilometres to Chanthaburi in 4½ hours from Bangkok. Buses depart every half hour from the Eastern Bus Terminal and approximately every hour from the Northern Bus Terminal. The fare is Bt130 for a 1st class air-conditioned bus and Bt101 for a 2nd class air-conditioned bus from the Eastern Bus Terminal and Bt135 for a 1st class air-conditioned bus from the Northern Bus Terminal. In addition, there are still some buses from the Eastern Bus Terminal which take the old route following round the coast and these take an hour longer to reach Chanthaburi.

There is a park and statue commemorating **King Taksin the Great** who used this town as his headquarters when repelling a Burmese invasion. There is also a shrine to the same king.

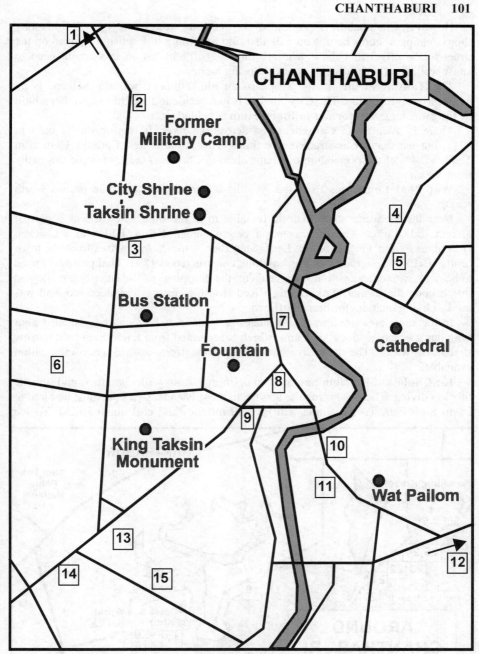

However, Chanthaburi is best known for **precious stones** and you will find many shops dealing in gems here. You will also find a warning in English displayed on the street to the effect that those who are thinking of gems as an investment need to know well about precious stones or risk losing money.

The **Taksin Shrine**, in the shape of an old-fashioned military helmet, is an impressive construction. The **City Shrine** is just beside it, thought to have been built by the same king. His **former military camp** is behind.

There is a Christian **Cathedral** just across the river. It was originally built in 1711, but has been reconstructed five times. This is the largest Catholic Church in Thailand. 4% of the population of Chanthaburi is Christian, mostly people originally from Vietnam.

Wat Phai Lom dates from the Ayutthaya Period and has some murals worth seeing.

Near the town are some historic remains from the time when it was a part of French Indo-China. The old detention centre named **Khuk Khi Kai** ('Chicken Droppings Prison') is just before Laem Sing Pier, some 25 kilometres from the town centre (Bt15 by *songtaew*). In this building, constructed in 1893, Thai protestors used to be held, with chickens living above them, the droppings of the latter being allowed to fall upon the former. **Tuk Daeng** ('Red House'), nearby, is indeed red, and was used as living quarters for French officers.

In the same area are attractive beaches and islands which can be visited. **Laem Sing** has a beach, as does **Ao Yang**, which is separated from Laem Sing by a narrow stretch of water. The latter is shaded with pine trees and has accommodation available.

Ko Chula and **Ko Nom Sao** are two offshore islands with coral reefs and suitable for skin diving. There is no regular service to these islands, so a boat must be hired at Laem Sing Pier. To Ko Chula will take 30 minutes and cost about Bt250. To Ko

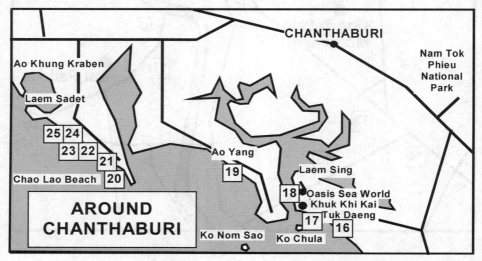

Nom Sao will take an hour and cost about Bt500. Boats hold approximately eight passengers. There are no facilities on either of these two islands.

Oasis Sea World is at Laem Sing. It has Dolphin Shows and attempts to breed and preserve rare species of this sea mammal. It also offers accommodation.

To the west, and reached by a different route from Chanthaburi, is **Chao Lao Beach**. It is 35 kilometres from town (Bt20 by *songtaew*) and has accommodation all of its length, mostly fairly expensive accommodation. Coral reefs lie just offshore. At the western end of Chao Lao is **Laem Sadet Beach**, which is much quieter and without accommodation. A little further still and you reach **Ao Khung Kraben** where there is a nature walk through salt marshes.

Outside the town to the east, at a distance of 17 kilometres, is the **Nam Tok Phliu National Park**, with waterfalls and the Alongkorn Chedi built in 1876 to commemorate the visit of King Chulalongkorn and Queen Sunantha. Poignantly, nearby another structure built by King Chulalongkorn in 1881 houses part of the ashes of Queen Sunantha, who was drowned in a boating accident near Bang Pa In.

Accommodation
Chanthaburi Town

Name	No. on Map	Rooms	Cheapest Price (Bt)	Name	No. on Map	Rooms	Cheapest Price (Bt)
Maneechan Resort	12	72	2,800	Travelodge	2	150	300
Caribou Highland	6	120	2,000	Chanthanimit	5	57	300
Riverside	4	48	1,600	Kietkhajorn	3	66	270
K.P. Grand	11	200	950	Ban Kaew	1	64	250
K.P. Inn	10	54	700	Kasemsarn	7	60	250
Eastern	14	142	650	Muang Chan	8	75	180
Royal Inn	15	61	500	Chanthaburi	9	70	150
Paris Inn	13	68	450				

Laem Sing Beach

Name	No. on Map	Rooms	Cheapest Price (Bt)	Name	No. on Map	Rooms	Cheapest Price (Bt)
Oasis Sea World	18	6	1,700	Laem Sing Beach	17	30	800
Ban Pak Sumboon	16	22	800				

Ao Yang

Name	No. on Map	Rooms	Cheapest Price (Bt)
Ao Yang Resort	19	18	800

Chao Lao Beach

Name	No. on Map	Rooms	Cheapest Price (Bt)	Name	No. on Map	Rooms	Cheapest Price (Bt)
Ban Had Pak Arang	20	15	2,800	Ban Sud Khob Fa	21	10	1,700
Maldeaf Beach Resort	25	18	2,800	Laem Sadet Resort	24	18	800
Chao Lao Sea Beach	22	48	1,900	Had Souy Resort	23	16	700

Moving On

The following bus services operate from Chanthaburi.

Destination	Route No.	Price (Bt)				Journey Time (hrs)		Frequency	
		V.I.P.	A/C 1	A/C 2	Ord	A/C	Ord	A/C	Ord
Bangkok	914	151	130/135	101	72	4.5	5.5	30 mins	11/day
Bangkok	9907		135			4		Hourly	
Bangkok	42			129	92	5.5	6.5	5/day	Hourly
Nakhon Ratchasima	340		187	146	104	6	7	2 hours	Hourly
Buriram	522		230		128	7	8.5	1/day	40 mins
Rayong	302			50	40	2	2.5	Hourly	30 mins
Saraburi	341			140	100	5	6	5/day	Hourly
Sakaeo	314				52		3.5		30 mins
Trat	301		55	40	30	1.5	2	3/day	30 mins

TRAT   ตราด

5 hrs 30 mins by bus from Eastern Bus Terminal

Trat has not always been a part of Thailand. At the end of the nineteenth century, King Chulalongkorn was forced to cede it to France in return for retaining the remainder of his country intact and having French forces withdraw from Chanthaburi. However, on 23rd March 1906 he regained possession in exchange for Siem Reap, Pratobong and Sri Sophon, which all lie to the east of the Mekong River. Accordingly, 23rd March is now celebrated in Trat as 'Independence Day'.

These days, Trat can be reached in only 5½ hours from Bangkok, using the new and shorter route. Cost is Bt169 by 1st class air-conditioned bus or Bt94 by ordinary bus, the latter taking an extra hour and a half.

This city too is well known for its gems. It is also near the Cambodian border. For that reason the author came here some years ago to see whether it was possible to enter Cambodia. (There was a war taking place at the time, so it was not a very intelligent adventure.) On my map, it looked as if Trat were located right on the border, so I was surprised after the eight hour journey, as it was then, to be told to take a taxi for another 75 kilometres to **Klong Yai**, a cheap but very uncomfortable journey with seven passengers in the wide American-made vehicle and the gear lever between my legs. Moreover, I was even more surprised when I reached Klong Yai to be told to take a *songtaew* for another twelve kilometres to the actual border at **Ban Hat Lek**. This time, it was a question of trying to negotiate several army road blocks without being noticed. I was finally spotted, but permitted to continue under escort to the army camp 500 metres from Cambodia, where I was told firmly that I could see the border from there, which I could, and not to be stupid because if I went any further I should quite certainly get shot, as somebody had been the previous week. I retreated. So now you know how to get to Cambodia. These days it is possible to cross legally from Ban Hat Lek, but you must be in possession of a visa, obtainable in Bangkok, a long way to go back if you forgot to get one. A shared taxi from Trat to Ban Hat Lek costs Bt100 and takes 1½ hours. A *songtaew* from Trat to Klong Yai costs Bt60, and then another Bt20 for a songtaew from Klong Yai to Ban Hat Lek.

On the way to Klong Yai, there are several beaches of note. In order, with kilometre post markings, these are **Sai Kaew Beach** (41km), **Sai Ngam Beach** (42km), **Mai Rut Beach** (57km), **Suk Sam Ran Beach** (57km) and **Ban Chuen Beach** (59km). It is said that the fine sand on Ban Chuen Beach makes it the best of all, but in reality there is not much reason to prefer one to another. All are relatively quiet. In terms of convenience, Sai Kaew and Sai Ngam are preferable because they are only some 300 metres from the main road, whereas the others are three to five kilometres away.

In fact, though, most people come to Trat to travel to Ko Chang (see next entry). If you reach Trat too late for that, you will find that the town itself is a pleasant enough one in which to stay and that there is accommodation available. Alternatively, you can take a *songtaew* to **Laem Ngop**, on the coast, from where one of the ferry services to Ko Chang operates, and where there is also accommodation. The *songtaew* leaves from the market just round the corner from the bus terminus and costs Bt20 for the 17 kilometre journey to Laem Ngop.

There is also a **TAT office** at Laem Ngop. It is conveniently located just a hundred metres from the pier and beside the *songtaew* terminus.

Accommodation
Trat

Name	No. on Map	Rooms	Cheapest Price (Bt)
Muang Trat	10	144	300
P.O. Resort	1	19	250
Pa Ploen	4	24	250
Thai Ruing Rot	7	76	250
Don Juan Resort	15	45	250
P.J. Villa Bungalow	6	30	200
Noen Sai Holiday	5	28	200
S.K. House	2	16	200

Name	No. on Map	Rooms	Cheapest Price (Bt)
Muang Trat O.K.	8	108	200
Sukhumvit Inn	3	18	190
Residang House	14	15	150
Trat Inn	9	52	120
Windy Guest House	11	5	120
Foremost Guest House	13	6	100
M.P. Guest House	12	11	60

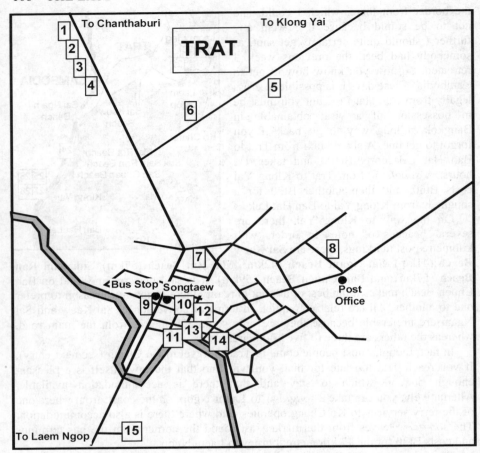

Laem Ngop

Name	No. on Map	Rooms	Cheapest Price (Bt)
Laem Ngop Resort	20	20	600
Paradise	16	20	450
Laem Ngop Inn	18	31	350

Name	No. on Map	Rooms	Cheapest Price (Bt)
The Camping	17	10	300
Chut Kaew G. H.	19	12	100

Ko Chang Pier

Name	No. on Map	Rooms	Cheapest Price (Bt)
Sipianak Guest House	21	12	350

Laem Ling (Near Ao Thammachat)

Name	No. on Map	Rooms	Cheapest Price (Bt)
T.K.K. Bungalow	22	14	800

Name	No. on Map	Rooms	Cheapest Price (Bt)
Ao Tal Koo Resort	23	10	600

Mai Rut Beach

Name	No. on Map	Rooms	Cheapest Price (Bt)
Duangnapa Resort	24	11	450

Klong Yai

Name	No. on Map	Rooms	Cheapest Price (Bt)
Ta Wan Ook Inn	25	25	300
Klong Yai	26	37	300

Name	No. on Map	Rooms	Cheapest Price (Bt)
Bang Inn Villa	27	44	200
Sok Sam Ran	28	37	150

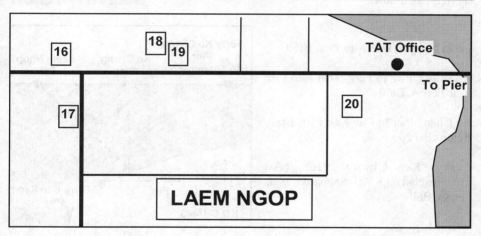

Moving On

The following bus services operate from Trat.

Destination	Route No.	Price (Bt)				Journey Time (hrs)		Frequency	
		V.I.P.	A/C 1	A/C 2	Ord	A/C	Ord	A/C	Ord
Bangkok	917		169	132	94	5.5	7	30 mins	Hourly
Bangkok (via Rayong)			197	158	113	6.5	8	2/day	2/day
Bangkok	9908		175			5.5		Hourly	
Chanthaburi	301		55	40	30	1.5	2	3/day	30 mins

KO CHANG เกาะช้าง

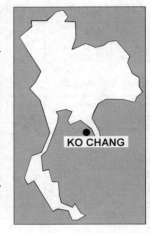

45 mins by ferry from Laem Ngop

Ko Chang is a large island just off the coast of Trat, the most important of the 52 islands in the Chang Group and part of the **Ko Chang National Park**. A battle was fought off the south of Ko Chang in 1941 when the French invaded Thai territorial waters. The **Battle of Ko Chang** resulted in the loss of three Thai naval vessels, the *Songkhla*, the *Chonburi* and the *Thonburi*, but a victory for the Thai Navy in that France withdrew.

Ko Chang is a quiet island with several pretty beaches, especially on the western side. There is quite a choice of ferries to reach the island. There are four main year-round services, as follows.

Laem Ngop to Dan Kao Pier, Bt50

Ko Chang Pier to Ferry Dan Kao Pier (Car Ferry), Bt60

Ko Chang Pier to Dan Kao Pier, Bt80, Return Bt120

Ferry Ko Chang Pier (Ao Thammachat) to Ao Sapparod (Car Ferry), Bt30

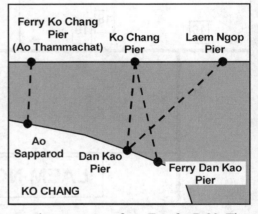

To reach any of these ferry services, you take a *songtaew* from Trat for Bt20. The *songtaew* leave from the market just round the corner from the bus terminus. To go to Laem Ngop, a distance of 17 kilometres, is not too difficult. Accommodation is available here, starting at Bt100. To go to Ko Chang Pier is also possible if you wait a little. However, to persuade a vehicle to go to Ferry Ko Chang Pier, from where the cheapest service leaves, is difficult. The journey is longer, and the similarity in names causes confusion, besides which there is no commission from the ferry company to the driver for bringing passengers to the cheapest service, so few westerners manage to get to Ferry Ko Chang Pier (also known as Ao Thammachat). If you try, you are likely to end up at Ko Chang Pier. If that occurs, note that there are two ferries from here. There is a large and reasonably priced car ferry and a smaller fishing boat which is expensive unless you limit your options by buying a return ticket. The *songtaew* driver will take you to the ticket office for the fishing boat, because it is in his interests to do so. However, note that you have a choice as to which vessel to take. The arrival points on Ko Chang are not far apart. The fishing boat carries nearly all foreigners and the car ferry carries nearly all Thais.

As to departure times for ferries, services currently operate at the following times.

From Laem Ngop:	7:00, 9:00, 11:00, 13:00, 15:00
From Ko Chang Pier (Fishing Boat)	6:30, 9:00, 11:00, 13:00, 15:00
From Ko Chang Pier (Car Ferry)	7:30, 10:30, 13:30, 16:30
From Ferry Ko Chang Pier	7:30, 10:00, 12:00, 14:30, 16:30

The crossing takes 45 minutes by any of the above ferries except the last, which can manage its reduced distance in 30 minutes.

At popular times (November until April), services sometimes operate to particular beaches on Ko Chang. However, such operations are not to be relied upon and are often subject to there being sufficient passengers. It is probably best to go with one of the regular services and enquire about a local service for the return journey.

Upon arrival at the ferry pier, your vessel will be met by *songtaew*. The fare is Bt30 to any place on the west side of the island as far as Kai Bae. Sometimes you are transferred from one vehicle to another on the way, but you pay only once.

Ko Chang is the second biggest island in Thailand (after Phuket) and is a beautiful place. It is relatively undeveloped and is therefore somewhat like the Ko Samui of a quarter of a century ago. It is well worth a visit. There is a multitude of places to stay. The west coast of the island is lined with accommodation, although the island is big enough for one never to feel crowded. Many of these guest houses and bungalows are in idyllic settings with sandy beaches on one side and forested mountains on the other. Just choose from the list, or from the current recommendations of others, or just keep going in the *songtaew* until somewhere takes your fancy. It should be noted that the roads on Ko Chang are not in very good condition and that it takes a long time to get anywhere. Allow at least an hour to get to any beach from the ferry terminal, or an hour and a half to the more distant places. The road does not go all the way round the island. In the south the eastern and western roads are not connected between Bang Bao and Salak Petch. Also note that many places do not have electricity during the day, only at night.

There is a small town on the island, at **Dan Mai**, on the east side. Occasional ferry services run here too in the busy season. *Songtaew* between Dan Mai and any of the beaches on the west down to Kai Bae cost Bt50.

There are also some other islands in the Ko Chang Group which have accommodation and regular ferry services. These are **Ko Wai, Ko Mak** and **Ko Kham**. Ferry services, all from Laem Ngop, leave to all of these islands at about 15:00 each day and return in the morning. Fares are Bt120 to Ko Wai, Bt150 to Ko Kham and Bt170 to Ko Mak.

Accommodation is available on Ko Lao Ya, Ko Wai, Ko Mak, Ko Kradat, Ko Kham, Ko Ngam and Ko Kut, in addition to Ko Chang, but, except in the case of the three islands mentioned above as having regular ferry services, this accommodation is only for those purchasing package tours to the islands.

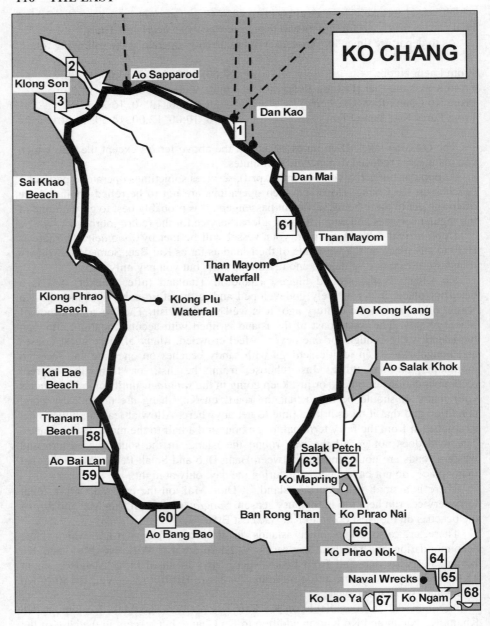

KO CHANG

2

Klong Son

3

Ao Sapparod

Dan Kao

1

Sai Khao
Beach

Dan Mai

61

Than Mayom

Than Mayom
Waterfall

Klong Phrao
Beach

Klong Plu
Waterfall

Ao Kong Kang

Kai Bae
Beach

Ao Salak Khok

Thanam
Beach

58

Ao Bai Lan

59

Salak Petch

63 62

Ko Mapring

60

Ban Rong Than

Ko Phrao Nai

Ao Bang Bao

66

Ko Phrao Nok

64

65

Naval Wrecks

68

Ko Lao Ya 67 Ko Ngam

Accommodation
Ko Chang
Dan Kao

Name	No. on Map	Rooms	Cheapest Price (Bt)
Ko Chang Cabana	1	24	700

Klong Son Beach

Name	No. on Map	Rooms	Cheapest Price (Bt)
Premwadee Resort	2	30	200
Racha Resort	3	26	350

Sai Khao Beach (White Sand Beach)

Name	No. on Map	Rooms	Cheapest Price (Bt)
White Sand Resort	4	73	230
Rock Sand Bungalow	5	10	200
K.C. Sand Resort	6		
Chita Bungalow	7	17	300
Ya Kah Bungalow	8	12	230
Arunee Resort	9	16	300
Sang Tawan Resort	10	19	450
Tiger Hut Bungalow	11	10	250
Cookie Bungalow	12	20	700
White House	13	4	250
Sabay Bar Bungalow	14	9	450
Mac Bungalow	15	19	700
Ko Chang Lagoon	16	45	1,000
Tan Tawan	17	12	150
Bamboo Bungalow	18	15	300
Apple Bungalow	19	13	250
Best Garden Resort	20	35	250
Ban Nuna	21	10	250
Ban Poo Ko Chang	22	28	250
Alina Resort	23	15	250
Sirin Guest House	24	7	250
Sea Sun Guest House	25	17	200
Harmony	26	3	250
Ko Chang Grand View	27	46	200
Moonlight Resort	28	19	200
Plaloma Cliff Resort	29	70	800
Paa Suk San Villa	30	10	250
Chang Tong Resort	31	5	700
No Name	32	5	250

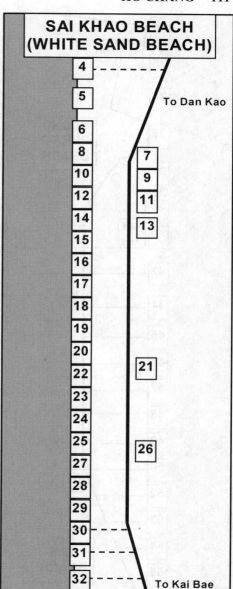

SAI KHAO BEACH (WHITE SAND BEACH)

To Dan Kao

To Kai Bae

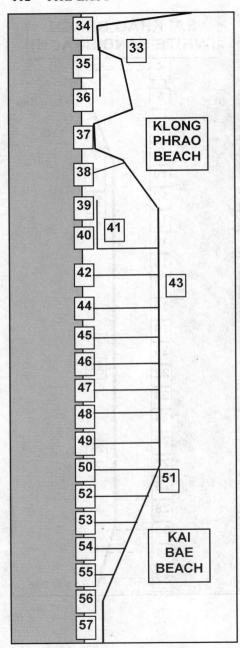

Klong Phrao Beach

Name	No. on Map	Rooms	Cheapest Price (Bt)
Boat Bungalow	33	9	350
Happy Time Resort	34	6	600
Coconut Bungalow	35	33	250
Chai Chet Bungalow	36	25	600
Ko Chang Resort	37	70	1,600
Klong Phrao Resort	38	72	800
P.S.S. Bungalow	39	10	120
K.P. Bungalows	40	28	200
Hobby Hut	41	3	200
Blue Lagoon	42	14	120
Cottage of Herbs	43	5	350
Erawan	44	4	200
Magic Resort	45	30	120
Chok Dee Bungalows	46	40	120

Kai Bae Beach

Name	No. on Map	Rooms	Cheapest Price (Bt)
Ko Chang Cliff Beach	47	16	3,800
Kai Bae Inn	48	15	120
Kai Bae Bar	49	5	300
Coral Resort	50	12	350
Kai Bae Garden	51	5	120
Nang Nual Bungalow	52	12	350
Kai Bae Hut	53	20	600
Kai Bae Beach	54	50	200
Porn's Bungalow	55	18	120
Sea View Resort	56	43	1,000
Siam Bay Bungalow	57	30	300

Thanam Beach (Lonely Beach)

Name	No. on Map	Rooms	Cheapest Price (Bt)
Tree House Lodge	58	24	190

Ao Bai Lan

Name	No. on Map	Rooms	Cheapest Price (Bt)
Bai Lan Beach Resort	59	6	120

Ao Bang Bao

Name	No. on Map	Rooms	Cheapest Price (Bt)
Bang Bao Blue Wave	60	14	230

Than Mayom

Name	No. on Map	Rooms	Cheapest Price (Bt)
Than Mayom Resort	61	10	600

Salak Petch

Name	No. on Map	Rooms	Cheapest Price (Bt)
Sang Aroon Bungalow	62	28	150
Salak Petch Bungalow	63	12	700

Sai Yao Beach

Name	No. on Map	Rooms	Cheapest Price (Bt)
Had Sai Yao Resort	64	42	150
Tan Tawan Bungalow	65	24	100

Ko Phrao Nok

Name	No. on Map	Rooms	Cheapest Price (Bt)
Ko Sai Kao Resort	66	63	Package

Ko Lao Ya

Name	No. on Map	Rooms	Cheapest Price (Bt)
Paradise Island Resort	67	32	1,800

Ko Ngam

Name	No. on Map	Rooms	Cheapest Price (Bt)
Twin Island Resort	68	55	1,300

Ko Wai

Name	No. on Map	Rooms	Cheapest Price (Bt)
Ko Wai Pak Arung	69	35	150
Ko Wai Paradise	70	23	200

Ko Mak

Name	No. on Map	Rooms	Cheapest Price (Bt)
Ko Mak Resort	71	48	350
Lazy Days	72	52	150
T.K. Hut Bungalow	73	30	450
Ko Mak Fantasia	74	23	120
Ao Kao Resort	75	15	150

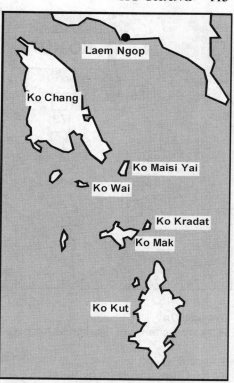

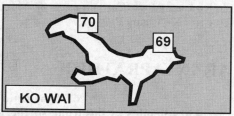

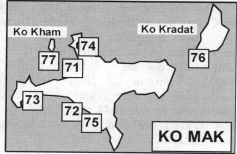

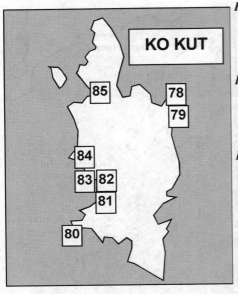

Ko Kradat

Name	No. on Map	Rooms	Cheapest Price (Bt)
Ko Kradat Resort	76	40	1,800

Ko Kham

Name	No. on Map	Rooms	Cheapest Price (Bt)
Ko Kham Resort	77	58	150

Ko Kut

Name	No. on Map	Rooms	Cheapest Price (Bt)
Kut Island Resort	78	42	4,500
Ko Kut Resort	79	25	Package
Klong Hin Hut	80	10	Package
S.B. Ngam Ko	81	20	Package
Klong Chao Resort	82	15	Package
Peter Pan Resort	83	20	Package
Ko Kut Cabana	84	60	Package
Ko Kut Sai Kao	85	25	1,400

Moving On

Here are the times of the regular ferry services from Ko Chang back to the mainland.

To Laem Ngop:	7:00, 9:00, 11:00, 13:00, 15:00
To Ko Chang Pier (Fishing Boat)	7:00, 9:00, 11:00, 13:00, 15:00
To Ko Chang Pier (Car Ferry)	9:00, 12:00, 15:00, 17:30
To Ferry Ko Chang Pier	8:30, 11:00, 13:00, 15:30, 17:30

ARANYAPRATHET   อรัญประเทศ

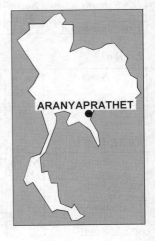

6 hrs by train from Bangkok
4 hrs 30 mins by bus from Northern Bus Terminal

The main claim to fame of Aranyaprathet is that it is very close to the Cambodian border. By train it takes six hours from Bangkok's Hualampong Station. There are only ordinary trains and they go as far as Aranyaprathet only twice a day, the 5:55 departure arriving at 11:40 and the 13:05 arriving at 18:30. The journey is not a particularly interesting one, but the train is, as usual, cheap. The fare is Bt48 third class. Usually only third class is available, but occasionally a second class carriage is also attached.

Buses leave from the Northern Bus Terminal, it should be noted, not the Eastern, and travel by two different routes. The faster bus takes 4½ hours and the slower five hours. Each service operates hourly. Fares are between Bt112 and Bt160 for air-conditioned buses.

The Cambodian border is only six kilometres east of Aranyaprathet and can be reached by *songtaew* or *samlor*. The *samlor*, however, ask the exorbitant price of Bt40. Until fairly recently, it was not possible to cross this border, but now this land entry is permitted (with visa). A few years ago, the author took the morning train to Aranyaprathet and

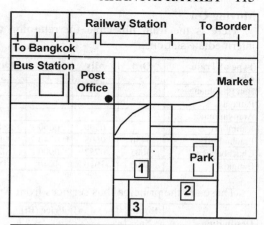

was surprised when the train did not terminate there, but continued right to the border, where a sizeable market was set up. This market is known as **Rong Klua Market**. The border is at a village called **Klong Leuk** and is just a stream with an impressive bridge marked 'Thailand-Cambodia-Australia Friendship Bridge'. (Presumably Australia paid for it.) At that time, there was a prominent notice advising that only locals and U.N. workers could cross, but nobody stopped me and, without formalities, I went into Cambodia. (The problems arose, however, when I later wanted to return to Thailand.) Now there will be no difficulties, as there are no restrictions on crossing this bridge, but the train does not at present continue to the border, although it may be reinstated at some time, so check to see.

There are also day trips by bus from Bangkok to Cambodia leaving early in the morning and returning in the evening and costing approximately Bt700. Since about eight hours is spent travelling, there is not a great deal of time remaining for Cambodia, but such an expedition can be useful if your time in Thailand has expired and you want another month.

If you are exploring the east and do not wish to return to Bangkok first, it is possible to reach Aranyaprathet directly by bus no. 522 from Chanthaburi (destination Buriram).

Accommodation
Aranyaprathet

Name	No. on Map	Rooms	Cheapest Price (Bt)
Aran Garden 1	1	25	150
Aran Garden 2	2	25	200

Name	No. on Map	Rooms	Cheapest Price (Bt)
Inter	3	40	500

Moving On

Here is the train timetable for returning to Bangkok from Aranyaprathet and intermediate stations.

Type of Train	Ord	Mix	Ord	Ord	Ord	Ord	Ord	Ord
Classes	3	3	3	3	3	3	3	3
Ban Plutaluang							1415	
Pattaya							1450	
Aranyaprathet				0630				1335
Kabinburi		0500	0650	0815		1225		1519
Prachinburi	0450	0605	0740	0902		1316		1617
Chachoengsao	0605	0752	0900	1025	1220	1438	1625	1731
Bangkok	0800	1010	1040	1150	1405	1610	1835	1915

These are the principal bus services from Aranyaprathet.

Destination	Route No.	Price (Bt)				Journey Time (hrs)		Frequency	
		V.I.P.	A/C 1	A/C 2	Ord	A/C	Ord	A/C	Ord
Bangkok	60/921		160/144	125/112		5/4.5		30 mins	
Buriram	522		130		80	3.5	4.5	1/day	40 mins
Chanthaburi	522		115		65	3.5	4	1/day	40 mins

POSTCARD HOME—Bangkok, 3rd March 1977

Dear Folks,

The flight from Rangoon was less than an hour late. An hour after leaving Rangoon, I was at Bangkok Airport, and three hours after that I was in Bangkok City. Bangkok is a city of Buddhas, so this is the enormous Reclining Buddha in Wat Pho, not quite as enormous as the one in Pegu, Burma, which is over 180 feet long, but this one has mother-of-pearl inlaid soles to his feet.

PART 4   THE NORTH-EAST

The north-east of Thailand is commonly known as I-san, the word coming from the Sanskrit name Isana which referred to the Mon-Khmer kingdom which flourished here centuries ago. I-san covers 170,000 square kilometres, which constitutes one-third of the total area of Thailand. It is bordered by Laos to the east and north and there are now several points at which a crossing to Laos can be made. The famous Mekong River forms much of the border.

This is a region of history. There are, at Ban Chiang, near Udon Thani, Stone Age excavations which have revealed pottery going back to 7,500 B.C., including what are probably the oldest earthenware designs yet discovered anywhere in the world. Then there are, for example at Phi Mai and Phanom Rung, Khmer ruins possibly predating those at Angkor Wat in Cambodia and very similar in design to that famous temple complex, although much smaller in scale.

The region is less developed than most of Thailand and retains its traditions more intact. It is the area that has least tourism and which visitors are most likely to neglect. As can be imagined, all of this makes it well worth exploring.

Let us start in the east of this region and gradually work our way round to the north, which is, in any case, quite a good way in practice to see what the area has to offer.

NAKHON RATCHASIMA (KORAT)
นครราชสีมา (โคราช)

NAKHON RATCHASIMA

5 hrs 30 mins by train from Bangkok
3 hrs 30 mins by bus from Northern Bus Terminal

There are eleven trains every day from Bangkok to Nakhon Ratchasima, a city sometimes referred to as Korat. They vary from ordinary trains to special expresses and air-conditioned railcars, and, of course, the price also varies accordingly. However, many of the trains depart at night and this is too short a journey to do at night really, so the best train to take is the 6:50 rapid train for Ubon Ratchathani. It is due to reach Nakhon Ratchasima at 12:22. The fare is Bt90 third class, or Bt155 second class, including the rapid supplement. If you are using a rail pass, the train to take is the 5:45, which is all air-conditioned second class and which will reach Nakhon Ratchasima at 10:28.

Bus no. 21 from the Northern Bus Terminal operates twenty-four hours a day and in the daytime it departs every ten minutes for the 256 kilometre trip to Nakhon Ratchasima, one of the best services in the country. The journey takes 3½ hours by air-conditioned bus and 4½ hours by ordinary bus and costs Bt139 and Bt77 respectively. Most of these buses arrive at the old bus station near the centre of the town. A few go to the new bus station, but stop in town. If you come from somewhere other than Bangkok, and arrive at the new bus station which is, of course, well out of the town, you can get back by air-conditioned city bus no. 15 (Bt6) or by *songtaew* no.7 (Bt4).

Nakhon Ratchasima is on a plateau and the train and, to a lesser extent, bus ride to the city is an attractive one. On the way you will pass **Lam Takhong Dam** and the artificial lake created by it. The dam was completed in 1968 and holds 300 million cubic metres of water. A resort town has grown up around the lake in the area of **Pak Chong** and there are many places to stay here, but all are relatively expensive.

You may also observe from bus or train a huge modern white seated Buddha statue on the hillside on your right. This is **Luang Po Khao** at Wat Thepphitak. He is made of reinforced concrete, 45 metres tall, and is very impressive, standing out conspicuously from the surrounding forest. He is reached by either of two flights of steps, in the shape of a Bhoti leaf, totalling 1,250 steps in all, representing the number of followers who assembled without prior arrangement on Maka Buja Day. The statue is 112 metres (56 wa) above the surrounding ground, representing the 56 goodnesses of Buddhism. The statue's height of 45 metres represents the 45 years that Buddha spent teaching following his enlightenment.

Nakhon Ratchasima can also be reached directly from Rayong and Pattaya, a journey of seven hours from Rayong and six hours from Pattaya. The fare from Rayong is Bt201 for a 1st class air-conditioned bus, Bt160 for a 2nd class air-conditioned bus and Bt110 for an ordinary bus. The scenery is spectacular for the last couple of hours as the ranges of mountains are negotiated.

The city itself is a little too large to be easy to explore. It can be divided into two parts: the old and the new. The old part is to the west, while the newer part is a moated area to the east.

Many people use Nakhon Ratchasima just as a base for visiting Phi Mai, but actually it has some interest in itself. Sights to see within the town include **Wat Phra Narai Maharat** on Prachak Road where there is a sandstone statue of the Hindu God Narayana. It is regarded as the city's most sacred statue. The city pillar is in the same temple.

The **Thao Suranari Monument** is in front of the old Pratu Chumphon Gate on the west side of the moated area. The monument itself is not old, however, having been erected in 1934. It commemorates Khun Ying Mo, who was the wife of the Deputy Governor during the time of King Rama III (1824 – 1851) and who managed to rally local citizens and repel a Lao invasion.

There is also the **Maha Viravong National Museum** (admission Bt30) displaying local objects of historical interest, many dating from the Khmer and

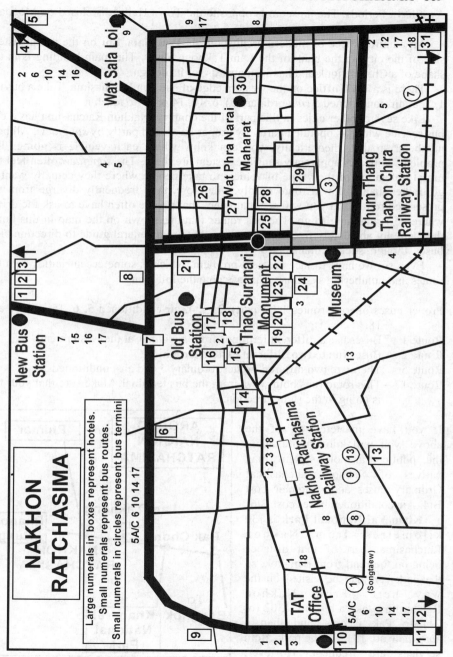

Ayutthaya Periods. The museum is opposite the Town Hall. It is closed on Mondays and Tuesdays.

An admired piece of modern architecture is **Wat Sala Loi** on the north-eastern side of the city on the bank of the Lam Takhong River. The main building is in the shape of a Chinese junk and has won awards for its design.

There is a **TAT office** on the western edge of Nakhon Ratchasima. Take a bus no. 1, 2, 3, air-conditioned 5 (*not* ordinary 5), 6, 10, 14 or 17 to reach it.

Like several other cities in this part of the country, Nakhon Ratchasima has a city bus service which is operated partly by proper buses and partly by *songtaew*. All bear numbers, so that, theoretically, you can know where each vehicle is going. The problems with this apparently sensible system are these. The *songtaew* often feel the moral obligation of their type of vehicle to take people where they actually want to go, rather than follow a route rigidly. Therefore, they frequently diverge from the prescribed route, and you will see that even Thai people often have to ask the driver where he is planning to go. The bus routes that are shown on the map in this book, then, are not absolutely fixed for *songtaew*, but are a general guide to direction. The buses, though, stick to their routes.

Even so, we have to face the next problem, which is some eccentricities with the routes and numbering systems, so please note the following.

Proper buses operate routes 1 (in part), 2, 3, 4, air-conditioned 5, 6, 15, 16, 17 and 18.

Route 1 –   Buses use a different terminus from *songtaew* at the western end.

Route 2 –   Buses run to two different eastern termini.

Route 5 –   There are two different routes: ordinary 5 and air-conditioned 5.

Route 17 – This route runs both ways from the bus terminal. Make sure that your bus is going in the right direction.

If you have mastered all of the above, you will know more about the public transport system than natives of Nakhon Ratchasima! Ordinary buses and *songtaew* cost Bt4. Air-conditioned buses cost Bt6.

Khao Yai National Park is 130 kilometres from Nakhon Ratchasima, part of that distance being on the road from Bangkok, so the park can also be visited on the way here. From Nakhon Ratchasima, take a bus no. 1302 (or 21) to Pak Chong, and then a *songtaew* no. 1317 to the park. Both services are frequent. However,

AROUND NAKHON RATCHASIMA

Phimai

Lam Takhong Dam

Pak Chong

NAKHON RATCHASIMA

Phanom Rung

To Bangkok

Khao Yai National Park

most of the *songtaew* terminate at the entrance to the park and other vehicles have to be taken from there on, as it is too large an area to be able to cover entirely on foot. This was Thailand's first national park, established in 1962. It is in the Dongrak Range. Its attractions include hiking trails, waterfalls such as the Heo Suwat Falls, Heo Narok Falls and Pa Kuay Mai Falls, and a wildlife observation tower. Accommodation is available, but advance booking is preferred (Tel: 02-5614292).

Accommodation
Nakhon Ratchasima

Name	No. on Map	Rooms	Cheapest Price (Bt)	Name	No. on Map	Rooms	Cheapest Price (Bt)
Royal Princess	4	35	1,850	Thai	8	147	400
Ratchapruk Grand	7	159	1,700	K. Star	26	70	350
Sima Thani	10	147	1,700	Sri Wichai	19	50	250
Korat Resort	31	15	1,400	Fa Sang	14	77	230
Sri Pattana	16	180	1,400	Cathay	21	48	230
K.S. Pavilion	6	59	1,200	Kings	9	116	200
Chompol Grand	30	154	1,200	Fa Thai	23	90	200
Pegasus	2	48	1,050	Tokyo B	17	40	150
Chom Surang	29	167	850	Tokyo A	18	40	150
Airport	13	65	800	Chumpol	20	72	150
Orchid	11	30	700	Thai Pokkapan	27	27	150
Tab Kaew Palace	5	44	600	Ek Nakhon	28	53	140
Best	12	65	600	Siri	15	60	120
Chao Phraya	24	99	550	Pho Thong	22	45	120
Gally White	1	66	450	Muang Thong	25	52	100
Boss	3	94	450				

Moving On

The railway timetable to places east of Nakhon Ratchasima, on the way to Ubon Ratchathani, and north of Nakhon Ratchasima, on the way to Udon Thani and Nong Khai, is on page 73. The timetable back to Bangkok is given below.

Type of Train	Exp *	Rap	Ord	Exp *	Rap	Ord	Ord	Exp *	Ord	Exp *	Rap *	Exp *†
Classes	2,3	2,3	3	2,3	2,3	3	3	2	3	2,3	2,3	1,2,3
Nakhon Ratchasima	0022	0234	0820	1037	1220	1328	1550	1820	1944	2244	2303	2332
Ayutthaya	0351	0741	1241	1339	1605	1741	2006	2133	0022		0302	0336
Bang Pa In			1253			1754	2016		0035			
Don Muang	0433	0840	1329	1416	1651	1836	2055	2211	0110	0310	0349	0425
Bangkok	0530	0935	1420	1505	1745	1930	2140	2255	0205	0400	0435	0520

* Air-conditioned 2nd class available   † 2nd class sleepers available

The following bus services operate from Nakhon Ratchasima.

Destination	Route No.	Price (Bt)				Journey Time (hrs)		Frequency	
		V.I.P.	A/C 1	A/C 2	Ord	A/C	Ord	A/C	Ord
Bangkok *	21		139		77	3.5	4.5	10 mins	Hourly
Khon Kaen	20/211		104		58	3	3.5	Hourly	30 mins
Udon Thani	22		162		90	5	6	Hourly	30 mins
Udon Thani	262		162		90	5	6	5/day	1/day
Nong Khai	23		189			6.5		Hourly	
Sri Chiang Mai	262		210		114	6.5	8	5/day	1/day
Ubon Ratchathani	25/285		220		121	5.5	6.5	3/day	4/day
Buriram	273		80		48	3	3.5	2/day	30 mins
Surin	31	275				3		4/day	
Surin (via Ban Ta Go)	274		84		60	3.5	4	5/day	30 mins
Chaiyaphum	204		70		39	2.5	3	Hourly	30 mins
Dan Khun Tut *	4391				19		1.5		30 mins
Phimai	1305				21		1.5		30 mins
Phimai	4542			28		1		90 mins	
Chok Chai	1307				12		1		30 mins
Phanom Wan *	4139				7		0.5		10/day
Pak Thong Chai *	1303				12		1		30 mins
Pattaya	589		200		100	5.5	6.5	7/day	7/day
Rayong	267		201		112	6	7	3/day	30 mins
Chantaburi	340		187	146	104	6	7	8/day	Hourly
Phitsanulok	635		258	221	133	7	8	9/day	5/day
Chiang Mai	635			325	218	13.5	15	4/day	3/day
Chiang Rai	651			464	258	14	16	4/day	1/day
Pak Chong *	1302				30		2		30 mins

* Departs from old bus station

PHI MAI   พิมาย

1 hr 30 mins by bus from Nakhon Ratchasima

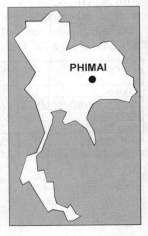

PHIMAI

Phi Mai is one of the historical monuments in Thailand which is not to be missed. Take a bus no. 1305 or 4542 from the new bus station in Nakhon Ratchasima for the 90 minute journey north. Bus no. 1305 is an ordinary bus running every half hour at a cost of Bt21. Bus no. 4542 is an air-conditioned service costing Bt28 which runs every 90 minutes. Neither bus terminates in the main town of Phi Mai. The 1305 continues quite a long way to Chum Puang. The 4542 goes on to the bus station in New Phi Mai, two kilometres away. If you do not want to stay in Nakhon Ratchasima, there are air-conditioned buses direct from Bangkok to Phi Mai four times a day. However, they run to New Phi Mai bus station without going through the main town. The cost is

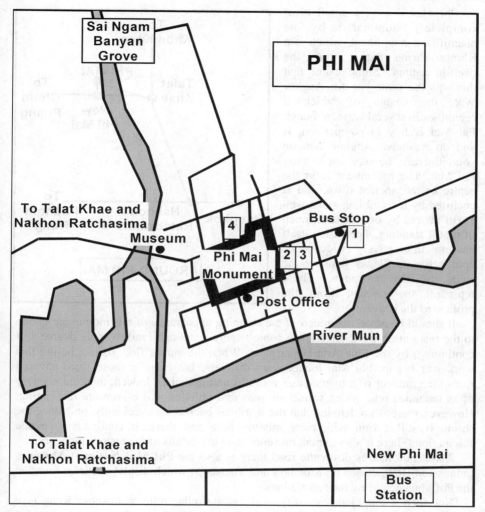

Bt170 for a 1st class air-conditioned bus or Bt130 for a 2nd class air-conditioned bus. You must walk two kilometres from the new town to the old or take a *songtaew* or motor-cycle taxi for Bt10. Alternatively, it is possible to take a bus from Bangkok to Khon Kaen and ask to be put off at the turn off to Phi Mai, reached about an hour after Nakhon Ratchasima. From this point to the town is twelve kilometres which takes only about fifteen minutes and costs Bt5, and there are *songtaew* operating from time to time in addition to the bus.

Phi Mai is a very small town completely dominated by its magnificent monument, which is a Khmer shrine dating from the twelfth century. Some claim that this was the prototype for Angkor Wat, the design of which it resembles in several ways, although Phi Mai is tiny in comparison. If you do not have Angkor Wat on your itinerary, be sure not to miss Phi Mai. The monument is in the centre of the ancient town, and is enclosed by a crumbling stone wall 1,030 metres by 665 metres, much of it still standing. The shrine itself has an impressively wide stone approach with Nagas flanking the steps to the entrance. These represent the passing from the profane to the heavenly.

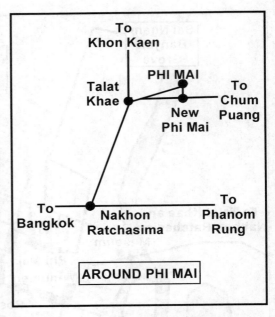

AROUND PHI MAI

It should be noted that much of the stunning appearance of this monument is due to the restoration work undertaken some twenty years ago (and to some degree still continuing) by the Fine Arts Department. When the author first visited, before this work was begun, Phi Mai looked very different, but even in those weed-covered ruins the grandeur of a bygone age was still unmistakable. Indeed, then the mystery of an untended relic which would not pass into oblivion was even more fascinating. However, there is no denying that the work has been done excellently, and since the shrine is still a ruin with parts missing here and there, it continues to exude fascination. There is also a small museum showing details of the restoration work.

About 500 metres down the road there is also the **Phi Mai National Museum** (admission Bt30, closed on Mondays and Tuesdays) which displays articles found at the Phi Mai site during the restorations.

Not such a long journey away, there is a similar relic at Phanom Rung (see under). To see both is a little repetitive (and many a discussion has centred on which is the better to see), but to see neither is truly to miss a part of Thailand. Without entering into the above discussion of merit, the author will merely mention that it is considerably easier to get to Phi Mai than to Phanom Rung. Admission to Phi Mai costs Bt40 for foreigners (Bt10 for Thais).

Another attraction here is Thailand's largest **grove of banyan trees** (but no single tree as large as the one in the Calcutta Botanical Gardens in India). The trees are about two kilometres from the town.

Accommodation

There is a hotel in Phi Mai, called, reasonably enough, the Phi Mai Hotel. Rooms are available from Bt200. The hotel is right next to the bus stop, just down the road from the Phi Mai monument. There are also three guest houses, one of them, the Old Phi Mai Guest House, being a youth hostel and offering members a 10% reduction.

Phi Mai

Name	No. on Map	Rooms	Cheapest Price (Bt)
Phi Mai Hotel	1	40	200
S and B Guest House	3	5	120

Name	No. on Map	Rooms	Cheapest Price (Bt)
J and B Guest House	4	8	120
Old Phi Mai G. H.	2	8	90

Moving On

The last bus back to Nakhon Ratchasima leaves at 18:00. If you are heading north from here, alight when the bus turns left at the main highway (Talat Khae) and take a bus travelling in the opposite direction. Most buses will stop at this point.

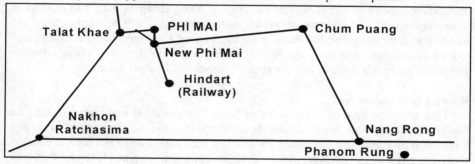

If you want to go east, there is a *songtaew* to Hindart four times a day, at 7:30, 9:30, 12:00 and 14:00, and from Hindart you can take a train eastwards, towards Ubon Ratchathani.

If you want to go to Phanom Rung, take the bus no. 1305 in the direction opposite to Nakhon Ratchasima, to its terminus at Chum Puang. From there take bus no. 516 to Nang Rong, which is the nearest town to Phanom Rung.

Here is a summary of buses running from Phi Mai. Remember that the Bangkok bus and also the *songtaew* to Hindart do not pass through the main town area. You must go to New Phi Mai to catch these services.

Destination	Route No.	Price (Bt)				Journey Time (hrs)		Frequency	
		V.I.P.	A/C 1	A/C 2	Ord	A/C	Ord	A/C	Ord
Bangkok	944		170	130		5.5		4/day	
Nakhon Ratchasima	1305				21		1.5		30 mins
Nakhon Ratchasima	4542			28		1		90 mins	
Chum Puang	1305				18		1		30 mins
Hindart					15		0.75		4/day

PHANOM RUNG

พนมรุ้ง

PHANOM RUNG

6 hrs by bus from Northern Bus Terminal

Phanom Rung is a very similar monument to Phi Mai, mentioned above. The difference is that it is considerably more difficult to reach, so let us start with ways to get there.

Route 1 (expensive)

First here is the traditional and most common route, which is likely to be recommended by any TAT office. Take a bus from Bangkok to Ban Ta Go. This will probably be a bus bound for Buriram, Surin, Sisaket or Ubon Ratchathani, but not all such buses travel via Ban Ta Go, so you need to check. If you cannot find a suitable bus, take any bus to Nakhon Ratchasima and then a bus no. 274 going to Surin. Ban Ta Go is fourteen kilometres beyond the town of **Nang Rong**. At Ban Ta Go, there is a road going off to the right beside which motor-cycle taxis will be waiting. Any one of them will be delighted to take you up to Phanom Rung and back, a distance of twelve kilometres each way, for Bt200. With persuasion they will come down to Bt150, an enormous price to pay for such a comparatively short distance.

Route 2 (less expensive)

Take a bus or train to Buriram, or to Nang Rong without continuing to Ban Ta Go. If you choose train, you can take the 6:50 rapid to Buriram, arriving at 14:20 and go to Phanom Rung next day. The fare is Bt107 third class and Bt195 second class. If you have a rail pass, however, use the 5:45, reaching Buriram at 11:45 and then you will be able to visit Phanom Rung the same day. If you are travelling from Nakhon Ratchasima, there is an ordinary train at 10:55, reaching Buriram at 12:58.

From Buriram or Nang Rong, take bus no. 522 (to Chanthaburi) or 510 (to Tha Phraya) as far as Ban Ta Pek. These buses go to Ban Ta Go and then turn right along the road towards Phanom Rung for 5½ kilometres. Get off at Ban Ta Pek and you will see the minor road to the monument on your left. From here it is only 6½ kilometres: four kilometres on the flat, then a steep 1½ kilometre climb and then one more kilometre almost flat at the top of the hill. Motor-cycle taxis can be found here too, and will ask an excessive Bt100. They can be persuaded to take you and bring you back for about Bt70.

Route 3 (almost free)

This is the most interesting way to go, and costs almost nothing for the trip to the monument and back. You need to stay overnight in the town of Nang Rong, the nearest town to Phanom Rung. That is no hardship, for there are two interesting guest houses with knowledgeable owners who speak excellent English. These two are

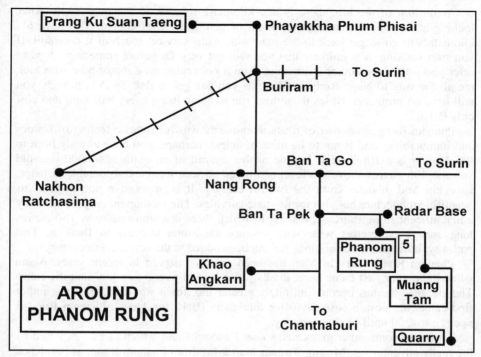

Honey Inn and California Park (see map). Take a bus from Bangkok to Nang Rong. It takes six hours to reach Nang Rong and costs Bt191 by 1st class air-conditioned bus. Alternatively, you can travel to Buriram or Nakhon Ratchasima by bus or train and make the journey to Nang Rong from there.

When the author first visited here some years ago, I was told to just wait in the town of Nang Rong until the Air Force came. It was a strange direction, but after a while a sturdy military truck turned up and everybody piled into the back, myself included, and we were transported as far along the road as we wished to go. At the top of the hill on which Phanom Rung is built, there is an Air Force radar station, and a truck goes up every morning carrying provisions. Returning to Nang Rong recently, the author was very pleased to find the same service still operating, although with many fewer passengers these days. Speak to the driver and he will be not just willing but pleased to take you up to Phanom Rung. There are some seats in the back of the truck. There is no charge for the rather exciting 26 kilometre trip, and you may even get a tour of the town first to pick up supplies here and there. The truck leaves every morning at 7:30. The only problem is to find it. Look at the map of Nang Rong, on which the departure point is marked. There is a prominent bank next door to the spot, but it is not a location with other obvious landmarks, although the truck itself is fairly conspicuous. If in doubt, seek help from the owner of your guest house in advance.

At the top of the hill, there is one kilometre to walk to the monument. After looking at it, you will have the problem of getting back of course. You have 6½ kilometres to go to get back to the road with a bus service, much of it downhill. If you start walking, it is unlikely that you will get very far before somebody stops to offer you a lift. The author's lift came from a policeman on a motor-bike who took me all the way to Nang Rong. As long as you can get to Ban Ta Pek, though, you will have no problems. Buses from there run to Nang Rong every half hour and cost only Bt10.

Phanom Rung is another of those monuments which exudes a feeling of history and immutability and is not to be missed, unless, perhaps, you have already been to Phi Mai. It is a Hindu style temple at the summit of an extinct 900,000-year-old volcano 400 metres above sea level and it can be seen from a considerable distance. Like Phi Mai, it dates from the twelfth century. It is impressive not only for its beautiful architecture but also for its stone carvings. The monument is approached by a magnificent stone staircase, leading to which there is a stone pathway 160 metres long and seven metres wide with seventy sandstone lanterns to flank it. This pathway, however, is not original, having been added in the seventeenth century.

Phanom Rung, like Phi Mai, has been greatly restored in recent years. Again when the author first came here, it was just a pile of overgrown but majestic ruins. The entrance fee has become infinitely greater too, for it was free when the author first came, but now it costs Bt40 for foreigners (Bt10 for Thais). Phanom Rung is open from 6:00 until 18:00 every day.

There are some other monuments near Phanom Rung which can be explored by the really adventurous. **Muang Tam** is 8km away from Phanom Rung, at Ban Khok Muang. Built in the eleventh century, this building was originally residential rather than religious in its purpose, but was later converted into a Buddhist temple and also has elaborate carvings. Admission costs Bt30.

There is a newly built and interesting temple at **Khao Angkarn**, 32 kilometres from Nang Rong.

At a distance of 68 kilometres, on the border with Cambodia, lies the **stone quarry** from which the materials for Phanom Rung were obtained. It is thought that they were dragged to the top of the volcano by hard-working elephants.

Prang Ku Suan Taeng is in Ban Don Wai, quite a long way north of Buriram. From Buriram take a bus for Roi Et until you reach Highway 202 at Phayakkha Phum Phisai after about an hour, and then you want to catch a bus going left towards Phutthaisong. The monument is reached 12 kilometres before Phutthaisong and consists of three pagodas of brick and mortar in Khmer style. It is famous because of the story of a lintel which was surreptitiously removed and re-discovered in Chicago. The lintel was eventually returned, under pressure, to the National Museum in Bangkok.

The owner of California Park Guest House has a minibus in which he will take visitors to Phanom Rung and back for a fee of Bt120 (better value than the exorbitant motor-bikes), subject to his having a minimum of three passengers. For a small extra fee he can include other nearby attractions.

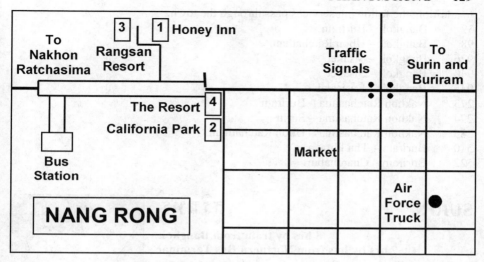

The owner of Honey Inn has motor-cycles for rent for Bt200 for half a day. Honey Inn, incidentally, also offers an excellent evening meal for Bt80, with much encouragement to "Eat up, eat up." Nang Rong is really not a bad little town in which to spend a night.

Accommodation
Nang Rong

Name	No. on Map	Rooms	Cheapest Price (Bt)
The Resort	4	12	400
Rangsan Resort	3	20	400
California Park G. H.	2	6	200
Honey Inn	1	7	150

Name	No. on Map	Rooms	Cheapest Price (Bt)
Kasemuk		13	120
Nang Rong		19	120
Sa Nguan Mit		19	90

Ban Ta Pek

Name	No. on Map	Rooms	Cheapest Price (Bt)
Phanom Rung Resort	5	11	700

Moving On
The following bus services commence from Nang Rong.

Destination	Route No.	Price (Bt)				Journey Time (hrs)		Frequency	
		V.I.P.	A/C 1	A/C 2	Ord	A/C	Ord	A/C	Ord
Chum Puang	516				30		2.5		Hourly
Sung Sang	521				25		2		Hourly

In addition, the following services pass through the town:

32	Bangkok – Buriram
98	Bangkok – Ubon Ratchathani
926	Bangkok – Sisaket
940	Bangkok – Sisaket
945	Bangkok – Rasisalai
273	Nakhon Ratchasima – Buriram
274	Nakhon Ratchasima – Surin
285	Nakhon Ratchasima – Ubon Ratchathani
510	Buriram – Tha Phraya
522	Buriram – Chanthaburi

SURIN   สุรินทร์

8 hrs by train from Bangkok
7 hrs by bus from Northern Bus Terminal

Surin has ten trains a day from Bangkok, including one at 21:00 with second class sleeping berths which reaches Surin at 4:52. During the day, there is the 6:50 rapid arriving at 15:07. This is the best train for economy, costing Bt113 third class or Bt209 second class. If you have a rail pass or want to be more comfortable and speedy, the 5:45 and 11:05 railcars from Bangkok both offer air-conditioned second class. The 5:45 covers the 420 kilometres in 6½ hours, which is comparable with the fastest buses, if you can get up early enough.

Air-conditioned buses leave the Northern Bus Terminal in Bangkok hourly. They take seven hours and cost Bt183. Ordinary buses take eight hours and cost Bt131.

Although Surin is famous for its **Elephant Round-up**, this takes place only once a year, on the third weekend in November, at which time everything is packed and it is very difficult to get seats on buses or trains or to find accommodation. If you want to see a lot of elephants in one place at the same time, this is your chance, but at other times Surin is a rather ordinary town.

To see elephants out of season, you need to go to **Ban Taklang**, north of Surin. Take a bus no. 3605 going to Kra Pho and alight at Ban Taklang (Bt20). The journey of 58 kilometres takes about 75 minutes and buses run approximately hourly. Of course, there are many places in Thailand where you can meet elephants, and this is not one of the easiest to reach, but here you will see elephants at home, rather than on display. They are not working elephants here, but animals kept as companions and for participation in the Round-up in November. There is an Elephant Show on Saturdays only at 9:30 (Bt200). There is also a small Elephant Museum in the village.

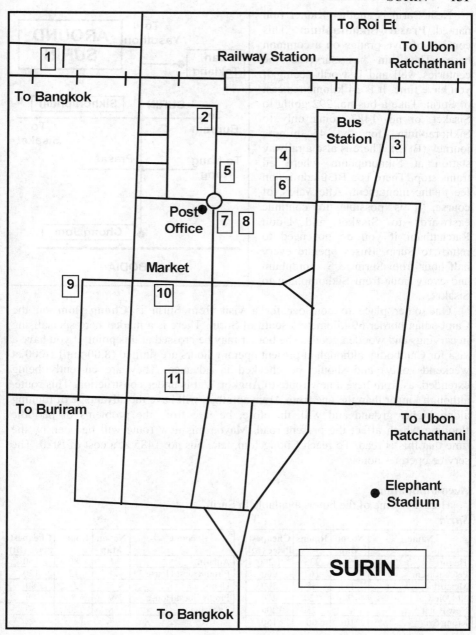

Near Surin is another Khmer ruin named **Prasat Sikhoraphum**. This consists of five prangs on a common base. The ruin has survived the centuries well and is worth seeing if you have time. It is 34 kilometres east of Surin. Take a bus no. 292 going to Sisaket, or no. 1487 going only to Sikhoraphum, for the 45 minute journey (Bt12). There is also a railway station at Sikhoraphum where all trains stop. There is a Bt30 admission fee to the monument. Afterwards, of course, it is possible to continue eastwards to Sisaket and Ubon Ratchathani if you do not need to return to Surin. Buses operate every half hour from Surin to Sikhoraphum and every hour from Sikhoraphum to Sisaket.

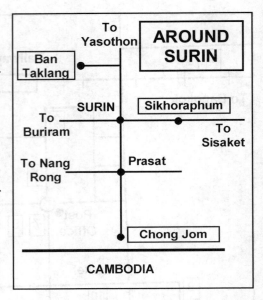

One other place to consider for a visit from Surin is **Chong Jom** on the Cambodian border 69 kilometres south of Surin. There is a market here specialising in carvings and wooden goods. The border may be crossed at this point, if you have a visa for Cambodia, although at present opening hours are limited (8:00 until 16:00 at weekends only) and should be checked in advance. They are currently being extended, as from here a new route to Angkor Wat is under construction. This route, although longer than the one from Aranyaprathet, will have the advantage of running along higher ground and will, therefore, be free from the problems of periodic flooding which affect the present road. Maybe this new route will be open by the time that this is read. To reach Chong Jom, take bus no. 1485 at a cost of Bt20. The service operates hourly.

Accommodation

Here are some of the hotels available in Surin.

Surin

Name	No. on Map	Rooms	Cheapest Price (Bt)
Tharin	3	233	1,200
Petch Kasem	4	162	900
Memorial	11	65	300
Nid Diew	7	124	200
New Hotel	2	75	200
Krung Sri	10	66	150

Name	No. on Map	Rooms	Cheapest Price (Bt)
Amarin	6	80	150
Pirom Guest House 2	1	12	120
Ubon	5	29	80
Pirom Guest House	9	8	80
Tanachai	8	20	50

Moving On

Now here is a summary of bus services from Surin.

Destination	Route No.	Price (Bt)				Journey Time (hrs)		Frequency	
		V.I.P.	A/C 1	A/C 2	Ord	A/C	Ord	A/C	Ord
Bangkok	31	355	225	183	131	7	8	Hourly	2/day
Bangkok	937			180	127	7	8	1/day	1/day
Nakhon Ratchasima	274		84		60	3.5	4	5/day	30 mins
Nakhon Ratchasima	563		77			3.5		5/day	
Rayong (via Pattaya)	588	400	350			9.5		4/day	
Pattaya	588/589	380	325	250	175	8.5	10	8/day	4/day
Roi Et	252				52		3.5		8/day
Roi Et	550				45		3		6/day
Yasothon	293				52		3		2/day
Rattanaburi	1483			30	20	2	2.5	30 mins	18/day
Chong Jom	1485				20		1.5		7/day
Sisaket (Sikhoraphum)	293				35		3		Hourly
Kra Pho, Na Klang	3605				20		1.5		Hourly
Satuk	524				40		3		13/day
Sangkha	292			30	20	1	1.5	3/day	30 mins
Khon Kaen	281				83		6		9/day
Sanom	4228				25		1.5		Hourly
Kok Krachai	558				23		2		8/day
Sikhoraphum	1487				12		1		15/day

There is also a minibus service, no. 4400, to Rattanaburi every 20 minutes.

UBON RATCHATHANI อุบลราชธานี

11 hrs by train from Bangkok
10 hrs by bus from Northern Bus Terminal

Ubon Ratchathani is the major city in the area east of Bangkok and bordering Laos and Cambodia. This is the final station on the north-eastern railway line, although there is another branch running north from Nakhon Ratchasima to Udon Thani and Nong Khai. There are seven trains per day from Bangkok to here. The 21:00 express departure has second class sleeping berths at a cost of Bt601 for an air-conditioned lower berth, Bt531 for an air-conditioned upper berth, Bt431 for an ordinary lower berth and Bt381 for an ordinary upper berth. It reaches Ubon Ratchathani at 7:20. By day, there is the rapid train, which is, as usual, economical. Third class

LONG-DISTANCE BUS TERMINI
(as shown on map opposite)

BUS TERMINUS 1	Amnat Charoen, Mukdahan
BUS TERMINUS 2	Khon Kaen, Udon Thani
BUS TERMINUS 3	Mukdahan, Nakhon Phanom
BUS TERMINUS 4	Bangkok
BUS TERMINUS 5	Local services
BUS TERMINUS 6	Kemmarat, Trakhan
BUS TERMINUS 7	Pattaya
BUS TERMINUS 8	Bangkok
BUS TERMINUS 9	Bangkok, Khon Kaen, Udon Thani
BUS TERMINUS 10	Bangkok, Chiang Mai, Pattaya, Rayong
BUS TERMINUS 11	Kantharalak
BUS TERMINUS 12	Sisaket, Phibun, Det Udom, Khong Chiam

costs Bt135 and second class costs Bt261. It leaves Bangkok at 6:50 and reaches Ubon Ratchathani at 18:10. Those with rail passes can use the overnight sleeper economically, or the air-conditioned express railcar at 5:45 which arrives at 14:05, less than 8½ hours later, a comfortable and speedy journey. Without a rail pass, this train costs Bt421.

Buses depart from the Northern Bus Terminal and travel to Ubon Ratchathani by four different routes. Air-conditioned buses take eight to ten hours, but most commonly the latter. Ordinary buses take 10½ to eleven hours. Air-conditioned buses cost Bt337 while ordinary buses cost Bt193. Air-conditioned buses leave hourly, but ordinary buses run only three times a day.

Ubon Ratchathani's attractions are a number of temples in different styles and some nearby National Parks and other attractive scenery. It is a long spread-out city, with the railway station at the southern extremity of the conurbation on the wrong side of the river in an area known as Warin, and no less than twelve different bus stations sprinkled round the city. Everything is linked together by a city bus service which runs quite frequently and efficiently, but stops at 18:30. The fare is Bt5, payable by inserting a coin into the turnstile by the entrance. If you do not have a Bt5 coin, the driver will give you change (which seems contrary to the main purpose of the system, but is convenient anyway). Numbers of bus routes are shown on the city map.

Ubon Ratchathani was founded in 1779 when a group of princes fled with their followers from Vientiane in Laos and sought asylum in Thailand under King Taksin. The city was recognised and given its name the following year. In more recent times it has been the site of a prisoner of war camp during the Second World War and subsequently of an American military base.

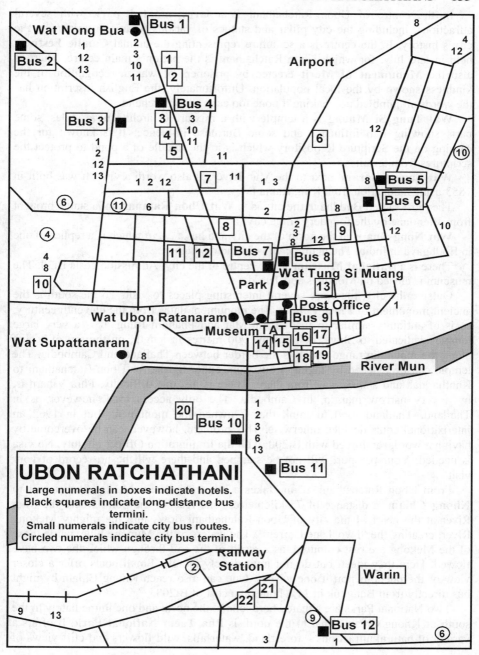

UBON RATCHATHANI

Large numerals in boxes indicate hotels.
Black squares indicate long-distance bus termini.
Small numerals indicate city bus routes.
Circled numerals indicate city bus termini.

In the centre of Ubon Ratchathani is a **large moated park** with several attractions, including the city pillar and statues of various figures prominent in the city's history. In the centre is a sculpture representing the annual **Candle Festival**, held in late July, for which Ubon Ratchathani is the nation's main centre. There is also the **Monument of Merit** erected by prisoners of war in recognition of the kindness shown by the local population. Unfortunately, the English inscription has the words all jumbled up, making it none too easy to comprehend.

Wat Tung Si Muang is a temple with a mixture of architectural styles, some parts showing Lao influence and some Burmese influence. It is known for the carving on the Scripture Repository which is in the middle of a pond to protect the scriptures from termites.

Wat Supattanaram, next to the Mun River, is also worth a visit. It was built in 1853 using a donation from King Rama IV.

The most sacred Buddha in the city is in **Wat Ubon Ratanaram**, a statue brought from Vientiane by the founders of the city.

Wat Nong Bua is in the north of the city and has a *chedi* which is a replica of one in Bodhgaya in India. The main *chedi* is 56 metres high.

There is a **National Museum** in the centre of the city. Admission costs Bt30. The museum is closed on Mondays and Tuesdays.

Outside the city, there are several interesting places to visit. To the south is the ancient monument of **Phra Viharn**. The monument dates from the eleventh century, so is of antiquity similar to that of Phi Mai and Phanom Rung. It is a very large temple, dedicated to Shiva, being some 900 metres in length, on the top of a cliff along the mountain range which is the border between Thailand and Cambodia. The temple can be reached by taking a bus from either Sisaket or Ubon Ratchathani to Kantharalak and a *songtaew* from there. There is just one difficulty. Phra Viharn is, by a very narrow margin, in Cambodia. The only access road, however, is in Thailand. Thailand used to think that it owned the monument, but in 1962 an international court decided otherwise. This problem, however, can be overcome by having a word, reinforced with Bt200, with the Immigration Officer on duty. No visa is needed. Your passport will not be stamped and there will be no record of your visit.

From Ubon Ratchathani, if one takes a bus from Warin Market further east to **Khong Chiam**, a distance of 75 kilometres, one reaches the point where the Mun River at the heart of the city of Ubon Ratchathani flows into the mighty Mekong River, creating the 'Two Tone Current'. The waters of the Mun are blue, while those of the Mekong are rust coloured, as a result of the soil through which the two have flowed. Here they meet, but do not immediately mingle. Small boats offer a closer view of the phenomenon if one wishes. One can also reach Khong Chiam by night bus directly from Bangkok in 11½ hours at a cost of Bt203.

Two National Parks are situated here, one to the north and one immediately to the south of Khong Chiam. That to the north is **Pha Taem National Park**. It offers a variety of natural attractions – forestland, waterfalls, wild flowers and cliff views of

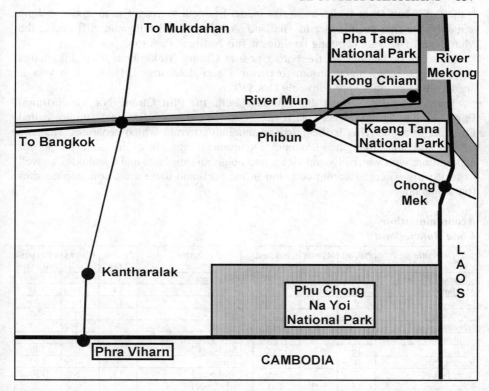

the Mekong River – but it is best known for its cave paintings, which are prehistoric colour drawings on the cliff faces next to the Mekong. There are four groups of paintings, the most accessible being the Pha Taem group which consists of some 300 drawings. Camping facilities are available in the National Park.

Just across the Mun River to the south of Khong Chiam is the **Kaeng Tana National Park**. At this point the Mekong River leaves Thai territory and, for the second time in its course, flows entirely within Laos. Before it does so, there is a narrow strip of land south of the Mun River which belongs to Thailand. This is the site of the Kaeng Tana National Park, which also includes **Don Tana**, an island 700 metres long in the middle of the Mun River. The island is connected to both shores by suspension bridges. Because the island constricts the course of the river, the current here is particularly strong and there are also dangerous rapids, with sharp rocks and underwater caves. It is claimed that 'Tana' is a corruption of 'Morana', meaning death, since many local fishermen have met with unfortunate accidents in this location. There is a beach on the island, but swimming is not recommended! In the midst of the rapids is a man-made structure put there by the French to assist navigation. Further upstream where the road to Khong Chiam crosses the Mun River is the **Pak Mun Dam** which has a fish ladder beside it to assist fish to spawn in June and July, the first such ladder in Thailand. A Nature Trail follows a cliff beside the Mun River. There are camping facilities in this National Park too.

Laos can be entered via the border post at **Chong Mek**, about thirty kilometres from this point, or ninety kilometres from Ubon Ratchathani. However, a visa is needed and that costs approximately U.S.$30.

There is a third National Park further south, the **Phu Chong Na Yo National Park**, in the triangle where Thailand, Laos and Cambodia meet, the so-called Emerald Triangle. This is the fairly mountainous terrain which separates Thailand from Cambodia, the Khao Phanom Dongram Range. It offers semi-jungle for exploration, with waterfalls and views into neighbouring Laos and Cambodia, as well as boat trips. There is accommodation in the park and there are also camping sites (but no tents).

Accommodation
Ubon Ratchathani

Name	No. on Map	Rooms	Cheapest Price (Bt)	Name	No. on Map	Rooms	Cheapest Price (Bt)
Ubonburi Resort	20	110	2,100	Somkhiat	6	25	350
Montana	12	30	2,050	Ubon	14	124	300
Laithong	9	124	1,200	Bodin	11	110	300
Tho Saeng	10	76	1,200	Racha	5	59	300
Nevada Grand	1	90	1,100	Tokyo	8	47	250
Pathumrat	3	169	1,050	New Nakhon Luang	17	56	250
Sri Kamol	16	42	1,000	Sri I-San 2	19	36	200
Regent Palace	4	116	1,000	Suriyat	7	50	150
Nevada Inn	2	63	750	Sri I-San 1	18	26	150
Ratchathani	15	103	400	Rivermoon G. H.	21	8	120
Krung Thong	13	116	350	Warin	22	10	100

Moving On

First, here is the return train timetable for the journey to Bangkok.

Type of Train	Ord	Exp *	Rap	Ord	Ord	Ord	Ord	Exp *	Exp	Rap	Exp *†	Rap
Classes	3	2,3	2,3	3	3	3	3	2	2,3	2,3	1,2,3	2,3
Ubon Ratchathani			0635	0655	0840	1245	1325	1435		1700	1815	1940
Surin	0500	0745	0920	1005	1201	1535	1629	1622	1930	1958	2050	2248
Buriram	0558	0835	1016	1100	1259	1626	1725	1656	2027	2056	2140	2353
Nakhon Ratchasima	0820	1037	1220	1328	1514	1835	1944	1820	2244	2303	2332	0234
Ayutthaya	1241	1337	1605	1741			0022			0302	0336	0741
Bang Pa In	1253			1754			0035					
Don Muang	1329	1416	1651	1836			0110	2211	0310	0349	0425	0840
Bangkok	1420	1505	1745	1930			0205	2255	0400	0435	0520	0935

There are bus services to the following places.

Destination	Route No.	Price (Bt)				Journey Time (hrs)		Frequency	
		V.I.P.	A/C 1	A/C 2	Ord	A/C	Ord	A/C	Ord
Bangkok	25/98	520	337		193	10	11	Hourly	1/day
Bangkok	931				180		10.5		2/day
Bangkok	944	601	311			9.5		4/day	
Bangkok	947	614		248		8		3/day	
Chiang Mai	587	630	540		300	17	19	5/day	1/day
Udon Thani (Mukdahan)	235		250		140	8	10	4/day	2/day
Udon Thani (Khon Kaen)	268		210	162	125	8	9.5	6/day	4/day
Mukdahan	255			75	55	3	4	6/day	Hourly
Mukdahan	241				55		4		Hourly
Khon Kaen	282			149	96	5.5	6.5	1/day	4/day
Pattaya	589		355		200	10	12	6/day	3/day
Rayong	588	450	375		220	11	13	7/day	2/day
Maha Sarakham	251				70		5		1/day
Roi Et	253				55		4		1/day
Nakhon Ratchasima	285		220		121	5.5	6.5	3/day	4/day
Yasothon	504/505				35		2.5		2/day
Pibun Mansahan	1459				20		1		20 mins
Det Udom	1460				15		1		20 mins
Sisaket	279				22		1.5		20 mins
Bun Tharik	4385				25		2.5		Hourly
Nacha Luai	4389				35		3.5		Hourly
Nam Yuen	4390				25		2.5		30 mins
Katharalak	511				20		1.5		20 mins
Pen Nakai	4328				15		1		20 mins
Kemmarat	290				50		3.5		Hourly
Amnat Charoen	222				35		2.5		Hourly

YASOTHON   ยโสธร

9 hrs by bus from Northern Bus Terminal

Yasothon is 522 kilometres from Bangkok and can be reached by a direct service in nine hours at a cost of Bt420 for a V.I.P. bus, Bt272 for a 1st class air-conditioned bus and Bt151 for an ordinary bus. However, most of these services run only at night. From Ubon Ratchathani, buses run to Yasothon four times a day, including those which go further, and take 2½ hours.

Yasothon is most famous for its **Rocket Festival** (Boon Bung Fai) which is held on the second weekend in May to encourage the Gods to send plenty of rain. The festival lasts for two days, the first day being occupied with such festivities as a procession of decorated rockets,

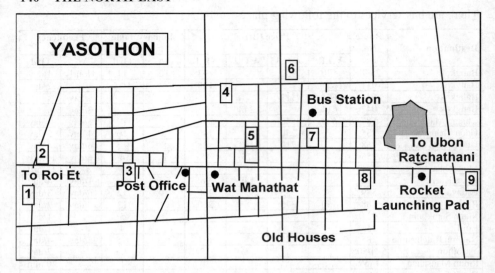

a contest to choose a Miss Rocket, a dinner and an exhibition of local handicrafts. On the second day, the rockets are actually launched from the park area in the south of the town known as Phraya Thaen. They are made of bamboo and filled with a mixture of saltpetre and charcoal. There are three categories: up to one kilogram of saltpetre, up to twelve kilograms of saltpetre, and up to 120 kilograms of saltpetre. When the manufacturers light the blue touch paper and retire, if the rocket fails to soar into the air, by tradition they are thrown by the crowd into a muddy rice field, causing considerable merriment.

If it does not happen to be the second weekend in May when you visit, you will find Yasothon to be a rather ordinary town, but, as usual, there are a couple of temples to look at. **Wat Mahathat** dates from the time when the first Lao immigrants settled here 200 years ago. The architecture of the older parts is Lao style. There is also **That Kong Khao Noi**, an old *chedi* from the Khom Era, but it is eight kilometres from the town on the road to Ubon Ratchathani. It is of an unusual shape resembling a rice container, which is what its name means. A legend attaches to it that a worker in the fields became annoyed when his mother was late bringing him his lunch and that when it arrived he considered it too small. In his rage he killed his mother, then ate his lunch. When he found that he could not eat it all, he realised what a terrible thing he had done and built the *chedi* as an act of atonement. Excavations here have revealed prehistoric human skeletons and pottery of similar antiquity to that found further north at Ban Chiang.

This town is also known for its weaving, basket making and production of 'Mon Khit' triangular pillows.

Accommodation
Yasothon

Name	No. on Map	Rooms	Cheapest Price (Bt)
J.P. Emerald	3	120	1,400
R.P. Mansion Park	7	56	800
99 Regent	6	43	400
Khum Bua Kham	4	8	400
Pen Tawan Resort	9	8	400

Name	No. on Map	Rooms	Cheapest Price (Bt)
Ratree Resort	1	3	250
Yodnakhon	5	66	230
Varothon	8	15	200
29 Bungalow	2	15	120

Moving On

There are bus services originating in Yasothon to the following places.

Destination	Route No.	Price (Bt)				Journey Time (hrs)		Frequency	
		V.I.P.	A/C 1	A/C 2	Ord	A/C	Ord	A/C	Ord
Bangkok	968/929	420	272		151	9	10	3/day	2/day
Ubon Ratchathani	504/505				35		2.5		2/day
Surin	293				52		3		2/day

In addition, buses pass through for Roi Et, Maha Sarakham, Khon Kaen, Udon Thani and Mukdahan.

MUKDAHAN   มุกดาหาร

10 hrs 30 mins by bus from Northern Bus Terminal
Mukdahan is a pleasant, rather than outstanding, city situated on the banks of the Mekong River. It is the first of many such places which we shall encounter from now on our journey round the North-East. On the other side of the river stands the Lao town of **Sawan Nakhet** and this is one of the points at which you are permitted to enter Laos, if you have a visa. The second bridge over the Mekong is currently under construction here, the first being at Nong Khai in the north of I-san.

Buses run directly from Bangkok, mostly overnight, in 10½ hours or a little longer, depending on the route, for there are four different routes used. Fares too vary according to the route, but most air-conditioned buses cost either Bt311 or Bt347. There are also plenty of buses from Ubon Ratchathani and Yasothon, if you are coming that way. From Ubon Ratchathani takes 2½ hours and from Yasothon two hours.

One of the attractions of Mukdahan is simply looking at the Mekong River, but since you are going to get plenty of chance to do that anyway, there is probably no need to spend a great deal of time here. Most people just pass through.

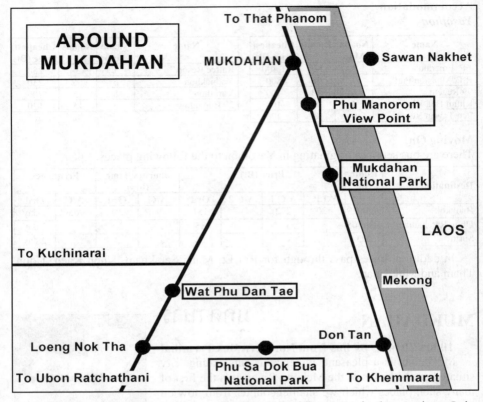

AROUND MUKDAHAN

To That Phanom

MUKDAHAN

Sawan Nakhet

Phu Manorom View Point

Mukdahan National Park

LAOS

To Kuchinarai

Mekong

Wat Phu Dan Tae

Don Tan

Loeng Nok Tha

To Ubon Ratchathani

Phu Sa Dok Bua National Park

To Khemmarat

In the centre of the town is the most sacred Buddha statue in the province. It is housed in **Wat Sri Mongkhon Tai**, on the bank of the river.

Also in the town, from a point near the same temple, boats leave for trips up and down the river.

Wat Phu Dan Tae is beside the road from Ubon Ratchathani (or Yasothon or Bangkok), 33km before the town of Mukdahan is reached. On a hill top it has a large and impressive Buddha statue named **Luang Pho Yai** depicting Buddha's first sermon.

Three kilometres south of Mukdahan, on the road to Don Tan which runs beside the river, is the **Phu Monorom View Point** which offers a view of Mukdahan, the Mekong and Sawan Nakhet on the other side.

Further along the same road is the **Mukdahan National Park**, the office of which is fifteen kilometres from town. The park has strange mushroom-shaped rocks, wildflowers and various types of forest.

Further still, beyond Don Tan and on the road going inland towards Loeng Nok Tha, lies **Phu Sa Dok Bua National Park** which contains the Phu Pha Taem rock paintings, as well as cliffs and wildflowers.

Accommodation
Mukdahan

Name	Rooms	Cheapest Price (Bt)	Name	Rooms	Cheapest Price (Bt)
Manorom Resort	30	350	Suni Bungalow	11	180
Hong Kong	23	200	Ban Thon Kasem	11	150
Mukdahan	55	200	Hua Nam	28	150
Sansuk Bungalow	17	200			

Moving On

There are bus services originating in Mukdahan to the following places.

Destination	Route No.	Price (Bt)				Journey Time (hrs)		Frequency	
		V.I.P.	A/C 1	A/C 2	Ord	A/C	Ord	A/C	Ord
Bangkok	927/928	540	347/311		191	10.5	11	8/day	2/day
Bangkok	946		419		193	11.5	11.5	1/day	1/day
Ubon Ratchathani	241				75		4		Hourly
Ubon Ratchathani	255			95	75	3	4	6/day	Hourly
Nakhon Phanom	555				34		2.5		Hourly
Khon Kaen	278				95		5		Hourly
Udon Thani	235							2/day	4/day

THAT PHANOM   ธาตุพนม

11 hrs by bus from Northern Bus Terminal

Proceeding further north, still beside the Mekong, we come to That Phanom, a small town with a very famous temple. This temple is, in fact, the most important religious monument in the North-East of Thailand and one which, although somewhat off the main tourist routes, should not be missed.

That Phanom can be reached from Bangkok by bus in eleven hours. The cost is Bt365 by 1st class air-conditioned bus and Bt203 by ordinary bus. There are also frequent buses from Mukdahan, Nakhon Phanom and Sakon Nakhon, and slightly less frequent ones from Ubon Ratchathani and Udon Thani.

Phra That Phanom is a particularly beautiful Lao-style temple, the equal of anything you will see in Vientiane or Luang Prabang. It stands back almost a kilometre from the river and is at its most resplendent when the early morning sunlight reflects off the gold decoration on its 52 metre *chedi*. It is at the same time a remarkably old and very new temple. The exact date of its foundation is uncertain, but estimates range between 1,200 and 1,500 years ago. However, it is only a quarter

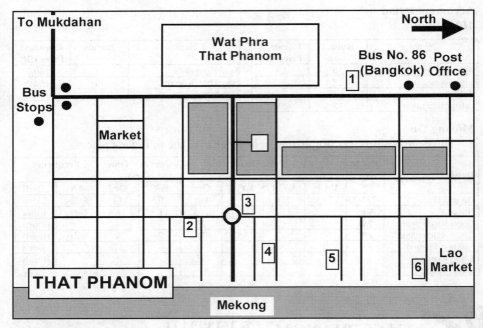

of a century since the whole edifice suddenly collapsed one day and had to be completely rebuilt. Thus, what you see now is, in fact, a modern construction. It is, however, a new and slightly improved copy of what was there before and an undeniably beautiful building. On top is a 110 kilogram ball of gold. Beside the temple is a small museum.

In front of Phra That Phanom is a wide open space with artificial lakes and then, quite a way away, an arched gateway to the town. The town does not have much depth, but it extends along beside the Mekong for a kilometre or more. At the northern extremity of the town is an area where the Lao market is held twice a week, on Mondays and Thursdays. Tradesmen come over in boats bringing their wares to sell, ranging from handicrafts to pigs.

There is a paved walkway beside the Mekong these days, as in many of the other towns which border the river, and that gives an attractive appearance. Beside the walkway are food and drink stalls which open in the evenings.

Accommodation

There are two guest houses in the town welcoming foreign visitors. One is Niyana Guest House, which has now moved to the northern edge, almost beside the Lao Market. Niyana claims to have opened the very first guest house in this part of Thailand, not here but in Nong Khai. She later moved to That Phanom. She is a placid, helpful lady. The guest house is cheap and friendly. The other guest house is

Pom's Guest House, which has been taken over recently by Otto, who is not a Pom at all, but a German who was previously running Erawan Guest House on Ko Chang. There is also a Chinese Hotel named the Chaivon Hotel near the arched gateway and there is the Limcharoen Hotel on the main road, for those who want a higher standard of accommodation. Near the river Rimkong Bungalow has some air-conditioned rooms. That Phanom is a pleasant small place to stay. Get up early in the morning, when the monks are still doing their rounds, and observe the beauty of the rising sun reflecting off the golden temple.

That Phanom

Name	No. on Map	Rooms	Cheapest Price (Bt)	Name	No. on Map	Rooms	Cheapest Price (Bt)
Rimkong Bungalow	5	8	250	Saeng Thong	2	17	150
Chaivon Hotel	3	19	150	Pom's Guest House	4	12	150
Limcharoen Hotel	1	23	150	Niyana G. H.	6	10	60

Moving On

There are bus services from That Phanom to the following places.

Destination	Route No.	Price (Bt)				Journey Time (hrs)		Frequency	
		V.I.P.	A/C 1	A/C 2	Ord	A/C	Ord	A/C	Ord
Bangkok	27	565	365		203	11	12	3/day	1/day
Nakhon Phanom	555				18		1.5		Hourly
Mukdahan	555				16		1		Hourly
Ubon Ratchathani	235		119		70	3.5	4.5	4/day	2/day
Sakon Nakhon	240				25		2		40 mins
Udon Thani	235		130		75	4.5	5.5	4/day	2/day

NAKHON PHANOM นครพนม

NAKHON PHANOM

11 hrs by bus from Northern Bus Terminal

Nakhon Phanom is 52 kilometres north of That Phanom and is a town of moderate size. It is another of the places lying beside the Mekong and here, as in several other locations, one may walk along beside the river and look at Laos on the other side. The name of the town means 'City of Mountains'. You will see the mountains referred to on the other side of the river in the distance. If you can get up early, sunrise is a good time for looking out across the Mekong.

Buses operate from Bangkok by two different routes, air-conditioned buses taking eleven hours and ordinary buses twelve hours or longer. The fares for the shorter route are Bt585 for a V.I.P. bus, Bt376 for a 1st class air-conditioned bus, Bt293 for a 2nd class air-conditioned bus and Bt209 for an ordinary bus. Other useful services operate to and from Ubon Ratchathani, Khon Kaen, Udon Thani, Nong Khai and Chiang Rai. Like many other towns, Nakhon Phanom has a nice new bus station on the edge of the town, but since it is not such a big town, it is possible to walk from the bus station to the centre in about twenty minutes, a distance of about one kilometre. If you prefer, a *samlor* or motor-cycle is available for Bt20.

The town itself, although pleasant, does not have very special sights to offer, its principal attraction being the Mekong River and the promenade beside it. On the other side of the river is the Lao town of **Tha Kaek**, another of the permitted crossing points for those with a visa.

Near the river is the **Indo-China Market** selling items brought across from Laos, and a lot of other things too, and next to that is **Wat Okatsribuaban** which contains two important Buddha statues. Not so far away, **Wat Sri Thep** has impressive murals.

A little further south is **Terdprakiat Park**. During the dry season, the water level in the river drops and there is quite an extensive beach here.

There is a **TAT office** in Nakhon Phanom, located quite accessibly beside the river, with a beautiful view across to the other side from the office itself. See the map.

If one needs to stay here, the River Inn is, as its name implies, right next to the river and has rooms from Bt200. Nearby, by the clock tower, is First Hotel at similar prices. There are also several rather more expensive hotels in the centre of the town.

Accommodation
Nakhon Phanom

Name	No. on Map	Rooms	Cheapest Price (Bt)
River View	11	120	1,000
Nakhon Phanom	4	79	700
Sri Thep	9	87	650
Mekong Grand View	10	114	500
Windsor	6	50	350
Lucky	2	27	250

Name	No. on Map	Rooms	Cheapest Price (Bt)
First	7	63	200
Charoensuk	5	38	200
River Inn	1	16	200
Grand	8	45	150
Vieng Inn	3	38	80

Moving On
Here is a list of bus services from Nakhon Phanom.

Destination	Route No.	Price (Bt)				Journey Time (hrs)		Frequency	
		V.I.P.	A/C 1	A/C 2	Ord	A/C	Ord	A/C	Ord
Bangkok (Udon Thani)	930		421	328	234	11	12.5	3/day	2/day
Bangkok (Direct)	26	585	376	293	209	11	12	12/day	4/day
Udon Thani (Nong Khai)	224			155	108	6.5	8	40 mins	40 mins
Udon Thani (Sakon Nakhon)	231			100	73	4.5	5.5	7/day	6/day
Khon Kaen	586		155		86	5.5	7	3/day	3/day
Ubon Ratchathani	256		146		81	5	6.5	2/day	3/day
Mukdahan	555				34		2.5		Hourly
Chiang Rai	661		536	417	298	10	12	4/day	1/day

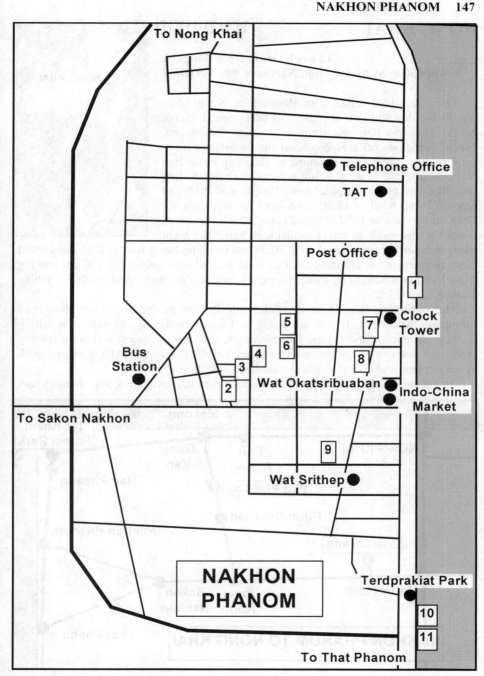

To Nong Khai

Telephone Office

TAT

Post Office

1

5

7   Clock Tower

6

4

3

8

Bus Station

2

Wat Okatsribuaban

Indo-China Market

To Sakon Nakhon

9

Wat Srithep

NAKHON PHANOM

Terdprakiat Park

10

11

To That Phanom

NONG KHAI   หนองคาย

NONG KHAI

12 hrs by train from Bangkok
9 hrs 30 mins by bus from Northern Bus Terminal

There are three trains from Bangkok to Nong Khai, one in the day and two at night. All take around twelve hours. They do not pass through Nakhon Ratchasima, instead branching off at Kaeng Khoi and following a more rural route further north, rejoining at Bua Yai. From Bua Yai onwards, the journey is not a particularly interesting one. The day train, a rapid, leaves Bangkok at 6:15 and reaches Nong Khai at 18:00. The fares for this train are Bt143 third class or Bt278 second class, which represents about the best value in travel available to here. The night express departing from Bangkok at 20:30 and reaching Nong Khai at 8:40 has second class sleepers and is probably the best train for rail pass holders. If you are coming from Nakhon Ratchasima, there is an early morning ordinary train at 6:15 reaching Nong Khai at 12:25.

The station in Nong Khai is, unfortunately, not in the town, but about two kilometres west of it. If you are going to Laos immediately, though, it is within walking distance of the bridge. Otherwise you can choose among a slightly lengthy walk into town, a *songtaew*, which should be obtainable for Bt10 if shared with several others, and a *samlor*, which should cost Bt20.

As for buses, the journey from Bangkok takes approximately 9½ hours by air-

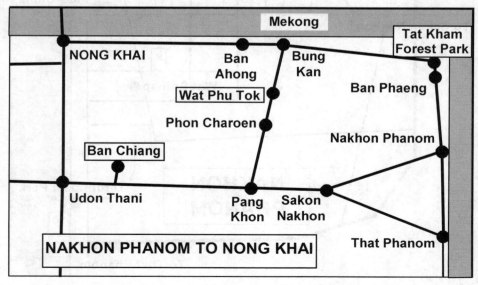

NAKHON PHANOM TO NONG KHAI

conditioned bus and an hour longer by ordinary bus, but nearly all of the buses run at night. V.I.P. buses cost Bt495. 1st class air-conditioned buses cost Bt319. 2nd class air-conditioned buses cost Bt248 and ordinary buses cost Bt177.

Assuming that you are following our plan from east to north, though, you may be coming from That Phanom or Nakhon Phanom. In that case you have a choice of routes. From That Phanom you can either take a bus no. 555 to Nakhon Phanom and then follow the Mekong River all the way round to Nong Khai with bus no. 224, or take a bus no. 240 to Sakon Nakhon, then no. 230 or 231 to Udon Thani, then to Nong Khai on no. 221 or 224. There is a similar choice from Nakhon Phanom – round the Mekong, or to Udon Thani first (no. 231), via Sakon Nakhon, then up to Nong Khai.

If you take the Mekong route, you will probably be a little disappointed, for you do not see the Mekong at all, except for a brief glimpse at a couple of points. Even so, it is a pleasant enough journey. On the way, there is **Tat Kham Forest Park**, an area of natural wooded beauty where streams flowing from Mt. Phu Langsa converge to form the Huai Kham River, offering a couple of pretty waterfalls. This park is just north of **Ban Phaeng**, about 1½ hours from Nakhon Phanom. Tat Kham Falls can be reached relatively easily, but the second waterfall, Tat Pho Falls, is five kilometres further on, about two hours walk each way.

Further still along the road to Nong Khai, a pleasant little guest house is located at **Ban Ahong**, which is 23 kilometres beyond **Bung Kan**. This guest house, just off the main road, is named, appropriately, Hideaway Guest House. Prices start at Bt100. 46 kilometres inland from Bung Kan is **Wat Phu Tok** ('Lonely Mountain Temple'), a temple and meditation centre well known for its remarkable wooden spiral staircase which took five years to complete. This staircase leads to the different levels of the meditation centre and to some caves which can be explored. This temple can be reached by taking one of the buses or *songtaew* from Bung Kan which run along the road to Phon Charoen passing nearby (Highway 222).

If you go the other way to Nong Khai, via Udon Thani, it is a relatively uninteresting journey, and an inconvenient change at Udon Thani, since the buses use different termini, but it is a quicker and shorter route. There is a direct bus from That Phanom to Udon Thani, but the first service is not until 10:00, so it may be more convenient to start earlier, using the green bus no. 240 from That Phanom to Sakon Nakhon and changing there.

If you are travelling between Sakon Nakhon and Udon Thani, you should note that you will pass very close to the **Ban Chiang** excavations where probably the oldest earthenware designs in the world have been found. If you want to look at the excavations and museum there, this is a good chance to avoid retracing your steps. Alighting at the 50km post (distance is from Udon Thani), you can take a *samlor* for the six kilometre journey to Ban Chiang (see Ban Chiang entry below).

Nong Khai is a pleasant little town, once again on the Mekong River, at the northern terminus of the North-Eastern Line of the State Railways of Thailand. It has always been the traditional place for crossing to Laos, for it lies almost opposite the

Lao capital of Vientiane. Indeed, this crossing seems to be the principal reason for the existence of the town. Until a few years ago, the crossing was made by ferry. The ferry still operates, from **Tha Sadet** in the middle of the town, but there is now a bridge too, the only bridge anywhere across the Mekong, although a second one is currently under construction in Mukdahan, and it is across the bridge that foreigners proceed to Laos. When the bridge was opened, the ferry crossing became restricted to locals. In recent months (mid-2000) there have been rumours that the ferry might be re-opened to foreigners too, so check if you prefer this method. The ferry is more conveniently situated on the Thai side, because to reach the bridge it is necessary to take a *songtaew* at a cost of Bt20 or have a long 4km walk. On the Lao side, however, transport is more convenient from the bridge.

If you go to the centre of Nong Khai, you will see the constant shuttling of goods, and some passengers, from Tha Sadet across the river in small boats. There is an observation point just to the left of the Customs and Immigration Office. When the author made this crossing, when it was permitted some years ago, I was surprised at the strength of the current in this apparently placid river. Notice how the boats head almost upstream to fight against it and are carried across in crab-like fashion seemingly against their wills. At the time, I was also advised to keep my head down, as snipers on the far bank had been firing at the ferries the previous day. Times have changed now, however, and fortunately peace prevails at present along this mighty river. Immediately outside the Customs and Immigration Building, a market spreads along the bank of the river selling everything that a Thai might want to purchase from Laos and everything that a Lao might want to take home from Thailand. It is worth strolling through this market. Beyond, the usual promenade stretches beside the river. If you walk along it and then follow the map shown below, you will come to a more remarkable location. It is quite a long walk, though, so hiring a bicycle might be a better idea.

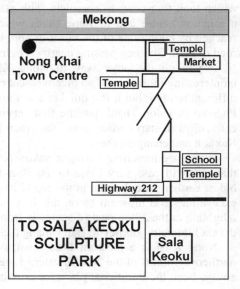

 Sala Keoku Sculpture Park is about 3½ kilometres from the centre of Nong Khai and should not be missed. Here you will find an amazing number of huge concrete sculptures, nearly all the work of one man, Boon Leua Sourirat, a Lao who came to Thailand when his own country fell into disorder and who died here in August 1996. The sculptures mostly have a Buddhist theme and many of them tower into the sky. Perhaps the most fascinating of the works is the

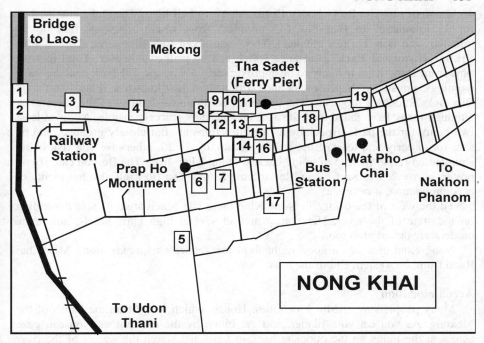

NONG KHAI

Wheel of Life in the farthest corner of the park. This depicts the different stages of life and is in an endless circle to demonstrate the Buddhist belief in reincarnation. Only by pursuing the path of redemption can we follow the Buddha figure which is stepping over the wall of the enclosure. Admission to Sala Keoku Sculpture Park costs Bt10.

The most important temple in the town is **Wat Pho Chai**, conveniently located next to the bus station. It contains a small but sacred Buddha statue named Luang Pho Phra Sai.

Outside the Town Hall, at the entrance to the town, is the **Prap Ho Monument**, built to honour those who lost their lives in a rebellion by the Ho hill tribesmen in 1886.

There is an historical park of some interest not far from Nong Khai, but to visit it needs a whole day and several changes of transport. First take a bus for the

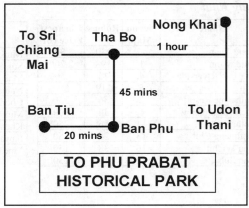

TO PHU PRABAT HISTORICAL PARK

45 kilometres to Tha Bo (1 hour). Buses run every half hour. Then take another bus for 35 kilometres to Ban Phu (45 minutes) from where *songtaew* run the 10 kilometres to Ban Tiu (20 minutes). They stop about two kilometres short of **Phu Prabat Historical Park**, a distance which can be walked however. Total journey time from Nong Khai is likely to be approximately 3½ hours. The park contains cave paintings, unusually shaped rocks and, within the *chedi* known as Phra Phutthabat Bua Bok, Buddha's footprint. The paintings are the most famous of the attractions, although many have faded over the ages and are now scarcely visible. Allow at least two hours for the park, especially as the attractions are not closely grouped, and be sure to go early and to start the return journey by 14:30, otherwise you risk being stranded *en route*. Instead of going back to Nong Khai, from Tha Bo you can, if you prefer, move west to Sri Chiang Mai or Sang Khom. Tha Bo itself also has plenty of accommodation, if necessary.

To the west of the bridge in Nong Khai there is a beach area, its size depending on the state of the river. Here one can find several high class hotels, and some moderately priced ones too.

Nong Khai also has a good night food market which spreads along Mee Chai Road from the western end of the town.

Accommodation

Many people stay at Mut Mee Guest House, which is right on the banks of the Mekong. As you eat your dinner, and get bitten by the mosquitoes, you can gaze across at the lights on the opposite bank in Laos and watch the waters of the river flowing timelessly past, perhaps considering how this mighty river has so influenced not only the geography but also the history and politics of the area. If mosquitoes are not for you, however, the conveniently located Panthawee Hotel can offer air-conditioned rooms from Bt400. There are several other choices available too, for which see the following list.

Nong Khai

Name	No. on Map	Rooms	Cheapest Price (Bt)
Grand Thani	17	130	2,300
Holiday Inn	1	198	2,200
Thai-Lao Riverside	4	72	1,500
Thip	5	119	800
Panthawee Resort	2	36	350
Prachak Bungalow	6	34	300
Panthawee	14	86	250
Banthoeng Chit	13	24	150
Pong Wichit	16	38	150
Poon Sub	12	12	150

Name	No. on Map	Rooms	Cheapest Price (Bt)
Rimkong G. H.	9	12	150
Suk San	7	30	150
Mae Kong G. H.	11	16	150
Naina Guest House	19	20	150
Chong Kong G. H.	10	10	100
Mut Mee G. H.	8	35	100
Kheng Huad	15	20	80
Sawasdee G. H.	18	17	80
Mae Kong	3	16	60

Moving On

First, here is the return train timetable for the journey to Bangkok, including journeys commencing in Udon Thani.

Type of Train	Ord	Exp *	Rap	Ord	Exp *	Exp *†	Rap
Classes	**3**	**2**	**2,3**	**3**	**2,3**	**1,2,3**	**2,3**
Nong Khai			0810	1305		1835	1925
Udon Thani	0610	0700	0922	1356	1925	1937	2034
Khon Kaen	0842	0832	1124	1622	2106	2126	2247
Nakhon Ratchasima	1240			1940	0022		
Ayutthaya		1439	1902			0430	0705
Don Muang		1519	1953		0433	0517	0810
Bangkok		1605	2050		0530	0610	0910

Here is a list of bus services from Nong Khai.

Destination	Route No.	Price (Bt)				Journey Time (hrs)		Frequency	
		V.I.P.	**A/C 1**	**A/C 2**	**Ord**	**A/C**	**Ord**	**A/C**	**Ord**
Bangkok	23/935	495	319	263	177	9	10	5/day	7/day
Rayong (via Pattaya)	590		385		220	13	15	7/day	7/day
Udon Thani	221				17		1.5		30 mins
Loei	507				80		5.5		5/day
Pak Chom	507				60		4		4/day
Sri Chiang Mai	507				20		1.5		Hourly
Nakhon Phanom	224			133	91	5.5	7	40 mins	40 mins

UDON THANI   อุดรธานี

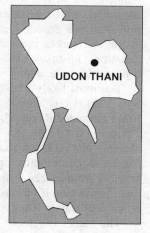

11 hrs by train from Bangkok
8 hrs 30 mins by bus from Northern Bus Terminal

Udon Thani lies one hour south of Nong Khai and is the major city of the area. Although Udon Thani has a long history, it is not in itself a place of great interest to the traveller. It is more of a transport centre for other nearby places of interest.

Udon Thani is served by the same trains as Nong Khai and reached one hour earlier. The rapid day train leaves Bangkok at 6:15 and reaches Udon Thani at 17:07. Fares are Bt135 third class or Bt259 second class. The night express carries second class sleepers. It departs from Bangkok at 20:30 and reaches Udon Thani at 7:49. In addition, there are two express railcars, one by day and one by night, which run to Udon Thani only, without continuing to Nong Khai. They leave Bangkok at 8:20 and

20:40 and reach Udon Thani in less than ten hours, at 18:00 and 6:25. The day train is a good one for rail pass holders, since it has air-conditioned second class carriages. From Nakhon Ratchasima, there is the morning ordinary train at 6:15 reaching Udon Thani at 11:35 and there is an afternoon ordinary train leaving at 15:00 and reaching Udon Thani at 21:40.

Bus no. 22 to Udon Thani leaves the Northern Bus Terminal in Bangkok approximately every half hour. Some buses are air-conditioned and some are ordinary. The fare is Bt292 for an air-conditioned bus and Bt162 for an ordinary bus. The journey takes 8½ hours by air-conditioned bus and about an hour longer by ordinary bus.

If you are coming from Nong Khai, there are frequent buses at a fare of Bt17 for ordinary buses, as most are. There are other useful services from Rayong, Pattaya, Khon Kaen, Ubon Ratchathani, Chiang Mai, Chiang Rai, Nakhon Phanom and Loei.

The main bus station in Udon Thani is well located, in the city centre and within walking distance of the railway station. The problem is that the onward connexions which many people want to take, to Nong Khai and Sri Chiang Mai, leave from a totally different bus station at Rung Sina Market in a distant part of the city. Moreover, there is a third bus station, the new bus station, on the western fringe of the city which is used by certain services. Some of the Nong Khai buses call in here too. This is thoroughly confusing, but the table at the end of this section shows where you can expect your bus to arrive or depart.

Fortunately, Udon Thani has a fairly well organised *songtaew* system, at least theoretically, with vehicles operating to fixed routes and bearing route numbers. Two of the routes, routes nos. 2 and 3, are actually operated by proper buses. As usual, the problem is that the *songtaew* do not stick to their routes, feeling free to deviate according to the convenience of their drivers and passengers. Nevertheless, the map shown gives a general idea of where you can expect the most useful of these services to go. All routes pass close to the city centre, so you cannot make any really disastrous mistakes. The fare is Bt5, irrespective of distance, and some routes continue for quite a long way beyond the main city area.

The most likely transfer to be needed is from the main bus station to the Rung Sina Market bus station. To make this change, walk down to the nearest point on Udon Dutsadee Road, which runs roughly north and south through the centre of the city, and take a *songtaew* no. 6 to Rung Sina Market at a cost of Bt5. Probably this nearest point on Udon Dutsadee Road will be the fountain or clock tower. Rung Sina Market is the terminus for most of these *songtaew* also. There are a few through bus services from places further south to Nong Khai and Sri Chiang Mai which use the main bus station if you are willing to wait for one of those, but usually it is quicker to make your way to Rung Sina.

The sights of Udon Thani itself include **Puya Shrine**, not far from bus and railway stations (see map). The shrine has two Chinese style pavilions over a lake and is dedicated to the God and Goddess of Mercy.

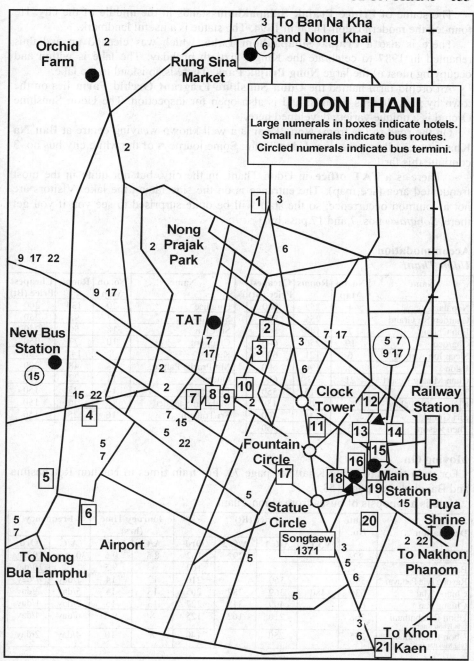

Orchid Farm

Rung Sina Market

To Ban Na Kha and Nong Khai

UDON THANI
Large numerals in boxes indicate hotels.
Small numerals indicate bus routes.
Circled numerals indicate bus termini.

Nong Prajak Park

TAT

New Bus Station

Clock Tower

Railway Station

Fountain Circle

Statue Circle

Songtaew 1371

Main Bus Station

Puya Shrine

Airport

To Nong Bua Lamphu

To Nakhon Phanom

To Khon Kaen

The statue of **Prince Prajak Sillapakhom** stands in the middle of the city. He founded the modern Udon Thani in 1894. The statue is a useful landmark.

There is also a **Prajak Sillapakhom Lake**, which was cleaned up and thus renamed in 1987 to celebrate the King's sixtieth birthday. The lake is within and occupying most of the large **Nong Prajak Park**. There is an island in the lake.

An orchid farm named the **Udon Sunshine Fragrant Orchid Farm** lies on the town by-pass. It sells orchids, and is also open for inspection. The Udon Sunshine Orchid is a unique variety developed here.

On the road to (or from) Nong Khai is a well known weaving centre at **Ban Na Kha**, sixteen kilometres from Udon Thani. Some journeys of the white city bus no. 3 continue this far.

There is a **TAT office** in Udon Thani, in the city, but not quite in the most frequented area (see map). The entrance is on the side facing the lake. Visitors are not a common occurrence, so the staff will be quite surprised to see you if you get there. *Songtaew* nos. 7 and 17 pass by.

Accommodation
Udon Thani

Name	No. on Map	Rooms	Cheapest Price (Bt)
Napalai	4	252	900
Charoen Sri Grand	12	255	850
Ban Chiang	7	149	850
Charoen	19	250	600
Sleep Inn Airport	6	121	600
Udon	3	190	600
Chan Muang Resort	21	33	600
Ton Koon	2	115	550
Charoen Sri Palace	9	98	450
Siri Grand	1	145	400
Phen Resort	5	50	350

Name	No. on Map	Rooms	Cheapest Price (Bt)
Paradise	20	134	300
Siri Udon	17	98	250
Sri Chai	18	50	250
Chaiporn	10	77	250
King	8	148	250
Mit Pracha Palace	13	48	200
Queen	11	22	150
Puttarag	14	25	150
Mala Sri Sangden	15	20	150
Sri Trakarn	16	25	150

Moving On

For train times to Nong Khai, see page 73. For train times to Nakhon Ratchasima and Bangkok, see page 153.

Here is a synopsis of buses from Udon Thani.

Destination	Route No.	Price (Bt)				Journey Time (hrs)		Frequency	
		V.I.P.	A/C 1	A/C 2	Ord	A/C	Ord	A/C	Ord
Bangkok	22			292	162	8.5	9.5	30 mins	10/day
Bangkok *	23				162		9.5		10/day
Rayong (via Pattaya) *	590		360		210	12	14	7/day	7/day
Chiang Mai *	636	480	369	287	205	13	14	5/day	2/day
Chiang Rai *	661		409	318	227	13	15	2/day	1/day
Ubon Ratchathani (via Khon Kaen)	268		210	162	125	8	9.5	6/day	4/day
Ubon Ratchathani (via Mukdahan)	235		250		140	8	10	4/day	2/day

Destination	Route No.	Price (Bt)				Journey Time (hrs)		Frequency	
		V.I.P.	A/C 1	A/C 2	Ord	A/C	Ord	A/C	Ord
Khon Kaen	226		68		38	2	2.5	15 mins	30 mins
Nakhon Phanom (via Sakon Nakhon)	231			100	73	4.5	5.5	7/day	6/day
Nakhon Phanom (via Nong Khai) *†	224			155	108	6.5	8	40 mins	40 mins
Sakon Nakhon	230			70	50	3	3.5	3/day	20 mins
Loei *	220				38		3		30 mins
Nong Khai *†	221				17		1.5		30 mins
Sri Chiang Mai †	223				28		2		30 mins
Non Sang	243/244				20		1.5		Hourly
Nakhon Ratchasima	211			125	90	5.5	6	Hourly	30 mins
Nakhon Ratchasima*	262		162		90	5	6	5/day	1/day
Phitsanulok *	644		198	154	110	8	9	2/day	1/day
Sophisai *	515				55		3.5		40 mins
Bung Kan	225				65		4.5		Hourly
Phen †	527				15		1		30 mins
Ban Pheng	280				70		4.5		6/day
Kalasin	562				60		4.5		50 mins
Roi Et	233				65		5		Hourly
Chumpae	232/809			55	40	2.5	3	5/day	2/day

*: From new bus station   †: From Rung Sina Market   No mark: From main bus station

BAN CHIANG   บ้านเชียง

BAN CHIANG

1 hr 30 mins by bus from Udon Thani

Ban Chiang is famous for the archaeological excavations there which have revealed pottery going back to 7,500B.C., including what are claimed to be the oldest earthenware designs yet discovered anywhere in the world. In 1992, it was declared by UNESCO to be a 'World Heritage Site'.

If you walk along Nittayo Road, to the south of Udon Thani Railway Station, you will find a place where large orange *songtaew* no. 1371 depart from the side of the road (see Udon Thani town map). Some, but not all, of these go to Ban Chiang. However, since it is a distance of 56 kilometres, you may find it more comfortable to take from the main bus station a bus no. 230 or 231 going to Sakon Nakhon and alight at the 50km post, from where *samlor* run the additional six kilometres to Ban Chiang. If you travel alone, the charge for the *samlor* is Bt20. If you are prepared to wait until there are three or four passengers, it will cost Bt10. There is also, near the 48km marker from Udon Thani, the modern pottery village of **Kham Or**, where reproductions of the Ban Chiang pottery are made.

The **Ban Chiang National Museum** is in two parts. There is a building where Ban Chiang pottery and other artefacts are on display and, further on, within the confines of **Wat Pho Si Nai**, there is an open-air section showing how the excavations were carried out and displaying *in situ* some typical findings of skeletal human remains, burial items and pottery. Most of the pottery which has been found was located in such graves.

Ban Chiang pottery is typically decorated with red painted designs. No other designs as old as this have yet been discovered anywhere in the world. There is also evidence of a primitive form of bronze casting, suggesting that this was a particularly advanced civilization. For all of this, the author may perhaps just mention that I found this a long way to come to see some old pots. Perhaps I was expecting too much.

Note that the museum is closed on Mondays and Tuesdays. On other days, admission costs Bt30.

Since Ban Chiang is some distance from Udon Thani, it can most conveniently be visited as a stop *en route* to somewhere else. Buses along the main road continue to Sakon Nakhon and Nakhon Phanom. That Phanom can be reached from Sakon Nakhon, and there are also buses running to Mukdahan and Ubon Ratchathani.

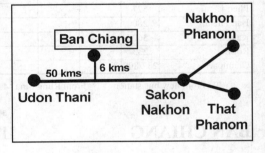

KHON KAEN   ขอนแก่น

9 hrs by train from Bangkok
6 hrs 30 mins by bus from Northern Bus Terminal

Khon Kaen is another rapidly developing city without so much interest to the traveller, but it can hardly be omitted from our book. It is served by the same trains from Bangkok as Udon Thani, but reached about two hours earlier. Fares to Khon Kaen by the morning rapid train, which is the most useful, are Bt117 third class and Bt219 second class. From Nakhon Ratchasima, there are departures at 6:15, 8:15, 11:20 and 15:00, arriving in Khon Kaen at 7:56, 9:58, 13:31 and 16:48.

By air-conditioned bus, the journey from Bangkok can be accomplished in 6½ hours at a cost of Bt232. By ordinary bus it takes an hour longer and costs Bt129.

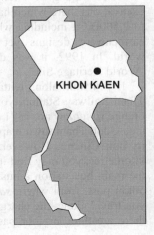

KHON KAEN

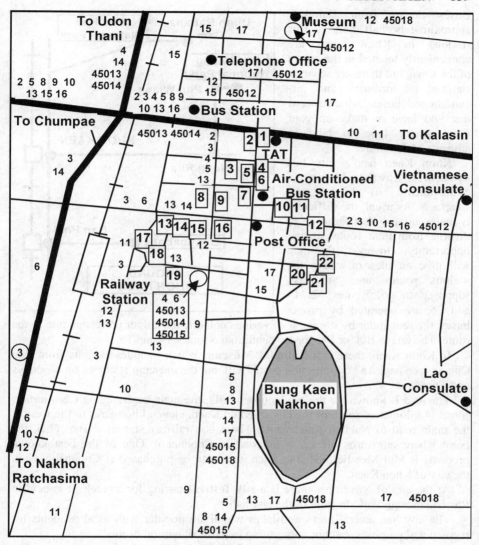

KHON KAEN

Large numerals in boxes indicate hotels.
Small numerals indicate bus routes.
Circled numerals indicate bus termini.

Buses depart from Bangkok approximately half hourly. Bus stations in Khon Kaen are conveniently located in the centre of the town, but there are separate stations for ordinary and air-conditioned buses, which means that you have to make up your mind which type to take in advance of departure.

Khon Kaen has a city bus system, operated by a combination of buses and *songtaew*. As usual, the difficulty is that *songtaew* feel the urge to diverge from their routes at any opportunity. However, the map will give an idea of where the various routes are, at least, supposed to go. Routes 12, 14 and 15 are operated by proper buses, the remainder by *songtaew* of various colours, the colour corresponding to the route. The fare is Bt4, or Bt5 for air-conditioned routes 14 and 15.

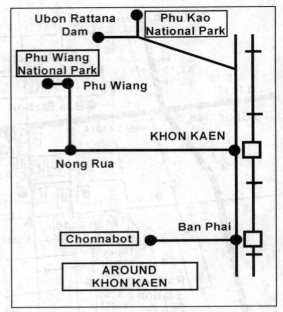

In Khon Kaen, there is a **National Museum** which includes exhibits from Ban Chiang (see page 157). Admission costs Bt30, but the museum is closed on Mondays and Tuesdays.

The area is known for the production of silk, the main centre being **Chonnabot**, some 54 kilometres south of the city of Khon Kaen, eleven kilometres to the west of the main road to Nakhon Ratchasima. There is a railway station at Ban Phai, the point where one turns off the main road to Chonnabot. One of the best known products is Mut Mee tie-died silk. Such items can be purchased at Chonnabot or in the city of Khon Kaen.

At the end of November there is a **silk festival** lasting for a week. It is held in Ratchadanusom Park, in front of the city hall.

The city has several parks and lakes which are popular with local residents for recreational purposes, but not outstanding in terms of natural beauty.

Phu Kao National Park, however, does have considerable natural beauty. It is a forested area 56 kilometres north of the city and has the additional attraction of rock paintings dating from the Ban Chiang Period. The national park can best be reached by bus no. 4174 which goes to the **Ubon Rattana Dam** just on the edge of the park.

The **Phu Wiang National Park** owes its fame to dinosaurs. A geologist drilling for uranium here came across a dinosaur bone and in 1994 a dinosaur fossil was found. The park is eighty kilometres north-west of Khon Kaen near the small town of Phu Wiang.

Accommodation
Khon Kaen

Name	No. on Map	Rooms	Cheapest Price (Bt)
Sofitel Raja Orchid	13	300	3,200
Charoen Thani	15	320	2,400
Chaipat	8	128	1,000
Kosa	14	254	1,000
Kaen Inn	7	160	900
Khon Kaen	3	130	800
Rossukund	1	78	800
Ruenrom	19	72	600
Pen Nuang	20	220	600
Muang Inn	9	37	550
Amarin Plaza	21	60	500

Name	No. on Map	Rooms	Cheapest Price (Bt)
Phu Inn	10	98	450
P.P. Hotel	17	150	400
Deema	22	120	300
Roma	5	197	300
Kaen Nakhon	12	150	250
Sawasdee	16	70	250
Grand	11	70	200
Saensum Rung	4	53	200
Thani Bungalow	18	20	150
Sri Mungkon	6	25	150
Suksawad	2	38	100

Moving On

For train times to Udon Thani and Nong Khai, see page 73. For train times to Nakhon Ratchasima and Bangkok, see page 153. Additional trains originating in Khon Kaen leave for Nakhon Ratchasima at 5:10 and 13:10, arriving at 10:10 and 17:11.

Here is a synopsis of bus times. Remember that ordinary buses and air-conditioned buses leave from different bus stations, although, just to complicate matters a little, a few 2nd class air-conditioned buses passing through Khon Kaen from and to other towns use the ordinary bus station.

Destination	Route No.	Price (Bt)				Journey Time (hrs)		Frequency	
		V.I.P.	A/C 1	A/C 2	Ord	A/C	Ord	A/C	Ord
Bangkok	20	360	232	181	129	6.5	7.5	Frequent	7/day
Chiang Mai (via Tak)	175		414	322	230	13	14	2/day	5/day
Chiang Mai (Uttaradit)	633		369		205	13	14	1/day	3/day
Chiang Rai	637		407	316	226	13	14	2/day	3/day
Phitsanulok	175/637		196	153	110	6	7	6/day	8/day
Nakhon Phanom	586		155		86	5.5	7	3/day	3/day
Udon Thani	226		68		38	2	2.5	15 mins	30 mins
Ubon Ratchathani	268/282			149	96	5.5	6.5	1/day	4/day
Rayong	590		311		180	10	12	7/day	7/day
Nakhon Ratchasima	211				58		3.5		30 mins
Surin	281				83		6		9/day
Phu Khieo	272				30		2.5		Hourly
Maha Sarakham	219/534				25		2		30 mins
Kalasin	264				25		2		20 mins
Bua Yai	270				35		3.5		Hourly
Mukdahan	278				90		5		Hourly
Phon Thong	289				40		3		40 mins
Loei	217			55	40	2.5	3	5/day	30 mins
Lom Sak	299				65		4.5		40 mins
Chaiyaphum	509				40		3		20 mins
Chiang Yuen	264				10		1		Hourly
Kosum Phisai	537				20		1.5		40 mins
Nong Rua	271				15		1.5		15 mins
Ban Phai	1352				15		1.5		Hourly
Phu Wiang	805				20		1.5		30 mins
Mancha Kiri	1358				20		1.5		20 mins

SRI CHIANG MAI ศรีเชียงใหม่

SRI CHIANG MAI

10 hrs by bus from Northern Bus Terminal

Sri Chiang Mai (not to be confused with its big brother Chiang Mai, from which it is very far distant) is the first of a number of very small communities hugging the Mekong River which have become popular with travellers in recent years.

It can be reached directly from Bangkok in ten hours by air-conditioned bus at a cost of Bt335 or in eleven hours by ordinary bus for Bt186. Most such buses operate at night. Readers are more likely to approach, however, from Nong Khai or Udon Thani. There are direct buses from both places.

From Udon Thani, green bus no. 223 runs to Sri Chiang Mai every half hour. The journey takes two hours and costs Bt28. The terminus in Udon Thani is at Rung Sina Market, for information on which see the section on Udon Thani (page 154).

From Nong Khai, bus no. 507 is also green. The journey to Sri Chiang Mai takes 1½ hours and costs Bt18. Many of these buses continue to Pak Chom and some to Loei.

One interesting feature to look for, as you make your way towards Sri Chiang Mai, is the **tree sculptures** beside the road. At first there is just one here and there, starting about ten kilometres before Tha Bo, and one wonders whether it was merely an accident, or even whether one imagined it, but then more and more appear, culminating in a whole park full of these fascinating works of art at **Hua Sai**, five kilometres before Sri Chiang Mai is reached. Keep your eyes open and be fascinated too.

Sri Chiang Mai is on the bank of the Mekong opposite the Lao capital of **Vientiane** and is, therefore, one of the most interesting places from which to look across the river. The lights of the city can be seen clearly on the other side at night

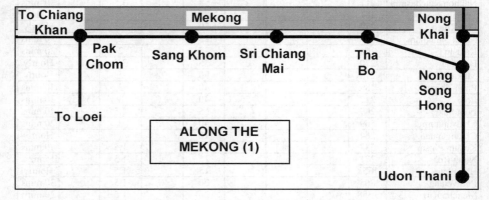

To Chiang Khan — Pak Chom — Sang Khom — Sri Chiang Mai — Tha Bo — Nong Khai — Nong Song Hong — Udon Thani

To Loei

Mekong

ALONG THE MEKONG (1)

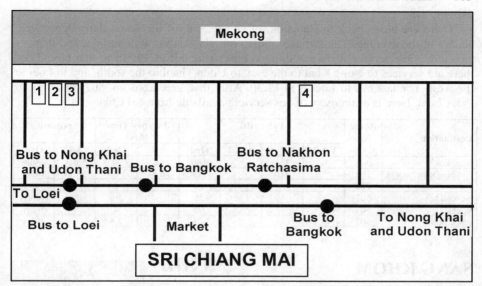

Bus to Nong Khai and Udon Thani
Bus to Bangkok
Bus to Nakhon Ratchasima
To Loei
Bus to Loei
Market
Bus to Bangkok
To Nong Khai and Udon Thani

SRI CHIANG MAI

and especially at dusk one feels that one wants just to pop across for the evening. In many places along the Mekong, one gets the impression that there is nothing much on the Lao side of the river, but here the roles are reversed, for it is Vientiane in Laos which is the big city and Sri Chiang Mai in Thailand which is the poor relation on the other side of the river. There used to be a ferry at this point and, in fact, the author once left Laos by this route. One could just walk down to the ferry pier in the midst of the city and be transported across, but that was many years ago and unfortunately this is no longer a legitimate crossing point.

As usual, there is a promenade beside the river, in the customary red bricks, and the small town is long and thin, following the contours of the river. Most of the accommodation is beside the Mekong, so that if you choose your room well, you will have a good view across.

Tim Guest House is the usual choice. It is operated by Daniel, a French speaking Swiss who has been here for a long time. If that does not appeal to you, there is the Sitthisuwan Hotel on one side and the Kusolsuek Hotel on the other and, a little further up (east), Maneera Resort offering air-conditioned rooms.

Here, as in several nearby towns, a French influence can be felt. For example, there are vendors selling sandwiches using tasty French style mini-baguettes.

Accommodation
Sri Chiang Mai

Name	No. on Map	Rooms	Cheapest Price (Bt)	Name	No. on Map	Rooms	Cheapest Price (Bt)
Maneera Resort	4	8	350	Sitthisuwan	3	11	100
Kusolsuek	1	15	150	Tim Guest House	2	8	90

Moving On

There are buses back to Bangkok, of course, but, of the seven daily departures, six are in the evening. The Bangkok buses run via Nakhon Ratchasima, and there is also a daytime service of five additional buses (the last at 10:30) to that city. Then there are services to Nong Khai to the east, to Udon Thani to the south, and to Loei to the west. The last bus to Loei is at 12:30. After that, green bus no. 507 runs only to Pak Chom. Here is a summary of bus services available from Sri Chiang Mai.

Destination	Route No.	Price (Bt)				Journey Time (hrs)		Frequency	
		V.I.P.	A/C 1	A/C 2	Ord	A/C	Ord	A/C	Ord
Bangkok	933		335		186	10	11	5/day	2/day
Nakhon Ratchasima	262		210		114	6.5	8	5/day	1/day
Udon Thani	223				28		2		30 mins
Nong Khai	507				20		1.5		Hourly
Loei	507				60		4		5/day
Pak Chom	507				40		2.5		4/day

SANG KHOM   สังคม

SANG KHOM

2 hrs 30 mins by bus from Nong Khai

A little further round the Mekong from Sri Chiang Mai is Sang Khom. It is, in fact, just one hour further on. There is no direct service from Bangkok, but it can be reached by taking the green bus no. 507 from Nong Khai (2½ hours), from Sri Chiang Mai (one hour) or from Loei (three hours). If you are following the suggested route, you will be coming from Sri Chiang Mai. It is a pretty road, keeping close to the Mekong all the way. You will pass an interesting temple at Wat Hin Mak Peng and Tan Thong Waterfall close to the main road before arriving in Sang Khom. Since buses run hourly, it is easy to stop and visit these on the way.

Sang Khom is a little spread out along the river, with two distinct areas for accommodation, one just as you enter the town and one just as you are about to leave it. See the map below. It is preferable to decide beforehand in which of these areas you wish to stay, since the distance between them is about two kilometres. Most famous of the accommodation is Mama's TXK River View Lodge and Mama is quite a well known character. However, her accommodation is no longer the best patronised, that honour falling to Bouy next door. Both of these bungalows had to be relocated after the originals were swept away, together with the land on which they were standing, by a flood a few years ago. At the other end of town, Dee Daeng is run by a Belgian, Rudi, and his Thai wife. If you stay there, perhaps you will even meet the patriarch of the town, Fred, if he is still there.

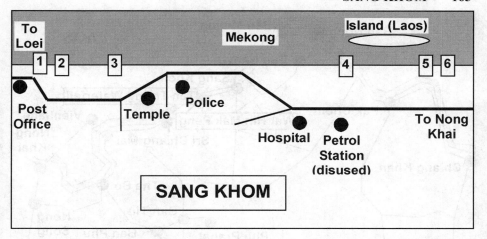

Sang Khom again offers views of Laos, of course, and again there appears to be nothing much on the other side of the river here. There is a beach, in season, and there is also an island, just near the Thai side of the river. Despite its proximity to Thailand, however, this island belongs to Laos. The Lao authorities are unlikely to complain if you visit it, though, and boat trips can even be arranged to the Lao side of the river, with a stay there, as long as you do not overstay your welcome.

Bungalow accommodation beside the river at all of the establishments starts at between Bt100 and Bt200. Just take your pick. The bungalows also have information on possible expeditions nearby and, in some cases, bicycles for hire.

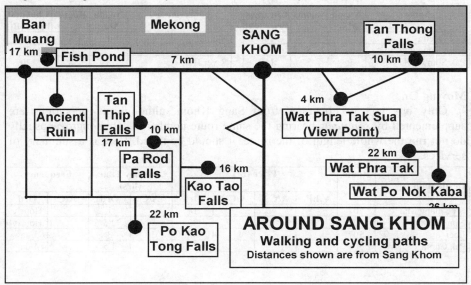

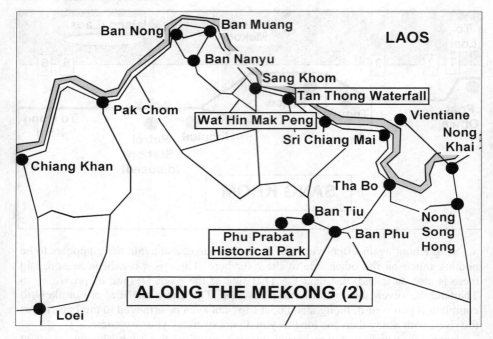

Accommodation
Sang Khom

Name	No. on Map	Rooms	Cheapest Price (Bt)
Dee Daeng	4	5	180
Siam Bungalow	4	5	150
Pak Som G. H.	5	5	150

Name	No. on Map	Rooms	Cheapest Price (Bt)
Mama's	1	4	120
Bouy	2	12	120
River Huts	3	8	120

Moving On

Only bus no. 507 operates from Sang Khom, although its operations are supplemented by *songtaew* bearing the same route number. These *songtaew* usually do not run the whole length of the route, it should be noted. Here is a summary of services.

Destination	Route No.	Price (Bt)				Journey Time (hrs)		Frequency	
		V.I.P.	A/C 1	A/C 2	Ord	A/C	Ord	A/C	Ord
Sri Chiang Mai	507				14		1		Hourly
Nong Khai	507				32		2.5		Hourly
Loei	507				45		3		5/day
Pak Chom	507				25		1.5		4/day

PAK CHOM

ปากช่อง

PAK CHOM

**3 hrs 30 mins by bus from Nong Khai
1 hr 30 mins by bus from Loei**

Once more proceeding west from Sang Khom, a scenic 63 kilometre journey taking an hour and a half will bring us to Pak Chom, again nestling beside the Mekong. There is no direct service from Bangkok to Pak Chom, but bus no. 507 runs from Loei to Pak Chom in 1½ hours.

As we travel from Sang Khom, the river seems to change character several times. Here it is wide and dotted with islands, there narrow and fast flowing. The road too ascends and descends beside the river, offering many different perspectives. To add to the entertainment, on the author's last journey here the bus driver spoke English well and was a football (soccer) enthusiast, knowing far more about the sport than I did. We also came across a large snake on the road which, to my surprise, he was careful not to run over. The fare for this journey is Bt25 (no surcharge for soccer and snakes).

Pak Chom too is very small and is a town at which travellers tend not to stay, but the river here is beautiful and there are guest houses which could hardly be closer to it. Pak Chom Guest House and Jumpee Guest House are side by side (see map) and both offer rooms for Bt100. If you prefer a higher standard of accommodation, though, ten minutes walk away at the Sang Khom end of the town is Pak Chom Resort with pleasant rooms for Bt300, or for Bt400 with air-conditioning. However, Pak Chom Resort is not beside the river, nor does it have any view of or direct access to the river. Also, it is marked with a sign only in Thai.

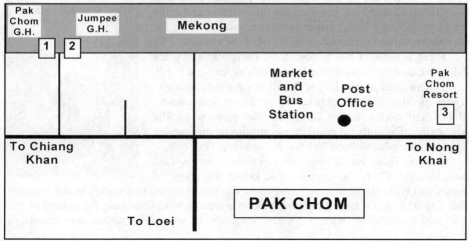

Accommodation
Pak Chom

Name	No. on Map	Rooms	Cheapest Price (Bt)
Pak Chom Resort	3	8	300
Pak Chom G. H.	1	6	100

Name	No. on Map	Rooms	Cheapest Price (Bt)
Jumpee G. H.	2	6	100

Moving On

Although not so many travellers stay here, many change buses at this point in order to proceed westwards to Chiang Khan. For this purpose, alight at the market and take a *songtaew* no. 4297. These run approximately every 40 minutes and the last is at 16:00. Bus no. 507 runs east to Sang Khom (1½ hours), Sri Chiang Mai (2½ hours) and Nong Khai (4 hours), and south to Loei (1½ hours). *Songtaew* no. 4213 also runs to Loei. Here is a summary.

Destination	Route No.	Price (Bt)				Journey Time (hrs)		Frequency	
		V.I.P.	A/C 1	A/C 2	Ord	A/C	Ord	A/C	Ord
Sang Khom	507				25		1.5		Hourly
Sri Chiang Mai	507				40		2.5		Hourly
Nong Khai	507				60		4		Hourly
Loei	507				20		1.5		5/day
Loei	4213				20		2		30 mins
Chiang Khan	4297				20		1.5		40 mins

CHIANG KHAN   เชียงคาน

11 hrs by bus from Northern Bus Terminal

Chiang Khan is our last stop for the moment along the Mekong. It lies a little further west still and is known for its nearby rapids and consequent fast flowing current.

There is a direct bus service from Bangkok taking ten hours by air-conditioned bus. However, this bus is a V.I.P. bus and so quite expensive, at Bt490. It runs only at night. There is also a night service by ordinary bus costing Bt176 and taking eleven hours for the journey of 809 kilometres. Recently an hourly air-conditioned bus service has been introduced from Nakhon Ratchasima via Loei.

Coming from Pak Chom, as mentioned above, take *songtaew* no. 4297. The journey of 41 kilometres takes 1½ hours and costs Bt20. You will pass near the above mentioned rapids in the river on the way. It is again a scenic journey along a narrow road following the course of the Mekong (sufficiently narrow for the *songtaew* in which the author was travelling

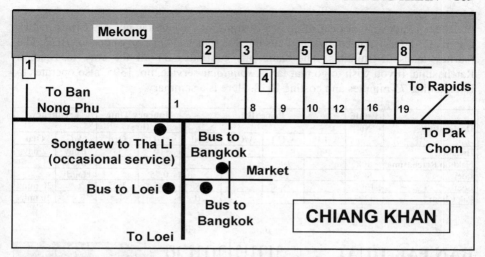

almost to have an accident). Unfortunately, though, the back of a *songtaew* does not really allow one to appreciate the scenery well.

Chiang Khan is slightly larger than the other places which we have visited along the Mekong, but still not very big. It is, however, one of the points at which a crossing to Laos is permitted.

There are several guest houses at which to stay, all close to the river. The original is Nong Sam Guest House, but it is some way from the town, in fact two kilometres down the road. It is perched on a small cliff giving a good view of the Mekong and used to be very popular, but its distance from the town, combined with the fact that it now has rivals with slightly lower prices, has meant that fewer guests make their way there these days. Prices start at Bt150. In town the various guest houses are to be found east of the central road junction, in the *soi* leading down to the river. Rim Kong Guest House is in Soi 8, Ton Hong Guest House in Soi 10, Zen Guest House in Soi 12, Nong Bon Guest House in Soi 16 and Chiang Khan Guest House in Chai Khong Road. All have rooms for Bt100. There are also two hotels: the Phun Sawat, also starting at Bt100, in Soi 9 and the Suk Sombun, starting at Bt200, in Chai Khong Road.

Accommodation
Chiang Khan

Name	No. on Map	Rooms	Cheapest Price (Bt)	Name	No. on Map	Rooms	Cheapest Price (Bt)
Suk Sombun	2	25	200	Zen Guest House	6	12	100
Nong Sam G. H.	1	12	150	Nong Bon G. H.	7	8	100
Rim Kong G. H.	3	15	100	Chiang Khan G. H.	8	10	100
Ton Hong G. H.	5	10	100	Phun Sawat	4	20	100

Moving On

There is not a great deal of choice of transport. *Songtaew* no. 4297 runs to Pak Chom (1½ hours). Air-conditioned bus no. 808 runs to Loei every hour for Bt22. The journey takes 45 minutes. The same bus continues on all the way to Nakhon Ratchasima, if you wish to go that far. A *songtaew* service, no. 1395, also operates to Loei, taking 75 minutes and costing Bt18. Here is a summary.

Destination	Route No.	Price (Bt)				Journey Time (hrs)		Frequency	
		V.I.P.	A/C 1	A/C 2	Ord	A/C	Ord	A/C	Ord
Bangkok	29	490			176	10	11	1/day	2/day
Nakhon Ratchasima	808		190			8.5		Hourly	
Loei	808		22			0.75		Hourly	
Loei	1395				18		1.25		20 mins
Pak Chom	4297				20		1.5		40 mins

BAN PAK HUAI   บ้านปากห้วย

BAN PAK HUAI

1 hr 30 mins by bus from Loei

Ban Pak Huai is near Tha Li and the reason for its inclusion here is that there is a guest house run by the daughter of Mama from Sang Khom. However, it is sometimes closed while the owner is away, so check, if possible, with other travellers to see the situation before going there, or else leave sufficient time to return to Loei if necessary.

To reach Ban Pak Huai, take a *songtaew* no. 1394 from Loei to **Tha Li**, a journey of 1¼ hours through scenic hill country (Bt20). Occasional rush-hour services continue to Ban Pak Huai (Bt25 from Loei), but most terminate at Tha Li. From the road junction there, you can take another *songtaew* to your right for the remaining nine kilometres to Ban Pak Huai (15 minutes, Bt10). O.T.S. Guest House is the only accommodation available. It consists of bungalows right beside the river at a cost of Bt100. It is a very pleasant quiet spot, if only it is open!

Ban Pak Huai is another village right on the border with Laos, but here there is a difference, for the Mekong has disappeared and now runs entirely within the territory of Laos. The border here is a much smaller river, the Huang River, so shallow in parts that one can walk across – and, indeed, that is what the locals do. You can join them if you wish. There are stepping stones. If the water happens to be too deep, there is a ferry across, mainly for goods being unloaded from trucks backed up to the water's edge, and a little beyond.

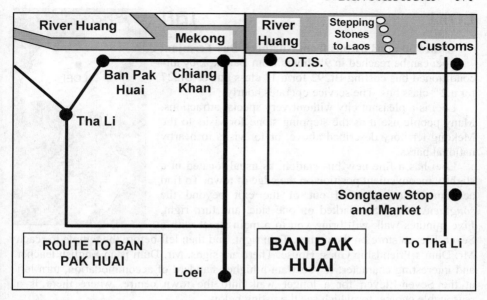

Accommodation
Ban Pak Huai

Name	Rooms	Cheapest Price (Bt)
O.T.S. Guest House	5	100

Moving On
Just the *songtaew* from here, back to Tha Li, or occasionally to Loei.

Destination	Route No.	Price (Bt)				Journey Time (hrs)		Frequency	
		V.I.P.	A/C 1	A/C 2	Ord	A/C	Ord	A/C	Ord
Tha Li					10		0.25		15 mins
Loei	1394				25		1.5		Few

POSTCARD HOME—Surat Thani, 12th June 1975

Dear Folks,

   Thailand. Not only a new language to cope with, but also a new alphabet. Few people can speak English, so not only am I unable to ask anybody anything, which isn't too bad, but I am unable to find anything out for myself, since I can't read anything, which is too bad. Rather than take the overnight express to Bangkok and miss everything, I am progressing by slow (not to say very slow) trains. Today's journey was a nine-hour one—10:00 until 7:00—to here, Surat Thani, 160 miles from Haad Yai. I enjoyed it. Steam trains are fun, even if one does end up black. These ones are Japanese, made about 1940, and they run on wood. Of course, we had to have extra stops for the engines to stock up on food and drink and to be changed. They even let me have a ride on the engine for part of the way, which was fun.

LOEI   เลย

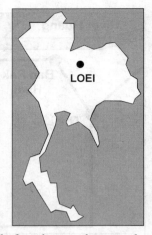

9 hrs 30 mins by bus from Northern Bus Terminal

Loei can be reached in 9½ hours from Bangkok by air-conditioned bus costing Bt292 for a 1st class bus or Bt227 for a 2nd class bus. The service operates hourly.

Loei is a pleasant city without very special attractions. Many people use it as the stepping stone for visits to the Mekong territory described above, or for visits to nearby national parks.

Loei has a fine new bus station, as usual located in a slightly inconvenient position on the edge of town. To find accommodation, proceed out of the exit beyond the *songtaew*, which are parked on one side, and turn right. Five minutes walk will bring you to a main street with a Seven-Eleven store on the corner. Turn right, and then left before the temple to reach Mr. Dum's Friendship Guest House. There are signs. Mr. Dum is an English teacher and interesting character. If you want a higher standard of accommodation, turn left at the Seven-Eleven for a longer walk into the town centre, where there is a reasonable choice, for which see the listing below.

Wherever one goes in Loei, there seems to be water. Not far from the city centre is the **Fitness Park**, on an island in the middle of a lake. At the corner of the same lake are the **City Shrine** and **Chao Phor Kud Phong Shrine**, both small but worth a look. There is a night market to see and, in the same direction lies **Wat Loei Lung**.

However, many of the attractions of Loei lie not in the city itself, but in the surrounding countryside, offering magnificent mountain scenery. Loei claims that it is the only province in Thailand in which temperatures down to zero are recorded.

Phu Rua National Park lies west of Loei and rises to 1,375 metres. To reach it, take a bus no. 286, 1391 or 1393 as far as Phu Rua, a distance of 48 kilometres. You will see a turning on the right leading to the park. It is a further four kilometres to the park entrance and then five kilometres more to the top of the mountain which lies at its heart. There is accommodation available in a guest house as one arrives in Phu Rua. Many years ago the author made this journey by bus (having been told that there was no through route to Lom Sak, but doubting it). It was the oldest bus I have ever seen in Thailand, with a long bonnet in front, and the road at that time was not paved. The bus could hardly crawl up the hills and I wondered whether it would ever complete the journey – but it did, although it took half a day to reach Lom Sak. These days, the bus still struggles with some of the slopes on this route, especially beyond Phu Rua, but the road is paved now, which makes the journey seem less romantic and adventurous! Phu Rua National Park offers waterfalls, viewpoints and various walks. There is accommodation available within the park (from Bt300) with prior reservation (Tel: 579-0529 or 579-4842).

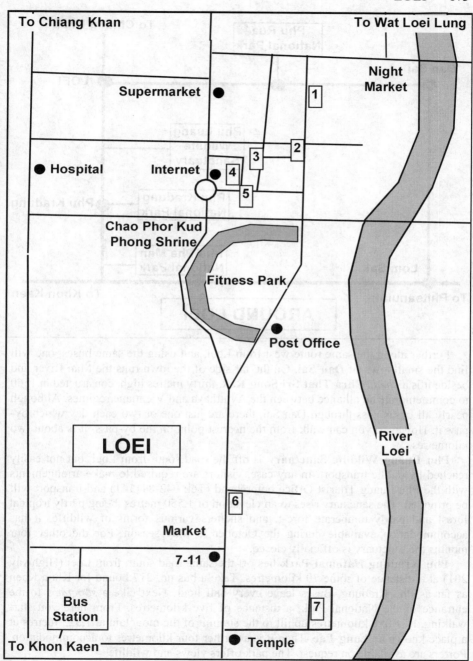

To Chiang Khan

To Wat Loei Lung

Supermarket

Night
Market

1

Hospital

Internet

2

3

4

5

Chao Phor Kud
Phong Shrine

Fitness Park

Post Office

River
Loei

LOEI

6

Market

7-11

Bus
Station

7

To Khon Kaen

Temple

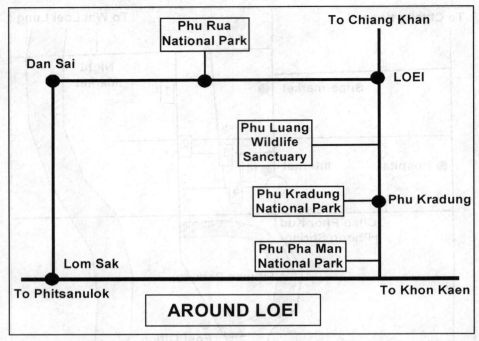

To Chiang Khan

Phu Rua
National Park

Dan Sai

LOEI

Phu Luang
Wildlife
Sanctuary

Phu Kradung
National Park

Phu Kradung

Phu Pha Man
National Park

Lom Sak

To Phitsanulok

To Khon Kaen

AROUND LOEI

Further along the same route west from Loei, and using the same buses, one will find the small town of **Dan Sai**. On the far side of the town runs the Man River and beside it is a *chedi*, **Phra That Sri Song Rak**, thirty metres high, constructed in 1560 to commemorate an alliance between the Ayutthaya and Vientiane régimes. Although nearly all buses pass through Dan Sai, there are just one or two each day which by-pass it. However, you can walk from the nearest point on the by-pass. It is about two kilometres.

Phu Luang Wildlife Sanctuary is off the road south from Loei, but not easily reached by public transport. In any case, visitors are required to make arrangements with the Phu Luang Tourist Office beforehand (Tel: 042-841141) and transport will be provided. The sanctuary rises to an elevation of 1,550 metres, being partly tropical forest and partly temperate forest, and shelters various forms of wildlife. It has accommodation available during the October to May season. For the other four months the sanctuary is officially closed.

Phu Kradung National Park lies off the same road south from Loei (Highway 201) at a distance of some 70 kilometres. Take a bus no. 217 bound for Khon Kaen as far as Phu Kradung. Buses leave every half hour. Next take a *songtaew* to the entrance of the National Park, a distance of five kilometres. From here you start walking. It is five kilometres uphill to the summit of the mountain at 1,325 metres at a place known as **Lang Pae**. Then it is a further four kilometres to accommodation. Porters are available on request. The park offers views and wildlife.

A recently adopted National Park is the **Phu Pha Man National Park**, further still along the same highway, a little beyond Pha Nok Khao. It has caves with stalagmites and stalactites, as well as ancient wall paintings and waterfalls. Again use bus no. 217, destination Khon Kaen, to reach this park.

Accommodation
Loei

Name	No. on Map	Rooms	Cheapest Price (Bt)
King	5	40	350
Royal Inn	4	45	350
Phu Luang	1	72	300
Thai Udom	2	74	250

Name	No. on Map	Rooms	Cheapest Price (Bt)
Friendship G. H.	7	10	150
Friendship Annex	6	15	150
Sri Sawat	3	16	80

Moving On
Here is a summary of bus services from Loei.

Destination	Route No.	Price (Bt)				Journey Time (hrs)		Frequency	
		V.I.P.	A/C 1	A/C 2	Ord	A/C	Ord	A/C	Ord
Bangkok	29	450	292	227	162	9.5	11	Hourly	1/day
Bangkok (via Nakhon Ratchasima)	938		338		188	10	12	4/day	3/day
Nakhon Ratchasima	808		170			7.5		Hourly	
Udon Thani	220				38		3		30 mins
Nong Khai	507				80		5.5		5/day
Khon Kaen	217			55	40	2.5	3	5/day	30 mins
Lom Sak	1393				56		4		6/day
Dan Sai	286/1391				32		2.5		5/day
Tha Li	1394				20		1.25		30 mins
Chiang Khan	1395				20		1.25		20 mins
Pak Chom	4213				20		2		30 mins

Other buses passing through include the following useful services:

636   Udon Thani – Chiang Mai
644   Udon Thani – Phitsanulok
661   Nakhon Phanom – Chiang Rai

POSTCARD HOME—Bangkok, 16th June 1975

Dear Folks,

   Bangkok! Every station from Butterworth to Thonburi (the part of Bangkok on the other side of the river). That 12-hour journey from Surat Thani to Prachuap Kiri Khan (11½ really, but I was being justifiably pessimistic) actually took 13½ hours. We arrived very sooty at 8:30p.m., and I left again for a 10½ hour trip, which took 12¼ hours, at 5:20a,m., a pretty tiring journey. As soon as I got here, I had something to eat, went to bed and spent yesterday recovering.

POSTCARD HOME—Vientiane, Laos, 21st June 1975

Dear Folks,

I have been lucky enough to acquire a map with the names in Thai, so, by a lengthy process of comparison between the names on the railway station departures board (when I have worked out which is departures) and those on the map, I can find a suitable train. My problem is how to ask for a ticket, since I do not usually know the name of my destination.

From Bangkok it was a pleasant 30/-, eleven hour, 400 mile ride by rapid train to Nong Khai, a quiet border town on the Mekong River. Next morning, an exorbitant five minute ferry ride, payments to the officials on each side and a taxi ride into Vientiane. Taxis here are of the variety which pick people up along the way, and so are quite cheap and, together with trishaws, the main means of local transport. Vientiane is a small French town, population 100,000 and shrinking, it seems, as the foreign rats leave what they believe to be a sinking ship. As I understand the situation, the Pathet Lao (communist) forces are now more or less in control even of this, the capital, city, although here there seems to be a sort of coalition, with each side tolerating the other. Tomorrow I have to go to the Pathet Lao office to try to get a road pass to visit Luang Prabang, the royal city. I suppose that there really is a civil war going on here, but, contrary to the impression being given to the world, everything seems very peaceful. Most people seem apathetic towards the conflict and for them life just continues as normal. There are many young travellers here, encouraged by the fact that marijuana is readily available and apparently legal. It is an interesting and likeable city, with even its own Arc de Triomphe, much more pleasant than noisy, dirty Bangkok! The picture on this card is of the Bridge on the River Kwai, back in Thailand.

BRIDGE OVER THE RIVERKWAE IN KANCHANABURI, THAILAND.

PART 5   THE NORTH

The north of Thailand is probably the most interesting area of the country, containing much of the nation's history as well as some beautiful scenery. For that reason it is well touristed, second in popularity only to the beaches.

Let us start from Bangkok and move gradually north, which is what the reader may well choose to do in any case.

AYUTTHAYA   อยุธยา

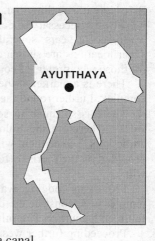
AYUTTHAYA

2 hrs by train from Bangkok
2 hrs by bus from Northern Bus Terminal

Ayutthaya is a truly fascinating historical city located 76 kilometres north of Bangkok. For more than four centuries, from 1350, when it was founded by King U-Thong, until 1767, when it was sacked by the Burmese, it served as the capital of the country and was ruled by 33 different kings. It was one of the most prosperous cities in Asia in its time, and its former opulence is reflected in the impressive grandeur of some of the remaining ruins, and also in the sheer extent of them. In 1991, the area was declared by UNESCO to be a World Heritage Site. The main part of the city lies on an artificial island formed by linking the Chao Phraya, Pa Sak and Lopburi Rivers with a canal.

Some people try to make a visit to Ayutthaya a day trip from Bangkok, but that is not really to be recommended, as there is just too much to see in one day and there is plenty of accommodation in Ayutthaya to suit all budgets. On the other hand, a day trip is infinitely better than not seeing the town at all. There are numerous trains running to Ayutthaya from Bangkok (Hualampong) Station. Journey time is two hours or a little less and the fare depends upon the type of train. Basic fare is Bt15 third class for an ordinary train. If you take a rapid or express train, however, there will be supplements to pay, so best to take just an ordinary train, and then it will be a very economical journey. When you arrive in Ayutthaya, ignore all the offers from *samlor* drivers and walk for one minute straight away from the station exit until you come to the river. From there two ferry services operate. Logically enough, the one on the left goes to the right, landing at a point opposite the market, while the one on the right goes straight across (so that the two ferries cross each other's paths). Either service will do to reach the town, but the one from the left is slightly preferable. The fare is Bt2.

Buses run from the Northern Bus Terminal in Bangkok and cost Bt43 for a 1st class air-conditioned bus or Bt34 for a 2nd class air-conditioned bus. These buses arrive at a reasonably convenient location within the town, whereas buses passing through Ayutthaya, but going further, use the bus station outside the town itself. If you should arrive at this bus station, there are air-conditioned town buses every few minutes to take you to the town centre, or to one of the historical sites, for Bt5.

Ayutthaya has recently introduced these two bus routes, labelled no. 5 and no. 6. Nobody knows what happened to 1, 2, 3 and 4. One of these two routes will take passengers to almost any place on the artificial island, and they also serve the bus station off the island. Buses operate every fifteen minutes on each route and in each direction. The rather complex routing is shown on the map. There are also *songtaew*, of course, and their fare is Bt10 to anywhere on the island and negotiable outside that. Some *songtaew* operate on fixed routes and will convey you on those routes for Bt5. Notwithstanding that, there are a lot of tourists in Ayutthaya, so, unfortunately, it is always necessary to confirm the fare before boarding.

In recent years, several guest houses have sprung up to supplement the hotels. Their locations are shown on the map. There is also more expensive accommodation for those who prefer, of course.

There is a market at the heart of the town, and, just opposite, a modern shopping complex. Further round the Pa Sak River is a night food market.

There is so much to see in Ayutthaya that it would take several days, or even weeks. Therefore the following itinerary covers just a few of the most interesting attractions. To see them will take half a day. If you wish to see more, use information provided by the tourist office, or study the map in this book, or just wander around at will.

From your lodging, walk or take a town bus down to **Wat Mahathat** first. This temple was constructed during the reign of King Borom Ratchathirat I in the fourteenth century. The ruins cover a wide area and it costs Bt30 for admission.

Proceeding further west, you will come to **Wat Phra Ram**, with a Buddha statue at its centre at the top of a steep staircase which may be climbed. This temple was constructed outside the Grand Palace compound by the command of King Ramesuan on the site where his father, King U-Thong, was cremated. Again, admission costs Bt30.

Now proceed west once more and you will find **elephants**, quite a number of them, eating banana trees and relaxing in an enclosure where they may be fed and ridden by visitors. They range in age from three to eighty. The three-year-old is free to roam around putting his trunk into everybody's business, while the senior heffalumps are employed to transport visitors to the next tourist attraction. Behind them rides a man with a cart to pick up any exhaust fumes emitted *en route*.

If you walk south a short distance, you will find a **TAT office** where you may pick up a better and larger map than the one given in this book, together with information on all of the ruins.

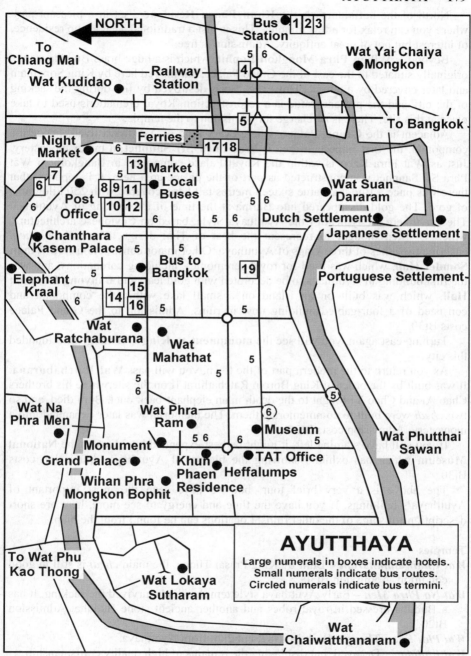

NORTH

Bus Station · 1 2 3

To Chiang Mai

Wat Yai Chaiya Mongkon ·

Wat Kudidao ·

Railway Station

5 6

4

To Bangkok

5

Ferries · 17 18

Night Market

6

13

Market Local Buses

6 7

5

6

8 9 11

Post Office

10 12

Wat Suan Dararam ·

5 6

Dutch Settlement ·

6

5

6

· Chanthara Kasem Palace

5

Japanese Settlement

Bus to Bangkok ·

5

19

Portuguese Settlement ·

· Elephant Kraal

5

14 15

6

16

Wat Ratchaburana ·

5

Wat Mahathat ·

5

5 6

5

· Wat Na Phra Men

Wat Phra Ram ·

5 6

6

· Museum

5

Monument · Grand Palace ·

5 6

6

5

Wat Phutthai Sawan ·

Wihan Phra Mongkon Bophit

Khun Phaen Residence

· TAT Office Heffalumps

To Wat Phu Kao Thong

AYUTTHAYA

Large numerals in boxes indicate hotels.
Small numerals indicate bus routes.
Circled numerals indicate bus termini.

· Wat Lokaya Sutharam

Wat Chaiwatthanaram ·

North of the heffalumps is the **Khun Phaen Residence**, set in a pleasant park where you can relax for a few minutes. This is just a traditional Thai group residence, of interest but not of great antiquity. Admission is free.

Beyond is **Wihan Phra Mongkon Bophit**, which is a huge brass Buddha statue, originally situated to the east of the Grand Palace, but moved here by King Songtham and later covered by a temple. However, it was destroyed by fire during the sacking of the city and the present statue is a reconstruction. Royal cremations used to take place at this site. There is no charge for admission to the temple.

Adjacent is the **Grand Palace**, where every king of Ayutthaya lived. Inside the compound, the first important area is **Wat Phra Sri Sanphet**, a major monastery. Just as Wat Phra Kaeo is within the Royal Palace compound in Bangkok, so Wat Phra Sri Sanphet was constructed as part of the palace area here. It is reported that there was once a Buddha statue sixteen metres tall here, covered with 250 kilograms of gold. The gold disappeared into Burma at the time of the sacking of Ayutthaya. The *chedi* here are typical of the Ayutthaya Style, based on Ceylonese architecture, which is often thought to represent the best of Thai design. These three *chedi* enshrine the ashes of three kings of Ayutthaya. Other major constructions are **Wihan Somdet Hall**, which was used for royal ceremonies, including coronations, and was the first building in Ayutthaya to be decorated with gold leaf, and **Banyong Rattanat Hall**, which was built on an island on a small lake within the compound and consisted of a four-gabled building now in ruins. Admission to the Grand Palace costs Bt30.

Turning east again, you will see the **monument to King U-Thong**, who founded this city.

As you return to the modern part of the town, you will pass **Wat Ratchaburana**. It was built by the order of King Borom Ratchathirat II on the site where his brothers Chao Ai and Chao Yi fought to the death in an elephant-back duel. Both died, and so two *chedi* were built to commemorate them. The memorial was later expanded into a monastery. Admission costs Bt30.

If you still have stamina left, it might be best expended by a look at the **National Museum** which has exhibits showing the history of Ayutthaya. Admission costs Bt30.

The above is a very brief tour, but we have seen the most important of Ayutthaya's buildings. If you have the time and energy to see more, here are short descriptions of some of the other ruins. Locations can be found from the map.

Temples

Wat Chaiwatthanaram – Built by King Prasat Thong, the main *chedi* is still in good condition. Admission Bt30.

Wat Na Phra Men – Early Ayutthaya style temple which survived the sacking. It has a Buddha dressed in royal robes and another ancient stone Buddha. Admission Bt20.

Wat Phu Khao Thong – Built in 1387, but 2km from Ayutthaya.

Wat Kudidao – Decayed, but displaying the remains of high quality craftsmanship.

Wat Yai Chaiya Mongkon – Contains a huge *chedi* built to commemorate the victory of King Naresuan in an elephant-back duel. Admission Bt20.

Wat Suan Dararam Ratchawora Wihan – Remains a royal temple, so is constantly renovated and improved.

Wat Lokaya Sutharam – Contains a Reclining Buddha 29 metres long.

Wat Phutthai Sawan – Marking the spot where King U-Thong supposedly decided upon the location of his new city.

Other Buildings

Chanthara Kasem Palace – Built half way through the Ayutthaya Period, but destroyed by the Burmese. Then reconstructed in the late nineteenth century by King Rama IV and used by him when visiting Ayutthaya. The main pavilion is now the Chanthara Kasem Museum. Admission Bt30.

Wanglang Palace – Originally the palace garden, but a residential building was later constructed and lived in by members of the royal family.

Elephant Kraal – A pavilion used for royalty to watch the elephant round-up. This is a modern reconstruction.

Dutch, Portuguese and Japanese Settlements – Areas assigned to visitors from these countries who came to trade with Ayutthaya.

Even this by no means exhausts the attractions of Ayutthaya. There are ancient ruins everywhere here, not only on and around the artificial island, but stretching far into the countryside. You could spend weeks and still not see all, but after one has seen the best, the remainder seem to pall in significance. A couple of days is a suitable time to spend, and then move on.

Accommodation
Ayutthaya

Name	No. on Map	Rooms	Cheapest Price (Bt)
Krung Sri River	5	206	1,600
Ayutthaya Grand	1	122	1,300
U-Thong Inn	4	190	1,250
Ayutthaya Hotel	13	101	1,000
Thai Thai Palace	2	122	700
My Garden	3	49	600
Wiang Fa	19	22	450
U-Thong Hotel	6	65	250
Youth Hostel	18	5	250
Iudea Guest House	17	10	250

Name	No. on Map	Rooms	Cheapest Price (Bt)
Cathay	7	26	200
Thai Thai Bungalows	15	20	150
T.M.T. Guest House	11	10	120
Ayutthaya G. H.	8	10	120
Toto House	9	10	120
B.J. Guest House	16	19	100
B.J.1 Guest House	10	8	100
Phatsaporn G. H.	14	8	100
P.U. Guest House	12	7	80

Moving On

The train timetable north is given on page 73.

There are three different places in Ayutthaya from which buses leave. The buses north and buses to Bangkok which have originated in other towns use the bus station outside the town. This can be reached by taking a town bus. Both routes go to the bus station. Buses to Bangkok originating in Ayutthaya (route no. 901) use the more convenient bus terminus in Naresuan Road. Immediately opposite, on the other side of the road, you will also find minibuses lined up to offer an alternative service. Local services depart from beside the market. Now here is a summary of bus services available from Ayutthaya.

Destination	Route No.	Price (Bt)				Journey Time (hrs)		Frequency	
		V.I.P.	A/C 1	A/C 2	Ord	A/C	Ord	A/C	Ord
Bangkok	901		43	34		2		10 mins	
Bangkok (Bang Pa In)	17			45	32	2	2.5	30 mins	12/day
Phitsanulok	100/913			120		5		3/day	
Sukhothai	965	230	148			6		8/day	
Chiang Mai	18	570		255		10		9/day	
Lopburi	607				25		1.5		20 mins
Suphanburi	703				30		2		40 mins
Wang Noi	1001				10		0.5		15 mins
Maharach	2174				15		0.75		20 mins
Sena	2212		20		10	0.5	0.75	30 mins	15 mins
Sena	2288		20		10	0.5	0.75	30 mins	15 mins

There are also minibuses to Bangkok every 20 minutes for Bt40.

BANG PA IN   บางปะอิน

BANG PA IN

1 hr 30 mins by train from Bangkok
1 hr 45 mins by bus from Northern Bus Terminal

Bang Pa In is the site of the Summer Palace of King Chulalongkorn (Rama V) and should not be missed.

The small town of Bang Pa In lies eighteen kilometres south of Ayutthaya and can easily and conveniently be visited on the way to or from that town, or as an excursion from the town. From Bangkok the fare is only Bt12 third class in an ordinary train, a very economical way to arrive. The journey takes 1½ hours. From the station, cross the main road and go a short distance to your left before taking the turning running away from the railway (i.e. on your right). Just keep following this road and you will come to the Bang Pa In Palace wall. Unluckily the entrance is on the other side, so you have to walk around this wall. From the station, it is a walk of about twenty minutes.

Buses run from the Northern Bus Terminal in Bangkok and take about 1¾ hours to arrive, costing Bt25 for ordinary buses and Bt35 for air-conditioned buses. The service is frequent.

Originally, the palace here was built by King Prasat Thong, on an island in the Chao Phraya River, probably in about 1632. The same king also constructed Wat Chumphon Nikayaram on the island. Thereafter the kings of Ayutthaya used the palace as a country residence.

Following the sacking of Ayutthaya, however, the palace fell into disrepair. The new capital was later established in Bangkok and Bang Pa In was deserted for eighty years. It was King Rama IV who brought it back to life. He had a new house built there and began visiting once more. His son, King Chulalongkorn, liked Bang Pa In, so, when he ascended the throne in 1868, he started to go there every year and to construct the Summer Palace which can be seen now. This is basically his creation and it features an amazing variety of beautiful architecture, copying styles that King Chulalongkorn liked from all over the world.

There is a Khmer style *prasat* (tower) dedicated to King Prasat Thong (whose name means 'King of the Golden Prasat'). There is a two-storey colonial style house for the King's relatives. There is a beautiful miniature Thai pavilion, a copy of one in the Royal Palace in Bangkok, in the middle of a lake. This pavilion now contains a statue of King Chulalongkorn. There is a neo-classical mansion where the King used to reside himself and which is still used by the present King when he is in residence at Bang Pa In.

Crossing a bridge with a louvered wall, so that the ladies of the court could watch what was going on without being seen, one comes to the Inner Palace. There are European style gardens here, since King Chulalongkorn liked gardening, and there is a Swiss chalet, which was one of his favourite places. The original chalet was accidentally destroyed by fire in 1938 and that which is there now is a reconstruction. Then there is a Chinese mansion presented to the King by an association of Chinese businessmen, with magnificent decoration and furnishings inside. Finally, there is an observation tower for the King to view the countryside.

This palace is not without its sadness too, for there are two memorials here. The first is to Queen Sunantha, who was drowned in the Chao Phraya River when her boat sank on the way to Bang Pa In in 1881. King Chulalongkorn wrote the words on the memorial, in both Thai and English, himself. The second is in memory of his consort Princess Saowapak Narirat and three of his children, who all died in the year of 1887.

When you have finished looking at this most memorable and impressive of palaces, do not leave immediately, for there is one more sight to see. Just outside the gates and to the south is Wat Niwet Thammaprawat, also built by King Chulalongkorn. To reach it, you must cross the water in a cable car. Just get into the car and soon, apparently by magic, it will whisk you across to the other side. The magic is, in reality, a monk in the control box on the other side. There is no charge for the transport or for visiting the monastery, but there is a box by the cable car in case you feel generous. Turn right and soon you will see, to your surprise, a Gothic church. Go inside and you will discover that it is, after all, not a church at all, but a unique Buddhist temple. King Chulalongkorn admired Gothic architecture, so decided in 1878 to construct this religious building just like a church, but to devote it to Buddhism. Therefore, he donated it to an order of monks who established a monastery here. It is a peaceful place to walk around, and perhaps take a rest in the grassy grounds.

When you have finished your visit to Bang Pa In, you will probably leave thinking, as the author does, and most Thais do too, that King Chulalongkorn was a fairly remarkable man. This is a palace which you will not easily forget. Admission to Bang Pa In Palace costs Bt50. It is open every day, but note that the last admission is at 15:30.

LOPBURI ลพบุรี

3 hrs by train from Bangkok
3 hrs by bus from Northern Bus Terminal

Lopburi is a town with a long history and some interesting sights to see, but one which is frequently overlooked on the long journey north. The problem is that, once you have broken your journey here, it is a little difficult to get going again, since most services do not start here and long-distance buses often do not pass through. However, it is not so inconvenient to stop on the return to Bangkok. If you are travelling on a long-distance bus which does not pass through Lopburi, you should alight at Singburi and take a bus from there. Such buses run every 15 minutes and cost Bt12 for the 27km journey.

Trains available from Bangkok include the 7:05 (destination Den Chai) and 8:35 (destination Phitsanulok) ordinary trains. Fare is only Bt28 third class, with arrival in Lopburi at 10:04 or 11:56. If you have a rail pass, you can take the 8:25 express railcar, arriving at 10:41, a very quick and comfortable journey. The railway station is right in town, near everything you need: hotels, shops, tourist attractions and **TAT office**. In fact, the main attractions are right outside the station.

Air-conditioned buses leave the Northern Bus Terminal in Bangkok every ten minutes for Lopburi. The fare is Bt86 or Bt57, depending on the class of bus. The journey takes three hours. The bus station, however, is not in the town. It is three kilometres down a long, straight, noisy highway next to a gigantic candle in the middle of the road. Walk outside the bus station to Narai Maharat Road and take any town bus from the near side. Any bus will go to the main part of the town and nearly all will terminate beside or behind the Palace there. The fare is Bt4. Some of the medium-distance buses (from Ayutthaya or Singburi, for example) will pass through the old town on their way to the bus station, so keep your eyes open and be ready to alight if you are using one of these services.

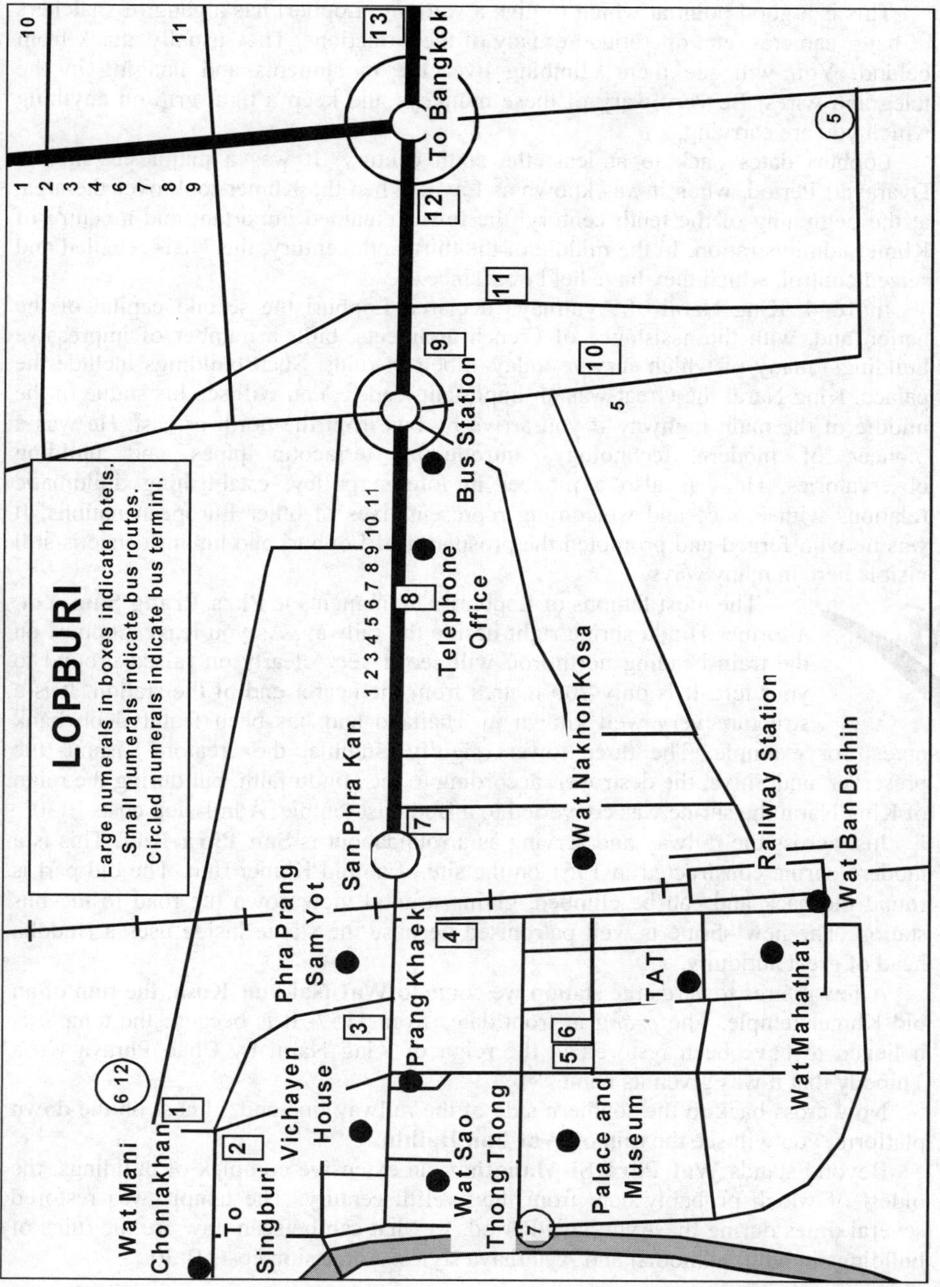

LOPBURI

Large numerals in boxes indicate hotels.
Small numerals indicate bus routes.
Circled numerals indicate bus termini.

Wat Mani Chonlakhan

To Singburi

Vichayen House

Phra Prang Sam Yot

Prang Khaek

San Phra Kan

Wat Sao Thong Thong

Palace and Museum

Telephone Office

Bus Station

Wat Nakhon Kosa

TAT

Wat Mahathat

Railway Station

Wat Ban Daihin

To Bangkok

This is a good point at which to give a warning. Lopburi has a gang of snatchers of bags, cameras, etc. operating at many of the attractions. They usually attack from behind. You will see them climbing over the monuments and hanging in the telegraph wires. Be very wary of these monkeys and keep a tight grip on anything which you are carrying.

Lopburi dates back to at least the sixth century. It was a major city in the Dvaravati Period, when it was known as Lavo. When the Khmer took over the area, at the beginning of the tenth century, the town remained important and a centre of Khmer administration. In the middle of the thirteenth century, the Thais rebelled and seized control, which they have held ever since.

In 1664, King Narai of Ayutthaya declared Lopburi the second capital of the nation and, with the assistance of French architects, built a number of impressive buildings, many of which survive today, albeit in ruins. Such buildings include the palace. King Narai the Great was an important leader. You will see his statue in the middle of the main highway if you arrive by bus from the north or east. He was a pioneer of modern technology, introducing terracotta pipes and building observatories. He was also a pioneer in foreign policy, establishing diplomatic relations with France and welcoming representatives of other European nations. It was he who forged and promoted the prosperity of Lopburi and his influence is still visible here in many ways.

The most famous of Lopburi's monuments is **Phra Prang Sam Yot**, a former Hindu shrine right beside the railway. As you leave Lopburi on the train heading north you will see it very clearly on raised ground to your left. It is only 200 metres from the nearer end of the station. It is a structure very well known in Thailand and has been featured on bank notes, for example. The three towers signify Brahma, the creator, Vishnu, the preserver, and Shiva, the destroyer, according to the Hindu faith, but during the reign of King Narai the shrine was converted to a Buddhist temple. Admission costs Bt30.

Just across the railway and serving as a roundabout is **San Phra Kan**. This is a modern shrine constructed in 1951 on the site of an old Khmer ruin. The old part is round the back and can be climbed, giving a good view down the road to the bus station. The new shrine is well patronised because the statue inside uses a Buddha head of great antiquity.

A few metres towards the station we come to **Wat Nakhon Kosa**, the ruin of an old Khmer temple. The *prang* in front dates from 1157. It is because the temple is believed to have been restored in the reign of King Narai by Chao Phraya Kosa Thibody that it was given its name.

Now cross back to the southern side of the railway line and, almost on the down platform, you will see the ruin of **Wat Ban Daihin**.

Beyond stands **Wat Phra Si Mahathat**, an extensive complex of buildings, the oldest of which probably date from the twelfth century. The temple was restored several times during the Ayutthaya Period, so what can be seen now are the ruins of buildings in both Sukhothai and Ayutthaya styles. Admission costs Bt30.

Walking away from the station for five minutes, we come to the **Narai Ratchaniwet Palace** built by King Narai and covering a very large piece of ground. Construction took twelve years and was completed in 1677. Buildings and ruins surviving from this time include the following. The Water Reservoir stored drinking water brought through terracotta pipes from a fresh-water lake. The twelve Treasure Houses stored royal treasures. The Stables were for both horses and elephants. The Chantara Phisan Pavilion was originally the royal residence, but later was used as an audience hall. The Dusit Sawan Thanya Maha Prasat Hall was an audience hall for high ranking foreign visitors. The Suttha Sawan Pavilion was King Narai's later residence, where he died on 11th July 1688. The Phra Chao Hao Building was a private audience hall, and the Banquet Hall was for entertaining important foreign dignitaries. In 1856, King Rama IV restored some parts of the palace and also constructed various new buildings. Within the palace compound is the **Lopburi National Museum** established in 1924. The palace is open from 7:00 until 17:30 every day, but the museum does not open until 9:00 and is closed on Mondays and Tuesdays. Admission costs Bt30.

Coming out of the main palace gate and turning left, we shall come in two minutes to **Prang Khaek** at the end of, and right in the middle of, the road. This is believed to be the oldest building in Lopburi. It is another Khmer ruin and was also once a Hindu shrine, but it is much smaller than Phra Prang Sam Yot. The architecture displays much Indian influence.

Just round the corner are the ruins of **Vichayen House**. This was built by King Narai as a residence for Louis XIV's ambassador, Chevalier de Chaumont. It was later used by Chao Phraya Vichayen (Constantin Phaulkon), until he was killed by revolutionary forces. Hence the name of the building. In fact, there are the remains of several buildings here, including a Roman Catholic chapel. Admission costs Bt30.

A few metres down the street from Vichayen House is **Wat Sao Thong Thong**, an old temple restored by King Narai. Parts of it may originally have been a Christian church or Islamic mosque. There are also buildings once used as reception places for Persian ambassadors.

Walking north for five minutes, we shall come to **Wat Mani Chonlakhan** on the Lopburi River. It was originally on a small island. Chedi Luang Pho Saeng stands beside the river on the south side of the road, while a large Buddha statue gazes across the river on the northern side.

Lopburi has a town bus service, but for most visitors it will not be needed, for all the main attractions are concentrated into one small area. The buses all link the old part of the town with the newer parts to the east. Therefore every route passes along the road to the bus station, which is the only journey likely to be useful to visitors. Thereafter, the buses go to different destinations, but many of the routes turn north and go to various points on the road to Khok Samrong. The routes are shown on the map. The fare for up to ten kilometres is Bt4. Over ten kilometres it is Bt6. There is a convenient bus stop just north of the palace where some town buses start, and also where a bus to Ayutthaya may be caught. Further north, there is a bus stop for buses to Singburi.

Accommodation

Lopburi has a reasonable range of hotels, but no guest houses. For those with limited budget, the Asia is a good bet. It is a typical Chinese hotel, not expensive, with a helpful owner who speaks English and distributes a map in English, and situated right outside the palace.

Lopburi

Name	No. on Map	Rooms	Cheapest Price (Bt)	Name	No. on Map	Rooms	Cheapest Price (Bt)
Lopburi Inn Resort	13	74	2,400	Muang Thong	3	37	150
Lopburi Inn	12	136	700	Wibunsi	7	38	150
Thep Thani	8	40	600	Nett	6	29	150
Piman	11	45	300	Lopburi City	4	40	150
Holiday	9	96	300	Youth Hostel	10	15	150
Rama Plaza	1	36	200	Asia	5	111	140
Tai Pai	2	104	190				

Moving On

The train timetable for moving north appears on page 73. Here is a summary of the bus services available.

Destination	Route No.	Price (Bt)				Journey Time (hrs)		Frequency	
		V.I.P.	A/C 1	A/C 2	Ord	A/C	Ord	A/C	Ord
Bangkok	11/12		85	57		3		10 mins	
Lom Sak	109				80		5.5		45 mins
Takli	106				35		2.5		20 mins
Saraburi	104				16		1		20 mins
Nakhon Ratchasima	108				64		4		Hourly
Ang Thong	105				25		1.5		30 mins
Singburi	159				12		0.5		15 mins
Ban Pahan	607				16		1		25 mins
Wang Muang	601				23		1.5		20 mins
Ayutthaya	607				25		1.5		40 mins
Suphanburi	462/653				35		2.5		Hourly
Ban Mee	655				28		1.5		20 mins

NOTICE IN MUT MEE GUEST HOUSE, NONG KHAI

THAI SHOWER INSTRUCTIONS
1. Throw water over body.
2. Apply soap to body.
   Do not put soap in water.
3. No swimming in water urn.
4. Wash off with more water.
5. Smell armpits.
   Consider repeating process.

POSTCARD HOME
Phitsanulok, 4th July 1975
Dear Folks,
   Yesterday, I was up in time to catch the 6:00 bus from Udon Thani to Loei, but the bus didn't make it, so I might as well have got up half an hour later and caught the 6:30 which I ended up on. Then along a pretty rough road, at an exorbitant price, to Lom Sak, and finally to Phitsanulok, which I reached at 5:00. Altogether an expensive day, costing 82 baht for travel, but scenic and exciting.

PHITSANULOK

พิษณุโลก

PHITSANULOK

7 hrs by train from Bangkok
6 hrs by bus from Northern Bus Terminal

From Lopburi to Phitsanulok is quite a big jump and, of course, there are towns on the way where it is quite possible to stay. However, the attractions of such places are limited, so let us keep moving north.

Phitsanulok is 372 kilometres north of Bangkok and is the half-way point on the journey to Chiang Mai. The railway passes through Phitsanulok, but buses to Chiang Mai usually do not. They stay on the main highway further west. Therefore, if you are travelling by bus and want to break your journey in Phitsanulok it is necessary to take a bus specifically bound for here.

For economy, the best train to take from Bangkok is the 7:45 rapid, which reaches Phitsanulok at 14:58. Cost is Bt109 third class or Bt199 second class. If you prefer the 8:35 ordinary train, arriving at 17:33, the cost will be only Bt69 third class, but the journey by ordinary train is a little long and tedious. If you are using a rail pass, there is a fast and comfortable air-conditioned railcar at 8:25, arriving at 13:37. (Cost without a pass is Bt359.) Alternatively, this journey is just long enough to consider use of a sleeper. The 22:00 departure from Bangkok reaches Phitsanulok at 5:15 and carries air-conditioned sleepers. If you are travelling without a pass, this will be a little expensive, though, at Bt469 for a lower air-conditioned berth, Bt419 for an upper air-conditioned berth, Bt349 for a lower ordinary berth or Bt299 for an upper ordinary berth.

By air-conditioned bus the journey takes about six hours and costs Bt194 or Bt160, depending on the class of bus. By ordinary bus, it takes an hour longer and costs Bt108. There are hourly departures from the Northern Bus Terminal.

The railway station is in the centre of town, but, as usual, the bus station is quite a long way out. However, there is a town bus service and routes 1, 6, 8, 10, 12 with red stripe, and 13 go through the bus station (see map for destinations), of which the most useful is the circular no. 1. If the destination board in the front window is red, the bus is running clockwise. If it is blue, it is running anti-clockwise. However, either direction will do from here and will take you into the town. The fare is Bt4 for an ordinary bus or Bt6 for an air-conditioned bus. These buses run every five minutes.

Phitsanulok is a town which gradually grows on one. It is of a size enabling one to walk to most places and it has been improved greatly by the recent cleaning up of some of the river bank areas. For a short time in the fifteenth century, the town even served as the temporary capital of Thailand. King Naresuan (1590 – 1605) and his brother Prince Ekathosarot were both born here.

Phitsanulok is most famous for its **Wat Phra Si Rattana Mahathat** (or simply Wat Mahathat) and for the **Buddha Chinnarat** statue within.

This is generally regarded as the most beautiful Buddha in Thailand. It was cast in 1357. The mother-of-pearl inlaid doors to the temple, dating from 1756, are also impressive. The temple is within easy walking distance of the town centre and lies just beside the Nan River. It is well worth a visit.

The river itself is an attraction, now that it has been improved. The riverside promenade is rather short, but appealing. Notice all the houseboats lining the banks, where they have not been displaced by floating restaurants. The river bank is also the scene of an interesting **night market**. This is the place for a good low-cost dinner, but a little further along there is also an extensive clothing market in the evenings. Just across the road is a day market of produce and behind and to the side of that, overflowing into the street, a small fruit market.

The night market has become famous for the long-established **Flying Vegetables** stall. The proprietor parks his truck and sends the waiters to stand on top of it. Then he cooks vegetables and hurls them skyward from the pan for the waiters to catch on their platters. It is a novel way to serve dinner. For variety, sometimes diners are invited to go and catch their own dinner, which is, of course, disastrous, and sometimes, for the *pièce de résistance*, one waiter stands on the shoulders of another on top of the truck to catch the main course. Understandably, this is a very popular stall, irrespective of the quality of its food, to which point, in fact, nobody seems to pay much attention.

Wat Ratchaburana is also beside the river, just near Wat Mahathat, and is of similar antiquity. There is an old *chedi* and some ancient tablets were found within, but there is little to see for the visitor.

Another temple of interest is **Wat Chulamani**. This is six kilometres south of the town, but can be reached by town bus. Bus no. 5 with a green destination board (not red) will terminate at Wat Chulamani. Bus no. 9, and bus no. 12 with a white destination board (not with a red stripe), will pass by. (Phitsanulok certainly seems to have made a determined effort to make its bus system confusing. Best to check with the conductor when boarding.) Wat Chulamani is the oldest building in Phitsanulok and has a unique architectural style. In particular, its ornate plaster designs are not found elsewhere.

There are also natural attractions around Phitsanulok, especially to the east. If you are coming from or travelling to the North-East of Thailand, you will pass many of these on the way. The journey to Lom Sak, and on to Khon Kaen, is a very scenic one. To travel to Lom Sak, take a bus no. 137 at a cost of Bt47. Buses run approximately hourly and the journey of 137 kilometres takes three hours or a little less.

The first point of interest along this road is the **Sakuno Thayan Waterfall** and Botanical Garden on the right near the 33km post. The waterfall is some ten metres in height.

At the 45km post, again on the right, is **Kaeng Song Falls**, right beside the road.

There are several places offering slightly up-market accommodation in this area, including Rain Forest Resort (from Bt1,100) at the 44km post, Wong Nam Yen

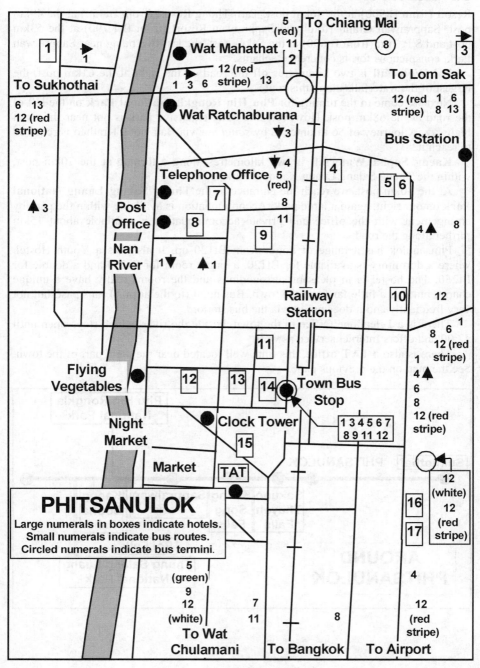

To Chiang Mai

Wat Mahathat

To Sukhothai

To Lom Sak

Wat Ratchaburana

Bus Station

Telephone Office

Post
Office

Nan
River

Railway
Station

Flying
Vegetables

Town Bus
Stop

Night
Market

Clock Tower

Market

TAT

PHITSANULOK

Large numerals in boxes indicate hotels.
Small numerals indicate bus routes.
Circled numerals indicate bus termini.

To Wat
Chulamani

To Bangkok

To Airport

Resort (from Bt900) at the 46km post, Tarn Thong Resort (from Bt450) at the 49km post, Sappraiwan Grand Hotel and Sappraiwan Resort (from Bt1,700) at the 53km post and S.P. Hut (from Bt600) at the 54km post, the last two being near Sappraiwan Park, conspicuous for its concrete elephants.

Poi Waterfall is two kilometres off the road on the right at the 61km post, the largest of the waterfalls along this route.

Next we come to the turning for **Phu Hin Rongkla National Park** on the left of the road at the 68km post. However, this quite extensive park is not near the main highway. A journey of 56 kilometres by *songtaew* via Ban Nong Krathao is required to reach it.

Kaeng Sopha Waterfall is two kilometres along a turning at the 70km post, within the Thung Salang Luang National Park.

At the 80km post, we reach the entrance to the **Thung Salang Luang National Park** on our right, again a large park. Accommodation is available within the park by arrangement with the office and private accommodation is available about 15km further along the road.

Phitsanulok has a range of hotels from Bt120 up. It also has a Youth Hostel, where a dormitory is available for Bt120, a single room for Bt200 and a double for Bt250. The hostel is in pleasant surroundings and the rooms really have a unique charm, but it is a little far from the town. Bus no. 4 (to the airport) runs past, but not very frequently and it does not go via the bus station.

There is a Telephone Office in the town, beside the river, which stays open until 22:00 and offers Internet service as well.

There is also a **TAT office**, this time well located near the main part of the town. See the map on the previous page.

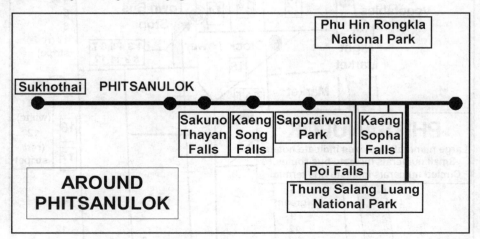

Accommodation
Phitsanulok

Name	No. on Map	Rooms	Cheapest Price (Bt)
Phitsanulok Thani	16	110	1,800
Amarin Lagoon	3	302	1,800
Pailyn	7	247	1,600
Topland	2	252	950
Ratchapruk	5	123	650
Amarin Nakorn	11	118	650
Thep Nakorn	15	150	600
Wang Kaew	1	85	600
U-Thong	10	96	500

Name	No. on Map	Rooms	Cheapest Price (Bt)
Samai Niyom	14	37	400
Sivathep	9	40	300
Ratchapruk G. H.	6	80	300
Chang Puak	4	52	280
Siam	8	40	150
Youth Hostel	17	24	120
London	12	11	120
Pan Sombat	13	23	120

Moving On

The train timetable for moving north appears on page 73. There is also an ordinary train to Chiang Mai leaving Phitsanulok at 7:25 and reaching Chiang Mai at 16:15. The fare to Chiang Mai by ordinary train, third class, is Bt65. The timetable for travelling south appears on page 228.

Here is a summary of bus services.

Destination	Route No.	Price (Bt)				Journey Time (hrs)		Frequency	
		V.I.P.	A/C 1	A/C 2	Ord	A/C	Ord	A/C	Ord
Bangkok (via Takfa)	100	302	194	160	115	6	7	Hourly	Hourly
Bangkok (Nakhon Sawan)	923	302		151	108	6	7	2/day	6/day
Chiang Mai (via Tak)	155/175	350	227	176	126	7	8	9/day	12/day
Chiang Mai (Den Chai)	623/635	350	205	160	114	6.5	7	4/day	3/day
Chiang Rai (Uttaradit)	651/663	400	250	195	139	7	8	8/day	5/day
Chiang Rai (Sukhothai)	622			195	139	8	9	3/day	3/day
Khon Kaen	175/637		196	153	110	6	7	6/day	8/day
Nakhon Ratchasima	635		258	221	133	7	8	9/day	5/day
Nakhon Ratchasima	572		258	221	133	8	9	3/day	3/day
Loei	644			110	69	5	6	2/day	5/day
Udon Thani	644		198	154	110	8	9	2/day	1/day
Sukhothai	131		40	27	19	1	1.5	Hourly	Hourly
Lom Sak	137				47		3		Hourly
Chattrakran	187				36		2.5		7/day
Nakhon Thai	187				28		2		Hourly
Tak	128			62	44	2.5	3	Hourly	Hourly
Mae Sod	128				100		5		6/day
Kampang Phet	193			52	37	2	2.5	Hourly	Hourly
Uttaradit	623			60	40	2.5	3	Hourly	Hourly
Phetchabun	136				56		3.5		Hourly
Phrae	613		103	80	57	3	4	2/day	1/day
Nakhon Sawan	99		80	60	42	2.5	3	3/day	6/day
Nan	613				91		5.5		4/day

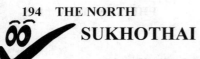

SUKHOTHAI   สุโขทัย

SUKHOTHAI

7 hrs 30 mins by bus from Northern Bus Terminal

Sukhothai is the birthplace of Thailand and was the nation's first capital. For anybody interested in history, it is an essential place to visit.

Sukhothai lies just over an hour west of Phitsanulok, through which trains to Chiang Mai pass, and just over an hour east of Tak, through which buses to Chiang Mai pass. From Phitsanulok buses depart every half hour bound for Sukhothai, and there are additional services which pass through on the way to other places. Air-conditioned buses can cover the 56 kilometres in just an hour. Ordinary buses take nearly 90 minutes.

If travelling by bus from Bangkok, you should take a service which comes directly to Sukhothai. These depart several times a day, and by night, for a journey which takes about 7½ hours. Fares are Bt230 for a 1st class air-conditioned bus, Bt179 for a 2nd class air-conditioned bus and Bt128 for an ordinary bus.

The name Sukhothai means 'Dawn of Happiness'. Originally the city was a major outpost of the Khmer Empire which controlled so much of South-East Asia. However, a rebellion by the Thais in 1238 drove out the Khmer, and Sukhothai was established as the first capital of the new Thai nation, with the leader of the rebellion installed as its first king – King Sri Indrathit.

In 1278, the second son of King Sri Indrathit ascended the throne as King Ramkhamhaeng (1278 – 1317) and became Thailand's first great ruler. Under his guidance, the Sukhothai kingdom expanded peacefully until it included most of current Thailand, and parts of modern-day Laos and Burma (Myanmar) as well. He established friendly diplomatic relations with China and made two visits there himself, meeting the Emperor Kublai Khan and bringing back craftsmen to teach the art of pottery, in particular, to his people. He was also responsible for introducing the Thai alphabet in 1283, using the old Khmer system as his basis. He tried not to overburden his subjects with taxes and promoted religion and culture. Buddhism began to flourish and some beautiful works of religious art were produced at this time. It is generally regarded as Thailand's golden age of peace and prosperity.

Eight kings ruled over the Sukhothai Kingdom, which lasted for 127 years. Towards the end, a gradual decline in power occurred and in 1365 it was taken over and incorporated into the new rising star named Ayutthaya. What we shall see here in Sukhothai is from that golden age when Thailand first emerged as a separate state and fostered its own art and architecture.

The first point to note is that modern Sukhothai is not in the same place as the ancient capital. It has shifted fourteen kilometres down the road. Thus, when you have found somewhere to stay in modern Sukhothai, you will have to go out and take

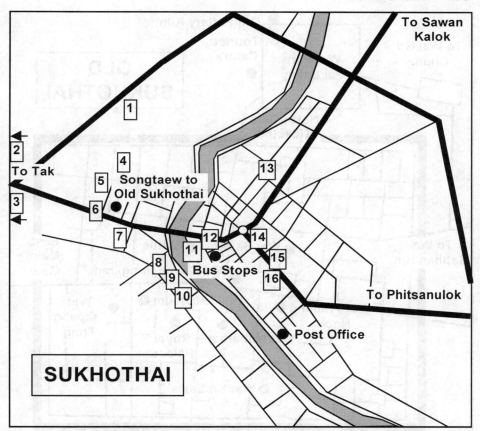

To Sawan Kalok

1

2
To Tak

4

5   Songtaew to
    Old Sukhothai

3

6

13

7

12   14

11

15

8

9   Bus Stops

16

10

To Phitsanulok

Post Office

SUKHOTHAI

a *songtaew* for those fourteen kilometres to the old city. *Songtaew* leave every ten minutes from a point just west of the river, near the cheaper guest houses in fact, and take about twenty minutes to make their way to Old Sukhothai at a price of Bt8.

Much of Old Sukhothai consists of an **Historical Park**. A few people live nearby, but this is only a village now. The Historical Park is extensive and well tended, and there are ticket offices at the east and north entrances (only) selling admission tickets at Bt30 a head. Some of the most important monuments within are as follows.

Royal Palace – This is the heart of the park and was the palace of King Ramkhamhaeng. It is surrounded by a moat.

Wat Mahathat – Wat Mahathat is the biggest and most important temple in the city. It lies within the palace compound and has a Buddha statue serenely gazing over the columns and pedestals of the ruined temple. There was originally a bronze Buddha made in 1362 in front of this temple, but King Rama I ordered that it be removed to Bangkok and now it sits in Wat Suthai there.

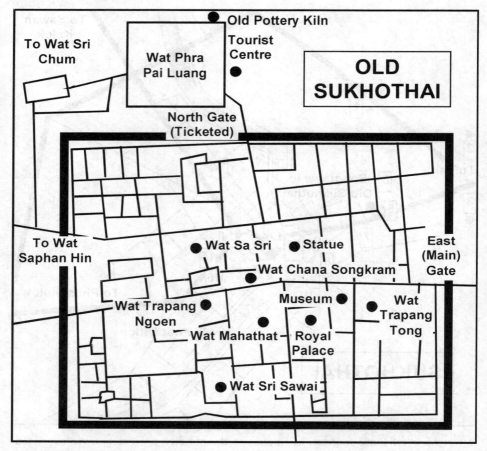

Old Pottery Kiln

Tourist Centre

Wat Phra Pai Luang

To Wat Sri Chum

OLD SUKHOTHAI

North Gate (Ticketed)

To Wat Saphan Hin

Wat Sa Sri

Statue

Wat Chana Songkram

East (Main) Gate

Wat Trapang Ngoen

Museum

Wat Trapang Tong

Wat Mahathat — Royal Palace

Wat Sri Sawai

Wat Sri Sawai – This was originally a Hindu shrine, so it has three Lopburi style *stupa*. Later additions, however, are Buddhist.

Wat Sa Sri – This temple is on an artificial island in the middle of a lake and has a Ceylonese style *chedi*, a stone Buddha and nine smaller *chedi* nearby.

Wat Trapang Ngoen – Only the crumbling ruin of this ancient temple remains.

Wat Chana Songkram – A Ceylonese style *chedi* remains, with the bases of twelve other smaller *chedi* and also an unusual *chedi* with three bases.

Wat Trapang Tong – A monastery in the middle of another lake, with a Ceylonese style *chedi* and a footprint of Buddha dating from 1390.

City Walls – These are intact to a considerable degree. They are 2,000 metres long on north and south, and 1,600 metres long on east and west, with four gates, one in each direction. An inscription states that King Ramkhamhaeng has set up a bell at one of the gates so that his subjects may summon him in case of need.

There is also a statue of King Ramkhamhaeng, with a history of his life, and the Ramkhamhaeng National Museum.

There are further monuments beyond the limits of the Historical Park and they include the following:

Wat Phra Pai Luang – 400 metres north. This temple was second in importance to Wat Mahathat and was also originally a moated Hindu shrine.
Wat Sri Chum – 1.5km north-west. The temple houses a huge stone seated Buddha.
Wat Saphan Hin – 500 metres west. The temple is on a 200 metre hill, giving a good view of the Historical Park. It also has a Buddha statue 12.5 metres tall.

You will probably have seen enough by now, but there is a tourist information office adjacent to Wat Phra Pai Luang giving details of other attractions, just in case you have stamina left. Beyond that there are the remains of an old pottery kiln, if you want to look at something different.

Accommodation

The more expensive hotels in New Sukhothai lie to the east of the Yom River, while the cheaper accommodation lies to the west of the river, mainly along its bank. The town is not so large, though, and it takes only five minutes or so to walk to the centre from almost any of the hotels or guest houses.

Sukhothai

Name	No. on Map	Rooms	Cheapest Price (Bt)	Name	No. on Map	Rooms	Cheapest Price (Bt)
Pailyn Sukhothai	3	238	900	Ban Thai G. H.	11	15	150
Ratchthani	6	81	600	Friend House	7	6	150
Northern Palace	15	57	525	No. 4 Guest House	4	10	150
Thai Village	2	100	450	Chinnawat	12	36	100
River View	9	48	370	Anasukho G. H.	5	5	100
Sawat Dipong	16	50	230	Somprasong G. H.	8	25	80
Sukhothai	14	42	200	Thai Guest House	13	5	70
Sky House	1	30	200	Yupa Guest House	10	6	60

Moving On

The following bus services operate to and from Sukhothai.

Destination	Route No.	Price (Bt)				Journey Time (hrs)		Frequency	
		V.I.P.	A/C 1	A/C 2	Ord	A/C	Ord	A/C	Ord
Bangkok	965		230	179	128	7.5	8	8/day	5/day
Phitsanulok	131		40	27	19	1	1.5	Hourly	Hourly
Sawan Kalok					15		1		30 mins
Tak	128			40		1.5		Hourly	
Mae Sod	128				80		3.5		6/day

There are also services to Uttaradit, Chiang Mai and Chiang Rai, but they do not usually start here. They simply pass through. Since Sukhothai is not the origin for most services, it should be borne in mind that times given by the bus offices will often be unreliable.

SRI SATCHANALAI   ศรีสัชนาลัย

1 hrs 30 mins by bus from Sukhothai

Sri Satchanalai is a repeat of Sukhothai, so you may very well think, "Then why do I need to see both?" And that is good reasoning. Really you do not need to see both. One is enough. The advantage with Sri Satchanalai is that everybody else goes to Sukhothai because it is easier to reach. When the author visited, I was the only person there. Admittedly, the whole area was flooded, but fewer people get here in any case.

Sri Satchanalai is 50 kilometres north of Sukhothai, dates from the same period, and was the seat of Sukhothai viceroys. It was the second city of the Thai nation. What remains is of a similar grandeur and in a similar condition to the ruins in its sister city, Sukhothai.

To reach Sri Satchanalai from Sukhothai takes 1½ hours by bus. The bus will not usually start in Sukhothai, but will have come from Phitsanulok. Its destination will be Uttaradit or Den Chai or beyond. Such services operate approximately hourly. It is important to note that Sri Satchanalai, like Sukhothai, has shifted, and the new town is eleven kilometres beyond the ruins of the old city. Impress on the conductor that you want to go to the old city, not the new, and do not get carried past your destination by mistake. The ruins are on the left. They can be seen from the bus, but the Yom River lies between so it is also quite possible to miss them.

On the way, 18 kilometres before Old Sri Satchanalai, you will pass through the small town of **Sawan Kalok**. There is a railway station here, the end of a branch line running, for no apparent reason, from Ban Dalar, which is on the main line to Chiang Mai. This is the only branch line anywhere on the Northern Line running from Bangkok to Chiang Mai and it used to be blessed with one ordinary train each way every day. It still has its one ordinary train, but recently an air-conditioned railcar service has also been introduced, running to and from Bangkok once every day. It leaves Bangkok at 23:10 and arrives here at 7:05, but, of course, has no sleepers – only reclining seats. It returns from Sawan Kalok at 7:40, reaching Bangkok at 15:15. Accommodation is available in Sawan Kalok.

Here are the most important of the 134 monuments in Sri Satchanalai.

Wat Phra Sri Rattana Mahathat – This temple is three kilometres south of Sri Satchanalai, situated in a bend in the river. It has a huge *prang* at its centre.

Wat Chang Lom – Has a very large bell-shaped *chedi* supported by 39 elephants, with the four at the cardinal points elaborately decorated.

Wat Chedi Chet Thaeo – Is regarded as a particularly beautiful temple. Its *chedi* are all of different design and the remains of some murals can still be seen.

Wat Suan Kaeo Utthayan Yai – Has a particularly large image hall.

Wat Nang Paya – This temple is known for its excellent stucco relief work.

Wat Suan Kaeo Utthayan Noi – Has an image hall almost intact.

Wat Khao Phanom Phloeng – Is mostly in ruins but offers a good view.

Wat Khao Suwan Khiri – Has a huge *chedi* on a five-tiered base and the remains of several statues. Because of the artwork, it is believed to have been constructed by King Ramkhamhaeng.

FROM SUKHOTHAI TO SRI SATCHANALAI

To Sri Satchanalai National Park
To Den Chai
To Uttaradit
Old Sri Satchanalai
To Ban Ko Noi
To Ban Dalar
Sawan Kalok
Sukhothai Airport
To Phitsanulok
To Tak
Sukhothai

Admission to the Sri Satchanalai Historical Park costs Bt30. Five kilometres further north, at **Ban Ko Noi**, are the remains of a pottery town where more than 500 kilns have been excavated. There is a museum, seven kilometres from Sri Satchanalai. Admission Bt30.

There is also a **Sri Satchanalai National Park**, but 45 kilometres away, at Ban Pa Ka. The park offers caves, waterfalls, viewpoints and wildife.

Accommodation

The following accommodation is available at Sawan Kalok.

Sawan Kalok

Name	No. on Map	Rooms	Cheapest Price (Bt)	Name	No. on Map	Rooms	Cheapest Price (Bt)
Suphalai Place	3	42	450	Muang Inn	2	29	200
Rai Im Aim (Airport)	4	30	400	Sangsin	1	34	200

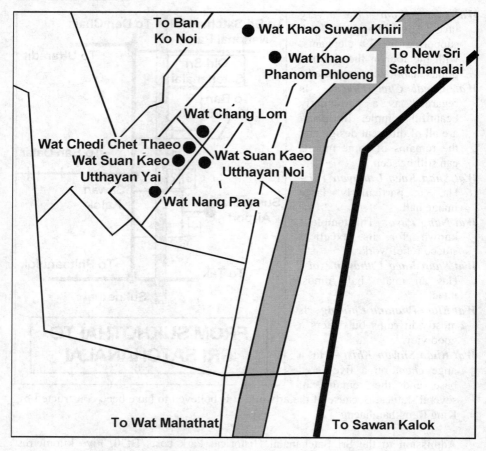

SRI SATCHANALAI

Moving On

There is little choice from here. By bus you can either go back to Sukhothai or Phitsanulok or go on to Uttaradit or Den Chai. Occasional buses go further, for example to Chiang Mai. No buses actually start or finish at Sri Satchanalai.

By train from Sawan Kalok, you can take the morning air-conditioned railcar at 7:40 to Bangkok or the afternoon ordinary train at 14:00 to Sila At (Uttaradit). The morning train option is particularly suitable for rail pass holders.

UTTARADIT

อุตรดิษฐ์

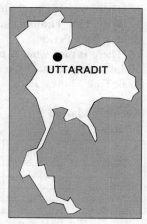
UTTARADIT

9 hrs by train from Bangkok
9 hrs by bus from Northern Bus Terminal

Uttaradit is a town in which you may find yourself if you visit Sri Satchanalai and continue north by bus. There are plenty of services from here.

There is a railway station with trains north and south. If you are going north, see the timetable on page 73. There is a rapid train to Chiang Mai at 7:13, arriving at 13:05, and an ordinary train at 9:39, arriving at 16:15. Those with a rail pass can also use the air-conditioned railcar at 14:52, arriving at 19:35, which would otherwise be rather expensive. Going south, there is a wide choice of trains. See the timetable on page 228.

There are buses to all likely destinations, including Bangkok, Chiang Mai, Chiang Rai, Nan, Phitsanulok and Udon Thani. However, most of these buses do not start here, but pass through from other towns.

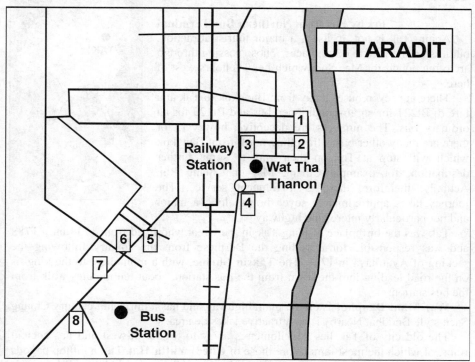

There are also places to stay. See accommodation list under.

Wat Tha Thanon, just near the station, has a bronze Buddha dating from the Chiang Saen Period.

There is also what is claimed to be the biggest teak tree in the world, but that is 60 kilometres east of the town itself, near Sirikit Dam. It is in **Ton Sak Yai** ('Big Teak Tree') Forest Park.

Accommodation
Uttaradit

Name	No. on Map	Rooms	Cheapest Price (Bt)	Name	No. on Map	Rooms	Cheapest Price (Bt)
Friday	5	147	1,100	Numchai	7	50	200
Seeharaj	6	152	1,100	Pro Wanit 2	2	66	200
Wiwat	8	90	300	Pro Wanit 3	4	25	200
Pro Wanit 1	3	24	220	Thano Thai	1	18	200

TAK   ตาก

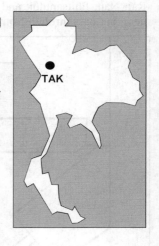

7 hrs by bus from Northern Bus Terminal

Again, Tak is not, in itself, a major tourist attraction, but it is on the way to other places. Those passing through are often bound for Mae Sod, which lies 1½ hours west of here.

There are seven buses a day from Bangkok to Tak at a fare of Bt221 for an air-conditioned bus and Bt123 for an ordinary bus. The numbers are deceptive, however, for there are many other buses travelling north from Bangkok which will stop at Tak on their way to some further destination, for example Chiang Mai or Chiang Rai. Actually, therefore, there is a frequent service. The journey takes approximately seven hours along a major and not particularly interesting highway.

Tak was the birthplace of King Taksin the Great who lived from 1734 until 1782 and was responsible for expelling the Burmese from the country following the sacking of Ayutthaya in 1767. The **Taksin Shrine**, with a monument to the king, is on the road leading into the town from the bus station, about ten minutes walk from the bus station.

Wat Mani Banphot is on the main highway and has a thirteenth century Chiang Saen style Buddha. Nearby is an attractive lakeside area.

The old city of Tak lies 25 kilometres away to the north-west and has ancient ruins, of which the most famous are those of **Chedi Yutta Hat Thi**, a hilltop pagoda supposedly constructed by King Ramkhamhaeng of Sukhothai. Also well known is

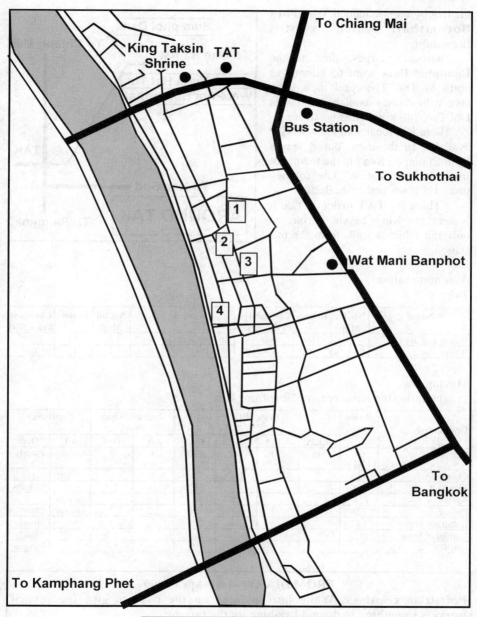

To Chiang Mai

King Taksin
Shrine

TAT

Bus Station

To Sukhothai

1

2

3

Wat Mani Banphot

4

To
Bangkok

To Kamphang Phet

TAK

the nearby temple named **Wat Phra Boromthat**, which is still flourishing.

Thailand's largest dam is the **Bumiphol Dam**, some 65 kilometres north of Tak. The result is a large lake with cruises available as far as Doi Tao, 140 kilometres upstream.

There is a local *songtaew* service available to the dam, but it leaves from Chompon Road in the town, not from the bus station. The journey takes 1½ hours and costs Bt20.

There is a **TAT office** in Tak. It is near the King Taksin Shrine, so only ten minutes walk from the bus station.

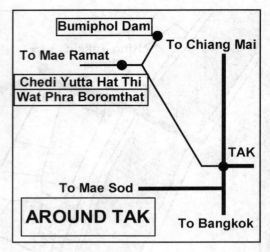

Accommodation
Tak

Name	No. on Map	Rooms	Cheapest Price (Bt)
Wiang Tak 1	1	100	600
Wiang Tak 2	4	50	600

Name	No. on Map	Rooms	Cheapest Price (Bt)
Sa Nguat Thai	2	44	270
Mae Ping	3	40	160

Moving On
The following buses are available from Tak.

Destination	Route No.	Price (Bt)				Journey Time (hrs)		Frequency	
		V.I.P.	A/C 1	A/C 2	Ord	A/C	Ord	A/C	Ord
Bangkok	91/ 114-119	345	221	172	123	7	8	Hourly	Hourly
Chiang Mai	118			122		4		5/day	
Mae Sod	128				33		1.5		30 mins
Sukhothai	128			40		1.5		Hourly	
Phitsanulok	128			62	44	2.5	3	Hourly	Hourly
Kampang Phet	642				25		1		Hourly
Bumiphol Dam	1152				20		1.5		Hourly
Ban Tak					10		0.5		30 mins

FROM DIARY—14th April 2000
Pedestrian crossings: White lines painted on the road to give the council workers something to do and brighten up the tarmac.

MAE SOD   แมสอด

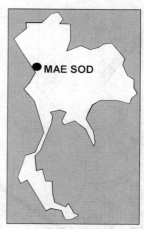

8 hrs 30 mins by bus from Northern Bus Terminal

Mae Sod is a gateway to Myanmar (Burma). If all were calm in that country, this would be the obvious place to enter. However, entry by land is currently prohibited except for brief local visits, so the border crossing does not fulfil its potential for travellers. Nevertheless, you may enter Myanmar here for the day, if you wish.

There are direct buses from Bangkok to Mae Sod. However, all except one run overnight. Most are air-conditioned buses. Fares vary with bus type, between Bt151 and Bt420, but the most common price is Bt211, for a 2nd class air-conditioned bus. The journey takes about 8½ hours.

There is also a regular service from Tak and a less frequent one from Phitsanulok via Sukhothai. These operations are by minibus, which is thought to suit the mountain road better. Fourteen passengers can be accommodated for each trip. From Tak the minibuses run half-hourly and from Phitsanulok they are hourly. Fares are Bt33 from Tak and Bt100 from Phitsanulok.

There are also two direct buses a day from Mae Sai, Chiang Rai and Chiang Mai to Mae Sod.

The road up is a wide, well constructed one, encouraging vehicles to travel too fast, so you can usually see one or two recent wrecks along the 86 kilometre route.

On the left at the 66km post (distance is from Mae Sod) is the entrance to **Lan Sang National Park**. Lan Sang Waterfall is three kilometres away, with Pha Phung and Lan Liang Ma Falls beyond. Accommodation is available in the park.

A little further on, at the 52km post, is the entrance on the right to **Taksin Maharat National Park** which has the biggest trees found in Thailand, a variety named *krabak yai*. Accommodation is available here too.

Also along the journey you will see the **Hilltribes Produce Village** selling wares produced by the natives of this area. There is a good view from this point, but the bus is not likely to stop to allow you to admire it for long.

Just before arriving in Mae Sod, you will see the **Shrine of King Khun Sanchom's Spirit** and then, on the left, **Tawi Chai Land**, which is known for its gardens of plants and flowers.

Mae Sod has a variety of accommodation available, including three guest houses. The town is not so big and any place is within walking distance.

To reach the border at **Moei River**, six kilometres away, take a blue *songtaew* at a cost of Bt10. They run every 10 minutes, and more frequently at rush hour, which is when the border closing time at 18:00 is approaching, At Moei River, there is a magnificent bridge across what is really quite a small river, with a palatial gate on the Thai side. Beneath the bridge is a market, spreading along the upper bank of the

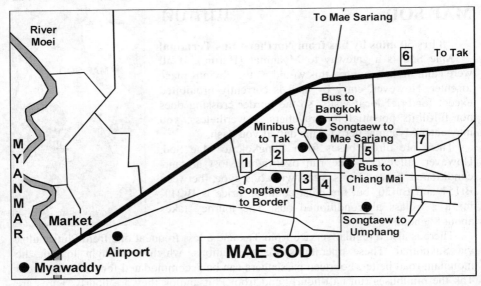

river. On sale are goods from Myanmar, including carved wooden furniture and other similar items (rather heavy to carry home in your bag), and jewellery. There are also goods for Burmese to take home from Thailand.

When you have looked at this official market, you can move down a level towards the river and see the unofficial one. Out in the open here, stalls with plastic canopies are selling clothing and other items and, beyond them, individuals with plastic bags are wading across from the other side of the river to hawk cigarettes and liquor at low prices. So much for border control!

If you wish to cross into Myanmar for the day, you may do so on payment of the required fee, at the Myanmar check point at the other side, of U.S.$10. It is best to bring this amount in U.S. funds, if possible, as any conversion into Thai currency will be carried out at a very unfavourable rate. You are required to leave your passport at the border and pick it up when leaving. That ensures that you do not stray too far. Note that the border closes at 18:00 and that Burmese time is half an hour behind Thai time.

Arriving in Myanmar at this point is something of a culture shock, for the standard of living is quite different from that in Thailand. **Myawaddy**, on the other side of the bridge, is just a poor village.

When you return to Thailand, you will be stamped back in and given another month's stay, so you will have something to show for your $10. Even if you do not intend to cross into Myanmar, you should still be sure to take your passport with you, as there is a police check point between the border and the town.

There are other places which can be visited from Mae Sod. You can move south to **Umphang**, an area on the Myanmar border remaining relatively unspoilt due to its

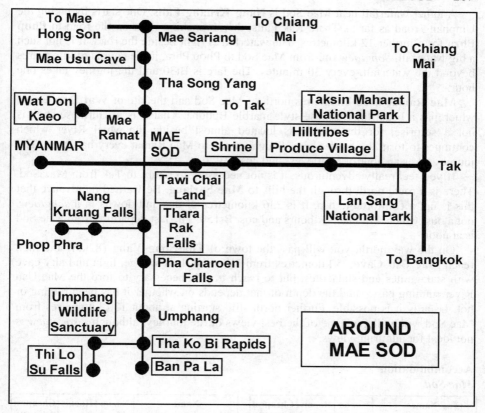

To Mae Hong Son

Mae Sariang

To Chiang Mai

To Chiang Mai

Mae Usu Cave

Tha Song Yang

Wat Don Kaeo

To Tak

Taksin Maharat National Park

Mae Ramat

MYANMAR

MAE SOD

Shrine

Hilltribes Produce Village

Tak

Nang Kruang Falls

Tawi Chai Land

Lan Sang National Park

Phop Phra

Thara Rak Falls

Pha Charoen Falls

To Bangkok

Umphang Wildlife Sanctuary

Umphang

Thi Lo Su Falls

Tha Ko Bi Rapids

Ban Pa La

AROUND MAE SOD

inaccessibility. Along the 167 kilometre route there, which rises to 1,200 metres above sea level, there are some beautiful views. There are also a couple of waterfalls. First is **Thara Rak Falls**, 26 kilometres from Mae Sod and 700 metres off the main road. The second is **Pha Charoen Falls**, 36 kilometres from Mae Sod and again about 700 metres from the road. There are *songtaew* available for the journey to Umphang. They leave every hour and take five hours over the journey. The fare is Bt100. Umphang is a sizeable town which offers plenty of accommodation ranging in price from Bt100 to Bt1,700. At the cheaper end of the scale are Boonchua Camping, Thawat Chai T.J. Tour, Hill Side Pension, Suk Satien, Pahlatha House and Tilosu Riverside, all starting below Bt200.

Beyond Umphang lie the **Umphang Wildlife Sanctuary** and the attractive **Thi Lo Su Falls**. There are also the **Tha Ko Bi Rapids** and cave and the Karen Hilltribe village of **Ban Pa La**, where traditional costume is still worn. These can be reached by *songtaew* from Umphang.

Another waterfall near Mae Sod is **Nang Kruang Falls**. One starts by taking the Umphang road as far as Thara Rak Falls, then branching right on the road to **Phop Phra** for a further 12 kilometres. The waterfall is right beside the road. It is not such a big waterfall. *Songtaew* run from Mae Sod to Phop Phra, just a couple of kilometres beyond the waterfall, every 30 minutes. The fare is Bt30 and the journey takes one hour.

Mae Ramat is 33 kilometres north of Mae Sod and the site of **Wat Don Kaeo**, which has a beautiful Burmese style marble Buddha. That it is in Burmese style is not a surprise, for the temple is located almost beside the Moei River which continues to form the border here. *Songtaew* run to Mae Ramat every half hour. The journey takes an hour or a little less and costs Bt20.

If you feel really adventurous, it is not necessary to return to Tak from Mae Sod. There is a route north through the hills to **Mae Sariang**. Be warned in advance that this is not a comfortable trip. It is 236 kilometres of ups and downs in a *songtaew*, not a bus, which will take six hours and cost Bt150. The last departure from Mae Sod is at noon.

On the way north, you will pass the town of **Tha Song Yang** (82km) and then reach **Mae Usu Cave** 95 kilometres from Mae Sod. It is a large, light and airy cave with stalagmites and stalactites, but to reach it, it is necessary to ford the Mae Usu River running past – and the depth of that depends on whether it has been raining or not. Usually it is possible. Further north still, starting at about 130 kilometres from Mae Sod, you will get some of the best views of the journey, although a *songtaew* is not ideal for admiring views.

Accommodation
Mae Sod

Name	No. on Map	Rooms	Cheapest Price (Bt)	Name	No. on Map	Rooms	Cheapest Price (Bt)
Maesot Hill	6	115	1,000	Mae Sod Guest House	7	12	150
Pornthep	4	160	500	Bai Fern's Home	2	8	150
Siam	3	85	300	No. 4 Guest House	1	5	60
Duang Kamon	5	50	300				

Umphang

Name	Address	Rms	Cheapest Price (Bt)	Name	Address	Rms	Cheapest Price (Bt)
Umphang Hill Resort	99 Moo 3	36	1,000	Wira Tour	106 Moo 6	25	350
Tu Ka Su Cottage	40 Moo 6	25	900	Gift House	166 Moo 1	15	350
Suan Reinkaew	41 Moo 6	15	900	Phu Doi Camp Side	9 Moo 1	16	350
Suan Bunyapron	106 Moo 6	18	600	Thawat Chai T.J. Tour	620 Moo 1	6	150
Huay Nam Yen Resort	107 Moo 3	8	500	Suk Satien	303 Moo 4	15	150
Umphang House Resort	443 Moo 1	14	350	Pahlatha House	49 Moo 1	5	150
Umphang G. H. Resort	438 Moo 1	14	350	Tilosu Riverside	7 Moo 1	5	150
Umphang Country Hut	Moo 1	18	350	Hill Side Pension	102 Moo 3	5	120
P.M. Resort	162 Moo 6	10	350	Boon Chua Camping	360 Moo 1	4	100

Moving On
The following buses are available from Mae Sod.

Destination	Route No.	Price (Bt)				Journey Time (hrs)		Frequency	
		V.I.P.	A/C 1	A/C 2	Ord	A/C	Ord	A/C	Ord
Bangkok	956	420	272	211	151	8.5	9.5	7/day	2/day
Chiang Mai	672		207		115	6	7	1/day	1/day
Chiang Rai	672		326		178	11	12	1/day	1/day
Mae Sai	672		348		193	12	13	1/day	1/day
Tak	128				33		1.5		30 mins
Sukhothai	128				80		3.5		6/day
Phitsanulok	128				100		5		6/day
Phop Phra					30		1		30 mins
Umphang					100		5		Hourly
Mae Ramad					20		1		30 mins
Tha Song Yang					50		2		Hourly
Mae Sariang					150		6		4/day

LAMPANG   ลำปาง

LAMPANG

11 hrs by train from Bangkok
9 hrs 30 mins by bus from Northern Bus Terminal

Lampang is famous for two things: its **taxis** and its **elephants**. The taxis are horse-drawn carriages imported from Victorian England and still in everyday use. The elephants are trained nearby for work in forestry.

Lampang can be reached by train from Bangkok in eleven hours. All trains going to Chiang Mai stop here approximately two hours before they reach that city. The fastest trains are the express railcars leaving Bangkok at 8:25 and 19:25. They arrive here at 17:53 and 5:35, at a cost of Bt444, the day train taking only 9½ hours. Cheaper is the rapid train leaving Bangkok at 7:45 and arriving 12½ hours later, at 20:20, for Bt146 third class or Bt284 second class.

Air-conditioned buses take only 9½ hours and cost Bt317 1st class or Bt246 2nd class. Almost all buses going to Chiang Mai from anywhere to the south will call in at Lampang.

The **Victorian carriages** are now overpriced, since they have become a tourist attraction. Instead of taking people where they want to go, they are now hired by the hour and generally end up where they began. It is just like New York, and not much cheaper either. Expect to pay Bt150 to Bt200 per carriage per hour. Taxi stands are located at Lampang Town Hall, the Wiang Thong Hotel and the Thip Chang Hotel.

The most important temple in the town is **Wat Phra Kaeo Don Tao**, an interesting Burmese style temple, famous because, for a period of 32 years, it housed

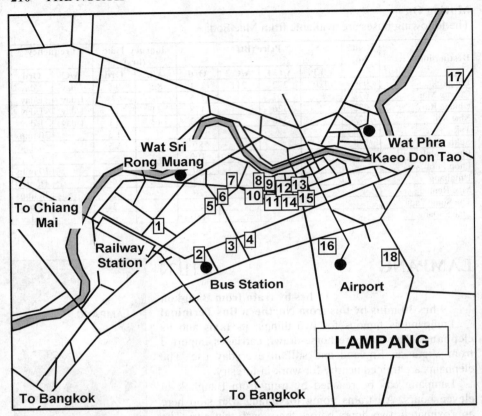

the **Emerald Buddha**, the most sacred Buddha in the country, now in Wat Phra Kaeo in Bangkok. Now it houses instead an attractive Burmese style Buddha.

Wat Sri Rong Muang is an old temple showing the art of stained glass decoration on its pillars.

The most important temple in the province is **Wat Phra That Lampang Luang**, which is twenty kilometres south-west of the town. It offers some attractive northern style architecture and houses a small Buddha with a solid gold base and a solid gold crown and necklace.

The elephants are to be found at the **Elephant Conservation Centre** at Ban Tung Kwian, which is 32 kilometres up the road towards Chiang Mai. The entrance is on the highway. Elephants are trained here for work in the forests. There are elephant shows at 9:30 and 11:00, and also at 14:00 at weekends and on holidays. Elephant rides are available too. This is not the only place offering elephant shows and rides, but it is one of the most popular.

Doi Khun Tan National Park is beside what is, in the author's opinion, the prettiest railway station in Thailand. Khun Tan station is at the northern end of the longest railway tunnel in the country. There are not many tunnels, in fact, and this one is only 1,362 metres long, but one often seems to have to wait here for an oncoming train. It is a beautifully lush and verdant station in a cutting, adorned with plants and smelling of nature. In fact, the park was first explored by the German engineers who excavated the tunnel a century ago. The park, which rises to an altitude of 1,272 metres, is within walking distance of the station. All trains stop except the express railcars. Accommodation, owned by the railway, is available.

Accommodation
Lampang

Name	No. on Map	Rooms	Cheapest Price (Bt)	Name	No. on Map	Rooms	Cheapest Price (Bt)
Wiang Lakor	4	100	1,050	Kelang Nakorn	14	102	380
Wiang Thong	3	235	1,000	Benjarong	18	46	350
Thip Chang	7	130	950	Siam	6	94	250
M.R. Palace	8	42	700	Rom Sri	12	40	250
Kim City	5	85	600	Kao Mithuna	9	48	200
Warissara Resort	17	35	600	Sakol	2	50	150
Asia	11	73·	500	Lampang	15	50	150
Pin	1	39	400	Arunsak	13	50	150
Kim	10	40	380	Super Highway	16	35	100

Moving On
Lampang is another town with few services originating or terminating, but many passing through. The following buses start here.

In addition, there are buses passing through to Chiang Mai, Uttaradit, Mae Sod, Tak, Sukhothai, Phitsanulok, Nan, Loei, Udon Thani, Nakhon Ratchasima and other towns en route.

Destination	Route No.	Price (Bt)				Journey Time (hrs)		Frequency	
		V.I.P.	A/C 1	A/C 2	Ord	A/C	Ord	A/C	Ord
Bangkok	91	490	317	246	176	9.5	10	10/day	4/day
Chiang Rai	146				70		5		20 mins

POSTCARD HOME—Bangkok, 10th July 1975

Dear Folks,

My bus from Chiang Mai to Bangkok was air-conditioned, which meant that the temperature was kept down to an average of about 85°F (30°C). The journey took about an hour longer than scheduled, and still an average speed of nearly 50 m.p.h. was maintained. Very dangerous it was too. On the way we saw the remains of several serious accidents, at least one involving a bus, which was not too reassuring.

CHIANG MAI   เชียงใหม่

CHIANG MAI

13 hrs by train from Bangkok
11 hrs by bus from Northern Bus Terminal

Chiang Mai is the second city of Thailand and the one place that those who take the trouble to make their way to the north inevitably visit. It is a much more likeable city than Bangkok, or indeed than most other big cities, and has a great deal of interest both in the city itself and in the surrounding area.

From Bangkok, it takes an average of thirteen hours to reach Chiang Mai by train. If you think that that is a long time, when the author first visited the fastest rail service took eighteen hours and it took me sixteen hours by mixed train just from the mid-point of Phitsanulok to Chiang Mai (see page 227). Now the air-conditioned railcar can reach here from Bangkok in a mere 11¼ hours. The day service leaves Bangkok at 8:25 and arrives at 19:35 at a cost of Bt481. If you want something cheaper, the rapid train leaves Bangkok at 7:45 and reaches Chiang Mai at 22:20 at a cost of Bt161 third class or Bt321 second class. There are also sleeper services on four different trains, at prices ranging from Bt421 for an ordinary upper berth on a rapid train to Bt681 for a lower air-conditioned berth on a special express.

The railway station is to the east of the city. There are some guest houses within walking distance (see map), but those within the city walls are a little too far away for comfortable walking. A *songtaew* should cost Bt10, but you will probably be required to pay Bt20.

Air-conditioned buses reach Chiang Mai in eleven hours from Bangkok at a cost of Bt369 1st class or Bt290 2nd class. They leave every half hour. However, there are also private buses operating, often at night, which undercut this price considerably. Such services can be found at travel agents along Khao San Road in Bangkok, for example.

The bus station, known as Arcade Bus Station, is in the north-east of the city, too far away to walk to most places. There used to be a city bus service in Chiang Mai, but it has been abolished, a retrograde step in the opinion of the author, because it leaves the city at the mercy of the *songtaew* drivers and, since there is an oversupply of vehicles, as you will soon see by looking in the corner of the bus station, those drivers are not very merciful. You will doubtless be accosted by a bevy of them keen to drive you to wherever you want to go for Bt60 or so. However, just walk over to the corner full of red vehicles and look for the next one to leave. You should be able to get anywhere within the city walls, or east of the walls but west of the river, for Bt10. Actually the statutory fare is Bt8, but you will find it impossible to travel for that price. An attempt was made by the authorities to regulate the *songtaew* to run on fixed routes at a standard price, but the result was a noisy protest by 5,000 *songtaew*, so the idea was modified. You will see on a board at the bus station a list of two *songtaew* routes. That does not mean, unfortunately, that the vehicles will run on these routes. In fact, they will ignore them completely. It is, however, a point for argument with the driver that you should be able to reach any point on the list for the standard Bt10 fare. The routes given are: Warorot Market, New Asia Hotel, Chang Puak Bus Station (local bus station), Teachers' College; and Thung Hotel, Railway Station, Sanpakhoy Market, Chiang Mai Gate, Suan Pung Hospital, Suan Dork Hospital. Note that red *songtaew* run to stops requested within the city area, while *songtaew* of other hues run from the city to other fixed destinations at prices determined by distance.

Chiang Mai is recorded as having been founded at 4:00 on 14th April 1296. King Mengrai ascended the throne of Northern Thailand (Lanna Thai) in 1259 and built a fortified capital at Chiang Saen on the Mekong. (We shall visit there later.) Then he built Chiang Rai on the Mae Kok River. Then he extended his influence further south and west and decided to build a new capital. He sought the advice of his friends King Ramkhamhaeng of Sukhothai and King Ngam Muang of Phayao in order to help him to choose a site and together they decided upon the area between Doi Suthep and the Ping River. Thus Chiang Mai was founded and became the capital of the Lanna Kingdom in its golden age.

The site was well chosen for a peacetime city, but in times of war Chiang Mai was vulnerable to attack because it lay so far west. The Burmese staged incursions repeatedly and Chiang Mai changed hands many times. Burmese power reached its zenith in the eighteenth century, when even Ayutthaya came under its control. The Lanna Kingdom was then obliged to seek an alliance with the southern Thai states in order to protect itself from the Burmese. It was this which eventually led to the unification of Thailand, with Bangkok as the capital.

Chiang Mai lies in a fertile valley surrounded by mountains, of which the highest is Doi (Mt.) Inthanon at 2,565 metres, the highest peak in Thailand. Chiang Mai itself is at 310 metres above sea level.

Sights in the City Area

There are so many things to see in Chiang Mai that it is difficult to know where to start and what to include in a book and what to leave out. There are, for example, more than three hundred temples in and around the city. Although this book mentions only the most important of the sights, these alone should keep you busy for several days. If you need more, though, and still have sufficient stamina, you should visit the tourist office and get additional information there.

Let us start with some of those 300 temples. They offer considerable variety of style, having experienced the influence of Lanna Thai, Burma, Sri Lanka and the Mon Empire.

Wat Chedi Luang is in the centre of the city and most impressive. You will be impressed when you enter the imposing gate and see the main temple building, but wait until you go round behind it and view the huge

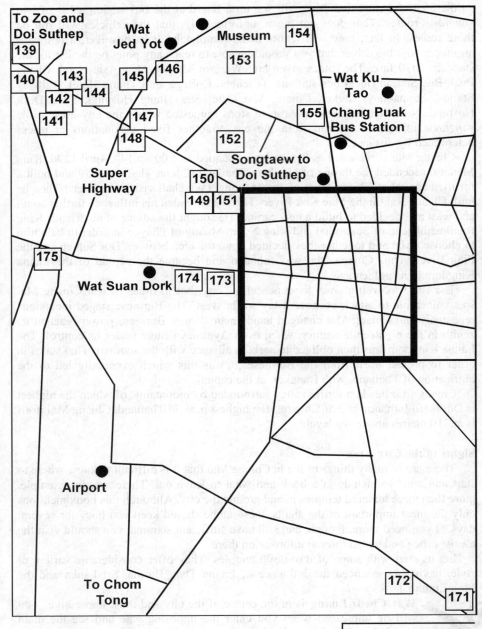

To Zoo and
Doi Suthep

139

140

**Wat
Jed Yot**

Museum

154

153

143

142

144

141

145

146

**Wat Ku
Tao**

147

148

155

**Chang Puak
Bus Station**

**Super
Highway**

152

**Songtaew to
Doi Suthep**

150

149 **151**

175

Wat Suan Dork

174 **173**

Airport

172

171

**To Chom
Tong**

CHIANG

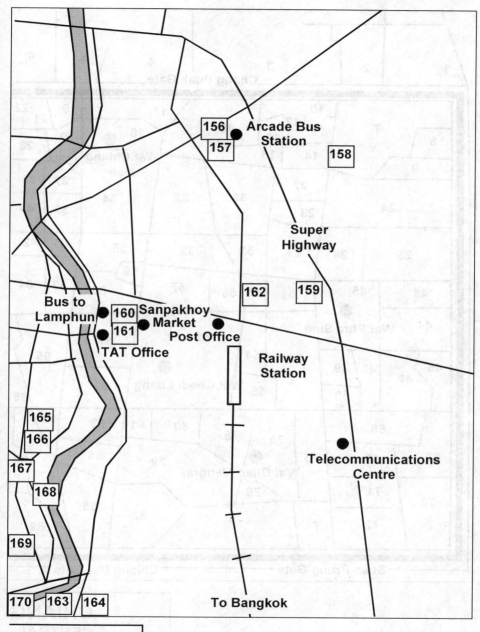

Arcade Bus
Station

156
157

158

Super
Highway

162 159

Bus to
Lamphun

160 Sanpakhoy
Market
161 Post Office

TAT Office

Railway
Station

165
166

167

168

Telecommunications
Centre

169

170 163 164

To Bangkok

MAI

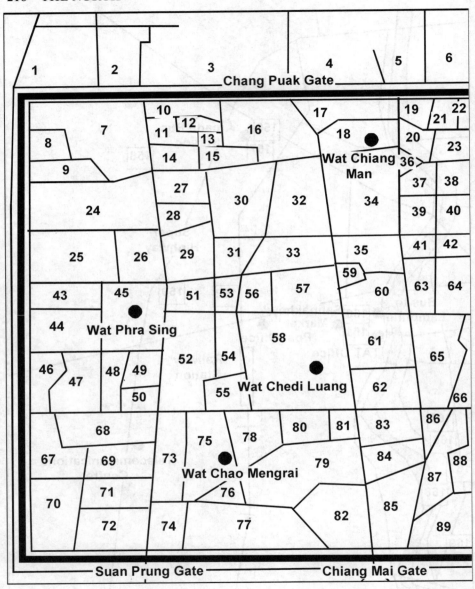

Chang Puak Gate

Wat Chiang Man

Wat Phra Sing

Wat Chedi Luang

Wat Chao Mengrai

Suan Prung Gate

Chiang Mai Gate

CHIANG
CENTRAL

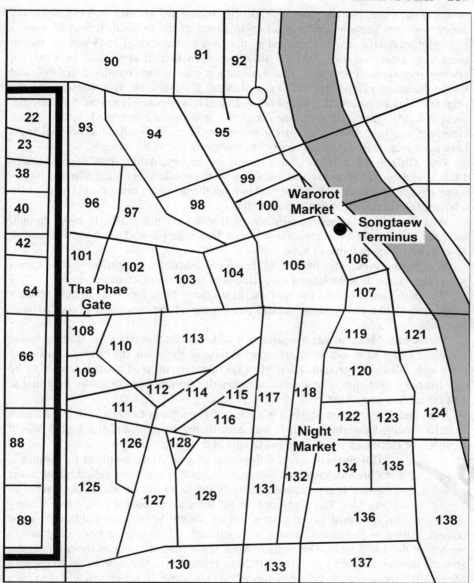

90
91
92
93
94
95
22
23
38
99
40
96
97
98
100
Warorot Market
42
Songtaew Terminus
101
102
104
105
106
64
103
Tha Phae Gate
107
108
113
119
121
66
110
120
109
112
114
115
117
118
111
116
122
123
124
88
126
128
Night Market
134
135
125
132
89
127
129
131
136
138
130
133
137

MAI
AREA

ruined *chedi* there. The temple was originally constructed in 1401. In 1454, the *chedi* which you now see was built, as an enlargement of the original. It was 86 metres high. Unfortunately, it was destroyed by the great earthquake of 1545 and has lain in ruins ever since, an awe-inspiring structure, even in that condition. In 1991, an attempt was made to restore it. The work took a year, being completed in 1992, and tourist literature claims that the restored *chedi* is 'every bit as impressive as the original'. Unfortunately, that is not really true. The concrete elephants, for example, look childish compared with the originals which have survived beside them. However, the ruin remains as strong testimony in itself to what the original must have been like. A Buddhist university operates from and in this temple.

Wat Chiang Man is the oldest temple in the city, dating from approximately 1300. It is thought to have served for a time as the residence of King Mengrai. It has a tiny crystal Buddha which is believed to have the power to bring rain. There is also a larger, finely crafted, Indian style Buddha.

Wat Phra Sing houses the most sacred Buddha in Chiang Mai. In 1992, though, the head of this statue was stolen and a copy is now in place. The *chedi* was built in 1345 to house the remains of King Kam Fu.

Wat Suan Dork dates from 1383, being constructed in the gardens of the Lanna Royal Residence. It is the largest royal chapel in the north of Thailand.

Wat Ku Tao is behind the stadium, near Chang Puak local bus station. It has a *chedi* shaped like five gourds stacked one on top of the other and decorated with porcelain.

Wat Chao Mengrai has a legend to it which states that when the Buddha statue for Wat Chiang Man was being transported through the town, the carriage broke and the statue fell to the ground. King Mengrai therefore ordered another temple to be constructed at that spot. The legend continues that he was later struck by lightning at that same place and killed.

Wat Jed Yot ('Seven Spires') is a copy of a temple in Bodhgaya in India where Buddha received enlightenment. It was constructed in 1477 and the Eighth World Revision of Doctrines was held in the temple at that time.

Doi Suthep is really the name of a hill. The temple at its summit is Wat Phra Borommathat Doi Suthep, but it is often just called by the name of the hill. It is a temple absolutely not to be missed and is the symbol of Chiang Mai. The problem is to get there at reasonable cost. Since Chiang Mai abolished its bus system and left the city at the mercy of the *songtaew* drivers, getting to places has become more difficult. There are plenty of *songtaew* to the top of the 1,678 metre Doi Suthep. Most leave from the foot of the hill near the zoo and they cost Bt30 to go up and Bt20 to come down. But how to get to the foot of the hill? There used to be a city bus to this point, for Bt3, but now it has to be a *songtaew* and the driver may well request as much as another Bt30 for this journey, although if you are lucky you may get it for Bt20. There are other possibilities though. If you do not mind a little waiting, there are also *songtaew* to the top of Doi Suthep leaving from the Chang Puak (north) Gate of the city. Cross the moat and you will see the *songtaew* just to your left. Those that go to Doi Suthep are few, so expect to wait half an hour or so for a departure. However, when the author last used this route, the fare was the same from here as from the foot of the hill. Another possibility is to find a group of people wanting to go to Doi Suthep and charter a *songtaew* to take you there and back and to wait while you look at the temple (which will take at least an hour, maybe longer). The charge for this should be about Bt200, so if you have three or more passengers it will be worthwhile. The ride is quite an exciting one if you enjoy being thrown around the back of a small vehicle. Admission to Doi Suthep is free, but if you do not want to walk up the long stairway to the entrance, there is a funicular railway for Bt10. The temple was built in 1383 by King Gue Na and the legend of Doi Suthep says that an elephant was sent to search for a suitable location. It climbed to the top of this hill, trumpeted, circled three times and fell on its knees. This was taken as an auspicious sign and Doi Suthep Temple was built in this place. The temple is truly beautiful, with its golden *chedi* glistening in the sunshine. Buddhist pilgrims from all over the world visit the site, and it is greatly revered. That means that one should be more careful than usual about clothing – no shorts or short skirts. No sleeveless shirts. Footwear is not so important, as you will have to take it off anyway. There is also a very fine view of the city of Chiang Mai from Doi Suthep.

Four kilometres further down the road from Doi Suthep is **Phu Ping Palace**, used as a winter palace by the royal family. It is open to the public on Fridays, Saturdays, Sundays and National Holidays only, except when royalty are in residence.

There is a **Meo Hilltribe village** a further three kilometres beyond Phu Ping Palace.

The **zoo** at the foot of Doi Suthep costs Bt100. **Huai Kaeo Waterfall** is nearby and near that is a **statue of Khruha Sivichai**, who made the plan for the construction of the road to the summit of Doi Suthep.

The **walls of the old city**, with their moats, have been preserved almost all the way round and are interesting to walk along, although a short distance will suffice.

Chiang Mai is famous for its **Night Market** which stretches along Charoen Prathet Road and into the minor roads which branch off. This market offers mostly clothing, handicrafts and souvenirs, but there is, of course, also a food section. Even if you do not want to buy anything, this market is worth looking at.

Trekking tours are easy to arrange from Chiang Mai, although most of the areas trekked are so accustomed to curious visitors that one could hardly call them pristine territory any longer. Nevertheless, it is interesting to view the way of life of the hilltribe people preserved even in the modern world and despite the daily incursion of van-loads of tourists. The principal cash crop produced by these hill people is opium, an industry which the government is under pressure to curtail. You will be able to judge how well such efforts are succeeding. Treks usually head north-west from Chiang Mai to the area on the border with Myanmar and, assuming a group of about six people, cost approximately Bt800 per day.

The main post office is near the railway station. It has international telephone and Internet facilities, but is open only for normal post office hours (8:30 – 16:30 on weekdays and 9:00 – 12:00 at weekends). Outside those hours, international telephone calls can be made from the Telecommunications Centre two kilometres further east on the Super Highway.

There is a **TAT office** in Chiang Mai in quite a convenient location just to the east of the river, beyond where the night market is held (see map).

Sights Outside the City Area
(i) Lamphun

To see more we must now look outside the city. One interesting nearby town to visit is Lamphun, which is only 26 kilometres away. Take a green bus no. 152 from near the TAT Office on the eastern side of Chiang Mai or a bus no. 181 or 182 from the Chang Puak Bus Station in the north of the city.

On the way you could, if you wish, visit **Wiang Kum Kam**, an old town founded by King Mengrai. This town is four kilometres to the south of the Chiang Mai city walls. The principal remains are **Wat Chedi Liam, Wat Chang Kham** and the bases of two other *chedi*. King Mengrai is reputed to have built the pyramid shaped pagoda known as Chedi Liam in 1288 in memory of the Queen, who had died while he was living here.

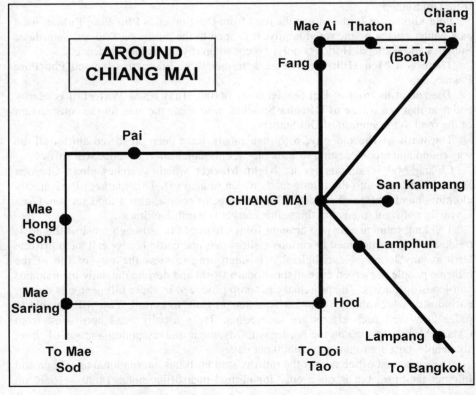

Lamphun is a city much older even than Chiang Mai. It was founded in 660 and its first ruler was Queen Chammathewi, whose statue stands in the town centre.

Not so far away is **Wat Phra That Hariphunchai** with a *chedi* 46 metres high which has 6.5 kilograms of gold on the top.

Wat Chammathewi, some way to the west of the main town, contains Chedi Ku Kut ('Topless Pagoda'). The temple dates from 755 and was built by the Khmer. The *chedi* is of Indian design and contains relics of Queen Chammathewi. It originally had a gold top, but the top has been broken off and stolen, hence its name.

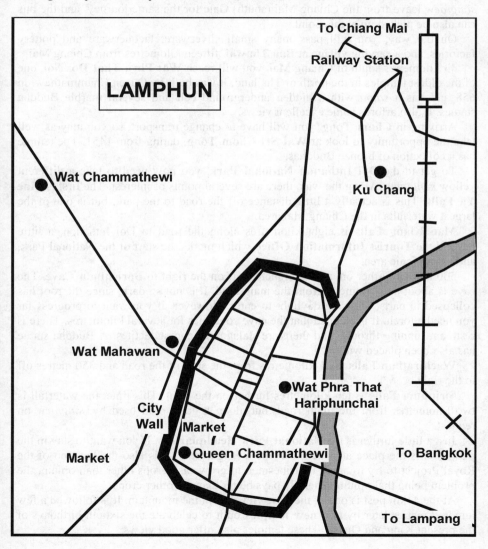

Wat Mahawan was built by Queen Chammathewi and is famous for its amulets.

Ku Chang ('Elephant's Grave') is to the north of the town and is thought to be the place where Queen Chammathewi's war elephant was buried.

(ii) Doi Inthanon

To start this journey south-west from Chiang Mai, take a bus or *songtaew* to Chom Tong. Blue bus no. 1232 leaves from the Chang Puak Bus Station every half hour for the 58 kilometre journey, taking 1½ hours and costing Bt20. Yellow *songtaew* leave from the Chiang Mai (south) Gate for the same journey, and the bus can also be picked up at this point.

On the way, you will pass many small silverware, lacquerware and pottery factories, and a carving village at **Ban Thawai**, fifteen kilometres from Chiang Mai.

43 kilometres south of Chiang Mai, you will reach **Wat Phra That Doi Noi**, one of the oldest temples in the north of Thailand. It was built by Queen Chammathewi in 658 and has a *stupa* with a hidden underground cell and several marble Buddha statues. It also affords some excellent views.

Arriving in **Chom Tong**, you will have to change transport, so you may as well take the opportunity to look at **Wat Sri Chom Tong**, dating from 1451. The temple has a collection of bronze Buddhas.

To get to the **Doi Inthanon National Park**, you now need to take a different yellow *songtaew*. Along the way, there are several points of interest. The first is **Mae Ya Falls**. This is actually a little distance off the road to the park, but is one of the largest waterfalls in the Chiang Mai area.

Mae Klang Falls is eight kilometres along the road to Doi Inthanon, a little beyond the **Tourist Information Office** which marks the start of the National Park, and has a picnic area.

500 metres further on, a road branches off on the right to **Borichinda Cave**. The cave is about one kilometre from the main road. It is not so dark, since the roof has collapsed in parts, allowing daylight to enter. However, if you want to progress far you need a torch. It is claimed that the cave continues for several kilometres. There is a stream running through and there are stalagmites and stalactites. A Buddha statue has also been placed within.

Wachirathan Falls is 21 kilometres from the start of the road and 350 metres off to the right.

Siriphum Falls is ten kilometres further on the right. This time, the waterfall is two kilometres from the main road, but along a good road used by *songtaew* on request.

Just a little further is the **National Park Headquarters**. If you want to stay in the park, this is the place at which to make arrangements. It is also the location of the Royal Project to try to assist hilltribesmen to grow cash crops other than opium, the problem being that opium generally pays better than the other crops.

At the 41km post is one of the **best views** from the mountain. It is followed a few hundred metres later by **two new temples** built to celebrate the sixtieth birthdays of the present King and Queen. These temples also offer good views.

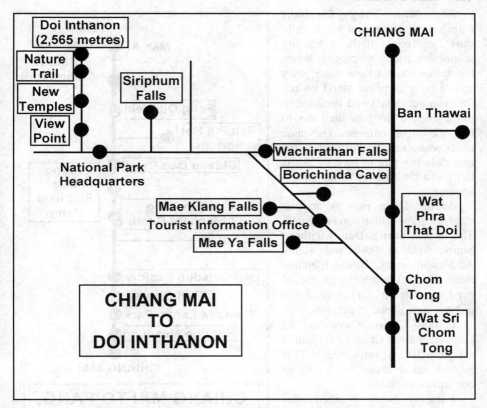

At 42km, a nature trail leads off to the right for a **three kilometre walk** through the forest.

The end of the road is a car park from which it is a short walk up to the summit of **Doi Inthanon**. At 2,565 metres, this is the highest point in Thailand.

(iii) Fang and Thaton

Fang lies 153 kilometres north of Chiang Mai and can be reached by bus no. 1231 or by an orange *songtaew*, both of which leave from Chang Puak Bus Station. The fare by bus is Bt48, but by *songtaew* it is Bt80, so better to take the bus. It is cheaper and more comfortable. The bus leaves every half hour. Here are the sights to look for, or at which to stop, on the way.

On the edge of the city is **Rama IX Lanna Park** and the **Hilltribe Museum** which illustrates the histories and cultures of the ten different hilltribes.

Lanna Golf Course is at the 4km post, evidence of the changes which have occurred in this country in the last few years.

The **Thai Celadon Factory** is near the 6km post. It produces pottery by traditional methods and can be visited.

The **Mae Tang Elephant Camp** is at 40km and has a daily show at 10:00. It is a training school for young elephants. When the author visited here some years ago, a baby elephant stood on my foot (no accident!) and declined to move even when I pointed out to him the inconvenience. The shoe never recovered, but fortunately the foot did. The fare to here by bus is Bt15 and the journey takes almost an hour.

At the 56km post is another elephant show which can be visited. This is the **Taeng Dao Elephant Show**, held at 9:00 and 10:00. Admission costs Bt60. Elephant rides are also available for Bt200 per hour. The bus fare is Bt20 and journey time about 75 minutes.

Chiang Dao Cave is 72 kilometres from Chiang Mai and is artificially illuminated. This journey takes about 1½ hours by bus and costs Bt25.

Fang is finally reached after three hours at a cost of Bt48. There are **hot springs** here, to visit which you should alight ten kilometres

```
                                    Thaton
                       Mae Ai  ●———————●
                                        (Boat to
                          Fang  ●        Chiang Rai)
              Fang Oil Well  ●
        Ban Pin Hot
          Springs    ●————————————●
        Chiang Dao Cave  ●
                          ●         Taeng
                                     Dao
             Mae Tang                Elephant
          Elephant Camp  ●           Camp
        To Pai ——————————

      Thai Celadon Factory  ●
           Golf Course  ●
      Rama IX Lanna Park  ●
        Hilltribe Museum  ●
                          ●
                  CHIANG MAI
```

CHIANG MAI TO FANG, MAE AI, THATON

before the town and take a *songtaew* for the eleven kilometre journey to **Ban Pin** (on the left). There are about fifty hot springs, of which three flow continuously.

There is also an **oil well** three kilometres before Fang. It can be visited, but usually only by request to the Northern Petroleum Development Centre in Fang.

Fang itself is just a small town, but it has accommodation if required. About half of the buses terminate here, while the others continue at least to **Mae Ai**, another small town, and five go on to **Thaton**, which is the most interesting destination for travellers, because from here there is a daily boat service along the Mae Kok River to Chiang Rai. The boat leaves Thaton at 12:30 and costs Bt170. It takes about five hours to reach Chiang Rai. To catch this boat, you need to take the 6:00 or 7:20 bus departure from Chiang Mai. The next bus, at 9:00, is likely to be too late as the bus ride takes four hours for the 177 kilometres. The bus fare is Bt55 to Thaton. Do not forget that this bus departs from the Chang Puak local bus station in Chiang Mai, not from the main Arcade bus station.

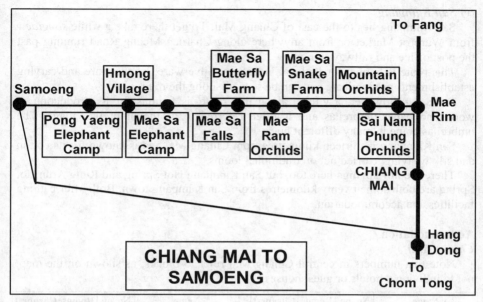

CHIANG MAI TO SAMOENG

(iv) Samoeng

To reach Samoeng, you need to follow route (iii) as far as Mae Rim, 16 kilometres from Chiang Mai, and then take a *songtaew* along the road which branches off left at that point (Highway 1096).

First you will come, after three kilometres, to **Mae Sa Snake Farm**, which has snakes from all over Thailand, breeding them and extracting venom. Demonstrations are given.

At almost the same point, there are three orchid farms, **Mountain Orchids, Sai Nam Phung** and **Mae Ram**, which accept visitors.

Mae Sa Butterfly Farm is at the 5km post.

At 7km is **Mae Sa Falls**, surrounded by large trees. It is just off the road to the left.

Mae Sa Elephant Camp is on the left at 10km and is the nearest of the elephant shows to Chiang Mai. This show is held at 9:30 every day.

Off to the right at the 12km post is a village of **Hmong Hilltribe people** following their traditional lifestyle (apart from the influx of several hundred tourists each day, of course).

A group of resorts now follows along this road, each offering accommodation in scenic locations at prices not at the lowest level.

Finally, at 19km from the start of the road and one kilometre off to the left are more elephants at the **Pong Yaeng Elephant Camp**.

If you continue all the way to the town of Samoeng, it is possible to take a *songtaew* back to **Hang Dong**, on the road south of Chiang Mai to Chom Tong, and return to the city that way. More resorts line the road from Samoeng to Hang Dong.

(v) San Kampang

San Kampang lies to the east of Chiang Mai. To get there take a white *songtaew* from Warorot Market or from anywhere along Charoen Muang Road running past the post office and railway station.

This route is known for its local industries. Silverware, lacquerware and carving establishments predominate and can be seen all along the road.

Bo Sang, however, a village along this route, is famous for its production of wood and paper umbrellas and is often referred to as the umbrella village. The umbrellas come in many different hues.

San Kampang is thirteen kilometres from Chiang Mai and is known for its cotton and silk weaving, carried out on traditional looms.

There are **hot springs** here too, but San Kampang Hot Spring and Rung Arun Hot Spring are both some twenty kilometres from San Kampang town. Both offer bathing facilities and accommodation.

Accommodation
Chiang Mai

Note that numbers in central Chiang Mai refer to blocks, as shown on the map, not to individual hotels or guest houses.

Name	No. on Map	Rooms	Cheapest Price (Bt)	Name	No. on Map	Rooms	Cheapest Price (Bt)
Al Farooq	168	80	700	Diamond Riverside	124	288	1,000
Amari Rincome	148	158	2,800	Dragon Guest House	133	13	500
Amity Green Hills	146	200	2,800	Duangtawan	131	50	450
Angket	158	100	1,500	Eagle Guest House	97	20	110
Anodard	83	120	300	Empress	165	375	3,300
Arcade Inn	156	114	500	Eurasia Chiang Mai	159	97	700
Baan Jong Come G.H.	113	20	400	Family	172	391	450
Ban Kaeo G. H.	137	20	400	Family Trekking	40	18	250
Ben Guest House	160	16	200	Fang Guest House	114	26	250
Bualawong Residence	166	120	1,500	Flamingo Guest House	114	9	100
Bualuang	143	24	450	Galare Guest House	124	35	730
C and C	3	20	100	Garden Guest House	58	17	150
Candy House	124	31	230	Gold City G. H.	39	18	100
Centre Place G. H.	125	30	150	Golden Inn	169	110	600
Chang Puak	3	57	300	Green Lodge	123	24	300
Chang Thai	101	11	120	Happy House	101	16	120
Chiang Inn	118	170	1,900	Holiday Garden	144	165	1,050
Chiang Mai Inn G. H.	96	38	250	Holiday Tour	84	20	120
Chiang Mai Orchid	150	266	3,000	Home Place	110	27	250
Chiang Mai Phucome	140	576	500	Inter Inn Guest House	109	60	200
Chiang Mai Plaza	137	444	2,800	Iyara	154	101	600
Chiang Mai President	90	128	950	Jame House	87	7	200
Chiang Mai Y. H. 1	87	16	200	Kim House	123	12	250
Chiang Mai Y. H. 2	171	25	200	Kinaree Place	88	80	450
Chiangcome	174	148	400	Kong Court G. H.	114	40	330
Chomdoi House	141	56	300	Kritsada House	87	12	120
Darets Guest House	101	20	100	Lai Thai Guest House	125	110	500

Chiang Mai (continued)

Name	No. on Map	Rooms	Cheapest Price (Bt)	Name	No. on Map	Rooms	Cheapest Price (Bt)
Lan Chang House	20	8	100	Racha Guest House	124	4	350
Lanna Palace	167	205	1,800	Rama Guest House	42	18	150
Lanna Thai G. H.	134	28	300	Ratchada Guest House	113	18	120
Lek House	96	21	120	Rendezvous G. H.	63	20	230
Libra Guest House	22	24	120	River Front G. H.	170	8	350
Little Guest House	5	7	250	River View Lodge	124	36	1,300
Living House	110	20	120	Rose Garden G. H.	40	10	80
Mae Ping	129	50	500	Rose Guest House	83	20	80
Midtown Guest House	113	26	150	Royal Princess	132	198	3,300
Mitrapap	99	86	370	S.B. House	18	7	210
Money Guest House	21	10	80	S.K. Guest House	23	24	200
Monthri	64	75	700	S.S.S. Guest House	6	24	100
Mountain View G. H.	16	30	250	Saitam Guest House	66	15	110
Mr. John House	110	10	100	Sarah Guest House	110	12	150
Muang Thong	88	21	120	Sri Tokyo	151	111	300
Nakom Ping Palace	164	117	700	Star Inn	131	80	850
Nantawan G. H.	162	20	250	Suan Doi House	147	25	350
Nat Guest House	83	21	190	Suan Dork Kaew	173	72	700
New Asia	98	198	300	Sum Fuen Fah	157	40	350
Nice Guest House	22	22	190	Supreme Guest House	21	16	200
North Star House	87	30	200	Tana Guest House	113	23	210
Northern Inn	3	100	400	Tanya Guest House	22	18	100
Novotel Chiang Mai	155	159	3,100	Tapae Place	113	90	800
Pang Suan Kaew	149	690	1,100	Tarin	145	170	400
Pangpon Guest House	101	10	200	Thailand G. H.	87	14	150
Paocome Guest House	96	12	70	Top North G. H.	88	90	350
Park Inn Tana	136	102	600	Toy House	88	9	120
Patchara	153	20	400	Travel Lodge	114	40	600
Pha Thai Guest House	87	12	120	Vista	18	62	1,100
Ping Payom	175	50	900	Western House	16	43	300
Plaza Inn	98	32	400	Westin Chiang Mai	163	526	3,400
Ploi Guest House	88	10	120	White Guest House	161	18	200
Pornping Tower	120	325	1,900	Winner Inn	130	50	500
Prince	94	106	900	Y.M.C.A. Chiang Mai	152	85	160
Providence	139	82	350	Your House	40	5	150
Quality Hills	142	249	1,800				

POSTCARD HOME—Chiang Mai, 6th July 1975

Dear Folks,

Yesterday I caught the train from Phitsanulok to here. I arrived at the station at 5:15 a.m. to catch the 6:00 train and found it already crowded, so I elected to let it go. It was an 'ordinary' train. Instead I decided to catch the 6:30 'mixed' train (that is, mainly goods, but with one or two passenger carriages on the back). The ordinary train was scheduled to take ten hours, but the mixed was supposed to take 12 hours and 50 minutes. However, I am past believing such prophecies now. It actually took 16 hours and 15 minutes, arriving in Chiang Mai a mere 3 hours and 25 minutes late at 10:45 p.m., at which time I had some difficulty in finding accommodation, particularly as the station is well out of town.

Moving On

Here is the train timetable for the journey from Chiang Mai back to Bangkok.

Type of Train	Ord	Rap *	Exp *	Ord	Rap *	Ord	Exp *	Exp *	Rap *†	Rap *†	Exp *	S.E *†	S.E *†	Exp *	Rap *†
Classes	3	2,3	2	3	2,3	3	2	2	2,3	1,2,3	2	1,2	1,2	2	2,3
Chiang Mai					0635		0825			1450		1625	1725	2010	2330
Lampang					0844		1016			1702		1845	1932	2158	0140
Den Chai				0620	1109		1225		1900	1938		2107	2153	0001	0415
Sila At		0720		0735	1210				2002	2039		2201	2247		0546
Uttaradit		0728		0747	1215		1321		2008	2046		2207		0056	0552
Ban Dalar		0755	0818	0824	1242	1301			2033						
Sawan Kalok			0740			1345									
Phitsanulok	0605	0850	0925	0935	1351		1440	1735	2142	2218	2300	2327		0204	0721
Lopburi	1118	1244		1434	1819		1755	2112	0300	0325		0347			1155
Ayutthaya	1242	1400		1616	1930				0402	0420		0446	0510		1320
Bang Pa In	1257	1412		1628											
Don Muang	1340	1444	1426	1710	2018		1941	2254	0449	0504	0358	0533	0557	0648	1400
Bangkok	1435	1530	1515	1800	2120		2030	2345	0540	0555	0450	0625	0650	0745	1455

Now here is a summary of buses from Chiang Mai.

Destination	Route No.	Price (Bt)				Journey Time (hrs)		Frequency	
		V.I.P.	A/C 1	A/C 2	Ord	A/C	Ord	A/C	Ord
Bangkok	18	570	369	290	205	11	12	30 mins	5/day
Nakhon Sawan	118				71		6		2/day
Nan	169			160	114	7	8	3/day	3/day
Golden Triangle	166		155		86	5	5.5	1/day	1/day
Phrae	169		180	140	100	3	3.5	9/day	2/day
Phayao	198		106	83	59	3	3.5	5/day	6/day
Chiang Rai (Direct)	619		119	92	66	3.5	4	45 mins	7/day
Chiang Rai (Lampang)	148-150/166				83		6		20 mins
Mae Sai	619		149	116	83	4.5	5	7/day	3/day
Chiang Khong	671		194	151	108	6	7	2/day	1/day
Mae Sod	672		207		115	6	7	1/day	1/day
Phitsanulok (via Tak)	155		227	176	126	7	8	6/day	3/day
Phitsanulok (Den Chai)	623				114		7		1/day
Sukhothai	155		196	153	109	6	7	4/day	5/day
Khon Kaen (via Tak)	175		414	322	230	13	14	2/day	5/day
Khon Kaen (Uttaradit)	633		369		205	13	14	1/day	3/day
Mae Hong Son (via Mae Sariang)	170		239		133	9	10	2/day	2/day
Mae Hong Son (Pai)	612				93		8		3/day
Mae Sariang	170		106		66	5	5.5	3/day	4/day
Pai	612				51		4		4/day
Udon Thani	636	480	369	287	205	13	14	2/day	2/day
Ubon Ratchathani	587	630	540		300	17	19	5/day	1/day
Rayong	659	590	505		280	15	16	5/day	2/day
Nakhon Ratchasima	635	458	392		218	12	13	7/day	2/day
Thaton	1231				55		4		5/day
Fang	1231				48		3		30 mins
Doi Tao	1232				45		4		30 mins
Phrao	1201				49		3		Hourly
Lamphun	181/182				12		0.75		20 mins
Lamphun	152				12		0.75		15 mins

MAE SARIANG   แมสะเรียง

●MAE SARIANG

13 hrs by bus from Northern Bus Terminal
5 hrs by bus from Chiang Mai

One of the very pleasant places to visit in the far north is Mae Hong Son, nine hours by bus from Chiang Mai. There are two routes, the old southern circuitous road and the new northern road through Pai. Half way to Mae Hong Son along the old southern road is Mae Sariang, which is a pleasant small town in itself and a suitable place to take a break if nine hours seems like a long time on a bus. Mae Sariang can also be reached in thirteen hours from Bangkok. There are two buses per day going to Mae Hong Son and passing through here. It can be reached from Mae Sod too – by *songtaew* in six hours, an exciting and uncomfortable journey.

The journey from Chiang Mai, which is the most common approach, costs Bt106 by air-conditioned bus or Bt66 by ordinary bus. The bus will head south first from Chiang Mai along the road to Chom Tong which was described in the section on Doi Inthanon under Chiang Mai. Thereafter it will continue to **Hod** where it usually takes a meal break. Hod can also be reached by local bus from Chang Puak Bus Station in Chiang Mai, some such buses continuing on to **Doi Tao Lake**. This is the other end of the lake mentioned in the section on Tak as having been formed by Bumiphol Dam. Boats and rafts travel the length of the lake, but are quite expensive. There is also raft accommodation available at prices from Bt200 per person. Doi Tao Lake is 35 kilometres from Hod.

When the bus continues from Hod to Mae Sariang, the mountains begin in earnest. From here it is up and down hill all the way. The **Ob Luang National Park** is 17 kilometres beyond Hod. Its star attraction is the Ob Luang Gorge framed by teak trees and mountains. During the rainy season a fierce torrent rages through the gorge. In other seasons it is more restrained but still attractive. *Songtaew* run here from Hod, in addition to the bus service. There is accommodation too, in the form of Khao Kriraj Resort, on the right just past the entrance to the park. However, it is cheaper, if less spectacular, to stay in Hod or Mae Sariang.

Further along the road to Mae Sariang, you will find **Tha Phanom Hot Spring** off to the right, then the **Baw Gaow Experimental Crop Station**.

64 kilometres before Mae Sariang is Om Koi Resort off to the left, following which there is a sign to **Pan House**. If you want to stay somewhere away from noise and bustle, you can try this. It is 75 minutes walk along a path. There is no road. The **Bua Tong** wild sunflower fields are next (blooming in November and early December) and then one reaches Mae Sariang. It is quite a small town, with a river running through, offering some temples to look at, as usual, and a reasonable range of accommodation.

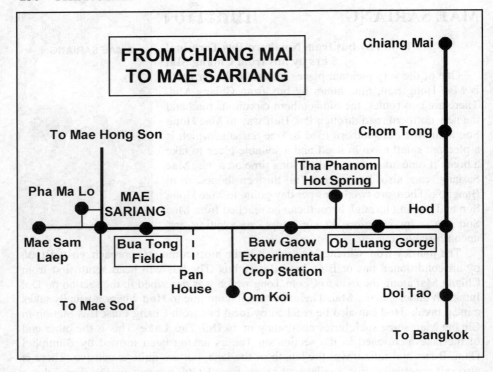

FROM CHIANG MAI TO MAE SARIANG

A Karen Hilltribe village is situated only three kilometres away at **Pha Ma Lo**. It specialises in the production of hand-woven fabric.

It is possible to take a *songtaew* west from Mae Sariang for one hour to the village of **Mae Sam Laep** on the Salween River, which forms the border with Myanmar. The village is in a deep valley, with Myanmar just across the river. There is a beach, and rafting on the river is also available and popular.

Accommodation
Mae Sariang

Name	Rooms	Cheapest Price (Bt)
Mit Aree	31	250
Kamolsorn	21	250
Mae Sariang Resort	10	250
Reungtara Guest House	18	250
Somsri Resort	10	250
Ekaluck	13	200

Name	Rooms	Cheapest Price (Bt)
Mit Aree Guest House	67	200
Seaview House	9	150
North-West Guest House	8	150
Salawin Inn	4	120
Riverside Guest House	10	80
Mae Sariang Guest House	16	60

Moving On

The following bus services are available from Mae Sariang.

Destination	Route No.	Price (Bt)				Journey Time (hrs)		Frequency	
		V.I.P.	A/C 1	A/C 2	Ord	A/C	Ord	A/C	Ord
Bangkok	961		400		235	13	14	1/day	1/day
Chiang Mai	170		106		66	5	5.5	3/day	4/day
Mae Hong Son	170		135		70	4	4.5	3/day	4/day
Mae Sod					150		6		4/day

MAE HONG SON   แมฮองสอน

MAE HONG SON

17 hrs by bus from Northern Bus Terminal
8 hrs by bus from Chiang Mai

Mae Hong Son can be reached by bus by two different routes from Chiang Mai. Both, however, involve long stretches of mountain road, not for the faint of stomach. The shorter and quicker is the new 274 kilometre northern route via Pai, which takes eight hours. The older southern route involves a distance of 355 kilometres and takes an hour longer. However, since our last stop was Mae Sariang, let us continue to describe the journey to Mae Hong Son from there (i.e. by the southern route).

At Mae Sariang, the road turns north and starts to aim for Mae Hong Son. On the way north one passes by hot springs on the right at **Ban Nong Hang**. There are also several hilltribe villages, but not immediately adjacent to the road.

Half way between Mae Sariang and Mae Hong Son is the town of **Khun Yuam**, with accommodation available. **Wat Muai Tor** has a large northern style pagoda and opposite is the Culture Centre with its **World War II Japanese Military Museum** displaying wartime artefacts and personal memorabilia. Seven kilometres away is the attractive Burmese style **Wat Tor Phae** ('Raft-Making Temple'), supposedly constructed by the workers who used to tie the teak logs together into rafts to float them down the river to the timber market.

Just beyond Khun Yuam, roads lead off to the left to a **wildlife sanctuary**, four kilometres away, and to the right to **Mae Surin National Park**. Within the park is **Doi Mae U-Kho** where wild sunflowers bloom in November and early December (only). Nearby is **U-Kho Falls**, 30 metres high and discovered only in 1987, where one can stand in the middle of the divided waterfall. The same road also leads to **Mae Surin Falls**, the highest known waterfall in Thailand. It drops 100 metres, but not in a single fall. Note that these sights are all a considerable distance from the main road. Mae Surin Falls, the farthest, is nearly 30 kilometres distant.

Pha Bong Hot Spring is reached some eleven kilometres before the town of Mae Hong Son, with **Pha Bong Falls** nearby. There is also **Pha Bong Dam**, which is used for a hydro-electric scheme.

So you will eventually arrive in the attractive isolated town of Mae Hong Son, a town which feels as much Burmese as Thai, except for its relative prosperity.

If you prefer an easier method of reaching here, Thai Airways flies from Chiang Mai three times a day (four in peak season) and the airport is in the heart of the town – round the back of the bus station, in fact. The cost is Bt390 for the 35 minute flight, which is not as expensive as one might anticipate. If you are going to fly anywhere in Thailand, this is not a bad choice, since it saves an uncomfortable eight hour bus journey at reasonable cost and gives the opportunity to view some beautiful mountain scenery from the air. Flights leave Chiang Mai daily at 10:00, 12:20 and 15:55.

Within the town, temples are the main attractions. The most famous is **Wat Phra That Doi Kong Mu**, which sits atop a hill overlooking the whole town. It can be reached either by road or by a set of steps leading up the hill. If you are on foot, do not try to walk up the road. It is much further, of course, and more arduous, than the steps. There are little rest houses at every corner of the steps, but actually the climb takes only ten to fifteen minutes. The temple is Burmese style and you will notice that here, as at most of the other temples, the inscriptions are written in Burmese as well as in Thai. The temple was built by King Phraya Singhanatracha, the first king of Mae Hong Son. There is a fine view from here not only of the town itself, but of range on range of surrounding mountains.

When you come down the steps from the hill, three more temples are waiting in line for you, **Wat Mai Hung, Wat Muai To** and **Wat Phra Non**, the last having a 12 metre long Burmese style Reclining Buddha, as well as the ashes of many of the kings of Mae Hong Son.

FROM MAE SARIANG TO MAE HONG SON

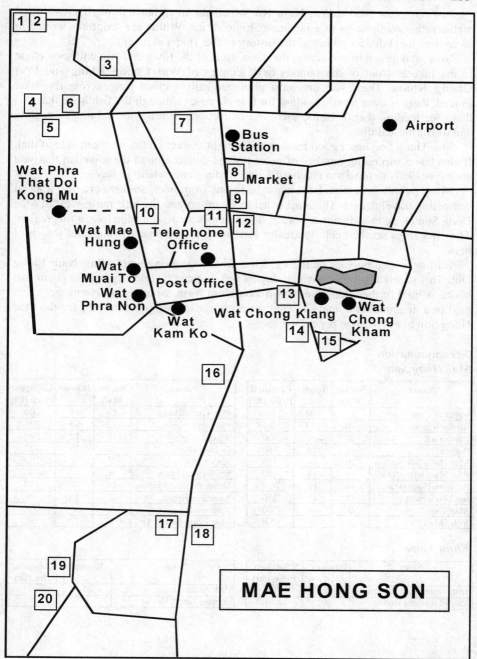

1 2

3

4 6

5

7

● Bus
Station

● **Airport**

Wat Phra
That Doi
Kong Mu

8 **Market**

9

10

11

12

Wat Mae
Hung ●

Telephone
Office

Wat
Muai To ●

Post Office

Wat
Phra Non ●

13

Wat Chong Klang

● Wat
Chong
Kham

Wat
Kam Ko

14

15

16

17

18

19

20

MAE HONG SON

Just across the road is **Wat Kam Ko**, which has an entrance through a row of red arches rather reminiscent of a Japanese Shinto shrine. Within are scriptures written in an ancient local dialect telling of the history of the Thai Yai people.

Now walk down to and across the main street of the town and you will soon come to the lake in front of the famous twin temples of **Wat Chong Klang** and **Wat Chong Kham**. These two are most photogenically viewed from across the lake. Indeed, there is even a little landing for that purpose (although the fish hope that it is there for feeding them). Inside there are collections of religious paintings on glass and of Burmese dolls.

Mae Hong Son has a good market and a night market on the northern side of that. It also has a surprising number of guest houses dotted around the town, so that you are never likely to have too much difficulty finding somewhere to stay.

Many people set off on trekking expeditions from here, so there are also a lot of competing travel agents. The most usual treks are up into the hills north-west of Mae Hong Son along the Myanmar border. The Long-Neck Karen tribe live in this region. They put rings on the neck, gradually increasing the number of rings and length of neck.

Rafting is also popular on the Pai River from Mae Hong Son to **Ban Nam Piang** Din. This scenic trip takes a whole day by raft, but can be done by boat in about two hours. A little further along the river is **Pha Hom Nam**, which is in Myanmar.

For a diagrammatic map showing the areas for trekking and rafting, see the Mae Hong Son to Pai map on page 236.

Accommodation
Mae Hong Son

Name	No. on Map	Rooms	Cheapest Price (Bt)	Name	No. on Map	Rooms	Cheapest Price (Bt)
Imperial Tara	17	104	2,000	Piya Guest House	13	11	200
Rooks Resorts	16	114	2,000	Pavillian	12	15	200
Panorama	8	36	900	River Lodge	15	12	200
Baiyok	11	40	750	Golden Hut	4	15	120
Mae Hong Son Resort	20	60	750	Jean's House	7	9	100
Rim Nam Klang Doi	19	39	450	Sri Wiang House	6	12	100
Penporn Bungalow	10	10	300	Diamond Guest House	14	6	100
Ing Doi Resort	18	12	250	Namapin House	1	10	80
Mae Thee	9	38	200	Rimtarn House	2	8	80
Yok Guest House	3	6	200	Mae Hong Son G. H.	5	12	60

Khun Yuam

Name	Rooms	Cheapest Price (Bt)	Name	Rooms	Cheapest Price (Bt)
Baan Farang Guest House	9	300	Mith Khun Yuam	25	120
Peek Mai Guest House	4	200	Holiday Guest House	3	120

Moving On

Here are the bus routes available from Mae Hong Son.

Destination	Route No.	Price (Bt)				Journey Time (hrs)		Frequency	
		V.I.P.	A/C 1	A/C 2	Ord	A/C	Ord	A/C	Ord
Bangkok	961		509		292	17	18	1/day	1/day
Chiang Mai (Mae Sariang)	170		239		133	9	10	2/day	2/day
Chiang Mai (via Pai)	612				93		8		3/day

If you choose to fly, there are flights to Chiang Mai at 11:10, 13:30 and 17:05.

PAI   ปาย

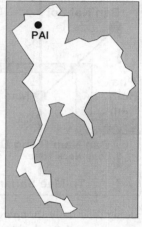

PAI

4 hrs by bus from Chiang Mai

At the time of writing, Pai is an 'in' place. Everybody who gets to Chiang Mai seems to want to go to Pai and the bus is crowded with foreigners. Of course, these things change, so by the time that this is read, Pai may well be going off the boil and some other small town may be 'in'.

Pai is the halfway point on the trip by the relatively new northern route from Chiang Mai to Mae Hong Son. It is 137 kilometres from Chiang Mai. Although the road to Mae Hong Son has been newly upgraded and paved, it was always possible to reach Pai by this route. It is the section between Pai and Mae Hong Son which is new (ish). One should not misunderstand, however, and think that it is a gleaming new four-lane highway. What it is is a twisting, turning, ascending and descending, narrow mountain road, but tarred.

Let us continue from Mae Hong Son to Pai along this relatively new road. After 17 kilometres, one reaches a turning on the left. This leads to **Pha Sua Forest Park**, which is ten kilometres away and contains Pha Sua Waterfall. If you continue further along this road, you will come to a **Meo Hilltribe village** and some other tribal villages right on the Myanmar border.

Just a little further down the main road, one comes to the **Fish Cave** on the left. Here fish lie in pools within the relatively cool cave.

As you pass through Tam Wua, you will see **Tam Wua Forest Monastery** gleaming in the morning sunlight (if it be morning, of course), and **Susa Waterfall**.

Accommodation is available a little further on at Wilderness Lodge, 1½ kilometres off to the left from a turning by a police check point (68kms from Pai).

Mae La Na Cave is six kilometres off to the left on a turning reached 55 kilometres before Pai.

And then we arrive in **Pang Ma Pha**, the mid-point between Mae Hong Son and Pai. The market here has many hilltribe folk, conspicuous in their tribal costumes,

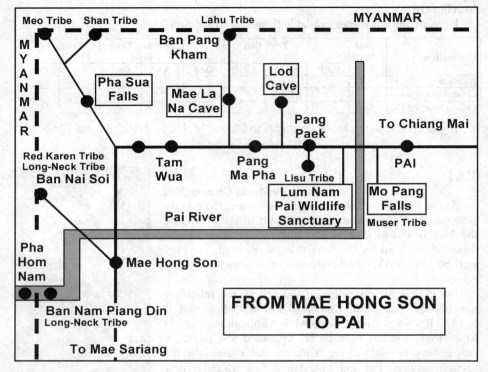

Meo Tribe   Shan Tribe   Lahu Tribe   MYANMAR

M
Y   Ban Pang
A   Kham
N
M   Pha Sua   Lod
A   Falls   Mae La   Cave
R   Na Cave
                                    Pang
                                    Paek   To Chiang Mai
Red Karen Tribe
Long-Neck Tribe   Tam   Pang   PAI
Ban Nai Soi   Wua   Ma Pha   Lisu Tribe
                                    Lum Nam   Mo Pang
                                    Pai Wildlife   Falls
                   Pai River   Sanctuary   Muser Tribe
Pha
Hom   Mae Hong Son
Nam
                                    FROM MAE HONG SON
         Ban Nam Piang Din   TO PAI
         Long-Neck Tribe

         To Mae Sariang

doing their daily shopping. There are several places to stay in Pang Ma Pha – in order
as we pass through the town, Jungle Guest House, Lemon Guest House, Remarim
Garden, Cave Lodge and Charming Home. There is a road off to **Lod Cave**, where
prehistoric remains have been discovered. It is eight kilometres to this site.

The **Lisu Tribal Village** is next, a little off the road to the right at Pang Paek.

As we approach Pai, the **Lum Nam Pai Wildlife Sanctuary** is on the right some
twelve kilometres before the town.

There are, of course, some sights to be seen around Pai. Nine kilometres away is
Mo Pang Falls, with a **Muser tribal village** nearby. **Muang Soi Waterfall** is in the
same area.

Wat Nam Hu is only three kilometres away from the town centre. It has a
Buddha dating from the Chiang Saen Period, the top of whose head opens, holy
water being kept within.

Then there is more rafting along the Pai River which runs almost through the
town. It is even possible to travel by raft all the way to Mae Hong Son, a journey of
some 70 kilometres which requires five or six days and the use of two rafts, as there
is one point in the river which cannot be traversed.

If we continue from Pai along the road to Chiang Mai, eight kilometres from Pai
we encounter **Pai Canyon** 200 metres off to the right.

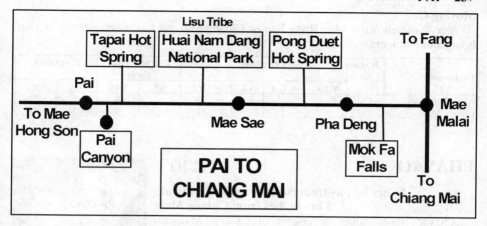

Tapai Hot Springs is ten kilometres from Pai, and then two kilometres more on a side road.

Huai Nam Dang National Park is at the 65km post (measured from Mae Malai). The park is six kilometres off the main road to the left and is planted with flowers and trees from temperate zones. There are several waterfalls, including the 50 metre Huai Nam Dang Falls. There is a Lisu Hilltribe village and there is a fine viewpoint at Doi Gew Lom, near the park office. Accommodation is available in the park.

Mae Sae is the halfway point between Pai and Chiang Mai. It is only a village, but accommodation is available at a Mae Sae Guest House right next to the bus stop.

At the 42km post, Pong Duet Hot Spring is 6½ kilometres off to the left. It is the biggest hot spring in Thailand. The geyser there spouts up to four metres in the air.

Pha Deng village is at the 29km post and, just on the Pai side of the village, accommodation is available at Pha Deng Cabin.

To reach Mok Fa Waterfall, at the 18km post, it is necessary to follow a side road on the right for two kilometres. It is a popular picnic spot. Freeland Resort offers accommodation one kilometre further on along the main road.

Finally, at Mae Malai, we rejoin the Chiang Mai – Fang highway and follow it for the last 38 kilometres back to Chiang Mai.

Accommodation
Pai

Name	Rooms	Cheapest Price (Bt)
Pai Skandia Resort	15	500
Rimpai Cottage	19	450
Hut Ing Pai Resort	25	450
Pai Resort	6	150
Pai Valley Rooms & Camp	10	150
Wiang Pai	15	100
Duang Guest House	10	100

Name	Rooms	Cheapest Price (Bt)
Golden Hut	8	100
Shan Guest House	10	100
River Corner Guest House	8	100
Pai In The Sky	15	80
Charlie's House	8	80
Chan Guest House	11	60
Kim Guest House	10	40

Moving On

Very little choice – Mae Hong Son or Chiang Mai, by bus. Each journey is four hours along mountain roads.

Destination	Route No.	Price (Bt)				Journey Time (hrs)		Frequency	
		V.I.P.	A/C 1	A/C 2	Ord	A/C	Ord	A/C	Ord
Mae Hong Son	612				45		4		3/day
Chiang Mai	612				51		4		3/day

PHAYAO   พะเยา

11 hrs by bus from Northern Bus Terminal
3 hrs by bus from Chiang Mai

Phayao, three hours north-east of Chiang Mai, is situated beside a large fresh water lake and is a place where travellers occasionally make a stop. There are direct buses from Bangkok taking eleven hours to reach this point. In addition, most buses from Bangkok to Chiang Rai stop at Phayao.

The main attraction is the lake itself. There are many restaurants along its shore, doing good business in the evenings especially.

Phayao was formerly a separate kingdom and during the late thirteenth century golden age of Sukhothai and Lanna, Phayao too was having its golden age under **King Ngam Muang**. His statue, standing beside the lake, attests to his influence here. Since his time, Phayao has lost in stature, however. It did not even become a province of modern Thailand until 1977, being previously administered by Chiang Rai.

Wat Sri Khom Kham is also on the lake shore. It is the principal temple of the town and has a very large Buddha within.

Further south along the lake is an area of old **traditional teak houses** which is worth visiting.

Accommodation available in Phayao includes Bungalow Siriphan, not far from the bus station on the lake shore, and there are other cheap to moderately priced hotels in the main street.

Accommodation
Phayao

Name	No. on Map	Rooms	Cheapest Price (Bt)
Gateway	2	108	1,400
Bua Resort	3	28	800
Phayao	1	75	800
Phayao Northern Lake	5	76	750

Name	No. on Map	Rooms	Cheapest Price (Bt)
Tan Thong	7	124	200
Bungalow Siriphan	4	20	150
Wattana	6	34	150

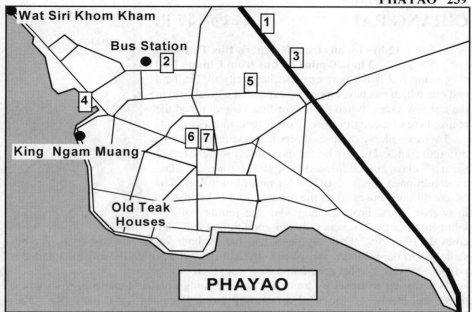

PHAYAO

Moving On

For trains, the nearest station is Den Chai, 141 kilometres to the south. There are bus services to the following towns.

Destination	Route No.	Price (Bt)				Journey Time (hrs)		Frequency	
		V.I.P.	A/C 1	A/C 2	Ord	A/C	Ord	A/C	Ord
Bangkok	922	565	365	284	203	11	12	5/day	3/day
Chiang Mai	198		106	83	59	3	3.5	5/day	3/day
Chiang Rai	621				30		2.5		
Nan	243				40		3		

POSTCARD HOME—Chiang Mai, 16th September 1980

Dear Folks.

An exciting event happened today. Somebody, a Thai, came and asked whether I would help him to use a stolen credit card. He needed somebody who might reasonably correspond to the name on the card, Mr. John Eaton, and was prepared to offer fifty per cent of the proceeds, although I should not be too confident of getting my share from such a person. He said that the card had been acquired in Bangkok and that it would be three days before anybody in Chiang Mai was alerted of its disappearance. I declined the generous offer, but had a look at the card and memorised the number (not so easy, because it was quite long—9458 096 040 941). Then I went to see what I could do. The police do not speak English, but I never had much expectation that they would be interested, so next I toured the banks, but they were disinterested too. One of them even assured me that the card had not been stolen because it was not yet on their list. Eventually I gave up and concluded that the man had been quite right when he told me that these were absolutely safe business transactions.

CHIANG RAI   เชียงราย

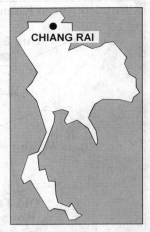

CHIANG RAI

12 hrs by bus from Northern Bus Terminal
3 hrs 30 mins by bus from Chiang Mai

Chiang Rai is the northernmost large city in Thailand and one which has developed and expanded a great deal in the last few years. When the author first visited, it had the atmosphere of a country town. Now it feels like a city.

There are plenty of buses direct from Bangkok, by two different routes. The fare by the more direct route is Bt412 for a 1st class air-conditioned bus, Bt321 for a 2nd class air-conditioned bus and Bt229 for an ordinary bus. The air-conditioned buses cover the distance of 805 kilometres in twelve hours. From Chiang Mai, the journey of 180 kilometres takes 3½ hours by air-conditioned bus and costs Bt119 or Bt92. Ordinary buses take half an hour longer and cost Bt66. The bus station is in the southern part of the city, but it is well within the city area and it is possible to walk to most accommodation from there.

If you want to travel by train, the best alighting point is Lampang, from where there are plenty of buses. The journey from Lampang to Chiang Rai takes approximately four hours.

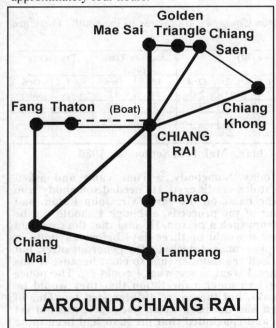

AROUND CHIANG RAI

Chiang Rai was founded by King Mengrai in 1262 and was the capital of his Lanna Thai kingdom until the construction of Chiang Mai in 1296. However, the city was later captured by the Burmese, and it was not until 1786 that it became part of Thailand once more.

Chiang Rai sits immediately to the south of the Mae Kok River and can be reached by boat along the river from Thaton, north of Chiang Mai. There is a daily service for those who would like to try this different mode of access. The boat leaves from and arrives at the Mae Fa Luang Bridge in the north-west of the city. From Chiang Rai, departure is at 10:30 and the fare is Bt170. The journey takes five hours.

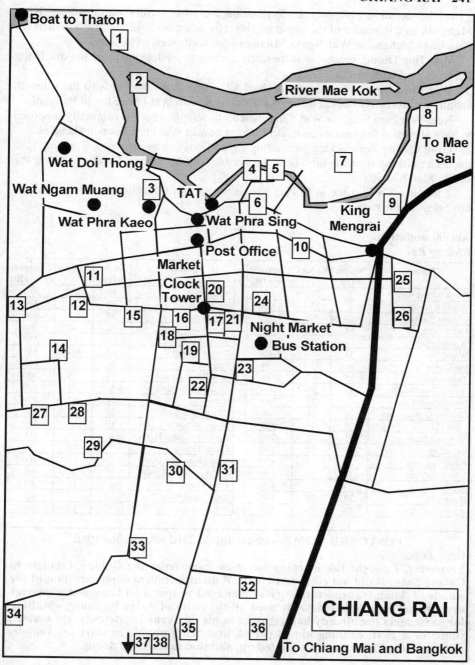

Boat to Thaton

River Mae Kok

To Mae Sai

Wat Doi Thong

Wat Ngam Muang

Wat Phra Kaeo

TAT

Wat Phra Sing

King Mengrai

Post Office

Market

Clock Tower

Night Market

Bus Station

CHIANG RAI

To Chiang Mai and Bangkok

In the northern part of the city, beside the road further north, stands **King Mengrai**, as a reminder of the city's origins. His ashes are held in a stupa named Ku Phra Chao Mengrai at **Wat Ngam Muang** in the north-west of the city.

Wat Doi Thong, nearby, is sufficiently ancient to predate the founding of Chiang Rai by King Mengrai.

Wat Phra Sing, almost opposite the TAT office, dates from at least the fifteenth century and formerly housed a Buddha which is now in Wat Phra Sing in Bangkok.

Near Wat Phra Singh is **Wat Phra Kaeo**, the temple which is originally supposed to have sheltered the famous Emerald Buddha now in Wat Phra Kaeo in Bangkok.

From Chiang Rai trekking and rafting expeditions can be arranged. Trekking is in the area north-west of the city, near the border with Myanmar. Rafting is along the scenic Mae Kok River.

There is a **TAT office** in Chiang Rai. It is in a useful location in the north of the city, close to the river.

Accommodation
Chiang Rai

Name	No. on Map	Rooms	Cheapest Price (Bt)	Name	No. on Map	Rooms	Cheapest Price (Bt)
Dusit Island Resort	2	271	3,000	Suknirand	16	105	350
Rimkok Resort	1	256	1,900	Paen Kiet Villa	34	28	330
Chiang Rai Inn	10	77	1,400	Napa Lodge	37	23	300
Little Duck	38	330	1,400	Tanapat	6	34	300
Wang Come	17	219	1,400	Tourist Inn	22	23	250
Wiang Inn	23	258	1,400	Krung Thong	18	110	230
Inn Come	36	110	750	Malina Ville	26	26	230
Thima Inn	13	47	750	Ben Guest House	14	26	200
Amorn Inn Resort	33	30	700	Gratom Rim Kok	8	20	200
Baan Khun Yom	11	22	700	Siam	21	52	200
Golden Triangle Inn	24	31	700	Chiang Rai Hotel	20	68	160
Saen Phu	15	100	650	Boon Bundan G. H.	19	53	100
Nim See Seng	31	78	600	Bowling Guest House	4	7	100
Ruenthip	35	78	600	Chian House	7	12	100
Baan Tue Son	32	20	450	Mae Hong Son G. H.	5	10	100
Yoo Suk Villa	30	20	450	T.P.K. Guest House	25	6	90
Art Ann	29	37	400	Chat House	3	15	80
Baan Silp	28	30	350	Lek Guest House	12	14	80
Bang On Court	27	30	350	White House	9	14	80

POSTCARD HOME—Phitsanulok, 23rd September 1980

Dear Folks,

Yesterday, I caught the morning *songtaew* back from the Golden Triangle to Chiang Saen. It did not come until 8:20. With an excellent demonstration of the whims of Asian transport, the driver managed to spend an hour and a quarter over the seven mile journey. He used all the ploys of Asian ingenuity - waiting for passengers (he already had eighteen in his tiny vehicle), detours, tea breaks, stops for a chat, running out of petrol, and being unable to start the vehicle, until even the locals were getting fed up, and that takes some doing.

Moving On

Here is a summary of buses from Chiang Rai.

Destination	Route No.	Price (Bt)				Journey Time (hrs)		Frequency	
		V.I.P.	A/C 1	A/C 2	Ord	A/C	Ord	A/C	Ord
Bangkok	90/909	640	412	321	229	12	13	11/day	5/day
Chiang Mai (Direct)	619		119	92	66	3.5	4	12/day	7/day
Chiang Mai (via Lampang)	148-150 /166				83		6		20 mins
Lampang	146				70		5		20 mins
Mae Sai	1241				20		1.25		15 mins
Chiang Saen	1245				20		1.5		15 mins
Chiang Khong	2127/2224 /2243				39		3.5		Hourly
Fang	675				40		3.5		1/day
Phayao	621				30		2.5		20 mins
Nan	611				90		6		1/day
Phitsanulok (Uttaradit)	651/663		250	195	139	7	8	8/day	5/day
Phitsanulok (Sukhothai)	622			195	139	8	9	3/day	3/day
Mae Sod	672		326		178	11	12	1/day	1/day
Pattaya	660	575	510		280	15	16	3/day	1/day
Rayong	660	600				16		1/day	
Nakhon Ratchasima	651	504	432		240	14	15	3/day	1/day
Nakhon Phanom	661		442		245	16	17	3/day	1/day
Khon Kaen	637		407	316	226	13	14	2/day	3/day

MAE SAI

แม่สาย

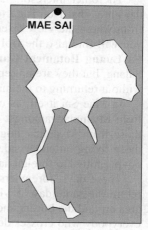

MAE SAI

13 hrs by bus from Northern Bus Terminal
1 hr 15 mins by bus from Chiang Rai

Mae Sai is the northern tip of Thailand, 62 kilometres north of Chiang Rai. The bridge across the small Mae Sai River at the end of the town is the border with Myanmar. Therefore, it is a frontier town and has a special character.

There are direct buses from Bangkok all the way to Mae Sai, a total of eleven buses a day, most of which, however, travel by night. The journey takes thirteen hours for the 856 kilometres and costs Bt 441 for a 1st class air-conditioned bus, Bt343 for a 2nd class air-conditioned bus and Bt245 for an ordinary bus. There are also buses from Chiang Mai, Fang, Mae Sod, Rayong, Pattaya and Nakhon Ratchasima, and, of course, a frequent service from Chiang Rai.

Although Mae Sai is a one street town, it has still been found necessary to join the club of towns with bus stations on the fringe of the populated area. The bus station in Mae Sai is five kilometres away from the town centre. The good point about Mae Sai is that there is a well organized system to deal with this situation so that one does not have to fight to get to town at a reasonable price. Red *songtaew* shuttle up and down between the bus station and the border. When you reach the bus station, you transfer, together with most of the other passengers, to the *songtaew* bearing the notice which says, 'This one next'. If there are sufficient passengers, two or three *songtaew* depart. Since each vehicle is full, the drivers do not need to overcharge and there is no dispute. The fare is a very reasonable Bt5. When you need to return, or to go any distance along the main street, there is a *songtaew* passing every two or three minutes and all rides cost Bt5.

There are hotels along the main street and a number of guest houses mostly congregated along the small river which forms the border with Myanmar. Of these, the most interesting are Mae Sai Guest House and Mae Sai Plaza Guest House. The former is right on the river bank, with Myanmar just across the narrow stretch of water. The latter climbs up the hill just back from the river, with each room designed to represent a traditional house of one of the various hilltribes. The higher rooms also have a view across to Myanmar.

Just west of Mae Sai are two interesting places. One is **Santi Khiri**, a hilltop village on **Doi Mae Salong** settled by Chinese nationalist soldiers who fled from their country in 1940 and sought refuge in Thailand. Their descendants now tend coffee plantations and orchards in this scenic area. There are places to stay and horse and elephant rides available. On the way to Doi Mae Salong, you will pass the **Hilltribe Development and Welfare Centre**, set up to assist the various tribes living in the area. Handmade products, including cloth and silverware, are on sale.

The other interesting spot is **Doi Tung**, a mountain rising to 2,000 metres with the Phra That Doi Tung temple at its summit. A road winds its way up to the top, from where the view extends into not only Myanmar but Laos too. Along this road you will find also the **Doi Tung Royal Villa**, which can be seen from afar, and the **Fa Luang Botanical Gardens**. *Songtaew* go up to Doi Tung, and also to Doi Mae Salong, but they are on separate roads and one cannot easily get from one to the other without returning to the main Chiang Rai – Mae Sai highway.

In Mae Sai itself, as one approaches the border there is a market selling goods from Myanmar, amongst other things. There are also sales of Thai products which those from Myanmar might want to take back with them, for it is not difficult for those living on either side of the border to cross here. Even when the crossing was not permitted to foreign nationals, locals could still go.

These days, foreigners can cross without the formality of a visa as long as they return the same day. A visa will give a longer stay, but one is still restricted to the area around the border and not permitted to travel across Myanmar. Therefore nearly everybody who crosses does so just for the day. If you wish to avail yourself of this opportunity, note that there are two different procedures according to one's purpose in crossing, as follows.

If you simply want to see what it is like on the other side, proceed to the border and, from a shop nearby which will be pointed out to you, obtain for Bt10 two copies of the identification pages of your passport. Then go to the Thai checkpoint and

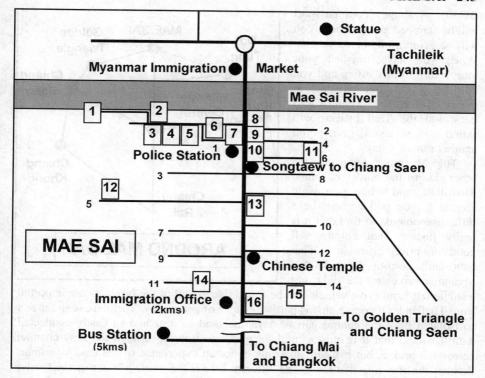

Statue

Tachileik
(Myanmar)

Myanmar Immigration ● Market

Mae Sai River

Police Station

Songtaew to Chiang Saen

MAE SAI

Chinese Temple

Immigration Office
(2kms)

Bus Station
(5kms)

To Golden Triangle
and Chiang Saen

To Chiang Mai
and Bangkok

present passport and photocopies. The official will stamp one of the photocopies, but he will not put any stamp in your passport. You then cross the border and leave your passport with the official on the other side, who puts the entry stamp on the other photocopy. He also requests in return for his services the sum of U.S.$5 or Bt250. Since the latter is considerably greater, try to remember to have $5 available for this purpose. When returning, you pick up your passport from the Myanmar office in exchange for the stamped photocopy, which you surrender. You cross the river and present your passport and the photocopy stamped by the Thai official. He retains the latter. Thus there is no record in your passport, or on any other document that you have, of the visit. It is as though it never happened. You do not get any extra time in Thailand.

If your purpose is to stay longer in Thailand, the procedure is different. Do not go to the border first. Instead, go to the Immigration Office, which is two kilometres back down the road (see map). There you present your passport and get yourself stamped out of Thailand. You are now officially nowhere – in limbo – so you are committed to the crossing at this point. Now proceed to the border. The Thai official will inspect your passport and let you pass. Cross the bridge and pay your U.S.$5 (or

Bt250), as above. Your passport will be stamped and retained. You will be given a numbered receipt. When you have finished your tour, return to this office and you will be given your passport in exchange for the receipt. Cross back and the Thai official will stamp you in again, giving you another month's stay.

The Myanmar town on the other side of the border is named **Tachileik**, and when you walk around it, you will perhaps be a little disappointed to find that it is really just a Thai colony. All goods are priced primarily in Thai baht and, despite the fact that Myanmar drives on the right, not a single left hand drive vehicle can be found. Nearly all of the products are imported from Thailand. Of course, this is partly a matter of geography. Tachileik is so far and so isolated from the central part of Myanmar and so near and so easily connected with Thailand that it is only natural for goods to flow in through the easy channel across the bridge, but it means that this is not an experience of the true Myanmar. Perhaps the only hint that things are different here is the statue just across the border of the Burmese king who conquered much of Thailand and was responsible for the sacking of Ayutthaya. That seems a little tactless, and then we charge Bt5 admission to rub salt into the wound! One notices that all the visitors are foreigners, not Thais.

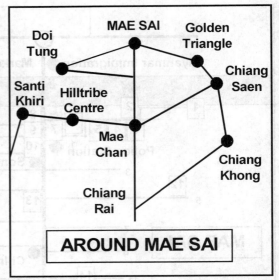

AROUND MAE SAI

Down to the right of the bridge as one crosses is another market – this time of all the things that one might want to bring back to Thailand. Here there is another little reminder that this is Myanmar, not Thailand, for one must think carefully about the appropriate price to pay. Unlike in Thailand, an item offered for Bt100 might well prove to be purchasable for Bt10 after some severe negotiation. There are certainly bargains available here for Thais, but for other visitors the appeal is limited. However, it is interesting to be able to say that one has been to Myanmar, and this is the cheapest place to go, for most of the other border crossings charge U.S.$10, instead of the $5 here.

POSTCARD HOME—Chiang Rai, 20th September 1980

Dear Folks,

From Fang, I decided to return by bus to Chiang Mai and then catch another bus to Chiang Rai. On reflection, I think that it was a cowardly way to do things. It would have been more interesting to try to cut directly through the hills. I am sure that it could have been done - with patience. I like Chiang Rai. For a start, it is a cheap place to stay - 15 baht for a single room, including free mosquitoes. It is also small enough to be able to walk round and see all the sights.

Accommodation
Mae Sai

Name	No. on Map	Rooms	Cheapest Price (Bt)
Wang Thong	8	148	1,000
Yunnan	16	30	700
Tai Thong	9	47	450
Ginpin Yunan G. H.	11	25	400
Top North	7	45	300
Mae Sai Hotel	10	40	300
Chonticha G. H.	15	15	200
Thip Sukon House	6	15	150

Name	No. on Map	Rooms	Cheapest Price (Bt)
Sin Wattana	13	31	150
Daw Guest House	5	15	150
Mae Sai Plaza G. H.	3	30	150
King Kobra G. H.	4	25	120
Chad Guest House	14	8	100
Mae Sai Guest House	1	25	100
Tom's Guest House	12	12	100
Northern Guest House	2	40	60

Moving On
Here is a summary of buses from Mae Sai.

Destination	Route No.	Price (Bt)				Journey Time (hrs)		Frequency	
		V.I.P.	A/C 1	A/C 2	Ord	A/C	Ord	A/C	Ord
Bangkok	957	685	441	343	245	13	14	7/day	4/day
Chiang Mai (Direct)	619		150		83	5	5.5	3/day	2/day
Chiang Mai (Lampang)	149				92		7		6/day
Chiang Rai	1241				20		1.25		15 mins
Fang	676				39		3		1/day
Pattaya	660	600	540		300	16	17	3/day	1/day
Rayong	660	630				17		1/day	
Nakhon Ratchasima	651		464		258	15	16	3/day	1/day
Mae Sod	672		348		193	12	13	1/day	1/day

GOLDEN TRIANGLE (SOP RUAK)
สามเหลี่ยมทองคำ (สบรวก)

GOLDEN TRIANGLE

4 hrs by bus from Chiang Mai
45 mins by *songtaew* from Mae Sai

The Golden Triangle is the famous point where Thailand, Myanmar and Laos all meet. The border between Myanmar and Laos is the mighty Mekong, while the border between Thailand and Myanmar is the Mae Sai River. Where the Mae Sai flows into the Mekong, at a place called Sop Ruak, is the point of the Golden Triangle and here Myanmar finishes and the Mekong becomes the border between Thailand and Laos.

When the author first visited the Golden Triangle, there was but a single isolated guest house there, the Golden Hut, and only one songtaew a day from Chiang Saen to this point along an unpaved road. The songtaew was at 17:00 and one sat and waited patiently at the junction at Chiang Saen until it appeared. The guest house did not have electricity and it felt like an adventure. Today that guest house lies sadly in ruins and luxury hotels are perched on the cliffs. Songtaew pass every thirty minutes and all the world knows of the Golden Triangle. Things change. Perhaps it is not for the worse, for in those days, twenty years ago, the trip was a hard one.

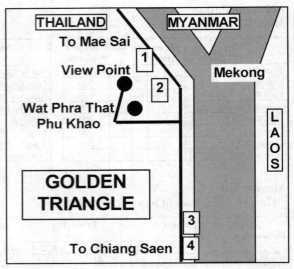

Now it is so much easier and so many more people can visit without too much difficulty. It is probably an improvement, but it is just a little sad to see the ruins of the Golden Hut, just as it is sad to see the ruins of a kingdom founded a millennium ago at Chiang Saen just down the road.

Blue songtaew run every half hour between Mae Sai and Chiang Saen. From Mae Sai they start at 9:00, but from Chiang Saen at 7:00. Our last stop was Mae Sai, so let us continue from there. The starting point for songtaew is, luckily, in the main street, not at the bus station (see map of Mae Sai). To the Golden Triangle costs Bt25 and takes 45 minutes. A single photograph can look from Thailand across the point of Myanmar into Laos – very economical!

Boats are available for hire, either for just a trip around the junction of the rivers or down the Mekong to Chiang Saen. Try not to take them, as their main purpose seems to be to create a degree of noise that will let everybody know just how important they are. This used to be a tranquil spot, and we can certainly manage without those whose whole purpose is to destroy tranquillity.

At the Golden Triangle, a road leads up to **Wat Phra That Phu Khao**, an old temple with ruins on the top of the hill. There is also a good viewpoint across the Golden Triangle, so it is worth walking up. You may find a group of children there too, dressed in hilltribe costume and chanting in unison, "Take a photo, twenty baht", for the benefit of every minibus-load of foreigners which arrives.

When you have finished, songtaew run on to Chiang Saen, a distance of nine kilometres, for Bt10. There are also hotels and guest houses in the vicinity of the Golden Triangle if you prefer.

Two buses a day run from Chiang Mai directly to the Golden Triangle. Both arrive in the early evening and return in the early morning, which may be useful.

Since these buses sleep in Chiang Saen, there is also an early evening and early morning bus service in the opposite direction between Chiang Saen and the Golden Triangle. One bus is an air-conditioned bus and one an ordinary bus.

Accommodation
Golden Triangle

Name	No. on Map	Rooms	Cheapest Price (Bt)	Name	No. on Map	Rooms	Cheapest Price (Bt)
Le Meridien Ban Boran	1	110	2,400	Akha Guest House	3	15	150
Imperial Golden Triangle	2	73	1,700	Bamboo Hut G. H.	4	12	150

Moving On
Only the following limited services are available from the Golden Triangle.

Destination	Route No.	Price (Bt)				Journey Time (hrs)		Frequency	
		V.I.P.	A/C 1	A/C 2	Ord	A/C	Ord	A/C	Ord
Chiang Mai	166		155		86	5	5.5	1/day	1/day
Mai Sai	Blue				25		0.75		30 mins
Chiang Saen	Blue				10		0.25		30 mins

CHIANG SAEN　　　เชียงแสน

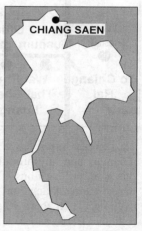

CHIANG SAEN

13 hrs by bus from Northern Bus Terminal
1 hr 30 mins by bus from Chiang Rai

The Chiang Saen Period existed prior to the founding of the Lanna Thai Kingdom and the establishment of Chiang Rai by King Mengrai. It is amazing to think that this sleepy little town was once the centre of a civilization and has given its name to a period of history. The present town consists of two streets, one parallel to and beside the Mekong and one, the main street, running at right angles to the river. It is a town of ruins. They are everywhere – in the main street and in every little road running off it – many of them overgrown with trees, but fascinating to wander around. It seems as though there are just so many ancient ruins that historians are overwhelmed by them and cannot take care of all. The old city is surrounded by a three-sided eight kilometre wall, the Mekong forming the fourth side. This wall far outstretches the limits of the present town.

There are two direct night buses from Bangkok to Chiang Saen, one air-conditioned and one not. The air-conditioned bus does the trip in thirteen hours, at a cost of Bt470. The ordinary bus takes an hour longer, but costs only Bt261. There is also a frequent service from Chiang Rai, costing Bt20 and taking an hour and a half.

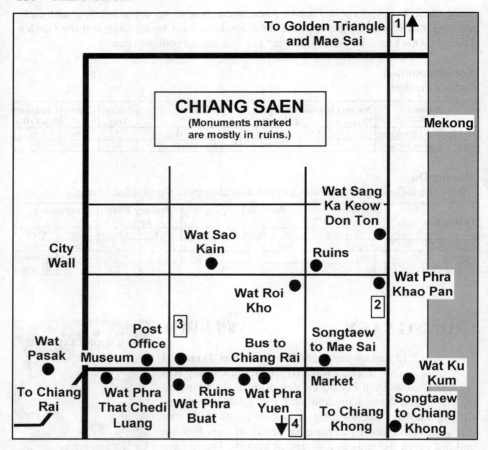

CHIANG SAEN
(Monuments marked
are mostly in ruins.)

To Golden Triangle
and Mae Sai [1]

Mekong

Wat Sang
Ka Keow
Don Ton

City
Wall

Wat Sao
Kain

Ruins

Wat Phra
Khao Pan

Wat Roi
Kho

[2]

Post
Office
[3]

Wat
Pasak

Museum

Bus to
Chiang Rai

Songtaew
to Mae Sai

Wat Ku
Kum

To Chiang
Rai

Wat Phra
That Chedi
Luang

Ruins
Wat Phra
Buat

Wat Phra
Yuen

Market

To Chiang
Khong

Songtaew
to Chiang
Khong

[4]

Two green buses leave in the early morning, actually originating at the Golden Triangle, and run through to Chiang Mai. One of these buses is air-conditioned and one is an ordinary bus. The journey to Chiang Mai takes about five hours. The same buses leave Chiang Mai in the early afternoon and reach Chiang Saen in the early evening. Then there is a *songtaew* service to and from the Golden Triangle (15 minutes, Bt10) and Mae Sai (1 hour, Bt30) and one to and from Chiang Khong (2 hours, Bt30). The Mae Sai *songtaew* is blue and the Chiang Khong one green.

The principal attraction of Chiang Saen, of course, is the ruins and it does not require much walking to reach them. See the map above for the ruins in the central area of the town. There are plenty more, though, if you want to go further afield. The best preserved of the ruins is **Wat Pasak**, just outside the city wall, and for this alone there is a charge of Bt30. All the other sites are free.

Nearby and just inside the walls is **Wat Phra That Chedi Luang**. The temple is still in use and the *chedi* in good condition.

Beside the temple is the **Chiang Saen National Museum** which has a good collection of Buddha statues and other local historical items. Admission costs Bt30.

Apart from the history, the town has a pleasant atmosphere because of its location next to the Mekong. There is the usual red brick promenade here beside its banks and in the evening a night market of food stalls arrives and sets up tables along the promenade.

Accommodation

As for accommodation, Chiang Saen Guest House is right beside the river and conveniently close to the centre of the town. Jin's Guest House is further along towards the Golden Triangle, pleasantly rural, but rather a long walk from the town. J.S. Guest House is right in town, but not adjacent to the river. Much more expensive is Chiang Saen River Hill Hotel, which is also a way from the town centre.

Chiang Saen

Name	No. on Map	Rooms	Cheapest Price (Bt)	Name	No. on Map	Rooms	Cheapest Price (Bt)
Chiang Saen River Hill	4	63	1,500	J.S. Guest House	3	9	120
Jin's Guest House	1	13	120	Chiang Saen G. H.	2	15	100

Moving On

Here is a summary of bus services available.

Destination	Route No.	Price (Bt)				Journey Time (hrs)		Frequency	
		V.I.P.	A/C 1	A/C 2	Ord	A/C	Ord	A/C	Ord
Bangkok	910	730	470		261	13	14	1/day	1/day
Chiang Mai	166		150		83	5	5.5	1/day	1/day
Chiang Rai	1245				20		1.5		15 mins
Mai Sai	Blue				30		1		30 mins
Golden Triangle	Blue				10		0.25		30 mins
Chiang Khong	Green				30		2		Hourly

CHIANG KHONG   เชียงของ

CHIANG KHONG

14 hrs by bus from Northern Bus Terminal
3 hrs 30 mins by bus from Chiang Rai

Chiang Khong is a small town 53 kilometres south from Chiang Saen along the Mekong. Buses run directly from Bangkok, taking fourteen hours over the 875 kilometre journey. The fares are Bt450 for a 1st class air-conditioned bus, Bt350 for a 2nd class air-conditioned bus and Bt250 for an ordinary bus. There are also services from Chiang Rai and Chiang Mai. From Chiang Rai buses take 3½ hours and cost Bt39. The service operates hourly.

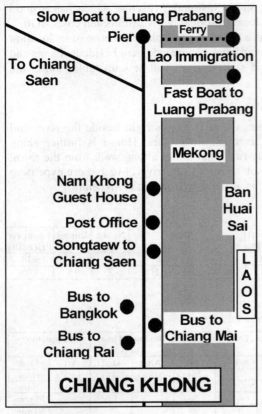

Slow Boat to Luang Prabang

Pier

Ferry

To Chiang Saen

Lao Immigration

Fast Boat to Luang Prabang

Mekong

Nam Khong Guest House

Post Office

Songtaew to Chiang Saen

Bus to Bangkok

Bus to Chiang Rai

Ban Huai Sai

L A O S

Bus to Chiang Mai

CHIANG KHONG

From Chiang Mai there are three buses every day costing Bt194, Bt151 and Bt108. The journey takes six to seven hours. There is also a *songtaew* service from Chiang Saen taking two hours and costing Bt30.

Chiang Khong is another of the pleasant little towns beside the Mekong. The most common reason for a visit here is that it is a crossing place to Laos. A short itinerary in Laos often involves entering at Nong Khai, visiting Vientiane, proceeding to the royal city of Luang Prabang, then by bus or boat to **Ban Huai Sai**, which is immediately opposite Chiang Khong, and leaving the country by that crossing point.

Chiang Khong is also known for its cloth production and for the giant Pla Buk fish which are caught in the river here. They are claimed to be the biggest freshwater fish in the world, growing to as long as 2½ metres and weighing as much as 300 kilograms – a pretty good lunch.

If you decide to cross into Laos at this point, from Ban Huai Sai you can take boats to Pak Bang and Luang Prabang. There is both a fast boat and a slow one, each operating daily. The fast boat leaves at 9:00 and the slow one at 11:00. To Pak Bang the journey takes four hours by fast boat and nearly a day by slow boat. To Luang Prabang takes eight hours by fast boat and two days and one night by slow boat.

Accommodation
Chiang Khong

Name	Rooms	Cheapest Price (Bt)	Name	Rooms	Cheapest Price (Bt)
Ban Golden Triangle	5	750	Nam Khong Guest House	10	120
Chiang Khong Hotel	35	150	Ruen Thai Sopaphan	25	90
Ban Tammila	9	120	Orchid Garden G. H.	10	60

Moving On

Buses from Chiang Khong are as follows.

Destination	Route No.	Price (Bt)				Journey Time (hrs)		Frequency	
		V.I.P.	A/C 1	A/C 2	Ord	A/C	Ord	A/C	Ord
Bangkok	962		450	350	250	14	15	8/day	8/day
Chiang Mai	671		194	151	108	6	7	2/day	1/day
Chiang Rai	2127/2224 /2243				39		3.5		Hourly
Chiang Saen	Green				30		2		Hourly

NAN

น่าน

NAN

11 hrs by bus from Northern Bus Terminal

Direct buses from Bangkok take eleven hours to reach Nan by two different routes. Most of these buses operate by night. Fares by the route most frequently used are Bt351 for a 1st class air-conditioned bus, Bt273 for a 2nd class air-conditioned bus and Bt195 for an ordinary bus. There are also services from Chiang Mai, Chiang Rai, Phitsanulok and intermediate towns.

Within Nan, several different bus terminals are used (see map), but the town is small enough to make this no major problem.

Nan is a pleasant town of an agreeable size, which had its time of great popularity with travellers a few years ago and has now calmed down to be a place visited if time permits. It is an old city, so, predictably, many of the attractions are temples.

Wat Chae Haeng is one of the oldest temples, dating from the fifteenth century. However, it lies three kilometres east of the town centre, across the river.

In the town is **Wat Suan Tan** which has an impressive decorated *chedi* and a large bronze Buddha.

Wat Chang Kham is a royal monastery founded in 1426, with a golden Buddha and a *chedi* decorated with sculpted elephants.

Almost opposite is **Wat Phu Min**, with an unusual design and beautiful architecture, including carved wooden doors made by Lanna Thai craftsmen, and mural paintings.

Wat Khao Noi sits on top of Khao Noi Hill, some 250 metres high, two kilometres to the south-west of the town.

Near Wat Chiang Kham and Wat Phu Min is the **Nan National Museum**. Its most famous exhibit is a black ivory elephant tusk 94cms long and 18kg in weight.

Other attractions lie outside Nan and need time to visit. One hour (44km) north by bus is **Wat Nong Bua** which was built by migrants from South China. There are

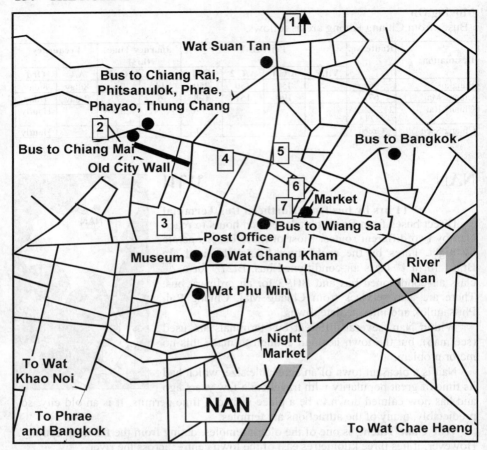

Wat Suan Tan

Bus to Chiang Rai,
Phitsanulok, Phrae,
Phayao, Thung Chang

2

Bus to Chiang Mai
Old City Wall

4

5

Bus to Bangkok

6

7

Market

3

Post Office

Bus to Wiang Sa

Museum   Wat Chang Kham

River
Nan

Wat Phu Min

Night
Market

To Wat
Khao Noi

NAN

To Phrae
and Bangkok

To Wat Chae Haeng

mural paintings of a style similar to that in Wat Phu Min. Take a bus no. 2187, going
to Thung Chang, to reach Wat Nong Bua. The bus to Chiang Rai also passes this
point, but there is only one such bus each day.

On the same route, but only twelve kilometres from Nan, is the **Pha Tup Forest
Park**, which contains a number of caves, as well, of course, as many trees.

To the north-east of Nan, along the border with Laos, is the **Doi Phu Kha
National Park**, rising to a height of 1,980 metres. It also contains the **Ban Bor
Kleua Salt Wells**, where salt can be extracted from the ground simply by
evaporation. On the road there, you will pass **Ton Tong Falls** and **Pha Khong Cave**,
both also within the park.

38 kilometres north-east of Nan at **Ban Nam Yao** is a former refugee camp for
people fleeing from Laos. At one time, this camp held as many as 60,000 displaced
people.

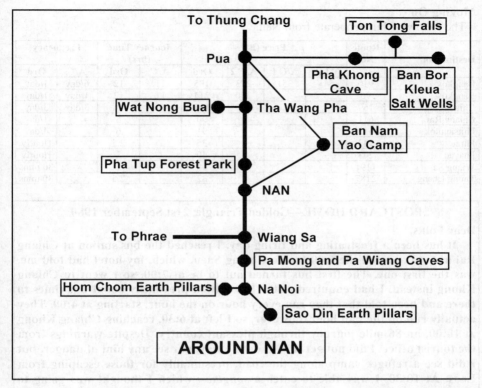

AROUND NAN

South of Nan are the **Hom Chom and Sao Din Earth Pillars** formed by wind erosion of surrounding softer ground. First take a bus no. 1191 to Wiang Sa, from where it is a further 36 kilometres by *songtaew* to Na Noi, the nearest town to this feature. The Hom Chom pillars are about one kilometre from this point, and the Sao Din pillars six kilometres.

On the same route, ten kilometres beyond Wiang Sa, are the **Pa Mong and Pa Wiang caves**, with stalagmites and stalactites.

Back in the town of Nan, the Nan River flowing through is an attraction in itself, and has parkland on the city bank. In the evenings it is the site of a night market.

Accommodation
Nan

Name	No. on Map	Rooms	Cheapest Price (Bt)
Dhevaraj	7	154	600
Fah Thanin	2	56	450
Nan Fah	6	14	450
Suk Kasem	4	43	200

Name	No. on Map	Rooms	Cheapest Price (Bt)
Amon Sri	5	16	150
Amazing Guest House	1	12	120
Nan Guest House	3	15	120

Moving On

The following buses operate from Nan.

Destination	Route No.	Price (Bt)				Journey Time (hrs)		Frequency	
		V.I.P.	A/C 1	A/C 2	Ord	A/C	Ord	A/C	Ord
Bangkok	910	545	351	273	195	11	12	6/day	1/day
Bangkok	96			300	214	11	12	1/day	1/day
Chiang Mai	169			160	114	7	8	3/day	3/day
Chiang Rai	611				90		6		1/day
Phitsanulok	613				91		6		4/day
Phrae	143				35		2.5		Hourly
Phayao	243				40		3		Hourly
Wiang Sa	1191				15		1		30 mins
Thung Chang	2187				32		2.5		30 mins

POSTCARD HOME—Golden Triangle, 21st September 1980

Dear Folks,

It has been a frustrating and tiring day. I reached the bus station at Chiang Rai at 5:40 to catch the 6:00 bus to Chiang Saen, which, my hotel had told me, was the first one. The first bus turned out to be at 7:00, so I went to Chiang Khong instead. I had enquired at the bus station previously about bus times to there and been told that they ran every hour on the hour, starting at 4:00. They actually run on the half hour, however, so I left at 6:30, reaching Chiang Khong at 10:00, an 86 mile journey through pleasant country. Despite warnings from the tourist office, I did not get shot at on the way, nor see any hint of danger, but I did see a refugee camp along the road, presumably for those escaping from Laos. At 10:30, I was able to catch a *songtaew* which I thought was going to Chiang Saen. In fact, however, it went only half way, about nineteen miles, along a very poor road through some magnificent hill countryside beside the Mekong. The nineteen miles took two hours and ten minutes, which gives some idea of road conditions, and it was a very expensive journey (20 baht). However, it was worth it because it was such a beautiful and interesting ride and we stopped at a village of one of the local hill tribes, different in dress, customs, appearance and behaviour from the Thai people. From the *songtaew* terminus, there was a bus to Chiang Saen. The remaining fifteen miles took another hour and there I had to wait patiently for 2½ more hours to find transport for the final seven miles to the Golden Triangle, the place where Thailand, Burma and Laos all meet and which is most famous for its part in the opium trade. So I reached here at 5:30 p.m., having spent eleven hours travelling, covering 127 miles, yet being actually just about forty miles from my starting point in Chiang Rai. From here one could literally throw a stone across the small river into Burma (and start an international incident?), while Laos is about half a mile away on the other side of the Mekong.

PART 6   THE SOUTH

The south of Thailand is most famous for its beaches. The long pan-handle stretches right down to Malaysia, making for some of the longest journeys in the country, and all the way down are beaches – on the east coast facing the Gulf of Thailand, on the west coast once it becomes part of Thailand (the more northern part belonging to Myanmar) and on the islands to the east and south. Let us start from Bangkok and make our way south.

KANCHANABURI   กาญจนบุรี

KANCHANABURI

3 hrs by train from Thonburi
2 hrs 30 mins by bus from Southern Bus Terminal
Kanchanaburi is famous for the **Bridge on the River Kwai**, part of the notorious **Thailand and Burma Railway** built during the war by forced prisoner-of-war and other labour. It is surely appropriate, therefore, to go to Kanchanaburi by train. Note, then, that trains leave from Thonburi Station, across the river from Bangkok, not from the main Bangkok (Hualampong) Station (except for a special excursion railcar which sometimes runs at weekends). Take a ferry to get to Thonburi Station, either the ferry from Phra Chan pier almost opposite, or an express boat from any pier. Trains leave at 7:40 and 13:50. The journey takes about three hours and costs Bt25.

The line from Thonburi joins the main line from Bangkok after twelve kilometres at a station called Thaling Chan Junction. It is actually a short cut. Then the train proceeds west along the main line to Nakhon Pathom and on to Nong Pla Duk, a tiny village, but an important railway junction with plenty of sidings. This is where the line built by the prisoners of war begins. As soon as you leave Nong Pla Duk, you will feel the train being switched to the middle track of three. The left one is the main line and the one on the right soon runs off to Suphanburi (one train each way every day). Strangely, we now run beside the main line for a further two kilometres before it curves off to start its long journey south. We proceed westwards for about another hour over flat and ordinary terrain before reaching the town of Kanchanaburi. It is quite likely that somebody will board the train at the previous station to look for recruits for a guest house. The author's opinion is that if somebody takes the trouble to do this and if one has no particular preference in mind, why not accept the offer? On the other hand, it should be mentioned that the Jolly Frog Backpackers is good value for money. Rooms are available from Bt80 and good food is offered at reasonable prices. The River Kwai is just across the lawn. There is even a film to watch in the evening if you wish. If there is a criticism to be made, it is that there are so many westerners around that it seems not to be part of Thailand any more, but that is hardly the fault of the management. If you prefer somewhere smaller and quieter, though, there are very many other similar establishments all along the river.

Kanchanaburi has developed rapidly in the last couple of decades. When the author first visited, none of this long line of guest houses existed, almost nobody visited the famous bridge, and I was the only westerner on the train to the end of the line. Trains across the bridge were still steam-hauled. Now the mid-morning train is just packed with visitors and thousands swarm around the famous bridge. This is not intended as criticism, just an indication of how quickly Kanchanaburi has become a major attraction. Quite apart from the famous railway, the potential of the beautiful river has suddenly been realized. It is a good place to relax, so, if you have a day or two to spare, why not spend it here?

If you decide to travel by bus instead of train, ordinary buses leave from the Southern Bus Terminal every fifteen minutes and take 3½ hours over the 119 kilometre journey, costing Bt41. Air-conditioned buses also leave every fifteen minutes, take 2½ hours and cost Bt68 1st class or Bt53 2nd class.

The Bridge next. It is at the far end of town, a long, but possible, walk of three kilometres. If that is too far, take an orange *songtaew* which starts in the centre of the town and runs there for Bt5. You may be surprised when you see the bridge, for it is a steel structure, nothing like the bamboo bridge in the film. So the film has been cheating you, has it? Twisting the facts again? Well, not entirely, for actually a temporary bamboo bridge was constructed by the prisoners to allow trains to pass while the permanent steel bridge was being assembled. When the steel bridge was finished, the bamboo one was dismantled, since it obstructed the river traffic. A photograph taken here by the author in 1975 shows quite distinctly the clearing where the bamboo bridge had been, to the left of the current structure, but now it is difficult to discern the place.

The ending of the film is fictitious, but the bridge was the target of much allied bombing and was eventually hit. You will notice that most of the bridge is constructed of rounded spans (which were actually stolen by the Japanese from a bridge in Java). In the middle, though, are two angular sections. These replace three of the original rounded spans which were destroyed by bombing. Near the bridge there is a display of engines used in its construction and a brief history of the Thailand and Burma Railway. It ran just over 400 kilometres and connected at Thanbyuzayat in Burma (now Myanmar) with a line already in use between Moulmein and Ye. The Thailand and Burma Railway was built for the Japanese, who were being permitted to use Thai territory without actually occupying the country. The thought of the Japanese was that if Thailand and Burma could be thus linked, a rail system could haul supplies all the way from Indo-China to India. There remained, however, the problem of building a bridge across the wide Salween River

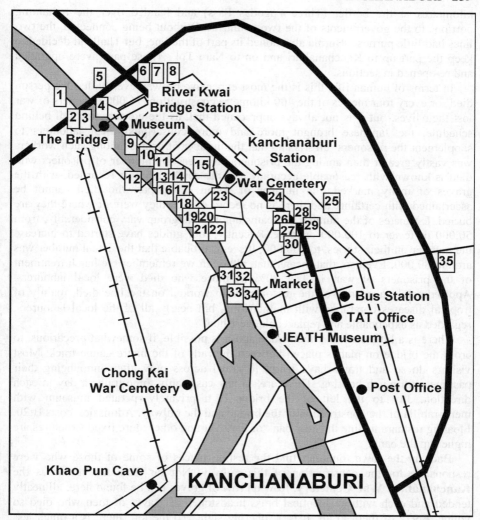

KANCHANABURI

estuary at Moulmein in Burma. That bridge was never completed, mainly due to repeated bombing raids and to the location's exposed position, so all goods had to be shipped across by ferry (as they still are), causing a bottle-neck.

The decision to build the railway was made in June 1942 and work started in October of the same year. It took just a year to build, being completed in October 1943, although the original target was August 1943, and then was in use for less than two years before the war finished and the British decided that it was no longer desirable to have Thailand and Burma thus connected. They dismantled four kilometres at the border (Three Pagodas Pass) and handed over the remaining portions to the governments of the two countries. Without being connected, the two lines had little purpose. Burma abandoned its part of the line, but Thailand decided to keep the part up to Kanchanaburi and on to Nam Tok. Those parts were upgraded and re-opened in sections.

In terms of human life, this is the most expensive railway ever built. One person died for every four metres of the 400 kilometre construction. 16,000 prisoners of war lost their lives, but it is not always appreciated that, as the construction fell behind schedule, the Japanese brought more and more conscripted local labourers to supplement the prisoners' efforts and that the number of deaths among such workers was vastly greater than among the prisoners. Whereas the number of prisoners who died is known with reasonable accuracy and the deaths of most recorded, with the graves of many marked, the number of Asian conscripts who died cannot be ascertained with certainty and there is no record of who they were or where they are buried. Estimates of the number of deaths among this group vary considerably, from 50,000 or fewer to 100,000 or more. Recently, tour guides have started to increase the number, in their stories, to 200,000. It seems probable that the actual number was around 80,000. Even so, that means that, although we remember the harsh treatment of the prisoners of war, in fact 80% of those who died were local labourers. Approximately a quarter of the prisoners who worked on the line died, mainly of tropical diseases combined with malnutrition, but nearly all of the local labourers, regarded as expendable and replaceable, perished.

There is a little station at the bridge and it is possible, if somewhat precarious, to cross the bridge on planks placed between the rails of the metre gauge track. Most visitors do so and trains have learnt to crawl across only after announcing their passage with much hooting. There are, in any case, only three trains a day in each direction. Just to the left of the bridge is a privately-operated museum with memorabilia of the construction of the bridge and the railway. Admission costs Bt20. Floating restaurants line the near bank of the river and other more fixed structures are higher up the bank.

Back in the town, one can find the resting places of some of those who were responsible for the construction of this railway. Not far from the station is the **Kanchanaburi War Cemetery**. Row on row of graves can be found here, all neatly tended and each with an identical brass headstone, all graves of men who died so young, 6,972 of them in all. It is a sobering sight. To the left, there is a much less neat Chinese cemetery. This contains later graves also, but a few are the graves of labourers who died during the war. Most such men are unremembered, however.

There is a second cemetery across the river and two kilometres away at **Chong Kai**. At this quieter spot, 1,750 more prisoners are interred.

Khao Pun Cave is about a kilometre further on. The cave contains Buddha statues, as well as stalagmites and stalactites.

By the river at the southern end of town is the **JEATH Museum**, started in 1977 by the late abbot of Wat Chai Chumphon, which is just across the road. The museum is a reconstruction of conditions in the prisoner-of-war camps, with photographs and equipment from that time. Admission costs Bt20, a price which has not changed, incidentally, since the museum opened.

There is a conveniently situated **TAT office** in Kanchanaburi. It is right beside the bus station.

 Other interesting sights are out of the town, some of them quite a way out. What you should do, of course, is to take a ride on the remaining part of the Thailand and Burma Railway. After all, it would be a pity if so many men had died for a railway that nobody was interested in any more.

Fortunately, though, people are interested. The 11:00 train is packed with interested parties, most of whom have come from Bangkok by bus on group tours. There is a special carriage attached to this train, offering the assurance of a seat, a free drink and a little certificate at the end. The price is Bt150 for the return journey. However, if you can do without these luxuries, it will cost Bt34 for the round trip.

If you use the above train, all you will see is the line, because at the end the engine is transferred to the other end of the train and the train comes straight back. However, if you can get up in time to catch the early morning train from Kanchanaburi at 6:11, you will have time to explore at **Nam Tok** between 8:40 and 13:00. Incidentally, this early train cannot be caught from Bangkok. It starts in Nong Pla Duk. Alternatively, you can catch the 11:00 from Kanchanaburi, arriving at Nam Tok at 12:50, and then catch the 15:15 train back, giving a little more than two hours for looking around.

The journey to Nam Tok is an exciting one, for suddenly you get a glimpse of the geographical difficulties which had to be overcome in building the railway. Up to Kanchanaburi, the terrain was flat and simple. The Bridge over the River Kwai was the first major difficulty, but from there on more and more obstacles presented themselves. The railway follows the course of the Kwai Noi River, hugging its bank. However, in places there is just no space to put a railway, so the line is constructed on trestles and supported by wooden girders forced into holes drilled into the cliff face. As the train creeps past these spots, one can lean out of the window and touch the rocks. The reason for the crawling, of course, is so that the train does not touch those rocks itself. The river lies below, and these days there are restaurants and raft accommodation all along it. This is an historic and scenic journey not to be missed.

Nam Tok, the name of the final station, means 'waterfall' and, true enough, there is a waterfall here. This is the **Sai Yok Noi Waterfall**. *Songtaew* will meet the train and take you there for Bt10. However, you can walk if you prefer. It is about two kilometres, and basically it is straight along where the railway used to continue. However, nature has taken back that route now and you have to go to the left to approach along the main road. It is a very pleasant little spot, with the waterfall splashing down the rocks and, at its foot, the bed of the old railway. In recent years, an engine has been installed here on a few metres of track reinstated specially for the purpose and it looks just as though a train is coming round the curve as it did more than half a century ago. There was a plan to extend the operational railway to here, but it has never been done and presumably it never will be now.

If you go up to the top of the cliff and walk a short distance, you will find an illuminated cave used as a small temple, with even a Buddhist monk in residence there.

Some three kilometres away is **Wang Ba Darn Cave**. For this one, though, you need a torch, which can be hired from the office at the entrance for Bt20. You first climb up the cliff face to the cave and then descend steeply within down narrow passages with bamboo ladders. It is quite exciting and the cave goes down a long way. The author never saw any sign of the bottom before deciding that he had gone far enough. Moreover, to add to the excitement, there were snakes within the cave (but there were mosquitoes outside, so which is worse?).

There are trains back to Kanchanaburi at 13:00 and 15:15, arriving at 14:51 and 17:51. The former continues to Thonburi, arriving at 17:40. However, the main road passes the Sai Yok Noi Waterfall, so if you wish, and have sufficient time, you can go on to other attractions and return later by bus.

On the way to Nam Tok by bus no. 8203 is the **Ban Kao National Museum**, beside the Kwai Noi River. It was constructed at the location of a 4,000-year-old Neolithic burial site discovered by a Dutch prisoner during the construction of the railway. The museum contains skeletal remains, artefacts and jewellery dating from the stone age. Admission costs Bt30, with the museum closed on Mondays and Tuesdays.

Lawa Cave can be reached by *songtaew* from Nam Tok Station, or by boat from Kanchanaburi. It is a large cave with the usual stalagmites and stalactites.

Hell Fire Pass is a part of the old railway built under the most difficult conditions. The cutting, some 80 kilometres from Kanchanaburi, is disused now, but can be walked through. Nearby is the Hell Fire Pass Memorial Museum, built by the Australian Government to commemorate those who perished in the harsh conditions here. The museum is on National Security Command land right next to the main road, and takes almost two hours to reach by bus no. 8203. The fare is Bt30.

Beyond Hell Fire Pass is another waterfall, **Sai Yok Yai Waterfall**, within the Sai Yok National Park, one of the prettiest falls in the area. It runs directly into the Kwai Noi River, so can be viewed best by boat. Again bus no. 8203 will take you there – or almost there. The waterfall is three kilometres from the main road. The distance from Kanchanaburi is 104 kilometres and the fare Bt35. The journey takes 2½ hours.

Thong Pha Phum is the next town of any size beyond Kanchanaburi. There is rafting on the river nearby and there is accommodation here (as there is at several places along the road, as well as on rafts on the river). The half-hourly service of ordinary buses finishes here and only four ordinary buses each day continue to Sangklaburi. However, there are also three air-conditioned buses and four minibuses which continue. Thong Pha Phum is 147 kilometres from Kanchanaburi. The journey takes 3½ hours by ordinary bus or 2½ hours by air-conditioned bus or minibus. The fare is Bt50 by ordinary bus.

Proceeding on from Thong Pha Phum, one reaches **Kao Lam National Park** on the right. The road from this point becomes full of twists and turns and ascents and descents, some of them very steep. The **Kao Lam Dam**, part of a hydro-electric project, has created a huge lake on the left of the road, flooding much of the countryside round here, including the path of the old Thailand and Burma Railway, which is a pity. Progress along the road is slow, but after another 70 kilometres **Sangklaburi** is reached. This is the last town in Thailand. It is a small one, but accommodation is available. There are guest houses by the lake about one kilometre from the town centre.

From here to the border at **Three Pagodas Pass** (*Chedi Sam Ong* in Thai) is 24 kilometres. *Songtaew* depart every 40 minutes, taking 40 minutes over the journey and charging Bt30. If you want to save time, you will see the turning to Three Pagodas Pass six kilometres before Sangklaburi is reached on the bus. You can alight and wait for the *songtaew* here if you prefer.

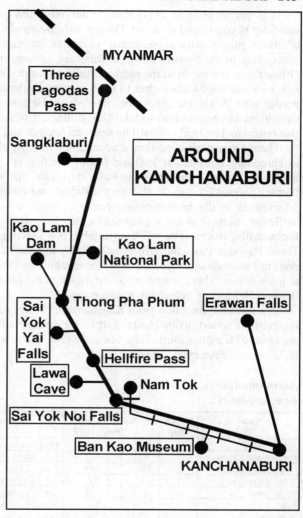

MYANMAR

Three Pagodas Pass

Sangklaburi

AROUND KANCHANABURI

Kao Lam Dam

Kao Lam National Park

Sai Yok Yai Falls

Thong Pha Phum

Erawan Falls

Hellfire Pass

Lawa Cave

Nam Tok

Sai Yok Noi Falls

Ban Kao Museum

KANCHANABURI

When you reach the border, you will see the three pagodas. They are not very big, but, we are told, bigger than they used to be. There is also a small market here, selling mostly antiques and furniture. Across the border runs a few metres of Thailand and Burma Railway track. Since this was the first part of the railway to be dismantled at the end of the war, it is obviously a modern reconstruction, but one presumes that the location is accurate. One can see the old path continuing round the back of the Myanmar Customs Office.

It is permissible to cross this border on a day pass, but read this paragraph carefully if you intend to do so. Do not just go straight to the border. This is another of those places where you must visit the Immigration Office in town before proceeding to the border. Town, in this case, is Sangklaburi. Go to the Immigration Office there, not far from the market, and get stamped out of Thailand. Then take the *songtaew* for the 24 kilometres to the border and submit your stamped passport at the border post. Walk the 20 metres into Myanmar and pay U.S.$10 (or over-valued equivalent in baht, so best to take U.S. dollars, if possible) for your day pass. When you return to Thailand you will be stamped back in and given another month's stay.

There are two air-conditioned buses a day running all the way from Kanchanaburi to Three Pagodas Pass, at 9:00 and 13:00. The first is a possible way of paying a very brief visit to the Three Pagodas Pass, if you do not want to cross the border. The journey takes 4½ hours by this very efficient and comfortable service and gives you 30 minutes at the border before returning at 14:00. It is not very long, but just sufficient, as there is not a great deal to see here really. The fare is Bt140 each way. Incidentally, if you take this comfortable bus leaving Sangklaburi at 13:00 for the Three Pagodas Pass, the fare is only Bt20, instead of Bt30 by *songtaew*. This bus does not stop along the road from Kanchanaburi to Three Pagodas Pass. It stops only at main towns. There is also accommodation at the pass. Three Pagodas Guest House is some 500 metres before the bus stop there.

In a different direction from Kanchanaburi is **Erawan Falls**, thought to be one of the prettiest waterfalls in Thailand. It is in Erawan National Park, 65 kilometres from the town of Kanchanaburi. Take bus no. 8170. The journey takes two hours and costs Bt25. Buses leave every 50 minutes.

Accommodation
Kanchanaburi

Name	No. on Map	Rooms	Cheapest Price (Bt)
Felix Resort	3	255	3,500
Pung-Waan Resort	4	111	3,000
Duen Shine Resort	2	80	1,400
Kwai Riverside	1	52	1,400
River Kwai	28	159	1,000
R.S.	6	209	800
Mettaphan	7	130	750
Sudjai Riverside Hse.	12	16	600
Modern Inn	25	36	600
Khao Tong View	35	35	450
Luxury	24	20	400
River Inn	29	38	360
Mit Muang Kan	8	138	320
M.K.	26	49	300
Singsonboon	5	48	300
R.S.P. Mansion	23	30	300
Prasopsuk	27	41	250
Bamboo House	9	20	250

Name	No. on Map	Rooms	Cheapest Price (Bt)
Don Ruk Bungalow	15	46	200
V.L. Guest House	30	25	180
Sam's Place	33	20	170
Mr. Tee Guest House	10	15	150
Apple's Guest House	18	20	150
Vimol G.H. (Rick's Lodge)	19	10	150
Good Corner G. H.	31	15	150
Nitaya Raft House	32	15	150
Supakornchai	34	15	150
C and C Guest House	11	15	120
Blue Star G. H.	13	12	120
Sam's House	14	10	120
Sugarcane House	16	8	120
V.N. Guest House	20	8	120
River Guest House	21	8	100
J. Guest House	22	12	100
Jolly Frog Backpackers	17	45	80

Sangklaburi

Name	Rooms	Cheapest Price (Bt)
Lake Valley Resort	28	2,400
Aramkitphotha Raft	6	1,700
Mitsampan Raft House	6	900
Ponnatee Resort	19	900
Sangkla Garden	9	700
Forget Me Not Resort	14	600
Songkalia River Hut	36	450

Name	Rooms	Cheapest Price (Bt)
Poy Long Resort	10	400
Sam Prasob Resort	25	350
Three Pagodas Resort	58	350
Porn Pilin	50	250
Burmese Inn	10	100
P. Guest House	20	100

Moving On

Here is the train timetable both to and from Kanchanaburi and Nam Tok.

Type of Train	Ord	Ord	Ord
Classes	3	3	3
Thonburi		0740	1350
Nakhon Pathom		0920	1459
Nong Pla Duk	0425	0947	1519
Kanchanaburi	0611	1100	1625
River Kwai Bridge	0618	1108	1642
Nam Tok	0840	1250	1840

Type of Train	Ord	Ord	Ord
Classes	3	3	3
Nam Tok	0525	1300	1515
River Kwai Bridge	0718	1443	1743
Kanchanaburi	0727	1451	1751
Nong Pla Duk	0833	1550	1920
Nakhon Pathom	0853	1619	
Thonburi	1035	1740	

Here is a summary of buses from Kanchanaburi.

Destination	Route No.	Price (Bt)				Journey Time (hrs)		Frequency	
		V.I.P.	A/C 1	A/C 2	Ord	A/C	Ord	A/C	Ord
Bangkok	81		68	53	41	2.5	3.5	15 mins	15 mins
Nakhon Pathom	81				25		2		15 mins
Ratchaburi	461				31		2.5		15 mins
Suphanburi	411				30		2		20 mins
Dan Chang	325				40		3.5		12/day
Erawan	8170				25		2		11/day
Three Pagodas Pass	8203		140			4.5		2/day	
Sangklaburi	8203		121	105	80	4	6	7/day	4/day
Thong Pha Phum	8203				50		3.5		30 mins

POSTCARD HOME—Bangkok, 28th August 1980

Dear Folks,
  I am staying at a different, and even cheaper, hotel. It suffers from the usual defects of accumulated filth and grime and a complete lack of maintenance. A calendar for 1956 hangs on the wall downstairs. It is obviously not very safe here either, for somebody had apparently tried to get into my room during the night, presumably with the intention of theft. There is so much noise in Bangkok that one would hardly notice someone trying to get in. There is a panel missing on the door, through which somebody had evidently reached the bolts. However, it appeared that he or she had been unable to undo the screen door within. When I pointed out to the management the fact that my room was not secure, they discussed the matter at great length, decided who the culprit was, but declined to mend the door, considering the problem solved.

CHA-AM

ชะอำ

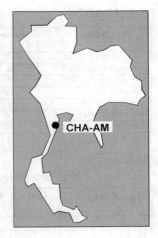

4 hrs by train from Thonburi
3 hrs 30 mins by bus from Southern Bus Terminal

The coastline facing the Gulf of Thailand has many good beaches. One of the more popular is at Cha-Am. Although there is a railway station here, only four ordinary trains and one rapid train stop. The most useful trains are the 7:20 from Thonburi station, destination Lang Suan, arriving in Cha-Am at 11:27, and a train starting in Chachoengsao, to the east of Bangkok, destination Hua Hin, which does not pass through Hualampong station in Bangkok, but stops at Sam Sen (9:28) and Bang Sue (9:36) stations, both in the metropolitan area. It reaches Cha-Am at 13:24. The fare is Bt38 from Thonburi.

Buses leave from the Southern Bus Terminal and take about 3½ hours. The fare is Bt97 by air-conditioned bus. There are some ordinary buses passing through also to other destinations, by which the fare is Bt55. Except for five buses a day, services do not terminate in Cha-Am. They usually run to Hua Hin or beyond. Because so many buses pass through, the service is frequent.

The railway station is about two kilometres from the beach and the bus stop about a kilometre and a half from the beach. Motor bikes are waiting to take you to the beach for Bt10 if you do not feel like walking. The hotels and guest houses are, as you might, perhaps, expect, strung out along the beach front. There is plenty of choice. Cha-Am is not a big town, and is quieter than Hua Hin, just down the road, for example.

There is a **TAT office**. It is in a somewhat inconvenient position, quite a long way down the main road south towards Hua Hin. Getting there is healthy exercise, but, if you prefer, a motor cycle taxi will ask Bt20 from the railway station or beach.

Accommodation
Cha-Am

Name	No. on Map	Rooms	Cheapest Price (Bt)	Name	No. on Map	Rooms	Cheapest Price (Bt)
Cha-Am Lagoon	1	59	1,500	Thapthari Place	13	15	900
Cha-Am Cabana	2	36	900	Sam Resort	14	15	650
Long Beach Cha-Am	3	40	2,800	Kwan Hut	15	10	300
Methawalai	4	220	2,000	Cha-Am Villa	16	11	250
Markland	5	25	2,800	Holiday Lodge	17	19	400
P.R. Beach House	6	15	200	Cha-Am Phoemsuk	18	18	300
Phai Siri	7	12	700	Rua Makam Villa	19	40	600
Santikam	8	28	450	St. Cha-Am	20	20	450
Happy Home	9	16	300	Niran Resort	21	20	300
Mankong Resort	10	25	200	Cha-Am Golden Villa	22	11	350
Kaen Chan	11	58	700	Arun Thip	23	15	250
Scandy Resort	12	20	350	White	24	34	350

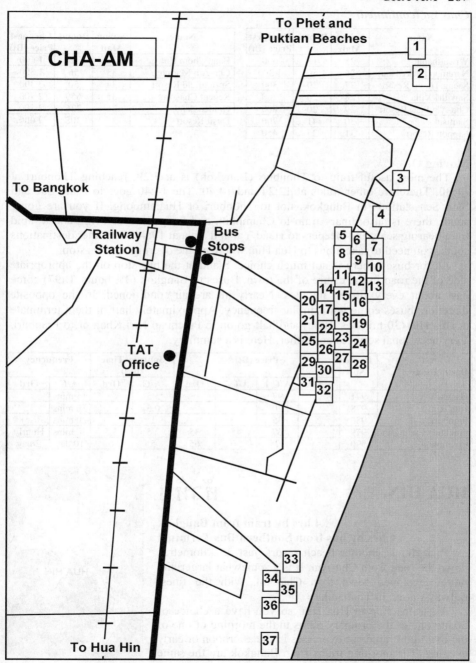

CHA-AM

To Phet and
Puktian Beaches

To Bangkok

Railway
Station

Bus
Stops

TAT
Office

To Hua Hin

Cha-Am (continued)

Name	No. on Map	Rooms	Cheapest Price (Bt)
Wiwatthana	25	15	600
Narumon Lucky House	26	50	1,300
Saeng Thong Resort	27	20	300
Sawittri Villa	28	20	700
Cha-Am Park Resort	29	20	800
Santisuk	30	41	700
Nippon Resort	31	25	450

Name	No. on Map	Rooms	Cheapest Price (Bt)
Baan Chom Hut	32	15	1,600
Cha-Am Marina	33	56	1,500
Springfield Resort	34	50	3,300
Regent Cha-Am	35	650	2,700
Golden Sands	36	226	3,300
Dusit Resort	37	308	4,000

Moving On

The most useful train to Thonburi (Bangkok) is at 7:29, reaching Thonburi at 11:30. There are other trains at 12:24 and 14:40. The 14:40 goes to Bang Sue and Sam Sen stations in Bangkok, not to Thonburi or Hualampong. If you are going south, there is an ordinary train to Chumphon and Lang Suan at 11:27 and a rapid train bearing seats and sleepers to Haad Yai and Yala at 19:44. For other destinations south, you need to take a bus to Hua Hin, where all the overnight trains stop.

As for buses, there is not much choice. Stand at the bus stop on the appropriate side of the road in the centre of the town. Buses to Bangkok (3½ hours, Bt97) come past about every fifteen minutes. Nearly all are air-conditioned. In the opposite direction, buses come with similar frequency. Approximately half of them terminate at Hua Hin (30 minutes, Bt20) and half go on to Prachuap Kiri Khan or to Pranburi. Very occasional services go further. Here is a summary.

Destination	Route No.	Price (Bt)				Journey Time (hrs)		Frequency	
		V.I.P.	A/C 1	A/C 2	Ord	A/C	Ord	A/C	Ord
Bangkok	971		97			3.5		15 mins	
Hua Hin	978		20			0.5		30 mins	
Pranburi	985		35			1		20 mins	
Prachuap Kiri Khan	979		67	45	35	2.5	3.5	30 mins	Hourly
Chumphon	990		125	90	65	5	6	10/day	2/day

HUA HIN   หัวหิน

4 hrs by train from Bangkok
4 hrs by bus from Southern Bus Terminal

Hua Hin is another beach resort, just 25 kilometres down the road from Cha-Am. It is a somewhat larger and more developed town than Cha-Am, with the finest railway station in Thailand.

All trains stop at Hua Hin, so you have a choice of taking one of the ordinary trains in the morning or one of the overnight rapids or expresses in the afternoon or early evening. The morning trains from Bangkok are the same

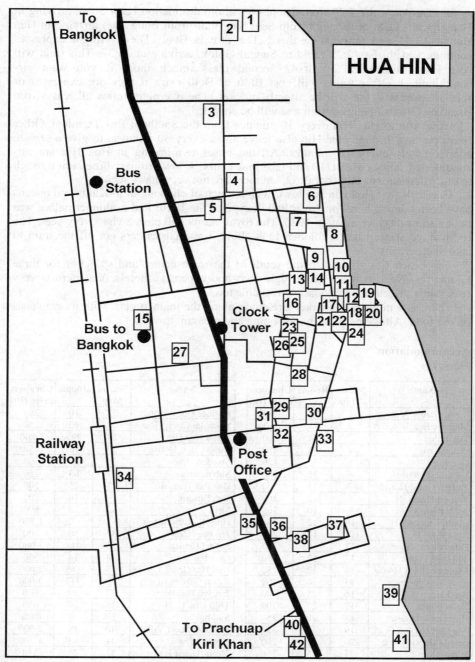

To
Bangkok

1
2

HUA HIN

3

Bus
Station

4

6

5

7

8

9

10

13
14

11
12
19

16

17

21
22
18
20

15

Clock
Tower

23
25
24

Bus to
Bangkok

27

26

28

29
31
30

32
33

Railway
Station

34

Post
Office

35
36
37

38

39

To Prachuap
Kiri Khan

40
42

41

as for Cha-Am – the 7:20 from Thonburi station, destination Lang Suan, arriving in Hua Hin at 11:58, or the 9:28 from Sam Sen (9:36 from Bang Sue) arriving in Hua Hin at 13:45 and terminating there. The fare is Bt44. The overnight expresses commence with the 12:25 rapid to Sungai Golok, arriving at 16:37. This train will cost Bt84 third class or Bt142 second class (much more if you want air-conditioning). Other trains will cost Bt20 or Bt40 extra if they are expresses or special expresses, but will be slightly quicker. The overnight trains all leave from Bangkok (Hualampong) station and will be crowded.

Buses run to Hua Hin every 30 minutes from the Southern Bus Terminal. Other buses passing through Hua Hin also leave about every 30 minutes, to give a service approximately every 15 minutes. All the buses terminating in Hua Hin are air-conditioned. They cost Bt110 and take four hours. A few ordinary buses run through to other destinations and cost Bt62, but there are not very many such.

One feels that Hua Hin is a town with a touch of class about it. Kings and queens have been coming here for Royal Paddling since the 1920s and a summer palace was built a short distance away in 1926. The royal family still pays a visit every year. The red painted **station** has a colonial look about it and passengers get off the train to take photographs.

The beach lies slightly to the south of the town centre and stretches for three kilometres. Next to it are some high class and expensive hotels. Yet there is very reasonably priced accommodation available too.

There is a night food market stretching along the main streets, with its emphasis on sea food. Altogether it is an interesting and pleasant town.

Accommodation
Hua Hin

Name	No. on Map	Rooms	Cheapest Price (Bt)
Royal Garden Village	1	162	3,900
Majestic Beach Resort	2	100	1,500
Tananchai	3	41	300
Phananchai	4	33	450
Dumrong	5	35	150
Tik Guest House	6	15	200
Pattana Guest House	7	15	300
Karoon Hut G. H.	8	12	200
All Nations G. H.	9	10	300
Chom Kluen G. H.	10	12	250
Rom Ruen G. H.	11	12	250
Fulay Guest House	12	10	250
21 Guest House	13	12	100
Memory Guest House	14	12	250
Siri Phet Chakasem	15	30	200
Sand Inn	16	25	300
Fulay Hotel	17	25	300
Bird Guest House	18	10	250
Sea Breeze Mod G. H.	19	10	250
Sirima Guest House	20	12	200
White House	21	15	250
K Place Guest House	22	10	250
Sukwilai Guest House	23	12	250
Melia Hua Hin	24	297	1,800
Nuvo Guest House	25	12	250
Sweden House	26	10	300
Subhamitra	27	83	250
Ban Pak Hua Hin	28	25	500
Ban Busarin	29	10	800
Sirin	30	25	890
Hua Hin City Beach	31	172	1,200
Jed Pee Nong	32	50	500
Sofitel Central	33	218	3,000
Golf Inn	34	14	550
Hua Hin Grand Plaza	35	168	2,000
Royal Garden Resort	36	217	3,000
Janchai Bungalow	37	29	600
Thip Urai G. H.	38	20	650
Sailom	39	70	1,800
Hua Hin Sport Villa	40	19	2,000
Chom View	41	43	1,700
Vegus Guest House	42	25	350

Moving On

To go to Bangkok, there are ordinary trains at 7:04 and 11:57 which run to Thonburi, arriving at 11:30 and 16:50, and another at 14:20 which runs to Bang Sue (18:45) and Sam Sen (18:54). The fare is Bt44. There is also a second class air-conditioned railcar running to Bangkok at 16:05 and arriving at 20:00. The fare for this train is Bt302. To go south, all the night expresses stop at Hua Hin. See the timetable on page 74.

There are two bus stations in Hua Hin. One is exclusively for air-conditioned services originating here and running to Bangkok. These buses operate every half hour, cost Bt110 and take four hours. The other bus station is for all other services. Only the Bangkok buses start in Hua Hin, so all other services are just passing through. They include very occasional services to Chumphon, Haad Yai, Phuket and Krabi, but mostly at night. Here is a summary.

Destination	Route No.	Price (Bt)				Journey Time (hrs)		Frequency	
		V.I.P.	A/C 1	A/C 2	Ord	A/C	Ord	A/C	Ord
Bangkok	978		110	67/85		4		30 mins	
Pranburi	985		20			0.5		20 mins	
Prachuap Kiri Khan	979		47	35	25	2	3	30 mins	Hourly
Chumphon	990		110	80	55	4.5	5.5	10/day	2/day
Haad Yai	982/992		420/390	300	229/212	12	13.5	6/day	3/day
Phuket	949/63		357	280	200	11	12.5	2/day	1/day
Krabi	950/983		321			10		1/day	

PRACHUAP KIRI KHAN
ประจวบคีรีขันธ์

6 hrs by train from Bangkok
6 hrs by bus from Southern Bus Terminal

Prachuap Kiri Khan is another seaside resort town, but this time one frequented mostly by Thais, which makes it interesting to visit. It is situated some 90km further south than Hua Hin. The railway station is right in the town, with the cheapest accommodation just nearby. The morning train leaves at 7:20 from Thonburi Station in Bangkok and reaches Prachuap Kiri Khan at 13:43, and there is an afternoon train leaving Thonburi at 13:05 and reaching Prachuap Kiri Khan at 18:55. The overnight

expresses from Bangkok (Hualampong Station) begin with the 12:25 rapid to Sungai Golok, which arrives at Prachuap Kiri Khan at 17:55, followed by several others (see page 74). The trains from Thonburi cost Bt56 third class, while the rapid costs Bt98 third class or Bt175 second class.

If travelling by bus, you should take a vehicle which is actually terminating in Prachuap Kiri Khan. That means bus no. 979. 1st class air-conditioned buses operate every hour and cost Bt157. 2nd class air-conditioned buses leave every half hour and cost Bt122. The two types of bus are operated by different companies, but both terminate near the railway station in Prachuap Kiri Khan. If you use a bus which is merely passing through on the way to another destination, you will be dropped on the main road two kilometres from the town, which is less convenient.

Prachuap Kiri Khan is situated on a bay, with a relatively little used beach continuing both to north and to south of the town itself. The southern part is occupied by an air force base, but the northern beach extends for several kilometres and has accommodation available. It too is only lightly used.

The town is dominated by a hill named **Khao Chong Krachok** ('Mirror Mountain'), with Wat Thannikaram Woravihara at its foot and Phra That Chedi at its summit. Monkeys play in the fountain at the bottom, so beware of your possessions. If you climb the 395 steps to the top of the hill, you will be rewarded with a fine view of bay and town, as well as a look at the *chedi*. Actually, however, the *chedi* looks at its most impressive viewed sparkling in the sunshine from a little distance, particularly from the train if you happen to pass by. Since the hill rises from flat ground, the buildings at its peak and the white steps leading upwards appear all the more beautiful.

Accommodation

The cheapest places to stay are around the railway station. If those are too cheap, a few minutes walk towards the sea will bring you to two good class hotels right on the sea front with fine views. A little to the north, but still in the town, is a group of bungalows (Thaed Saban Bungalow), suitable for family rather than individual occupation, but with a few rooms available too at Bt300. All of the accommodation mentioned is within walking distance of bus or train. There is also accommodation as you move north along the beach leaving the town. The nearer places (shown on the map) are within about 20 minutes walk of bus or train.

Prachuap Kiri Khan

Name	No. on Map	Rooms	Cheapest Price (Bt)	Name	No. on Map	Rooms	Cheapest Price (Bt)
Had Thong	8	120	650	Suk Sant	7	100	200
Kum Chao Lai	4	25	450	Yuttichai	5	20	200
Golden Beach	2	10	400	Prachuap Suk	9	20	150
Thaed Saban Bungalow	3	35	300	Inthira	6	25	150
Happy Inn	1	12	300				

Moving On

To return to Bangkok, there is a morning train originating in Prachuap Kiri Khan at 5:00 and arriving in Thonburi at 11:30. There is a second ordinary train at 10:20 reaching Thonburi at 16:50. The fare on these trains is Bt56 third class. The express

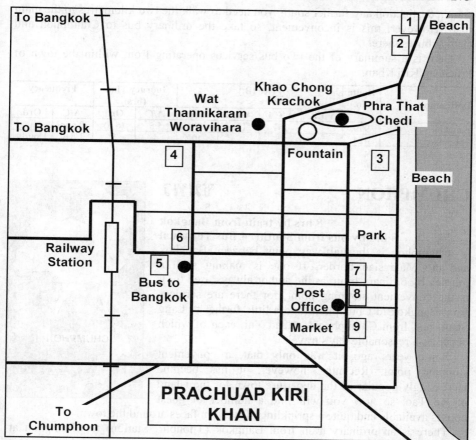

trains pass through in the middle of the night, but if you want to be reasonably comfortable and save time, you could consider taking a sleeping berth on the rapid train passing at 22:49 and reaching Bangkok at 5:05. Fare would depend on the type of berth chosen, but would be a minimum of Bt275 for an upper berth without air-conditioning. An air-conditioned lower berth would cost Bt445.

Going south, there is the ordinary train to Chumphon and Lang Suan at 13:43 from Prachuap Kiri Khan, reaching Chumphon at 17:25 and Lang Suan at 18:50. Then there are the various express trains to Haad Yai, Sungai Golok, Butterworth and other destinations, which pass through Prachuap Kiri Khan in the evening. These trains will be crowded, so you should consider them only if you have an advance reservation for a sleeper. Full details of the timetable south are shown on page 74.

As for buses, there is the excellent service to Bangkok at least every half hour from 4:00 until 1:30, and there is also an ordinary bus running to Chumphon. If you want a destination any further south, you need to walk the two kilometres to the main road. However, this is inconvenient, so take the ordinary bus to Chumphon and change buses there.

Here is a summary of the two bus services operating from within the town of Prachuap Kiri Khan.

Destination	Route No.	Price (Bt)				Journey Time (hrs)		Frequency	
		V.I.P.	A/C 1	A/C 2	Ord	A/C	Ord	A/C	Ord
Bangkok	979		157	122	(87)	5.5	(6.5)	30 mins	
Chumphon	426		75		40	4	5	2/day	Hourly

CHUMPHON

ชุมพร

8 hrs by train from Bangkok
8 hrs by bus from Southern Bus Terminal

Chumphon is the half-way point between Bangkok and the Malaysian border. If one is making such a journey by ordinary train, as the author always used to, it is the convenient stopping point, for there are services from Bangkok to Chumphon (and a little further to Lang Suan) and from Chumphon to Haad Yai, each of which occupies a reasonable day's travel.

Some years ago, it was only that, a convenient stopping point. Recently, however, it has become increasingly popular as the departure town for the island of Ko Tao, so now you will find a number of guest houses available and quite a sprinkling of western faces around the town.

There is an ordinary train from Bangkok (Thonburi Station) to Chumphon at 7:20, arriving at 17:25. Fare is Bt80 third class. Then there are overnight expresses with sleeping berths, but most of them arrive rather inconveniently early. The best one to take is the 19:15 from Bangkok (Hualampong Station) to Nakhon Si Thammarat, which will reach Chumphon at 4:13. This will be reasonably convenient if you want to take the morning boat to Ko Tao without staying in Chumphon. The fare for a lower air-conditioned sleeping berth on this train is Bt520.

By bus, there are air-conditioned departures early in the day and by night from the Southern Bus Terminal. Cost is Bt245 for a 1st class bus and Bt190 for a 2nd class bus. There are other buses passing Chumphon on the way to further destinations. However, Chumphon has two bus stations, one conveniently located in the centre of the town and one several kilometres away on the by-pass. Buses passing Chumphon often call only at the latter. There are *songtaew* into the town for Bt10. If you cannot find one at the bus station, cross the main road and stand at the start of the road almost opposite, leading into town.

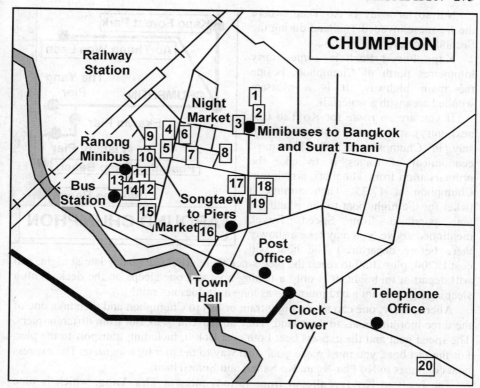

The town of Chumphon is pleasant, but not particularly interesting. Those who stay for more than a single night usually do so for interest in diving opportunities from nearby islands, of which there are many, particularly **Ko Mattra, Ko Rat, Ko Thong Lang, Ko Ngam Yai, Ko Ngam Noi and Ko Maphrao**. There is no shortage of travel agents in town offering these opportunities, but one convenient and friendly such agent is Speed Travel, located right next to the bus station and open even in the middle of the night when overnight buses and trains are arriving.

There is a well known beach named **Hat Sai Ree**, some fifteen kilometres from the town. *Songtaew* are available for the journey there for Bt15, and there is accommodation at the beach. Also there is the **shrine of Prince Chumphon**, regarded as the father of the modern Thai Navy, with a World War II vessel on display, the *Royal Chumphon*, a large torpedo ship decommissioned in 1975. Prince Chumphon died at this location in 1923.

On the way to Hat Sai Ree is another beach, **Hat Pharadon Phap**, fringed with coconut palms and with accommodation also available.

Sixteen kilometres to the north of Chumphon is **Ao Thung Wua Laen**, yet another attractive beach and also a diving spot. Once more, *songtaew* transport (Bt20) and accommodation are available.

Not so far away is Ao Thap, where the Japanese invaded Thailand during the Second World War.

Kapo Forest Park is some thirty kilometres north of Chumphon, beside the main highway. It is a pleasant wooded area with a waterfall.

If you are *en route* for Ko Tao (see next entry), it is actually not necessary to stay in Chumphon at all. The most economical of routes is to take the ordinary train from Thonburi, arriving in Chumphon at 17:25. Then arrange a ticket for the night boat to the island. (If you purchase from Speed Travel, mentioned above, you may take a shower there before departure.) The boat will

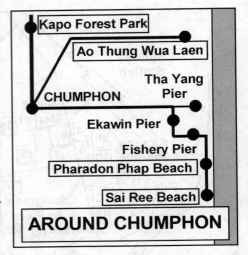

AROUND CHUMPHON

cost Bt200, plus Bt50 to reach the pier, since there are no *songtaew* late at night, and will depart at midnight. It is only a fishing boat and one sleeps on the deck. With a sleeping bag it is not a bad journey – as long as it does not rain!

Alternatively, one can take a night train or bus to Chumphon and then take one of the three morning boats to the island. They all leave at 7:30, but from different piers. The speed boat and the express boat both cost Bt400, including transport to the pier. For the fast boat, you must make your own way to the pier by *songtaew*. The express boat continues to Ko Pha-Ngan, Ko Samui and Surat Thani.

The boats to Ko Tao all sail from various piers at **Tha Yang**, which is nine kilometres from the town. *Songtaew* leave from near the town hall (see map) and cost Bt5. Most of the same *songtaew* continue to the beaches of Hat Sai Ree and Hat Pharadon Phap.

Accommodation
Chumphon

Name	No. on Map	Rooms	Cheapest Price (Bt)
Jansom Chumphon	8	210	550
Paradon Inn	7	106	500
Chumphon Palace	16	90	500
Mix	20	40	400
Tha Taphao	14	55	350
Mayazes Guest House	12	10	300
Suriwong	5	78	250
Sri Chumphon	4	95	200
Sri Taifa	15	45	200
Morakot Guest House	9	15	150

Name	No. on Map	Rooms	Cheapest Price (Bt)
Infinity Guest House	10	12	120
Infinity Travel G.H.	1	8	120
Ekawin Travel	3	5	100
New Chumphon G. H.	2	10	100
Jaroen Phong	6	12	100
Suda Guest House	11	15	100
Palm Guest House	17	10	100
Sooksamer G. H.	18	12	100
Chomkae G. H.	19	10	100
Speed Travel	13	5	80

Hat Sai Ree

Name	Rooms	Cheapest Price (Bt)
Suan Pha Daeng	28	2,400
Sai Ree Lodge	6	1,700

Name	Rooms	Cheapest Price (Bt)
Porn Sawan Resort	6	900

Ao Thung Wua Laen

Name	Rooms	Cheapest Price (Bt)
Suan Pha Daeng	28	2,400

Moving On

To return to Bangkok, there is a morning train at 7:00 reaching Thonburi at 16:50. The fare on this train is Bt80 third class. The express trains pass through Chumphon in the late evening and the sleepers attached offer a pleasant and comfortable method of travel. One or two trains have additional sleeping accommodation added in Chumphon. The fare would be a minimum of Bt330 for an upper berth without air-conditioning on a rapid train. An air-conditioned lower berth on an express would cost Bt520.

Going south, there is an ordinary train to Haad Yai originating in Chumphon at 6:35 and reaching Haad Yai at 17:10. Then there are the express trains to Haad Yai, Sungai Golok, Butterworth and other places, which pass Chumphon in the late evening and early hours of the morning with sleeping accommodation available. These need prior reservation, however.

There are buses to Bangkok every hour during the morning, and also by night. Here is a summary of services available.

Destination	Route No.	Price (Bt)				Journey Time (hrs)		Frequency	
		V.I.P.	A/C 1	A/C 2	Ord	A/C	Ord	A/C	Ord
Bangkok	990	286	245	190	136	8	10	10/day	2/day
Haad Yai	721		265	209	147	9	10	3/day	2/day
Ranong	429				39		3		Hourly
Surat Thani	474			91	70	4	5	Hourly	30 mins
Prachuap Kiri Khan	426		75		40	4	5	2/day	Hourly
Phuket				176		7		3/day	

There are also minibus services to Bangkok (13:00 only, 6 hours, Bt350), Surat Thani (every 30 minutes, 3 hours, Bt120) and Ranong (hourly, 2 hours, Bt80). The departure points for these services are shown on the map.

Then there are the boat services to Ko Tao, as shown below.

Type of Boat	Pier	Departure	Arrival (Ko Tao)	Fare (Bt)
Speedboat	Ekawin	07:30	09:30	400
Express	Fishery	07:30	10:30	400
Fast	Tha Yang	07:30	10:00	300
Slow	Tha Yang	24:00	06:00	200

The speed boat continues to the other islands and on to Ko Samui, as follows.

Chumphon	Ko Tao		Ko Pha-Ngan		Ko Samui		Surat Thani
Depart	Arrive	Depart	Arrive	Depart	Arrive	Depart	Arrive
07:30	10:30	10:35	12:15	12:30	13:15	14:00	16:30

KO TAO

เกาะเต่า

KO TAO

3 hours from Chumphon by express boat

In 1983, there was one guest house on Ko Tao ('Turtle Island'). Within the space of two decades it has become one of the most flourishing of Thailand's diving resorts and there are no fewer than 72 guest houses dotted around the island. The permanent population, however, is only 700.

As detailed above, there are four daily ferries to the island from Chumphon, one at night and three early in the morning. There are also five daily ferries from Ko Samui, via Ko Pha-Ngan, ranging in price from Bt250 to Bt450. From Surat Thani, 115 kilometres away, there are a night boat and a daily express boat. The night boat has two standards of accommodation at Bt250 and Bt350. Non-Thais are encouraged to take the higher class, which includes a straw mat and pillow. The boat leaves at 23:00 from Ban Don (see map on page 281). The express boat leaves from Ta Thong, just outside Ban Don. It sails at 8:00 and reaches Ko Tao, via Ko Samui and Ko Pha-Ngan, at 14:00, at a cost of Bt495.

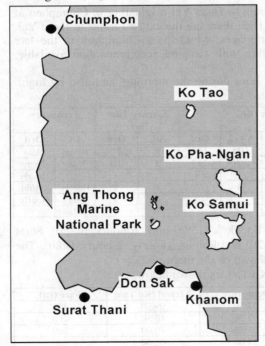

ISLANDS BETWEEN CHUMPHON AND SURAT THANI

Although Ko Tao is most famous for its diving resorts, it is not necessary to be a diver to visit rewardingly. There are plenty of beaches and there is no shortage of pleasant scenery, including some steep hills and even places for rock climbing. Ko Tao has an area of 21 square kilometres, making it the twentieth island in the country in terms of size.

The main town is **Mae Had**, towards the southern end of the west side of the island, where the ferries all arrive. Then there are two principal beach areas: **Had Sai Ree** (the same name as the beach on the mainland near Chumphon) stretching up the west of the island, and **Had Chalok Ban Kao**, in the south. There are also other little bays dotted around the island with a few huts in each.

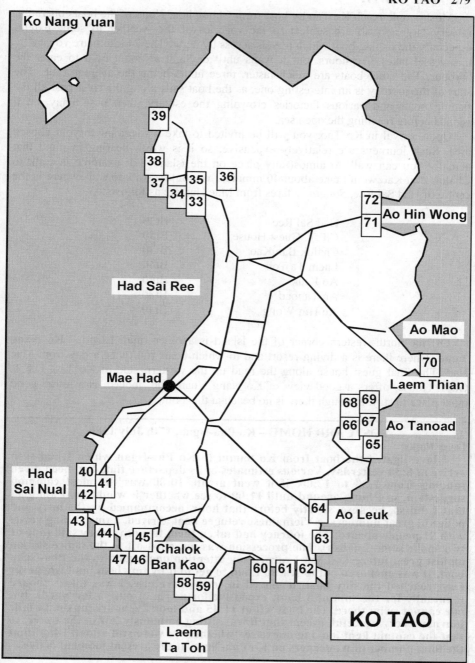

Most people reach Ko Tao by boat from Chumphon. None of the boats operating is very large, so all are subject to the vagaries of the weather to some extent, especially the fishing boat which travels across by night. The 74 kilometre voyage by this vessel takes five hours, but it waits until daylight at about 6:00 to enter the harbour. The other boats are much faster, three hours being the average time. The start of the journey is an interesting one, as the boat sails along the river past all the fishing boats and various factories crowding the estuary, then past many small islands before reaching the open sea.

Upon arrival in Ko Tao, you will be invited to take a *songtaew* to your chosen area. Such journeys are relatively expensive, so it is worth bearing in mind that actually you can walk to almost any place on the island. For example, a walk to Chalok Ban Kao would take about 40 minutes, as would a walk to somewhere in the centre of Had Sai Ree. *Songtaew* fares from Mae Had are as follows:

Had Sai Ree	Bt30
C.F.T. Guest House	Bt50
Chalok Ban Kao	Bt30
Laem Ta Toh	Bt40
Ao Leuk	Bt40
Ao Tanoad	Bt80
Ao Hin Wong	Bt40

Off the north-western corner of the island is another small island – **Ko Nang Yuan**, where there is a diving resort and to which boats run twice a day from Mae Had. The final guest house along the road up the western side of Ko Tao, C.F.T. Guest House, offers a good view of Ko Nang Yuan, and, indeed, is a rather good quiet place to stay, although there is no beach at this point.

POSTCARD HOME—Ko Pha-Ngan, 17th July 1980

Dear Folks,
   I investigated the boat from Ko Samui to Ko Pha-Ngan which I had seen arrive at 8:30 yesterday. Various estimates of its departure time had been given ranging from 7:30 to 12:00, if it went at all. 10:00 was the most common suggestion, so I hung around until 11:00 to see whether it would go. I am glad that I did so, because, shortly before that hour, accompanied by the navy and police in great numbers, a Vietnamese refugee boat arrived, a tiny fishing vessel with 81 people aboard. The journey had taken them five days, they said (one or two spoke some English). The procession was marched off to the police station amidst great interest. Then I turned my attention once again to the Pha-Ngan boat. It was anchored out to sea, so I had to get to it by tiny boat, and whenever I approached the tiny boat, it moved to somewhere else. I was taken aboard eventually for the sum of 3 baht, expensive for a trip of only a few yards, but one cannot swim there. The boat left at 11:45 and took 2¼ hours for the 14 mile journey - very peaceful, except that it was sitting ominously low in the water, so that the captain kept looking out to see whether we were still afloat. I find that the total number of westerners on Ko Pha-Ngan at the present moment is five.

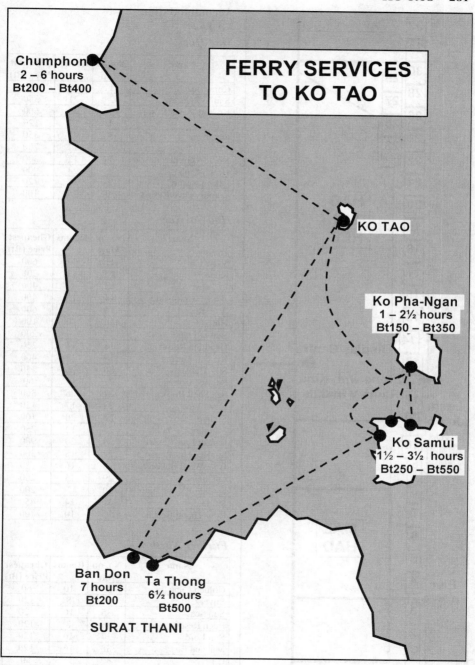

FERRY SERVICES TO KO TAO

Chumphon
2 – 6 hours
Bt200 – Bt400

KO TAO

Ko Pha-Ngan
1 – 2½ hours
Bt150 – Bt350

Ko Samui
1½ – 3½ hours
Bt250 – Bt550

Ban Don
7 hours
Bt200

Ta Thong
6½ hours
Bt500

SURAT THANI

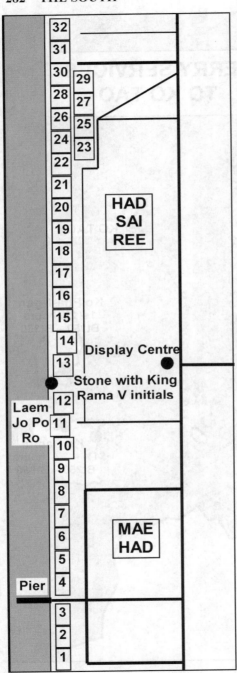

Accommodation
Ko Tao
Mae Had

Name	No. on Map	Rooms	Cheapest Price (Bt)
Coral Beach	1	18	100
San Si Paradise	2	21	350
Ko Tao Royal Resort	3	12	600
C.L.	4	17	120
Nanthiya	5	7	350
Crystal Dive Resort	6	17	700
Ko Tao Garden Resort	7	12	300
Beach Club	8	24	900
Queen Resort	9	12	120
Tommy Dive Resort	10	25	100

Had Sai Ree

Name	No. on Map	Rooms	Cheapest Price (Bt)
View Cliff	11	17	600
Khao	12	11	200
In Touch	13	5	400
A.C. Two Resort	14	12	400
A.C. Resort	15	23	600
Bing	16	10	100
Ban Diving Resort	17	10	200
Haad Sai Resort	18	14	250
Ko Tao Marina	19	18	400
S.B. Cabana	20	26	350
Sai Ree Cottage	21	19	60
Sea Shell Resort	22	26	350
New Way	23	17	120
Suthep	24	20	100
Simple Life Villa	25	12	250
Sunset Buri Resort	26	20	900
Sai Ree Hut Resort	27	18	300
Blue Wind Bakery	28	16	120
O-Chai	29	15	200
O-Chai II	30	7	200
Pranee	31	14	450
Bow Thong Beach	32	10	400

Further North

Name	No. on Map	Rooms	Cheapest Price (Bt)
Golden Cape	33	10	60
Silver Cliff	34	8	120
Sun Sea	35	10	120
Eden Resort	36	8	120
Sun Lord	37	16	120
Mahana Bay	38	16	120
C.F.T.	39	15	80

Had Sai Nual

Name	No. on Map	Rooms	Cheapest Price (Bt)
Sai Thong	40	24	120
Siam Cookie	41	14	120
Char	42	12	100

Ao Kul Jeua

Name	No. on Map	Rooms	Cheapest Price (Bt)
Sunset	44	15	120

Ao Chalok Ban Kao

Name	No. on Map	Rooms	Cheapest Price (Bt)
Leam Klong	48	24	250
Sunshine II	49	20	350
Sunshine	50	22	450
Buddha View Resort	51	23	250
Carabao Dive Resort	52	9	100
Ko Tao Tropicana	53	10	750
Pond Dive Resort	54	30	350
Big Fish Dive Resort	55	9	60
Ko Tao Garden Resort	56	37	350
Aud Resort	57	10	250

Had Ta Toh Yai

Name	No. on Map	Rooms	Cheapest Price (Bt)
Ta Toh Lagoon Resort	58	18	200
Freedom Beach	59	10	120

Ao Thian Ok

Name	No. on Map	Rooms	Cheapest Price (Bt)
Rocky Resort	60	37	100

Had Sai Daeng

Name	No. on Map	Rooms	Cheapest Price (Bt)
Coral View Resort	61	10	350
Sai Daeng Cape	62	20	90

Laem Je Ta Kang

Name	No. on Map	Rooms	Cheapest Price (Bt)
Tao Thong Villa	43	13	120

Had Saal Chao

Name	No. on Map	Rooms	Cheapest Price (Bt)
Black Bock	45	6	80
Taraphon	46	14	250
View Point Dive Resort	47	26	120

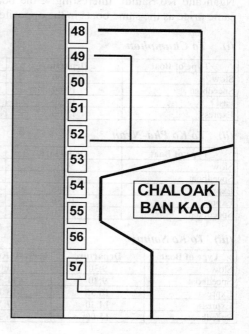

Ao Leuk

Name	No. on Map	Rooms	Cheapest Price (Bt)
Nice Moon	63	4	300
Ao Leuk	64	7	60

Ao Tanoad

Name	No. on Map	Rooms	Cheapest Price (Bt)
Reef Cave	65	6	400
Poseidon	66	15	120
Diamond Beach	67	12	120
Bamboo Huts	68	11	100
Ta Note Bay Resort	69	25	100

Laem Thian

Name	No. on Map	Rooms	Cheapest Price (Bt)
Laem Thian	70	15	120

Ao Hin Wong

Name	No. on Map	Rooms	Cheapest Price (Bt)
Hin Wong	71	8	100
Green Tree Resort	72	8	100

Moving On

There are boats to Chumpon and Surat Thani and to the nearby islands of Ko Pha-Ngan and Ko Samui. Interestingly, the boats to Chumphon are not necessarily the same price as the same boats in the opposite direction. Here are details.

(i)   To Chumphon

Type of Boat	Departure	Arrival (Chumphon)	Fare (Bt)
Slow	10:00	15:00	200
Speedboat	10:00	12:00	450
Fast	10:30	13:00	300
Express	15:00	18:00	400

(ii)   To Ko Pha-Ngan

Type of Boat	Departure	Arrival (Ko Pha-Ngan)	Fare (Bt)
Slow	9:30	12:00	150
Speedboat	9:30	10:30	350
Express	10:35	12:15	200
Express	14:30	16:00	200
Speedboat	15:00	16:00	350

(iii)   To Ko Samui

Type of Boat	Departure	Arrival (Ko Samui)	Arrival Port	Fare (Bt)
Slow	9:30	13:00	Maenam	250
Speedboat	9:30	11:30	Nathon	450
Express	10:35	13:15	Nathon	345
Express	14:30	17:15	Maenam	295
Speedboat	15:00	16:30	Bo Phut	450

(iv)   To Surat Thani

Type of Boat	Departure	Arrival (Surat Thani)	Arrival Port	Fare (Bt)
Express	10:35	16:30	Ta Thong	395
Slow	20:30	6:00	Ban Don	350

KO PHA-NGAN   เกาะพงัน

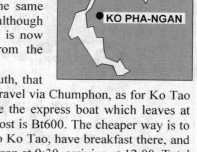

KO PHA-NGAN

3 hrs by ferry from Don Sak or Khanom

When the author first visited Ko Pha-Ngan, there was just one guest house there (and the ruins of another, which had failed, on the far side of the island). The guest house did not have electricity. There were no roads, so no vehicles, except a few motor bikes which could negotiate the sandy tracks around and across the island.

Today Ko Pha-Ngan is unrecognisable as the same island. The roads are not all of high quality, although some are, but almost every corner of the island is now accessible and large car ferries run to and from the mainland several times every day.

Most people reach Ko Pha-Ngan from the south, that is via Surat Thani, although it is also possible to travel via Chumphon, as for Ko Tao above. From Chumphon, the easy way is to take the express boat which leaves at 7:30 and which reaches Ko Pha-Ngan at 12:15. Cost is Bt600. The cheaper way is to take the slow boat at midnight from Chumphon to Ko Tao, have breakfast there, and then take the slow boat from Ko Tao to Ko Pha-Ngan at 9:30, arriving at 12:00. Total cost will be Bt350, plus transport from Chumphon town to Tha Yang Pier (Bt5, if you go before dark, Bt50 if you wait until late in the evening).

From Ko Tao to Ko Pha-Ngan, there are five boats per day, as detailed above at the end of the entry for Ko Tao. Costs vary between Bt150 and Bt350. Note that Thai people do not necessarily pay the same fares. You could, for example, try getting on the slow boat without a pre-booked ticket, as most Thais do, and tendering Bt100, as they do. The chances are that you would still be requested to pay Bt150, but because the commissions to the ticket agents would be saved you might get away with paying the same as the locals.

From Surat Thani in the south, four different types of service operate. First of all there are two companies operating car ferries.

Raja Ferries operates three times a day from Don Sak Port, at 10:00, 13:00 and 18:00. The fare is Bt120 and the journey is direct, taking 2½ hours. Note that Don Sak is not near the main town of Surat Thani, so first a bus must be taken to the port. For departures to Ko Pha-Ngan, a minibus is operated, leaving from Surat Thani (Ban Don main town) 1½ hours before the ferry departure. The actual minibus journey takes a little over one hour and costs Bt70. If you want to reduce this cost, Raja Ferries also operates ferries from Don Sak to Ko Samui, and for these services a large ordinary bus is used at a cost of Bt40 to the port. The morning departure, for example, coincides with a departure for Ko Samui, so the big bus can be used without any addition to total journey time. For information regarding the location of the bus departure point, see the Surat Thani entry below.

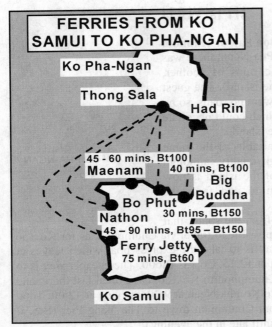

FERRIES FROM KO SAMUI TO KO PHA-NGAN

Ko Pha-Ngan

Thong Sala

Had Rin

45 - 60 mins, Bt100
Maenam
40 mins, Bt100

Big Buddha

Bo Phut

Nathon
30 mins, Bt150

45 – 90 mins, Bt95 – Bt150

Ferry Jetty
75 mins, Bt60

Ko Samui

The second car ferry service is operated by Songserm and travels from Khanom port via Ko Samui. A bus is operated between Surat Thani and Khanom. Although the ferry fare is the same as for Raja, Khanom is further from Surat Thani and the stop in Ko Samui also adds to the journey time. There are two services per day. For the first, the bus leaves Surat Thani at 8:00 and the ferry sails from Khanom at 10:00, reaching Ko Pha-Ngan at 13:15. For the second, the bus leaves at 16:00 and the ferry sails at 18:00, arriving at 20:45.

The third service is an express boat from Ta Thong (near the heart of Surat Thani in Ban Don, but still a short bus ride is involved). This is operated under the name of Ferry Line, but is actually the same company as Songserm. The boat sails at 8:00 and travels via Ko Samui, reaching Ko Pha-Ngan at 11:45. The fare is Bt245.

The fourth service is the slow night boat which departs from Ban Don port in the heart of Surat Thani at 23:00. It arrives at Ko Pha-Ngan at 5:00. The fare is Bt200.

From Ko Samui, just to the south of Ko Pha-Ngan, there are no less than eight different services.

The first is a car ferry operated by Raja Ferries. There is one sailing per day, at 8:30, reaching Ko Pha-Ngan 75 minutes later. The departure point on Ko Samui is the Ferry Jetty, ten kilometres south of the main town of Nathon. The fare is Bt60 and this is the cheapest service between the two islands.

The second service is the car ferry operated by Songserm. There are two departures, at 12:00 and 19:30, for the 25 kilometre crossing. The journey time is 90 minutes and departure point the centre of the main town of Nathon. The fare is Bt80 for Thais and Bt95 for foreigners.

The third service is the express boat operated by Ferry Line (Songserm). It leaves from the town of Nathon at 11:00 and reaches Ko Pha-Ngan at 11:45. The fare is Bt95.

Next there is a speedboat from Nathon to Ko Pha-Ngan. It leaves at 12:00 and takes 45 minutes at a cost of Bt150.

Now from the northern coast of Ko Samui, there are four more services. From Maenam, there is an express boat at 9:00, taking 45 minutes for the 16 kilometres and costing Bt100.

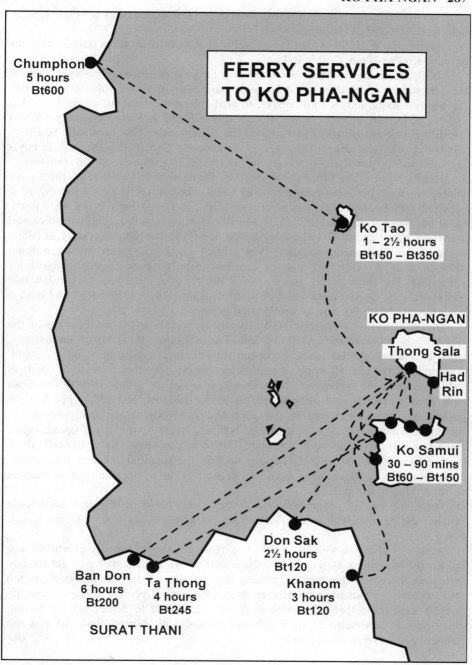

FERRY SERVICES TO KO PHA-NGAN

Chumphon
5 hours
Bt600

Ko Tao
1 – 2½ hours
Bt150 – Bt350

KO PHA-NGAN

Thong Sala

Had Rin

Ko Samui
30 – 90 mins
Bt60 – Bt150

Don Sak
2½ hours
Bt120

Ban Don
6 hours
Bt200

Ta Thong
4 hours
Bt245

Khanom
3 hours
Bt120

SURAT THANI

Also from Maenam, there is a slow boat at 14:00 which reaches Ko Pha-Ngan an hour later, at a cost of Bt100.

Moving east to Bo Phut, there is a speedboat at 8:30 which takes only 30 minutes to reach Ko Pha-Ngan. Cost is Bt150.

Finally, from Big Buddha Pier, there is a ferry service to Ko Pha-Ngan. This is the only service which does not arrive at the main town of Thong Sala. Instead it uses the shortest route, only 12 kilometres, to Had Rin at the southern extremity of Ko Pha-Ngan. Usually it berths on the western side of Had Rin, but occasionally tide and weather conditions oblige it to berth on the eastern side. This boat sails at 10:30, 13:00 and 16:00 and takes 50 minutes for the crossing. Considering the short distance involved and the popularity of the service, Bt100 seems expensive for this crossing.

Ko Pha-Ngan is the fifth largest island in Thailand. It has an area of 168 square kilometres and a permanent population of 8,500. The main town of Ko Pha-Ngan, at which all services except the last mentioned arrive, is **Thong Sala**. It is a small town, but it has most of the facilities which one would expect, including a post office and numerous travel agencies. From Thong Sala, it will probably be necessary to take a *songtaew* to your accommodation. The nearest guest houses are within walking distance, but you will find that the beaches near the town are not so good for swimming. The slope is very gentle, so that the sea goes out a long way at low tide and is shallow. On the other hand, if you just want to lie on the beach and have a quiet time, they are fine and generally good value.

The 'in' place at present is **Had Rin**, the peninsula at the southern tip of the island twelve kilometres from Thong Sala. For the author, this is much too touristy, with a beach covered with European bodies and hardly a Thai in sight. Accommodation can be found at reasonable prices, but other necessities, such as food and drink, are expensive. The peninsula is so narrow at this point that one can walk between eastern and western beaches in five minutes. The eastern beach is the popular one, the western narrow and quiet. The population here is totally devoted to the holiday industry. Shops, restaurants, bars and guest houses make up the entire community. If this is not what you want, however, you need only walk north along the western beach as far as necessary to gain the required level of tranquillity. Moreover, as you move away from the 'scene', prices of accommodation become correspondingly reduced.

There is plenty of accommodation at locations other than Had Rin, on or near beaches dotted round the island. Just pick what appeals, and if you do not like it, move on.

What will give you a shock is the price of the *songtaew*, not only exorbitant, but constantly increasing as the drivers discover that westerners will pay almost any price and, moreover, that they are at their mercy, since most of the distances are too great to walk without serious inconvenience. On the positive side, this overcharging does at least mean that the *songtaew* drivers can afford to depart without having every square centimetre of their vehicles packed with human flesh, so that the frequency of services is improved.

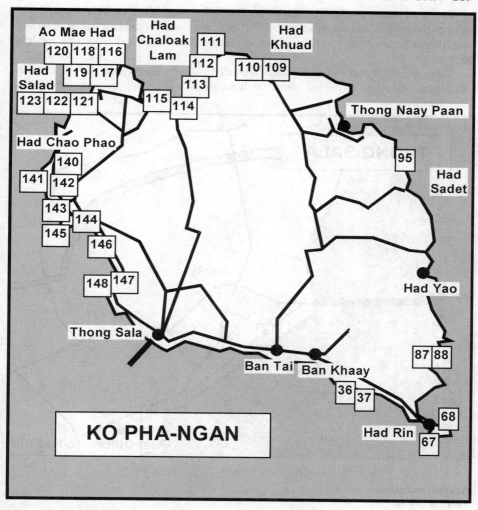

Here is a list of the principal *songtaew* fares from Thong Sala:

Ban Tai	Bt20
Ban Khaay	Bt30
Had Chao Phao	Bt30
Had Sadet	Bt40
Had Chaloak Lam	Bt40
Had Rin	Bt50
Had Yao	Bt50
Thong Naay Paan	Bt80

There are tours available to reach various interesting but relatively inaccessible parts of the island. Although, at Bt400 to Bt600, they are not exactly cheap, it would cost almost as much in *songtaew* fares to reach these places and would be far less convenient.

There are also boats to nearby small islands, in some cases regular services and in some cases charters. However, none of these small islands has accommodation or other facilities.

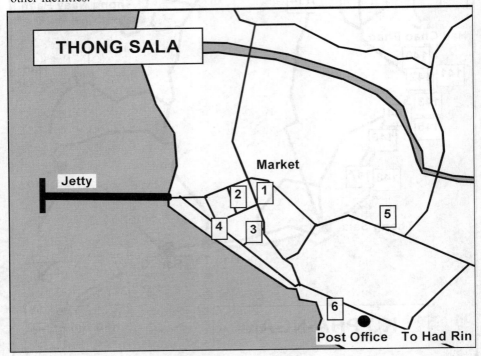

Accommodation
Ko Pha-Ngan
Thong Sala

Name	No. on Map	Rooms	Cheapest Price (Bt)
Buakao Inn	1	5	300
Black House	2	5	300
Shady Nook	3	3	150
Pha-Ngan Central	4	65	1,700
Chao Guest House	5	20	300
Phunum Pattana	6	6	250
Petch Cottage	7	12	60
Sundance	8	24	60

Name	No. on Map	Rooms	Cheapest Price (Bt)
Pha-Ngan Villa	9	11	60
Moonlight	10	12	60
Weang Thai	11	12	100
Charm Beach Resort	12	24	60
Chokana Resort	13	25	100
First Villa	14	17	600
King	15	10	60
Dew Shore	16	16	60

Ban Tai

Name	No. on Map	Rooms	Cheapest Price (Bt)
Birdville	17	5	60
S.P. Resort	18	13	60
Pink	19	17	60
Triangle Lodge	20	10	60
Liberty	21	7	150
Mac's Bay Resort	22	30	120
Bay Hut	23	9	120
Phargan Lodge	24	10	100
Lee Garden	25	25	100

Ban Khaay

Name	No. on Map	Rooms	Cheapest Price (Bt)
Sramanora Resort	26	5	250
Pha-Ngan Rainbow	27	16	80
Green Peace	28	9	90
Golden Beach	29	25	80
Sun Sea Resort	30	17	80
Beer	31	12	60
Banja Beach	32	7	60
Thong Yang	33	18	60
Pha-Ngan Island Resort	34	20	400
Boom's Café	35	17	60

Ao Hin Lor

Name	No. on Map	Rooms	Cheapest Price (Bt)
Silvery Moon	36	10	60

Laem Bangson

Name	No. on Map	Rooms	Cheapest Price (Bt)
Bang Son Villa	37	19	60

Had Rin West

Name	No. on Map	Rooms	Cheapest Price (Bt)
Blue Hill	38	10	120
Tiara Palace	39	14	100
Bird	40	12	80
Sun Beach	41	25	80
Sandy	42	15	80
Seaside	43	15	60
Rainbow	44	25	80
Coral	45	18	120

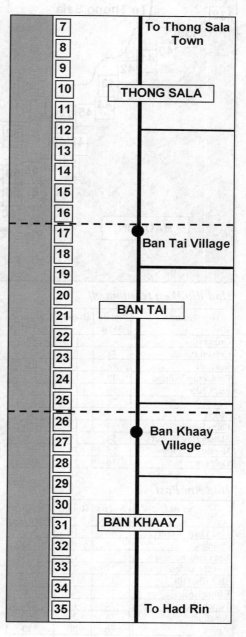

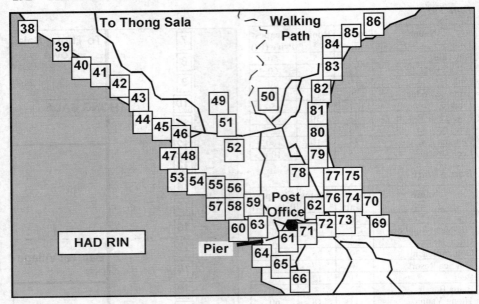

Had Rin West (continued)

Name	No. on Map	Rooms	Cheapest Price (Bt)
Grammy	46	11	80
Crystal Palace	47	13	120
Suksom	48	10	100
Pool Trup Village	49	13	60
Mr. Chaa	50	15	80
Nees	51	14	80
Moon	52	5	60
Palm Beach	53	13	120
Sunset Bay Resort	54	19	100
Neptune's Villa	55	30	60
Dolphin	56	21	100

Name	No. on Map	Rooms	Cheapest Price (Bt)
Charung	57	20	100
Had Rin Village	58	17	100
Black and White	59	22	120
Friendly	60	20	200
Top Gold	61	11	120
Oasis	62	10	250
Family House	63	20	60
Rin Beach Resort	64	20	300
Sun Cliff	65	30	200
Sea Breeze	66	10	120
Light House	67	10	120

Had Rin East

Name	No. on Map	Rooms	Cheapest Price (Bt)
Hua Laem Resort	68	10	250
Paradise	69	40	350
Sea Garden	70	19	200
Royal Garden	71	11	80
Had Rin Hill	72	7	120
China Rose	73	4	100
Beach Blue	74	15	200
Jonathan	75	22	200
Anant	76	80	120
Had Rin Resort	77	20	200

Name	No. on Map	Rooms	Cheapest Price (Bt)
Bumble Bee Hut	78	8	200
Pha-Ngan Orchid	79	18	350
Sunrise	80	26	120
Pha-Ngan Bay Shore	81	42	250
Tommy's Resort	82	30	100
Palita Lodge	83	35	200
Sea View	84	30	300
Mountain Sea	85	25	250
Serenity Hill	86	28	120

Had Thian

Name	No. on Map	Rooms	Cheapest Price (Bt)
Sanctuary	87	10	50
Had Tien Resort	88	30	150

Had Sadet

Name	No. on Map	Rooms	Cheapest Price (Bt)
Thong Reng Resort	89	20	120
Thaan Wung Thong	90	13	90
Mai Pen Rai	91	10	200
Nid's	92	8	60
Silver Cliff	93	12	80
Mai Pen Rai II	94	7	80
Somrak	95	10	40

Thong Naay Paan

Name	No. on Map	Rooms	Cheapest Price (Bt)
White Sand	96	12	120
A.D. View	97	15	120
Nice Beach	98	30	250
Central	99	12	400
Pen's	100	26	150
Ping Jun Resort	101	25	120
Chang Chit Dreamland	102	24	120
White Winds	103	10	120

Had Thong Naay Paan Nui

Name	No. on Map	Rooms	Cheapest Price (Bt)
Panviman Resort	104	38	1,200
Star Hut	105	26	120
Honey	106	20	120
Star Hut II	107	14	250
Thong Ta Pong	108	19	120

Had Khuad

Name	No. on Map	Rooms	Cheapest Price (Bt)
Bottle Beach	109	47	120
Bottle Beach II	110	43	120

Had Khom

Name	No. on Map	Rooms	Cheapest Price (Bt)
Coral Bay	111	18	110
Thai's Life	112	12	50

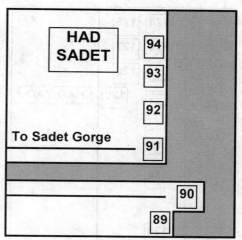

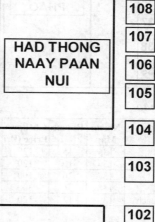

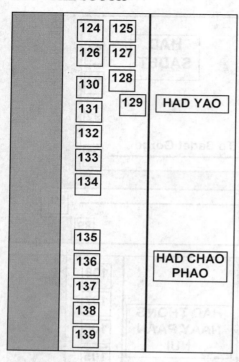

Had Chaloak Lam

Name	No. on Map	Rooms	Cheapest Price (Bt)
Try Thong Resort	113	18	60
Fanta	114	30	80
Wattana Resort	115	15	100

Ao Mae Had

Name	No. on Map	Rooms	Cheapest Price (Bt)
Crystal Island Garden	116	10	50
Mae Had	117	10	60
Mae Had Bay Resort	118	18	50
Island View Cabana	119	25	200
Wang Sai Resort	120	18	100

Had Salad

Name	No. on Map	Rooms	Cheapest Price (Bt)
Ko Pha-Ngan Resort	121	5	150
My Way	122	14	50
Salad Hut	123	10	50

Had Yao

Name	No. on Map	Rooms	Cheapest Price (Bt)
Ben Jawaan	124	10	80
Had Thian	125	16	50
Bay View Resort	126	25	150
Dream Hill	127	7	80
Blue Coral	128	10	80
Hide Away G. H.	129	3	100
Silver Beach	130	50	200
Had Yao	131	30	200
Ibiza	132	15	120
Sea Board	133	13	200
Sandy Bay	134	21	60

Had Chao Phao

Name	No. on Map	Rooms	Cheapest Price (Bt)
Great Bay	135	15	120
Had Chao Phao	136	10	120
Sea Flower	137	20	100
See Tanu	138	9	300
Nakhon Palm Beach	139	12	120

Ao See Tanu

Name	No. on Map	Rooms	Cheapest Price (Bt)
Laem Son	140	16	120
Laem Son Bay	141	6	200
Sea View Rainbow	142	12	200
Loy Fa	143	28	120
Chai	144	5	120
Nantakarn Resort	145	14	120

Ao Hin Kong

Name	No. on Map	Rooms	Cheapest Price (Bt)
Lipstick Cabana	146	7	60

Ao Wogtum

Name	No. on Map	Rooms	Cheapest Price (Bt)
Kiet	147	16	40
O.K.	148	24	120

Ao Plaaylaem

Name	No. on Map	Rooms	Cheapest Price (Bt)
Darin	149	18	80
Chuenjit	150	12	60
Sea Scene	151	18	150
Bounty	152	15	200
Porn Sawan	153	17	100
Cookie	154	18	80
Beach 99	155	11	100

Ao Naiwog

Name	No. on Map	Rooms	Cheapest Price (Bt)
Siriphun	156	30	350
Charn	157	8	120
Pha-Ngan	158	25	100

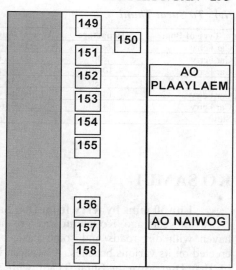

Moving On

There are boats to Chumpon, Surat Thani and the nearby islands of Ko Tao and Ko Samui. Again, fares for these boats are not necessarily the same as fares for the same boats in the opposite direction. Here are details.

(i) To Chumphon

Type of Boat	Departure	Arrival (Chumphon)	Fare (Bt)
Express	12:30	18:00	600

(ii) To Ko Tao

Type of Boat	Departure	Arrival (Ko Tao)	Fare (Bt)
Speedboat	9:00	10:00	350
Express	10:00	11:30	250
Slow	11:30	14:00	150
Speedboat	12:30	13:30	350
Express	12:30	14:00	250

(iii) To Ko Samui

Type of Boat	Departure	Arrival (Ko Samui)	Arrival Port	Fare (Bt)
Car Ferry	6:00	7:30	Nathon	95
Slow (Had Rin)	9:30	10:20	Big Buddha	100
Speedboat	10:45	11:30	Nathon	150
Slow (Had Rin)	11:40	12:30	Big Buddha	100
Slow	12:00	13:00	Maenam	100
Express	12:30	13:15	Nathon	95
Car Ferry	14:00	15:30	Nathon	95
Slow (Had Rin)	14:30	15:20	Big Buddha	100
Express	16:30	17:15	Maenam	95
Speedboat	16:00	16:30	Bo Phut	150
Car Ferry	16:00	17:30	Ferry Jetty	60

(iv)   To Surat Thani

Type of Boat	Departure	Arrival (Surat Thani)	Arrival Port	Fare (Bt)
Car Ferry	6:00	11:00 (by bus)	Khanom	120 + 105 (bus)
Car Ferry	7:00	11:00 (by minibus)	Don Sak	120 + 70 (minibus)
Car Ferry	10:00	14:00 (by minibus)	Don Sak	120 + 70 (minibus)
Express	12:30	16:30	Ta Thong	245
Car Ferry	13:00	17:00 (by minibus)	Don Sak	120 + 70 (minibus)
Car Ferry	14:00	19:00 (by bus)	Khanom	120 + 105 (bus)
Slow	22:00	5:00	Ban Don	200

KO SAMUI   เกาะสมุย

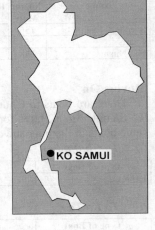

1 hr 30 mins by ferry from Don Sak or Khanom

A few years ago, Ko Samui was a rustic backpackers' haven with dirt roads and some basic accommodation erected on its various beaches. A boat ran from the centre of Ban Don town in Surat Thani with space for fifty passengers, and the overflow permitted to travel (dangerously) on the roof in the full glare of the sunshine. Once in a while this boat was stopped and robbed by pirates.

All that has changed. Now there are paved roads, and towns have sprung up where before there were tiny villages. There are classy hotels, large car ferries in operation many times a day, and even a small airport with direct flights from Bangkok.

Ko Samui is the third largest island in Thailand, after Phuket and Ko Chang, with an area of 247 square kilometres. It measures 25 kilometres from north to south and 21 kilometres from east to west, so it is still possible to find cheap accommodation on quiet beaches, if that is what you want, and, despite the erection of the high class hotels, the majority of visitors here are still looking for accommodation costing less than Bt500 per night, which is readily available at all locations.

What have changed noticeably over the last two decades are the occupations and pre-occupations of the permanent residents. Twenty years ago, they went about their agricultural business, glancing with interest and curiosity at the growing influx of western visitors, but regarding it merely as a temporary phenomenon. Now few people bother about coconuts any more. Tourism is the industry of Ko Samui, and everything revolves around that staple of the island. It has made Ko Samui into an importer, rather than an almost self-sufficient community, and, of course, that means that much of the rural atmosphere has been lost, but it has also brought prosperity to the society there and improvements in infrastructure.

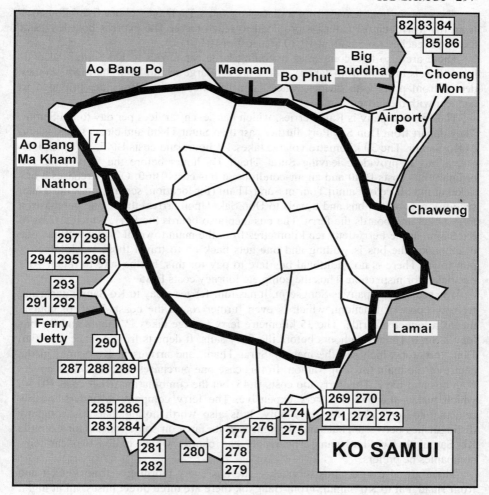

Ko Samui is usually reached by one of the ferry services, or ferry plus bus services, from Surat Thani which lies to the south-west of the island. First, therefore, it is best to understand the intricacies of reaching Ko Samui and how best to handle them.

Two ferry services still depart from near the area of Surat Thani known as Ban Don, which is the real heart of the town. These two are the express boat operated under the name of Ferry Line (actually the same company as Songserm) and the slow night boat. The night boat leaves at 23:00 from the centre of Ban Don, reaching Ko Samui at 5:00. It costs Bt100 for the upper deck, which includes a mat and pillow (Bt80 for the lower deck, but you will be encouraged to take the higher class).

The express boat leaves from a place known as Ta Thong, about five kilometres from the town centre. A bus is provided to reach there. The express boat leaves at 8:00 and reaches Ko Samui at 10:30 at a cost of Bt150.

There are also two companies operating large car ferries to Ko Samui (second-hand vessels brought from Japan). These are too large to sail from the town, so they depart from ports with deeper water some distance away. Buses are provided to connect with the ferries.

The first company is Raja Ferries, which has seven services per day to Ko Samui. They depart from Don Sak Port, further east than Surat Thani and closer to the island of Ko Samui. The 30 kilometre voyage takes 1½ hours and costs Bt45. To reach Don Sak a bus is provided, leaving Surat Thani 1½ hours before the ferry sails. An ordinary bus costs Bt40 and an air-conditioned bus costs Bt60. One purchases a bus ticket at the office of Samui Tour in Surat Thani (for location, see map in Surat Thani section), gets on the bus and travels to Don Sak. Upon arrival there, one purchases a ferry ticket and boards the ferry. The bus then also boards the ferry, which arrives in Ko Samui at the Ferry Jetty ten kilometres from the main town of Nathon. When one disembarks, the bus is waiting and one gets back on to travel those ten kilometres into town. There is no additional bus fare to pay for this, but be sure to retain your bus ticket for inspection. Thus the complete journey costs Bt85.

The second company is Songserm. It has four ferries a day to Ko Samui departing from the port of Khanom, which is even further round the coast. That, of course, means a longer bus ride. The 35 kilometre ferry voyage takes 1½ hours and the bus leaves Surat Thani two hours before the ferry sails. It departs from a place near Ban Don Port, for which see the map of Surat Thani, and arrives in Ko Samui in the centre of the main town of Nathon. In this case one purchases a ticket which covers both bus and ferry. This ferry too costs Bt45, but the combination ticket costs Bt150, which makes the bus ride very expensive. The ferry company is understandably reluctant to sell tickets for ferry only. It is also worth noting that this company distinguishes between Thais and foreigners in its fares on some routes (for example Ko Samui to Ko Pha-Ngan). The reader can choose which of the two car ferry companies he prefers.

There are also direct bus services – one bus every morning – from Phuket and from Haad Yai to Ko Samui. From Bangkok there are three direct buses, all at night. These buses run to the ferry terminal at Don Sak and then they too travel on the ferry across to Ko Samui where one re-boards for the last ten kilometres to Nathon. Bus tickets are sold inclusive of the ferry fare.

Ko Samui can also be reached by boats from the islands of Ko Pha-Ngan and Ko Tao (for details see the sections above relating to those islands) and by the express boat from Chumphon at 7:30, which arrives in Ko Samui (Nathon) at 13:15, at a cost of Bt745.

There is an air service operated by Bangkok Airways with no less than ten flights every day from Bangkok. The airport is on the north side of the island, near Big Buddha Beach.

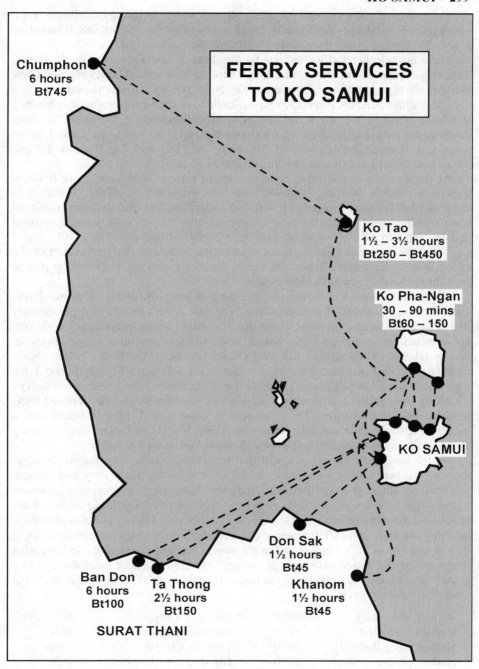

**FERRY SERVICES
TO KO SAMUI**

Chumphon
6 hours
Bt745

Ko Tao
1½ – 3½ hours
Bt250 – Bt450

Ko Pha-Ngan
30 – 90 mins
Bt60 – 150

KO SAMUI

Don Sak
1½ hours
Bt45

Ban Don
6 hours
Bt100

Ta Thong
2½ hours
Bt150

Khanom
1½ hours
Bt45

SURAT THANI

The principal town of **Nathon** offers all reasonable facilities including a **TAT office** just behind the post office with useful information for new arrivals. This office is only five minutes walk from the town pier and the bus terminal.

There is a telephone office with by far the cheapest Internet service on the island. This office is open from 8:00 until 22:00. There are also several hotels and one guest house in the town, for those who want to stay there. It is a town of a pleasant size.

The various beaches around Ko Samui each have their own character, governed to a large extent by the prices and density of accommodation in that area. The most developed is the six kilometre long **Chaweng Beach** on the east coast. **Lamai**, in the south-east, is moderately developed. **Maenam, Bo Phut and Big Buddha** are less so, and the little places in between are still quite tranquil.

At Big Buddha Beach, there is, as one might perhaps anticipate, a big Buddha. This is a modern creation, built on what was originally an island. However, a causeway has been constructed to join it to the mainland and land has been reclaimed to enlarge the island, so that the temple and meditation centre could gradually expand and develop into what is becoming quite an impressive complex worth a visit.

There are waterfalls, although not outstanding ones, and the central part of the island is quite hilly and offers good views. There are also some interesting phallic rocks at the southern end of Lamai Beach.

To the west of Ko Samui is the **Ang Thong National Marine Park**, encompassing a number of smaller islands. The park covers an area of approximately 250 square kilometres, of which about 20% is land. Various excursions to this area are operated by companies in Ko Samui, some of them providing opportunities for diving. Islands visited include Ko Wao Talab ('Sleeping Cow Island') which has a notable viewpoint, Ko Mae Ko ('Mum's Island'), Ko Prayat ('Miserly Island'), Ko Sam Sao ('Three-Legged Island'), Ko Nai Pud ('Mr. Pud's Island') and Ko Wao Tey ('Kicking Cow Island'). The islands are composed of limestone with forested cliffs reaching up to 400 metres. There are remote beaches and 'Mum's Island' has a beautiful emerald blue salt lake known as Talay Nai ('The Inland Sea'). It takes about two hours to reach the Ang Thong National Park from Ko Samui.

Dotted around Ko Samui you will find bus stops, which is interesting, because there are no buses, except the ones which run between the Ferry Jetty and Nathon, and they do not stop along the way. There are, however, the ubiquitous *songtaew* trying to get as much money from their passengers as possible. Inside every vehicle is posted a list of permissible fares. Thais are usually asked to pay about double these amounts and foreigners are frequently charged about three times the correct fares, if they do not object. It is a nuisance, but the way to proceed is to watch carefully what others are paying and to have enough change to be able to tender exact money. As a guide, here are the currently accepted prices (i.e. about double the posted fares, but what Thais usually pay):

Nathon – Maenam	Bt20	Nathon – Lamai	Bt30
Nathon – Bo Phut	Bt20	Nathon – Chaweng	Bt30
Nathon – Big Buddha	Bt30	Lamai – Chaweng	Bt30
Nathon – Choeng Mon	Bt30	Big Buddha – Chaweng	Bt30

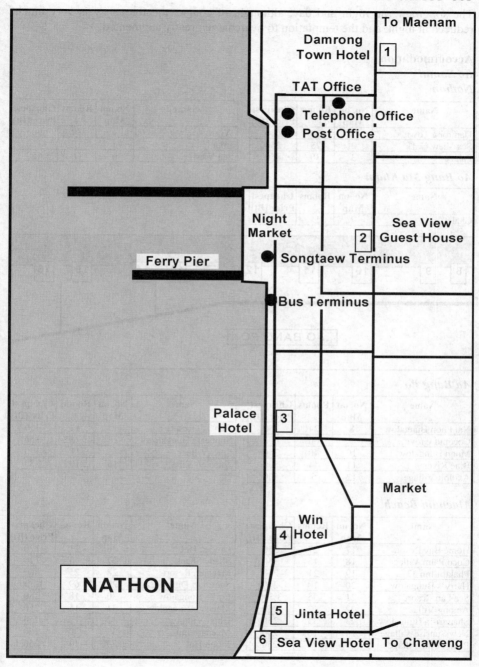

To Maenam

Damrong
Town Hotel [1]

TAT Office

● Telephone Office

● Post Office

Night
Market

[2] Sea View
Guest House

Ferry Pier

● Songtaew Terminus

● Bus Terminus

Palace
Hotel

[3]

Market

Win
[4] Hotel

NATHON

[5] Jinta Hotel

[6] Sea View Hotel To Chaweng

The *songtaew* run night and day, although, of course, the frequency is very much reduced at night, and the temptation to overcharge greatly augmented.

Accommodation
Ko Samui
Nathon

Name	No. on Map	Rooms	Cheapest Price (Bt)	Name	No. on Map	Rooms	Cheapest Price (Bt)
Damrong Town	1	20	600	Win	4	30	600
Sea View G. H.	2	25	250	Jinta	5	10	450
Palace	3	30	450	Sea View	6	16	450

Ao Bang Ma Kham

Name	No. on Map	Rooms	Cheapest Price (Bt)
Chalet	7	15	250

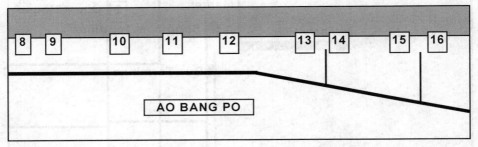

Ao Bang Po

Name	No. on Map	Rooms	Cheapest Price (Bt)	Name	No. on Map	Rooms	Cheapest Price (Bt)
Nai Phon Bungalow	8	24	250	Ban Tai Resort	13	12	450
Coconut Grove	9	60	600	Sunbeam Bungalows	14	25	350
Moon Bungalow	10	40	250	O.K. Village	15	11	120
Blue River	11	44	500	Napalan Villa	16	10	250
Axololt Village	12	5	500				

Maenam Beach

Name	No. on Map	Rooms	Cheapest Price (Bt)	Name	No. on Map	Rooms	Cheapest Price (Bt)
Home Bay Resort	17	27	350	Golden Hut	26	21	120
Coco Palm Village	18	15	350	Shady Shack	27	15	120
Phalarn Inn 33	19	21	250	Maenam Resort	28	25	800
Harry's Bungalow	20	10	250	Santiburi Dusit Resort	29	69	1,000
Sea Fan Resort	21	35	3,500	Lolita Bungalow	30	18	250
Among Villa	22	12	250	Maenam Bungalow	31	15	250
Shangri-la Bungalow	23	35	250	Ubon Villa	32	17	250
New Sunrise Village	24	10	200	Maenam Inn	33	30	250
Palm Point Village	25	16	250	Moon Hut	34	14	250

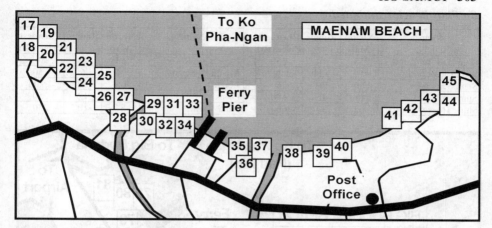

Maenam Beach (continued)

Name	No. on Map	Rooms	Cheapest Price (Bt)
Nature	35	17	150
Cleopatra Palace	36	18	200
Sea Shore	37	32	250
Near Sea Resort	38	20	600
New Lapaz Villa	39	30	600
Paradise Beach Resort	40	30	2,200

Name	No. on Map	Rooms	Cheapest Price (Bt)
Friendly Bungalow	41	16	250
Rose Bungalow	42	15	100
Silence	43	23	80
Maenam Villa	44	20	250
Laem Sai Bungalow	45	30	200

Bo Phut Beach

Name	No. on Map	Rooms	Cheapest Price (Bt)
Sunny Bungalow	46	26	80
Chalee Villa	47	17	200
Bo Phut Guest House	48	16	200
Star Fish and Coffee	49	15	350
Sandy Resort	50	72	950
World Resort	51	50	600

Name	No. on Map	Rooms	Cheapest Price (Bt)
New Sala Bungalow	52	15	150
Samui Palm Beach	53	50	3,500
Palm Garden	54	20	100
Calm Bungalow	55	24	250
Peace Bungalow	56	45	350
Fontana Resort	57	40	2,200

Bo Phut Beach (continued)

Name	No. on Map	Rooms	Cheapest Price (Bt)	Name	No. on Map	Rooms	Cheapest Price (Bt)
Chai Had Bungalow	58	10	250	New Boon Resort	63	13	80
Samui Euphoria	59	124	2,200	Miami Bungalow	64	6	150
Siam Sea Lodge	60	30	250	Lodge	65	10	1,200
Summer Night	61	15	600	Oasis	66	12	250
Smile House Resort	62	30	600	Sand View	67	10	250

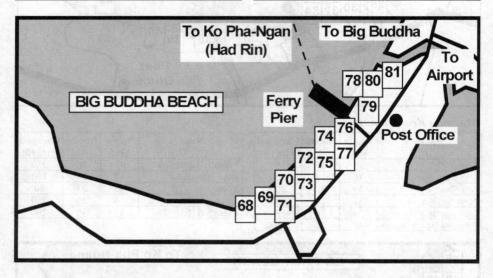

Big Buddha Beach (Bang Ruk)

Name	No. on Map	Rooms	Cheapest Price (Bt)	Name	No. on Map	Rooms	Cheapest Price (Bt)
Como's Bungalow	68	11	600	Phayorm Park Resort	75	11	250
Beach House	69	20	350	Sunset Song	76	19	300
L.A. Resort	70	10	350	Ocean View	77	17	250
Eden Inn	71	16	200	Sunset	78	12	200
Secret Garden	72	10	350	Pong Petch	79	30	600
Kinnaree Bungalow	73	15	350	M.P.S. Resort	80	12	450
Number One	74	10	250	Nara Garden	81	45	1,400

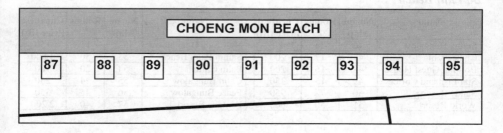

Choeng Mon Beach

Name	No. on Map	Rooms	Cheapest Price (Bt)
Bay View Village	82	135	2.200
Golden Pine	83	10	100
Samui Thong Son	84	11	250
Thong Son Bay	85	25	100
Ban Thong Sai	86	72	12,500
Au Soleil Bungalow	87	15	250
P.S. Villa	88	14	600
White House	89	40	2,700
Choeng Mon Bungalow	90	20	300
Phayorm Park View	91	18	350
Chat Kaew Resort	92	15	600
Island View Bungalow	93	21	250
Imperial Boat House	94	216	6,000
Sun Sand Resort	95	35	600

Chaweng Beach

Name	No. on Map	Rooms	Cheapest Price (Bt)
I.K.K. Resort	96	10	250
Coral Bay Resort	97	42	2,200
Papillon Resort	98	15	600
Samui Island Resort	99	20	700
Matlang Resort	100	35	600
Chaba Cabana Resort	101	78	3,500
Venus Resort	102	15	250
Marine Bungalow	103	35	350
Lazy Wave	104	20	350
Moon Bungalow	105	45	150
Family Bungalow	106	10	250
Samui Villa Flora	107	82	1,200
Chaweng Pearl Cabana	108	26	350
K. John Resort	109	20	150
Muang Kula Pan	110	50	3.200
Amari Palm Reef	111	84	6,000
Chaweng Blue Lagoon	112	61	4,000
Samui Natien Resort	113	25	1,300
Palm Island	114	45	1,300
J.R. Bungalow	115	75	250
O.P. Bungalow	116	35	1,100
Samui Cabana	117	57	350
Relax Resort	118	31	500
Samui Country Resort	119	45	600
Novotel Samui Resort	120	36	2,500
The Island	121	40	900
Chaweng Regent	122	120	5,000
Chaweng Villa	123	45	1,300
Mon Thien House	124	45	1,100
Lucky Mother	125	10	250
Lotus Bungalow	126	25	250
Sun East Bungalow	127	15	300
Coconut Grove	128	12	350

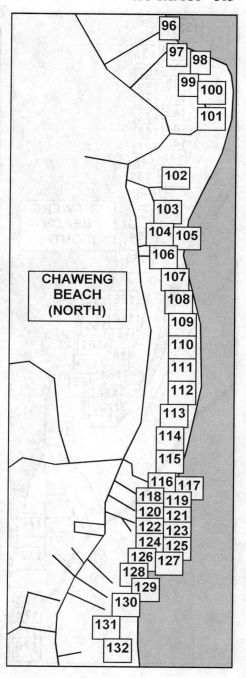

CHAWENG BEACH (NORTH)

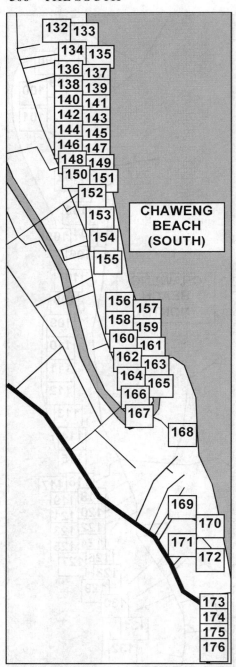

CHAWENG
BEACH
(SOUTH)

Chaweng Beach (continued)

Name	No. on Map	Rooms	Cheapest Price (Bt)
Samui Coral Park	129	20	200
Chaweng Garden Beach	130	39	600
Ban Chaweng Resort	131	20	450
J.R.	132	30	600
Anchor House	133	20	250
Best Beach Bungalow	134	10	350
Chaweng Inn	135	15	200
Chaweng Beach House	136	24	350
Samui Royal Beach	137	30	600
Malibu Beach Club	138	17	600
Chaweng Buri Resort	139	115	3,500
Long Beach Lodge	140	25	600
Ban Samui Resort	141	79	2,600
Thai Restaurant I	142	16	100
Thai Restaurant II	143	14	80
Dewdrop Hut	144	24	200
King's Bungalow	145	30	250
Chaba Samui Resort	146	45	3,500
Beachcomber	147	60	4,000
Silver Sand Bungalow	148	40	250
Thai House	149	20	250
Charlie's Hut	150	80	150
Viking	151	27	150
Central Bay Resort	152	20	600
Princess Village	153	12	1,600
Trade Winds Resort	154	20	1,600
Central Samui Beach	155	21	6,000
Chaweng Resort	156	40	2,200
Arabian Bungalow	157	20	600
Chaweng Cabana	158	40	1,200
Chaweng Cove	159	50	950
Poppies Resort	160	24	5,500
Joy Resort	161	45	250
Parrot Bungalow	162	20	600
Samui Resotel	163	50	1,600
Sans Souci Samui	164	138	1,600
Samui Paradise	165	32	1,200
Chaweng G. H.	166	25	600
Sea Side Bungalow	167	30	250
First Bungalow	168	60	2,200
New Star Resort	169	40	600
Imperial Samui	170	80	6,250
Santa Lucia	171	30	700
Victorian Resort	172	60	2,800
Mao Bungalow	173	16	80
Chaweng Noi	174	10	100
Pong Petch G. H.	175	30	600
Bird's Eye View	176	20	450
Samui Bay View Villa	177	74	2,200
Coral Cove Resort	178	20	300
Coral Cove Chalet	179	64	1,700

Chaweng Beach (continued)

Name	No. on Map	Rooms	Cheapest Price (Bt)
Blue Horizon	180	20	700
High Coral Cove	181	20	250
Beverley Hill Resort	182	15	350
Golden Cliff Resort	183	12	350
Orion (Little Mermaid)	184	6	600
Samui Silver Beach	185	20	350
Tong Ta Kian Villa	186	10	250
Samui Yacht Club	187	40	1,700

Lamai Beach

Name	No. on Map	Rooms	Cheapest Price (Bt)
Thong Gaid Garden	188	18	80
Royal Blue Lagoon	189	20	2,000
Bay View Villa	190	20	350
Comfort Bungalow	191	20	600
Jungle Park Resort	192	40	450
Flower Paradise	193	10	250
Long Island Resort	194	40	1,600
Rose Garden	195	20	400
New Weekender Villa	196	20	250
Spa	197	18	250
No Name Bungalow	198	10	250
My Friend Bungalow	199	10	250
Sukasem Bungalows	200	12	600
Tapi Bungalow	201	11	250
New Hut	202	10	250
Beer's House	203	10	400
Marine Park Bungalow	204	20	100
Lamai Villa	205	20	100
Lamai Resort	206	26	250
Sand Sea Resort	207	29	1,500
Garden Home	208	31	250
Platuna	209	20	250
Samui Laguna Resort	210	60	1,800
Pavilion Resort	211	50	3,000
Noi Bungalow	212	11	250
Utopia Bungalow	213	45	250
Samui Residence	214	20	350
Lily House	215	20	250
Magic Resort	216	20	450
Lamai Coconut Resort	217	30	700
Suan Thale Resort	218	20	250
Weekender Resort	219	64	2,000
Bonny	220	25	600
Sea Garden	221	20	120
Coconut Beach Resort	222	20	100
Lamai Inn 99	223	52	700
Rich Resort	224	15	250
Beach Side Bungalow	225	10	400
Best Resort	226	50	600

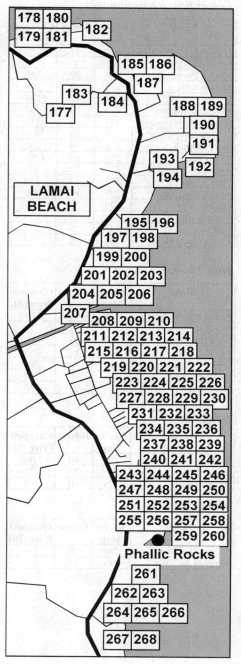

Lamai Beach (continued)

Name	No. on Map	Rooms	Cheapest Price (Bt)	Name	No. on Map	Rooms	Cheapest Price (Bt)
Holiday	227	12	250	Kanok Guest House	244	4	250
Sawasdee House	228	8	250	Lamai Pearl Bungalow	245	30	100
Marina Bungalow	229	20	250	Bill Bungalow	246	40	450
Marina Villa	230	40	700	Paradise Bungalow	247	45	600
Galaxy Resort	231	40	1,200	Green Canyon	248	15	350
Mira Mare Resort	232	20	250	Lamai Chalet	249	17	350
Sea Breeze Bungalow	233	30	250	B.R. Garden	250	9	200
Golden Sand Resort	234	80	600	Wanchai Villa	251	17	200
Som Thong Resort	235	20	250	Amity Bungalow	252	20	350
Aloha Resort	236	60	1,900	White Sand Bungalow	253	50	250
Amadeus Bungalow	237	20	300	Chain Bungalow	254	13	250
Phan's Garden	238	17	250	Nice Resort II	255	70	600
Koeng Bungalow	239	10	250	Nice Resort I	256	35	600
Casanova's	240	20	150	Palm Resort	257	30	250
Varinda Resort	241	20	250	Ban Thai Resort	258	16	450
Full Sun Resort	242	20	350	Sunrise Bungalow	259	29	300
Lamai Guest House	243	18	250	Grand Rock Resort	260	6	250

Hua Thanon

Name	No. on Map	Rooms	Cheapest Price (Bt)	Name	No. on Map	Rooms	Cheapest Price (Bt)
Samui Park Resort	261	64	2,200	Pine Beach Bungalow	268	10	250
Noi Bungalow	262	10	250	Cosy Resort	269	15	150
Jinta House	263	28	600	Samui Maria Resort	270	40	700
Floral House	264	12	250	Wanna Samui Resort	271	20	600
Best Wishes Bungalow	265	8	200	Samui Orchid Resort	272	40	1,200
Swiss Chalet	266	15	250	Central Samui Village	273	100	3,800
Rocky Resort	267	20	350				

Bang Kao

Name	No. on Map	Rooms	Cheapest Price (Bt)	Name	No. on Map	Rooms	Cheapest Price (Bt)
Butterfly Village	274	40	2,000	Diamond Villa	277	12	120
Laem Set Inn	275	20	2,200	Samui Coral Resort	278	20	200
River Garden	276	10	200	Waikiki Bungalow	279	10	350

Thong Krut

Name	No. on Map	Rooms	Cheapest Price (Bt)	Name	No. on Map	Rooms	Cheapest Price (Bt)
Thong Krut Bungalow	280	10	250	Coconut Villa	282	50	450
Simple Life Villa	281	15	150				

Taling Ngam

Name	No. on Map	Rooms	Cheapest Price (Bt)
Emerald Cove	283	20	250
Gems House	284	10	150
Pearl Bay	285	10	250
Seagull	286	15	250
Västervik	287	4	250
Wiesenthal	288	17	600

Name	No. on Map	Rooms	Cheapest Price (Bt)
Meridien Taling Ngam	289	60	12,000
Coco Cabana	290	20	250
R-An Palace Resort	291	10	400
Infoo Palace	292	10	350
Sunflower	293	25	100

Nathon Bay

Name	No. on Map	Rooms	Cheapest Price (Bt)
International Bungalow	294	23	600
Raja Pruek Resort	295	16	900
Lipa Lodge	296	24	350

Name	No. on Map	Rooms	Cheapest Price (Bt)
Siam Residence	297	20	6,500
Sawai Home	298	25	300

Moving On

There are boats to Chumphon, Surat Thani, Ko Tao and Ko Pha-Ngan. Here are the details.

(i)   To Chumphon

Type of Boat	Port	Departure	Arrival (Chumphon)	Fare (Bt)
Express	Nathon	11:00	18:00	745

(ii)   To Ko Tao

Type of Boat	Port	Departure	Arrival (Ko Tao)	Fare (Bt)
Speedboat	Bo Phut	8:30	10:00	550
Express	Maenam	9:00	11:30	350
Slow	Maenam	10:30	14:00	250
Express	Nathon	11:00	14:00	350
Speedboat	Nathon	11:30	13:30	550

(iii)   To Ko Pha-Ngan

Type of Boat	Port	Departure	Arrival (Pha-Ngan)	Fare (Bt)
Speedboat	Bo Phut	8:30	9:00	150
Car Ferry	Ferry Jetty	8:30	10:00	60
Express	Maenam	9:00	9:45	100
Slow (to Had Rin)	Big Buddha	10:30	11:20	100
Slow	Maenam	10:30	11:30	100
Express	Nathon	11:00	11:45	100
Speedboat	Nathon	11:30	12:15	150
Car Ferry	Nathon	12:00	13:30	95
Slow (to Had Rin)	Big Buddha	13:00	13:50	100
Slow (to Had Rin)	Big Buddha	16:00	16:50	100
Car Ferry	Nathon	19:30	21:00	95

(iv) To Surat Thani

Type of Boat	Port	Departure	Arrival (Surat Thani)	Fare (Bt)
Car Ferry	6:00	No bus	Don Sak (7:30)	45
Car Ferry	6:00	No bus	Khanom (7:30)	45
Car Ferry	8:00	11:00 (by bus)	Don Sak	85
Car Ferry	8:00	11:00 (by bus)	Khanom	150
Car Ferry	10:00	13:00 (by bus)	Don Sak	85
Car Ferry	12:00	15:00 (by bus)	Don Sak	85
Express	14:00	16:30	Ta Thong	150
Car Ferry	14:00	17:00 (by bus)	Don Sak	85
Car Ferry	14:00	17:00 (by bus)	Khanom	150
Car Ferry	15:00	18:00 (by bus)	Don Sak	85
Car Ferry	16:00	19:00 (by bus)	Khanom	150
Car Ferry	17:00	20:00 (by bus)	Don Sak	85
Slow	23:00	5:00	Ban Don	100

Buses run directly to Surat Thani, in conjunction with the Raja ferries via Don Sak, as listed above, and also to Bangkok, Haad Yai and Phuket. Here is a summary of bus services from Ko Samui. The fares for the buses include the ferry, except in the case of the Surat Thani buses.

Destination	Route No.	Price (Bt)				Journey Time (hrs)		Frequency	
		V.I.P.	A/C 1	A/C 2	Ord	A/C	Ord	A/C	Ord
Bangkok	991	802	396	308		14		3/day	
Haad Yai	729		240			7		1/day	
Phuket	727		230			8		1/day	
Surat Thani	8244		60		40	3	3	6/day	6/day

SURAT THANI สุราษฎร์ธานี

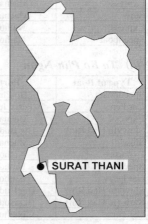

12 hrs by train from Bangkok
11 hrs by bus from Southern Bus Terminal

Surat Thani is most often visited as a staging post on the way to Ko Samui. Most people just pass through, but some find it necessary to stay overnight, and there is plenty of accommodation of various prices available for this purpose.

Surat Thani is actually a confusing town. The name Surat Thani refers to an area rather than a single conurbation and this leads to misunderstandings. The heart of the town is in a place known as **Ban Don**. When people refer to Surat Thani, without further qualification, this is usually where they mean. The railway station, however, is also called Surat Thani, but is in a place known as **Phun Phin** thirteen

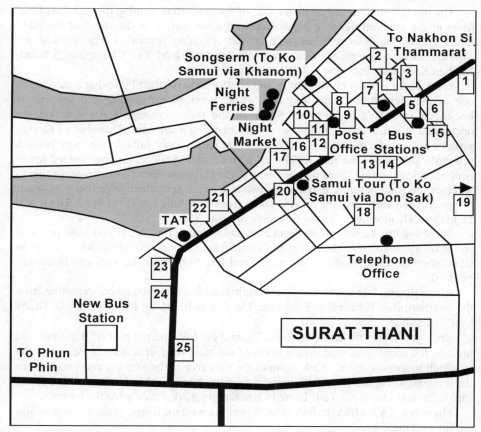

kilometres west of Ban Don. To get from Phun Phin to Ban Don, just walk outside the station and take a city bus no. 3 at a cost of Bt8. There are no other city bus services in Surat Thani, so it is obscure as to why this service is labelled 3. However, conveniently, Phun Phin and Ban Don are its two termini.

Bus stations are confusing here too. The government has recently built a beautiful new bus station, but it is in such an inconvenient location, seven kilometres from Ban Don on the road to Phun Phin, that nobody wants to use it. The result is that it stands there almost deserted while the old bus stations in the middle of Ban Don remain in use in a rather overcrowded area. The buses which do use the new bus station are the air-conditioned services to and from Bangkok, Haad Yai and Phuket. Theoretically, other buses call in also, but since this is only theory, you should catch other services from Ban Don town centre at present. If you do need to use the new bus station, the no. 3 bus between Phun Phin and Ban Don calls in (Bt5 from Ban Don or from Phun Phin to the bus station). Ascertain which way the bus is going, as services in both directions stop in the same place.

The old bus stations are on either side of the main road running through Ban Don. Most of the medium distance buses stop in the bus station to the south of the main road. Various minibus services have started operating from this area too and are offering speedy, if somewhat cramped, transport to Haad Yai, Chumphon, Phuket, Nakhon Si Thammarat, Don Sak, Khanom and Chaiya.

Surat Thani is most conveniently and comfortably reached by taking a sleeper on one of the night trains from Bangkok. These services are popular and need to be booked a few days in advance. Some of the trains convey sleepers which are uncoupled at Surat Thani, and these will be carrying a substantial number of foreign visitors heading for Ko Samui. Such trains are particularly suitable for those using a rail pass. Otherwise, the fare will be, as a guide, Bt558 for an air-conditioned lower berth on a rapid train. There will be some slight variation from this price according to whether the train is rapid, express or special express and whether the berth is upper or lower. If an early evening train is taken from Bangkok, arrival in Surat Thani will be in the early morning. See the timetable on page 74.

There are no ordinary trains from Bangkok running this far. If you wish to travel by ordinary train, use the 7:20 departure from Thonburi and spend a night in Chumphon (or Lang Suan) on the way. Total fare from Thonburi to Surat Thani will be Bt90.

Alternatively, one of the many air-conditioned buses can be taken, departing from the Southern Bus Terminal in Bangkok. The fare is Bt346 by 1st class bus and Bt269 by 2nd class bus.

Once you reach the centre of Surat Thani, you will find the port of Ban Don, and most of the accommodation, to the north of the main road. It is quite a pleasant town in which to spend a night. Walk down to the port area in the evening and you will see the three night boats tied up and preparing for departure: one to Ko Samui, one to Ko Pha-Ngan and one to Ko Tao. There is also a night market alongside the harbour.

There is a **TAT office** in Ban Don. It is at the western fringe of the town area, just within walking distance.

More than a millennium ago, Surat Thani ('City of Good People') was the centre of the Srivichaya Empire, and from this the nearby town of **Chaiya** derives its name. Chaiya is 54 kilometres north of the present centre of Surat Thani and has a temple, Wat Phra Borom That Chaiya, much restored, dating back some 1,200 years to the period when this was an imperial capital. There is also a National Museum in Chaiya.

Five kilometres south of Chaiya, so almost exactly 50 kilometres north of Surat Thani, is a modern temple, known variously as Wat Than Nam Lai ('Temple of the Flowing Water'), Wat Suan Mokkha Phalaram, or just **Wat Suan Mok**, founded on the 'back to basics' philosophy of the internationally famous Buddhist monk, the late Bhikku Buddhadasa. The temple is just off the main road (Highway 41), but constructed in a beautiful natural setting. The buildings avoid extravagance, but are decorated with murals and poems illustrating various Buddhist moral teachings. The temple is popular as a meditation centre.

Wat Traimit, Bangkok ▲

▼ **Phi Mai**

Summer Palace, Bang Pa In ▲

▼ Grand Palace, Bangkok

Track of Thailand and Burma Railway at Sai Yok Noi Falls, near Kanchanaburi ▲
▼ Guard performing his duties on ordinary train near Kanchanaburi

▲ Floating Market at Damnoen Saduak

Elephant taking a ride, from the bus
between Trang and Phuket (top left)

Typical budget riverside accommodatio
O.T.S. Guest House at Ban Pak Huai
(centre)

◄ Main road on Ko Chang, near Kai Bae

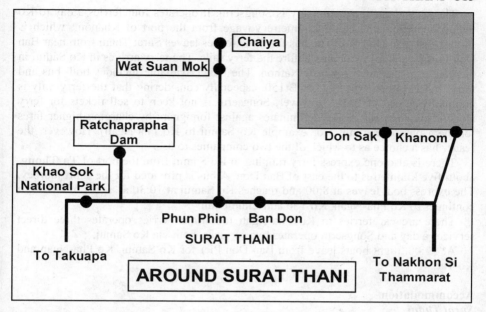

West of Surat Thani, on the road to Takuapa, is the **Khao Sok National Park**. The park is 109 kilometres from Surat Thani and offers forest land and wild life. Accommodation is available near the park entrance.

On the way to the National Park, you will pass by the **Ratchaprapha Dam**, part of a hydro-electric project and set in attractive countryside. However, the dam is twelve kilometres off the main road (Highway 401. Turning by the 52 kilometre post). Accommodation is available here too.

To reach Ko Samui from Surat Thani, you have a choice of two car ferry operators. The first company is Raja Ferries, with seven services per day to Ko Samui. They depart from Don Sak Port, 1½ hours east of Surat Thani by bus. Go to the office of Samui Tour in the main street of Ban Don (see map on page 311) and purchase a bus ticket. The bus leaves from opposite the same office 1½ hours before the ferry sails. An ordinary bus costs Bt40 and an air-conditioned bus costs Bt60. When one reaches the ferry terminal, one purchases a ferry ticket for Bt45 and boards the ferry for the 1½ hour voyage (30 kilometres). The bus makes the ferry trip too and arrives in Ko Samui at the Ferry Jetty ten kilometres south of the main town of Nathon. One disembarks and gets back on the bus to travel the remaining ten kilometres into town. Be sure to retain your bus ticket for inspection on this leg of the journey. The complete journey from Surat Thani to Nathon (Ko Samui) takes three hours and costs Bt85 including an ordinary bus or Bt105 using an air-conditioned bus. You will find that the ordinary bus is quite adequate, since the journey is made without stops and to tight deadlines.

The second car ferry company is Songserm. It operates four ferries a day to Ko Samui departing for the 35 kilometre voyage from the port of Khanom, which is further east than Don Sak. The bus for these ferries leaves Surat Thani from near Ban Don Port (see map) two hours before the ferry sails. The ferry arrives in Ko Samui in the centre of the main town of Nathon. The ticket available includes both bus and ferry, but is rather expensive at Bt150, especially considering that the ferry only is nominally priced at Bt45. However, Songserm is not keen to sell tickets for ferry alone. This company also discriminates against foreigners by charging higher fares for them on some routes (for example Ko Samui to Ko Pha-Ngan). However, the reader has a choice as to which of the two companies to use.

There is also one express ferry running to Ko Samui from the port of **Ta Thong**, about five kilometres to the east of Ban Don. A bus is provided for the short journey. The express boat leaves at 8:00 and reaches Ko Samui at 10:30 at a cost of Bt150. It continues to Ko Pha-Ngan, Ko Tao and Chumphon.

There are car ferries to Ko Pha-Ngan too. Raja Ferries operates three direct services a day and Songserm operates two services, both via Ko Samui.

At 23:00, night boats leave from Ban Don Pier for Ko Samui, Ko Pha-Ngan and Ko Tao.

Accommodation
Surat Thani

Name	No. on Map	Rooms	Cheapest Price (Bt)	Name	No. on Map	Rooms	Cheapest Price (Bt)
Siam Thara	20	172	450	Merry Time Resotel	19	90	500
Rung Tawan	24	64	650	Rat Thanee	7	105	330
Wang Tai	23	230	950	K.R. Apartment	18	40	330
Siam Thani	25	215	780	Ban Don	17	19	160
Tapi	12	120	300	In Town	16	48	350
Muang Tai	13	44	280	Grand City	11	120	260
Southern Star	14	120	1,200	Surat	9	30	350
Thai Thani	5	140	290	Phan Fa	8	58	190
Thai Rung Ruang	3	120	330	Thai	10	37	200
Saowaluk Thani	1	280	2,000	Seree	2	24	230
S.A. Guest House	22	24	120	T.H. Mansion	4	15	350
Cha Thip G. H.	6	15	150	Somlout Guest House	15	20	150
Samaporn	21	40	430	Queen	Phun Phin	35	200

Moving On

There are ferry, bus plus ferry, or boat services to Ko Samui, Ko Pha-Ngan, Ko Tao and Chumphon. Here are the details. Departure times are from Ban Don town.

(i)   To Ko Samui

Type of Boat	Depart (Surat Thani)	Arrival (Ko Samui)	Departure Port	Fare (Bt)
Car Ferry	6:30	9:30	Don Sak (8:00)	85
Car Ferry	No bus	9:30	Khanom (8:00)	45 (from Khanom)
Express	7:30	10:30	Ta Thong (8:00)	150
Car Ferry	8:00	11:30	Khanom (10:00)	150
Car Ferry	8:30	11:30	Don Sak (10:00)	85
Car Ferry	10:30	13:30	Don Sak (12:00)	85
Car Ferry	12:30	15:30	Don Sak (14:00)	85
Car Ferry	14:00	17:30	Khanom (16:00)	150
Car Ferry	14:30	17:30	Don Sak (16:00)	85
Car Ferry	15:30	18:30	Don Sak (17:00)	85
Car Ferry	16:00	19:30	Khanom (18:00)	150
Car Ferry	16:30	19:30	Don Sak (18:00)	85
Slow	23:00	5:00	Ban Don	100

(ii)   To Ko Pha-Ngan

Type of Boat	Depart (Surat Thani)	Arrival (Pha-Ngan)	Departure Port	Fare (Bt)
Express	7:30	11:45	Ta Thong (8:00)	245
Car Ferry	8:00	13:30	Khanom (10:00)	120 + 105 (bus)
Car Ferry	8:30	12:30	Don Sak (10:00)	120 + 40 (bus)
Car Ferry	11:30	15:30	Don Sak (13:00)	120 + 70 (minibus)
Car Ferry	16:00	21:00	Khanom (18:00)	120 + 105 (bus)
Car Ferry	16:30	20:30	Don Sak (18:00)	120 + 40 (bus)
Slow	23:00	5:00	Ban Don	200

(iii)   To Ko Tao

Type of Boat	Depart (Surat Thani)	Arrival (Chumphon)	Departure Port	Fare (Bt)
Express	7:30	17:30	Ta Thong (8:00)	850

(iv)   To Chumphon

Type of Boat	Depart (Surat Thani)	Arrival (Ko Tao)	Departure Port	Fare (Bt)
Express	7:30	14:00	Ta Thong (8:00)	500
Slow	23:00	8:30	Ban Don	350

There are convenient night trains with sleeping accommodation for the return journey to Bangkok also, of course. No fewer than eight such trains pass through during the course of the evening, but they are popular, so again it is wise to book a few days in advance if possible. Sleeping accommodation is added to some of the trains in Surat Thani and, if you can obtain a berth in such a carriage, you will be able to occupy it at your convenience some time before the scheduled departure and sit in air-conditioned comfort until your train arrives and you are coupled to it. The train timetable can be found on page 369.

Now here is a list of principal bus services originating in Surat Thani.

Destination	Route No.	Price (Bt)				Journey Time (hrs)		Frequency	
		V.I.P.	A/C 1	A/C 2	Ord	A/C	Ord	A/C	Ord
Bangkok	993	535	346	269	192	11	13	27/day	2/day
Haad Yai	490		185		103	5.5	6.5	5/day	5/day
Phuket	465		160		92	6	7	2/day	7/day
Chumphon	474			91	70	4	5	Hourly	30 mins
Ranong	469			90	75	5	6.5	4/day	Hourly
Nakhon Si Thammarat	475			60	45	3	3.5	5/day	20 mins
Songkhla				139		6		2/day	
Sungai Golok				240		10		1/day	
Phang-Nga	708				50		4		5/day
Krabi	482/710				70		5.5		4/day
Thung Song	488				50		4		Hourly
Ko Samui	8244		60		40	3	3	7/day	7/day

The following additional services are operated by minibuses departing from the old bus station in the centre of Ban Don.

Destination	Route No.	Price (Bt)				Journey Time (hrs)		Frequency	
		V.I.P.	A/C 1	A/C 2	Ord	A/C	Ord	A/C	Ord
Haad Yai	490		150			4.5		5/day	
Phuket	727		160			5		Hourly	
Chumphon	474		120			3		Hourly	
Nakhon Si Thammarat	475		80			2.5		30 mins	
Chaiya			35			1		Hourly	
Don Sak	717		40			1		8/day	
Khanom			50			1		Hourly	

NAKHON SI THAMMARAT

นครศรีธรรมรา

NAKHON SI THAMMARAT

16 hrs by train from Bangkok
13 hrs by bus from Southern Bus Terminal

Nakhon Si Thammarat is a sizeable city, but it is one of those places slightly off the tourist route, and so it tends to get missed out of busy itineraries. It is a pleasant city, with several historic sites, and one which is not difficult to reach.

From Bangkok, there are two night trains to Nakhon Si Thammarat. The rapid leaves Bangkok at 17:35 and reaches Nakhon Si Thammarat at 9:25. The Express leaves at 19:15 and arrives at 10:50. The fare for a lower berth in an air-conditioned sleeper on the rapid, for example, is Bt618. As if to emphasize the possibility of passing Nakhon Si Thammarat by, the city is not on the main railway line, but on a branch line which leaves the main southern line at the small station of Chum Thong and proceeds north-east for about thirty kilometres. There are also ordinary trains from Sungai Golok, Yala and Haad Yai in the south. From Sungai Golok the train departs at 8:55. From Yala departures are at 6:30 and 11:32, and from Haad Yai they are at 8:45 and 13:45. The two trains arrive in Nakhon Si Thammarat at 13:15 and 17:40.

There are buses from the Southern Bus Terminal in Bangkok. The journey of 805 kilometres takes twelve hours on the fastest services and costs Bt414 on a 1st class air-conditioned bus, Bt322 on a 2nd class air-conditioned bus and Bt230 on an ordinary bus.

Nakhon Si Thammarat is a city with a long history. It was the capital of the Tambralinga Kingdom, at which time the city was known as Ligor. Later, Ceylonese Buddhist monks established a monastery here and changed the name to Nakhon Si Thammarat ('Great City of the Righteous King') and thus the city became an important centre of Buddhism as long as 1,700 years ago. During the Srivichaya Period, starting in the eighth century, Nakhon Si Thammarat gradually gained in importance until, by the late thirteenth century, it had became a major trading centre, especially involved in commerce with Southern India and Sri Lanka. There was intermarriage with Indian merchants, so that the complexions and some of the religious beliefs of people in this area differ slightly from those in other parts of the country.

The city is famous for buffalo-hide shadow puppets, which were introduced to Thailand through Nakhon Si Thammarat's close connexions with the Indian sub-continent and with Java, and for neilloware jewellery techniques borrowed from China. These techniques produce a black surface with gold or silver designs.

The geography of Nakhon Si Thammarat is also unusual, for basically it consists of one main street some five kilometres long with all places of interest on or adjacent to this single street, known as Ratchadamnoen Road. *Songtaew* run along this road every minute or two and convey passengers any distance within the city limits (roughly the area shown on the map) for Bt5. Take a *songtaew* to the southern part of Ratchadamnoen Road and then walk back into the city looking at the various places of interest along the road.

First, the **Nakhon Si Thammarat National Museum** (admission Bt30) is near the southern limits of the city.

The most important site in the city is **Wat Phra Mahathat**, a few minutes walk to the north. It is a beautifully impressive complex of temple buildings dominated by a *stupa* originally constructed 1,700 years ago. However, it has been enlarged several times since. The current tower is of Sri Lankan style, 55 metres tall, with a solid gold ball on the top. There is also an example of high quality Ayutthaya-style architecture in the form of Viharn Luang, which is known for its elaborately decorated and painted ceiling. Viharn Phra Ma contains two national masterpieces: a bas relief of the life of Buddha and a carved door, several hundreds of years old, depicting the Hindu gods Brahma and Vishnu.

Phra Buddha Sing is a Buddha statue housed in a chapel of the same name, a little further into town, near the Town Hall. It is claimed that it dates from the year 157. There are three identical statues in Thailand, one kept here, one in the National Museum in Bangkok, and one in Wat Phra Sing in Chiang Mai.

Nearby, **Phra Isuan** and **Phra Narai** are reminders of the Hindu influence in this city. Phra Isuan is dedicated to the Brahman god Vishnu, while Phra Narai is also Brahman and was the site of the discovery of an ancient sandstone statue of the god Narai wearing a hat and holding a conch shell. This statue appears to date from about the seventh century and is now in the National Museum down the road.

Moving towards the town centre again, one comes to two walled areas. They seem to match each other well, but actually that on the left is the town gaol, while that on the right is more interesting, for it is the remains of the **old city wall**. This wall is very old, dating from the Srivichaya Period, and it used to enclose an area 2.2 kilometres long and 400 metres wide, but now the only section in a condition of good preservation (restored) is this 100 metre length with a moat beside it. At the near end is the Chai Nua northern gate to the city.

Almost opposite the city wall, but set back from the road by the width of a playing field, is the **TAT office**. Just to the right of the office you will find the attractive **city shrine**.

At the northern edge of the city are **Wat Pradu** and **Wat Chaeng**. Both date from the eighteenth century. The former is reputed to contain the ashes of King Taksin the Great and the latter is known for a Chinese-style building, Keng Jeen, decorated with wood imported from China.

Outside the city, there is the Khao Luang National Park, with several waterfalls, and there are also several beaches near Nakhon Si Thammarat.

Khao Luang National Park covers 600 square kilometres and contains the highest peak, Khao Luang, in southern Thailand. The summit is at 1,835 metres. The area is covered by natural rainforest and the mountain range is a watershed. Starting point for any hiking on the mountain is usually Ban Khiri Wong, a village which was hit by catastrophic flash floods on 21st November 1988, when more than a hundred houses were washed away and many residents perished. Some of the ruins have been retained as a reminder. The village can be reached by taking a *songtaew* from Nakhon Si Thammarat. The journey takes about 45 minutes and costs Bt20.

Although there are various beaches both north and south of Nakhon Si Thammarat, the best known are some way to the north. **Sichon Beach** and **Hin Ngam Beach** are about 70 kilometres away and can be reached by taking a bus no. 475 for Surat Thani. Such buses depart every 20 minutes. Sichon Beach is three kilometres off the main road. It is a rock-strewn beach, but with a wide curved sandy area suitable for swimming. Accommodation is available (see under).

Hin Ngam Beach is adjoining and is known for its round rocks of varying hues. Two kilometres further on is **Piti Beach** (also known as Kho Khao Beach). Accommodation is available at these beaches too.

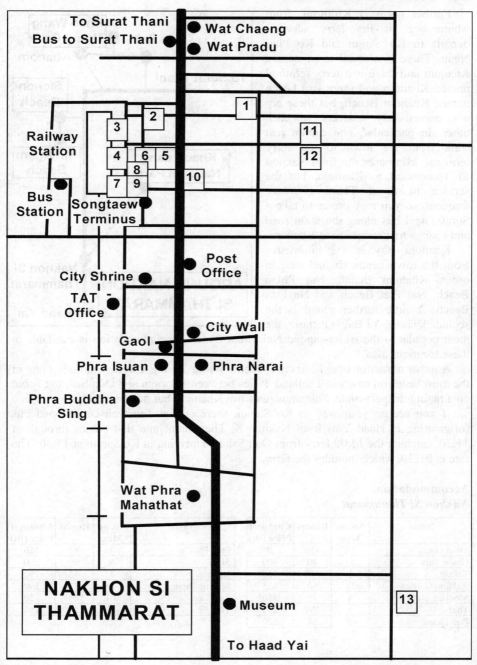

To Surat Thani
Bus to Surat Thani

Wat Chaeng
Wat Pradu

1

2

3

11

Railway
Station

12

4 6 5

8

7 9

10

Bus
Station

Songtaew
Terminus

Post
Office

City Shrine

TAT
Office

City Wall

Gaol

Phra Isuan

Phra Narai

Phra Buddha
Sing

Wat Phra
Mahathat

NAKHON SI
THAMMARAT

Museum

13

To Haad Yai

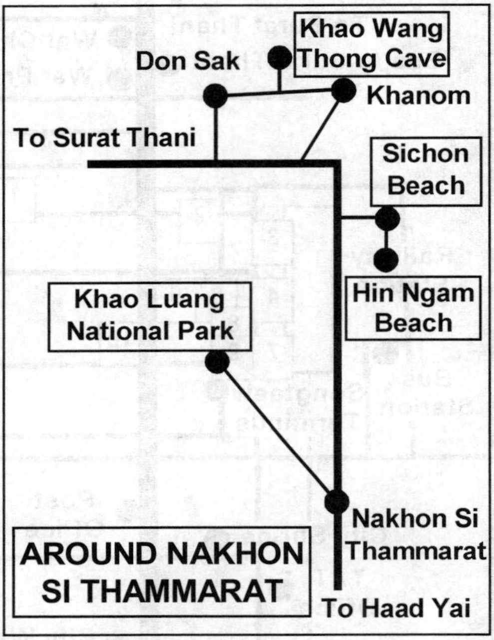

Further north is **Khanom**, from where one of the ferry services departs to Ko Samui and Ko Pha-Ngan. There is a small town named Khanom and there is a ferry terminal named Khanom and there is a beach named Khanom Beach, but these are not immediately adjacent to each other. In particular, one cannot just walk from the town to the ferry terminal. Minibuses run from Nakhon Si Thammarat to Khanom, but the service to Surat Thani is more frequent, so you may prefer to take a Surat Thani bus along the main road and change to a *songtaew* to Khanom.

Khanom Bay is 1½ kilometres from the town centre. It includes, in order, Khanom Beach, Nai Phlao Beach, Nai Pret Beach and Na Dan Beach. A little further round is the secluded Thong Yi Bay. Of these, the most popular is the white-sanded Nai Phlao Beach. Accommodation is available at these locations also.

Khao Wang Thong Cave

Don Sak

Khanom

To Surat Thani

Sichon Beach

Khao Luang National Park

Hin Ngam Beach

Nakhon Si Thammarat

AROUND NAKHON SI THAMMARAT

To Haad Yai

Another attraction near Khanom is **Khao Wang Thong Cave**, regarded as one of the most beautiful caves in Thailand. It lies between Khanom and Don Sak, but is not on a main transport route. *Songtaew* run from Khanom, but not frequently.

If you are on your way to Ko Samui, there is one direct air-conditioned bus (originating in Haad Yai) from Nakhon Si Thammarat and that passes through at 11:30, catching the 14:00 ferry from Don Sak and arriving in Ko Samui at 15:30. The fare is Bt130, which includes the ferry.

Accommodation
Nakhon Si Thammarat

Name	No. on Map	Rooms	Cheapest Price (Bt)
Twin Lotus	13	410	1,200
Grand Park	12	80	700
Taksin	1	110	550
Nakhon Garden	11	50	435
Montien	4	95	350
Thai	5	239	250
Bua Luang	9	84	220

Name	No. on Map	Rooms	Cheapest Price (Bt)
Phet Phailin	3	80	210
Siam	6	50	200
Nakhon	7	42	190
Muang Thong	8	52	190
Thai Lee	10	20	150
Thai Fa	2	13	150

Si Chon, Hin Ngam, Piti Beaches

Name	Rooms	Cheapest Price (Bt)
Piti Resort	46	1,400
Krua Poi	10	400
Prasansuk Villa	29	400
Wang Luang	23	250

Name	Rooms	Cheapest Price (Bt)
Hin Ngam Bungalow	5	250
Sun Thon	40	250
Sai Lom Bungalow	22	150

Khanom Town

Name	Rooms	Cheapest Price (Bt)
Sri Khanom	40	220

Name	Rooms	Cheapest Price (Bt)
Ek	12	230

Nai Phlao Beach

Name	Rooms	Cheapest Price (Bt)
Supha Royal Beach	70	950
Supha Villa	19	950
Kanap Nam Diamond Cliff	10	800

Name	Rooms	Cheapest Price (Bt)
Nai Phlao Day Resort	45	600
G.B. Resort	8	600

Nai Pret Beach

Name	Rooms	Cheapest Price (Bt)
Thip Montri Resort	8	600

Na Dan Beach

Name	Rooms	Cheapest Price (Bt)
Khanom Golden Beach	93	1,500
Alongkot Resort	41	800

Name	Rooms	Cheapest Price (Bt)
Tan Khu Resort	9	600
Rabiang Sai	28	450

Moving On

There are two overnight trains to Bangkok, both with sleeping accommodation, and three ordinary trains departing for southern destinations during the day.

Type of Train	Ord	Ord	Rap	Exp	Ord
Classes	3	3	1,2,3 *†	1,2,3 *†	3
Nakhon Si Thammarat	0600	0955	1220	1400	1500
Surat Thani			1620	1737	
Chumphon			1927	2040	
Prachuap Kiri Khan			2249	0016	
Hua Hin			0033	0147	
Nakhon Pathom			0320	0425	
Bangkok			0505	0625	
Pattalung	0830	1224			1750
Haad Yai	1022	1433			
Yala	1248	1705			
Sungai Golok	1505				

*Air-conditioned 2nd class available   †2nd class sleepers available

Now here is a list of principal bus services from Nakhon Si Thammarat.

Destination	Route No.	Price (Bt)				Journey Time (hrs)		Frequency	
		V.I.P.	A/C 1	A/C 2	Ord	A/C	Ord	A/C	Ord
Bangkok	981	640	414	322	230	12	14	7/day	5/day
Haad Yai	477			90	64	4	4.5	Hourly	Hourly
Phuket	740			155	115	7	8	2/day	Hourly
Krabi	743				60		4.5		4/day
Trang	448				36		3		1/day
Surat Thani	475			60	45	3	3.5	5/day	20 mins
Ko Samui	729		130			4		1/day	
Pattalung	476		63		35	2.5	3	4/day	30 mins
Songkhla	477			85	60	3.5	4	3/day	Hourly

The following additional services are operated by minibus.

Destination	Route No.	Price (Bt)				Journey Time (hrs)		Frequency	
		V.I.P.	A/C 1	A/C 2	Ord	A/C	Ord	A/C	Ord
Haad Yai	477				100		3		1/day
Phuket	727				150		6		Hourly
Krabi	743		80			3		1/day	
Trang	448				70		2.5		Hourly
Surat Thani	475		80			2.5		30 mins	
Khanom (for Ko Samui)			115			2		2/day	

RANONG ระนอง

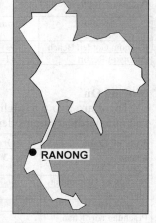

RANONG

10 hrs by bus from Southern Bus Terminal

The long, narrow 'pan-handle' which runs down to the south of Thailand is shared between Thailand and Myanmar, Myanmar to the west and Thailand to the east. It is not until one reaches Ranong, 583 kilometres from Bangkok, that the territory of Myanmar reaches its southern limit and Thailand at last extends westwards to the Indian Ocean.

Ranong's distinctions include being both the least populous and the rainiest province in Thailand. Until relatively recently, it was a place not much visited. However, in the last few years, a number of beaches and islands have been 'discovered'. The majority of the beaches are further south within the territory of Phang-Nga Province, but some are in Ranong, and the islands are mostly in Ranong. There is also a National Park and the possibility of paying a day visit to Myanmar (and getting a further month's stay upon return to Thailand).

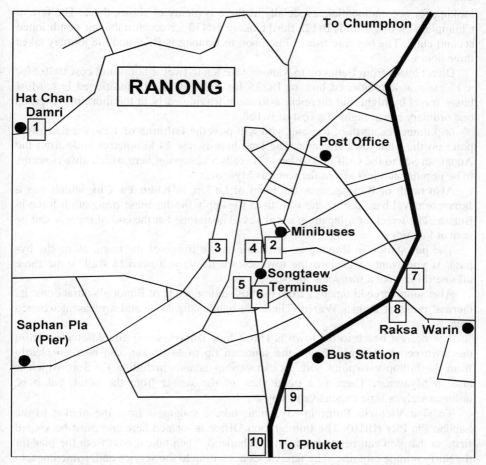

Ranong is not served by the State Railways of Thailand. If you want to go by train, you travel from Bangkok to Chumphon and take a bus for the remaining 120 kilometres from there. There are two possibilities for such a journey – the comfortable one and the cheap one. The comfortable one involves taking a sleeper as late as possible in the evening from Bangkok, so that you do not reach Chumphon any earlier than necessary. This latest train leaves Bangkok at 19:15 and is an express bound for Nakhon Si Thammarat. It still reaches Chumphon rather too early, at 4:13. Cost for a lower air-conditioned berth is Bt520. The cheap way is to take the ordinary train at 7:20 from Thonburi station in Bangkok. It will reach Chumphon at 17:25 and you can continue to Ranong the next morning. The fare to Chumphon is Bt80 third class. There is one more possibility, which is to take the 12:25 rapid from Bangkok, destination Sungai Golok, arriving in Chumphon at 20:47, which is not too late to be looking for accommodation, especially as there is plenty of choice there. The fare to Chumphon on this train is Bt122 third class or Bt430 for comfortable air-conditioned second class. The bus fare from Chumphon to Ranong is Bt39 and the journey takes three hours.

Direct buses from Bangkok to Ranong take ten to twelve hours and cost Bt302 for a 1st class air-conditioned bus, or Bt235 for a 2nd class air-conditioned bus. Most buses travel by night, but there are also some leaving early in the morning. There is one ordinary bus at night at a cost of Bt168.

66 kilometres north of Ranong, you will pass the **Isthmus of Kra**, the narrowest point on the Malayan Peninsula. The land here is just 44 kilometres wide from the Andaman Sea to the Gulf of Thailand. There is a viewpoint here which always seems to be popular and just across the water is Myanmar.

Also north of Ranong, near the town of La Un, is **Khao Fa Chi**, which was a Japanese naval base during the war, used to supply the Japanese occupation force in Burma. The wreck of a Japanese naval vessel abandoned at the end of the war can be seen at low tide.

The bus station in Ranong is, as usual, on the fringe of the town, along the by-pass. If you want to go into the town centre itself, you need to walk some three kilometres or take a *songtaew* for Bt5.

Also some three kilometres from the bus station is one of Ranong's attractions: its thermal pools at **Raksa Warin**. There are bathing facilities and a pleasant wooded area.

The nearest beach to the town is **Hat Chan Damri**, some nine kilometres from the town centre. Victoria Point, the southern tip of Myanmar, can be seen clearly from the hilltop viewpoint here, as can various islands including Ko Son, which is also in Myanmar. There is a good view of the sunset from the hotel, but it is, unfortunately, a little expensive to stay at.

To visit **Victoria Point** in Myanmar, take a *songtaew* from the market to the Saphan Pla Pier (Bt10). The Immigration Office is located here and must be visited first, so that you can be stamped out of Thailand. Then take a boat from the pier for the thirty minute crossing. The fare varies according to the service and, sometimes, to the number of passengers wishing to travel. The cheapest rate obtainable is about Bt50 and the most expensive Bt300. You will also be charged U.S.$10 (or an inflated equivalent in Thai currency) for admission by the Myanmar authorities. Only a day pass is available. One of the advantages of this journey, however, is that, as at other points where a crossing to Myanmar is permitted, upon return to Thailand, you will be given another month's stay. There is a market at Victoria Point selling local Myanmar products. Thai currency is acceptable.

From the same Saphan Pla Pier, there are regular boat services to **Ko Chang** and **Ko Phayam**, on both of which accommodation is available. It takes two to three hours to reach Ko Phayam. There is a choice of accommodation. For example, on Ko Phayam you can try Mr. Gao Bungalow and on Ko Chang Lae Tawan Bungalows (no electricity, however) or Ko Chang Bungalows.

Moving south from the town of Ranong, we come to **Bald Hill** on the right, which is just as it sounds, an unusual hill with only grass as the covering, and the small **Ngao National Park** on the right containing the Ngao Waterfall.

53 kilometres south of Ranong is the much larger **Laem Son National Park**, covering 315 square kilometres, including a considerable area of sea. There are several attractive beaches and small islands within the park. The main beaches are Bang Ben Beach (where the Park Headquarters are located, ten kilometres off the main highway south), Laem Son Beach and Prapat Beach. Islands included within the park boundaries are **Khang Khao**, **Kham Yai** and **Kham Noi**. Khang Khao has unusual rock formations at Ao Khao Kwai, while Kham Yai is known for its beautiful beach. Diving is popular here, too, to view underwater plants and fish. There is accommodation in the park, and also just outside. The Wasana Resort is at Sam Nak, some 200 metres from the entrance to the National Park.

Accommodation
Ranong

Name	No. on Map	Rooms	Cheapest Price (Bt)
Royal Princess	3	50	1,800
Jansom Beach Resort	1	40	1,250
Jansom Thara	8	220	1,100
Spa Inn	7	58	630
Ranong Garden	9	50	550

Name	No. on Map	Rooms	Cheapest Price (Bt)
Ranong Inn	10	74	270
Asia	5	130	240
Sin Thawi	4	63	150
Sin Ranong	6	60	120
Rattanasin	2	10	100

Moving On

Now here is a list of principal bus services from Ranong.

Destination	Route No.	Price (Bt)				Journey Time (hrs)		Frequency	
		V.I.P.	A/C 1	A/C 2	Ord	A/C	Ord	A/C	Ord
Bangkok	64	470	302	235	168	10	12	9/day	1/day
Chumphon	429				39		3		Hourly
Phuket	430		170		91	5	6	2/day	2/day
Phang-Nga	435				90		6		4/day
Surat Thani	469			90	75	5	6.5	4/day	Hourly

PHANG-NGA   พังงา

14 hrs by bus from Southern Bus Terminal

Phang-Nga is the name of the province lying between Ranong and Phuket, and is also the name of the principal town in that province. The province is one of considerable beauty, with hills and mountains rising almost vertically, a multitude of islands, and sandy beaches which have had only modest development and even that only in the last few years. 57% of the province consists of rainforest or mangrove swamps. Phang-Nga used to be a tin mining area, but now its main industry is rubber plantations.

The town of Phang-Nga lies at the southern end of the province, beside the sea, and is not on any railway line. The nearest railway station is Surat Thani, from where it is a four hour bus ride (Bt50). The most common approach, however, is by bus via Ranong. The description of attractions which follows is in the order corresponding to that route. From Bangkok the trip to Phang-Nga is a long fourteen-hour one, even on the most rapid of the services available. Most of the buses travel overnight, but there is one bus leaving very early in the morning.

Coming south from Ranong, the first attraction is the **Ko Surin National Park**, The Surin Islands are some 60 kilometres offshore and are reached by a boat leaving from Ban Hin Lat five kilometres north of the small town of Kuraburi. The voyage takes five hours. There are two main islands, Surin Nua and Surin Tai, and three smaller ones. Surin Tai is very undeveloped and is the home of some of the last 'sea gypsies', who live primitive lives on houseboats. These people do not know their own ages, nor can they count beyond ten, but they are excellent boatbuilders, fishers and divers. The island is also the site of Ao Luk ('Deep Bay') which has dark green water and a coral reef, and of Ao Mae Yai, a particularly peaceful bay. Basic accommodation is available. There are also boats to the Surin Islands from Ranong, but the voyage lasts seven hours from there, and from Thap Lamu further south along this coast. It should be noted, however, that none of these (including the service from Ban Hin Lat) is a regularly timetabled service and that it is necessary to wait until a sufficient number of passengers is available. The boat costs about Bt10,000, with the cost divided among the number of passengers wishing to travel.

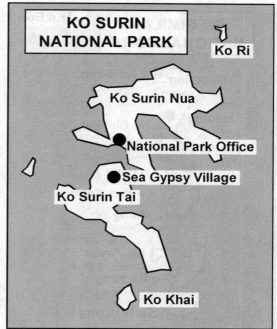

KO SURIN NATIONAL PARK

Ko Ri

Ko Surin Nua

National Park Office

Sea Gypsy Village

Ko Surin Tai

Ko Khai

From Kuraburi, a boat service operates to the inhabited, but unspoilt, island of **Pratong**, where accommodation is available. The voyage takes 75 minutes.

A little further south is the relatively new **Sri Phang-Nga National Park**. It is nearly all forested, with several waterfalls. The park is five kilometres from the main road.

The town of **Takuapa** is the next major point south. The bus station here, where most services pause for a few minutes, is one of the few in Thailand offering clean(ish) and free toilet facilities. You can also buy a rice meal here for Bt15 or Bt20.

Near Takuapa is the **Khao Lak - Lam Ru National Park** with Khao Lak (Mt. Lak, reached from the coastal Highway 4 at a point 25 kilometres south of Takuapa) and Lam Ru Waterfall (reached from a point near Ka Pong on the inland Highway 4090).

From Takuapa, a succession of small beaches starts to stretch down the coast: **Laem Pon Beach, Tap Tawan Beach, Bang Sak Beach, Pakwib Beach**, and others. All have accommodation available, mostly at a variety of prices, and none of these is too developed.

The **Ko Similan National Park** lies offshore here, covering an area of 130 square kilometres and comprising nine islands, of which Ko Similan is the largest. The boat service runs from Thap Lamu, a small town about 40 kilometres south of Takuapa, and takes three hours to cover the 50 kilometres to Ko Similan. There are also boats from Kuraburi, but this is the shorter crossing. Ko Similan is a horse-shoe shaped island with a large bay at the western end with relatively shallow water very suitable for diving. Ko Miang has accommodation, beaches and coral reefs. Ko Hu Yong also has a long sandy beach and is a favoured place for turtles to lay their eggs. Ko Hua Kalok ('Skull Island') looks like a skull and is a good diving location.

KO SIMILAN NATIONAL PARK

Ko Bon

Camping

Ko Bangu

Camping

Ko Similan

National Park Office

Ko Payu

Ko Hua Kalok

Ko Miang

Ko Payan

Ko Pa Yang

Ko Hu Yong

A little further down the road towards Phuket we reach the **Khao Lampi - Hat Thai Muang National Park**. To the left of the highway are two waterfalls, Lampi Falls and Ton Phrai Falls, about five kilometres apart, while on the right is Thai Muang Beach, a 13 kilometre long sandy beach good for swimming and used by turtles for egg-laying between November and February. Accommodation is available.

The beaches between here and the southern tip of the mainland, where the main road crosses onto Phuket, are more developed, but still accommodation to suit most pockets is available. Highway 4 now swings east at Kokkloi and continues to the town of Phang-Nga and beyond.

Attractions within, or very close to, the town of Phang-Nga are several caves. **Rusi Sawan Cave** ('Ascetic's Heaven Cave') and **Luk Sua Cave** are together in Somdej Phra Sri Nakarin Park, with the latter cave entered through the former. Outside is a statue of the monk Phra Rusi. Not far away, by Wat Prachimket, is **Pung Chang Cave** ('Elephant Belly Cave'), containing Buddhist statues. **Nam Phut Cave** is two kilometres away from the town. Eight kilometres from the town, just off the main road to Phuket is **Wat Suwan Kua**, a temple built inside a series of caves. The largest cave contains a very well executed Reclining Buddha some fifteen metres long.

The greatest attraction of town and province, though, is the **Phang-Nga National Park**, which consists of numerous islands, many of unusual shapes and formations. The park covers 400 square kilometres and can be reached by boat from Tha Dan Pier, 12 kilometres from the town centre. *Songtaew* are available for the journey to the pier, or buses on the main highway pass within four kilometres of it. There is accommodation at Tha Dan, but very little is available on the islands within the park. Ko Yao, however, outside the National Park boundaries, has places to stay. The National Park can also be reached by boats departing from Surakul Pier or Kasom Pier, a few kilometres further west than Tha Dan.

The islands within the National Park limits include the following. **Ko Panyi** is home to a Muslim fishing community with houses built on stilts over the sea and

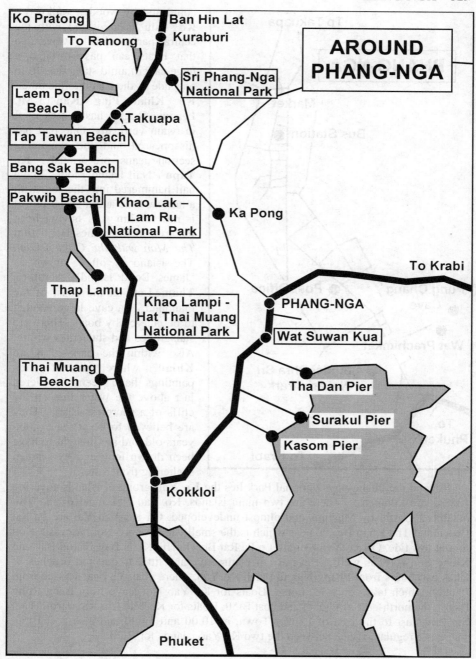

Ko Pratong

Ban Hin Lat

To Ranong

Kuraburi

AROUND
PHANG-NGA

Sri Phang-Nga
National Park

Laem Pon
Beach

Takuapa

Tap Tawan Beach

Bang Sak Beach

Pakwib Beach

Khao Lak –
Lam Ru
National Park

Ka Pong

To Krabi

Thap Lamu

Khao Lampi -
Hat Thai Muang
National Park

PHANG-NGA

Wat Suwan Kua

Thai Muang
Beach

Tha Dan Pier

Surakul Pier

Kasom Pier

Kokkloi

Phuket

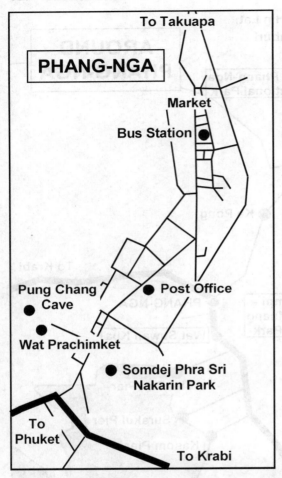

PHANG-NGA

To Takuapa

Market

Bus Station

Pung Chang
Cave

Post Office

Wat Prachimket

Somdej Phra Sri
Nakarin Park

To
Phuket

To Krabi

connected by wooden walkways. **Ko Talu** is an island with the central part eroded by waves, so that boats can pass through a huge cavern amid stalactites from one side of the island to the other. **Ko Khao Ping Kan** ('Mt. Leaning Rock') has a rock cleft in twain vertically. One part has disappeared and the remaining section leans precariously. **Ko Tapu** ('Nail Island') looks like a nail hammered into the sea, with a narrow base and a broad top. It is now a film star, having been featured in the James Bond film *The Man with the Golden Gun*. The island is often known as 'James Bond Island', therefore. **Tham Lot**, on the coast of the mainland, is a cave large enough to be entered by boats. There are stalagmites and stalactites within. Also within the park is **Khao Khian**, where ancient rock paintings have been discovered just above the water line on the cliffs of a shoreless island. They are believed to be at least 3,000 years old and are thought to have been drawn long ago by seamen sheltering from a storm.

Beyond the Phang-Nga National Park lies the **Ko Yao** group of islands covering 138 square kilometres. There are two main islands, Ko Yao Noi and Ko Yao Yai, inhabited mostly by Muslims and almost undeveloped. On Ko Yao Yai are Pa Sai Beach and Tha Khao Beach, near which is the small island of Ko Nok, accessible on foot at low tide. On Ko Yao Noi are Lo Pa Rat Beach, Hin Kong Bay, Tikud Bay and Klong Son Bay, as well as several other attractive and little frequented beaches. It takes two hours from Phang-Nga to reach Ko Yao. There is also a boat service from Phuket, which takes only 1½ hours. Boats for Ko Yao Noi leave from Bang Rong Pier in the north-east of Phuket and cost Bt50. Boats for Ko Yao Yai leave from Tien Sin Pier, just to the east of Phuket Town, at 10:00 and 14:00 and also cost Bt50. There is a regular service between the two Ko Yao islands for Bt20.

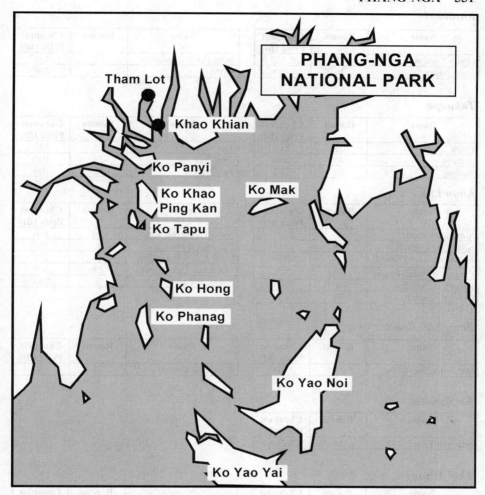

Accommodation
Ko Surin

Name	Rooms	Cheapest Price (Bt)
National Park	15	120

Ko Pratong

Name	Rooms	Cheapest Price (Bt)
Lost Horizon Resort	9	1,200

Name	Rooms	Cheapest Price (Bt)
Golden Buddha Beach	12	700

Kuraburi

Name	Rooms	Cheapest Price (Bt)
Green View Resort	25	2,400
Nang Nuan	14	300

Name	Rooms	Cheapest Price (Bt)
Sang Petch Bungalow	11	250
Extra	10	200

Takuapa

Name	Rooms	Cheapest Price (Bt)
Extra	75	250
Amarin	40	200
Padung	20	150

Name	Rooms	Cheapest Price (Bt)
Tan Yao	15	120
Suan Suk	11	100
Tan Prasert	9	100

Khao Lak

Name	Rooms	Cheapest Price (Bt)
Similana Resort	46	2,200
Khao Lak Laguna	76	2,000
Khao Lak Sunset Resort	31	800
Chong Fa Beach Resort	20	700
Khao Lak Seaview	4	700
Garden Beach Resort	79	450

Name	Rooms	Cheapest Price (Bt)
Nang Thong Bay Resort	70	450
Fair House Bungalow	6	350
Gerd & Noi Bungalow	38	350
Phu Khao Lak Resort	12	300
National Park	3	250

Bang Sak Beach

Name	Rooms	Cheapest Price (Bt)
Sun Splendour Lodge	15	1,200

Name	Rooms	Cheapest Price (Bt)
Bang Sak Resort	17	350

Ko Similan

Name	Rooms	Cheapest Price (Bt)
National Park	10	120 (Tent)

Thai Muang

Name	Rooms	Cheapest Price (Bt)
Thai Muang Marina	36	2,000
National Park	5	600
Poseidon Bungalow	6	600

Name	Rooms	Cheapest Price (Bt)
Sariroj	11	380
Sarirote	11	350
Ban Paradise	6	250

Kokkloi

Name	Rooms	Cheapest Price (Bt)
Ban Piyalai Resort	7	700

Name	Rooms	Cheapest Price (Bt)
Kokkloi Inn	30	250

Phang-Nga Town

Name	Rooms	Cheapest Price (Bt)
Phang-Nga Valley	10	650
Luk Muang 2	24	450
Sunimit Mansion	8	400
Riverside	5	300
Luk Muang 1	21	220

Name	Rooms	Cheapest Price (Bt)
Tawee Suk	8	200
Muang Thong	14	190
Rattanapong	29	150
Ruk Phang-Nga	12	120

Tha Dan

Name	Rooms	Cheapest Price (Bt)
Phang-Nga Bay Resort	79	650

Klong Kien

Name	Rooms	Cheapest Price (Bt)
House By the Bay	10	850

Ko Panyi

Name	Rooms	Cheapest Price (Bt)
National Park	3	400

Ko Lawa Yai

Name	Rooms	Cheapest Price (Bt)
National Park	3	400

Ko Yao Yai

Name	Rooms	Cheapest Price (Bt)
Halavee Bungalow	5	450

Name	Rooms	Cheapest Price (Bt)
Hin Kong Villa	10	200

Ko Yao Noi

Name	Rooms	Cheapest Price (Bt)
Long Beach Village	25	500
Thakao Bungalow	7	450
Sabai Corner	8	400

Name	Rooms	Cheapest Price (Bt)
Ko Yao Resotel	4	350
Ko Yao Cabana	2	250
Ko Yao Mansion	9	250

Moving On

Principal bus services from Phang-Nga are as follows.

Destination	Route No.	Price (Bt)				Journey Time (hrs)		Frequency	
		V.I.P.	A/C 1	A/C 2	Ord	A/C	Ord	A/C	Ord
Bangkok	61	625	403/419	326		14		5/day	
Phuket	437				31		3		5/day
Ranong	435				90		6		4/day
Surat Thani	708				50		4		5/day
Haad Yai	443		196			7		1/day	

<table>
<tr><td>

**NOTICE IN PHUKET
TAILOR'S SHOP**
Best Style. In the End.

</td><td>

**NOTICE AT NAI HARN BEACH,
PHUKET**
You Must Drop Lister

</td></tr>
</table>

PHUKET

ภูเก็ต

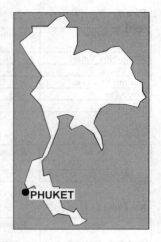

PHUKET

15 hrs by bus from Southern Bus Terminal

Phuket is the largest island in Thailand and one of the most popular beach resort areas. The island first became popular with backpackers many years ago, then gradually moved upmarket, and finally found that it was large enough to accommodate all budgets. Each beach has its own character, reflecting the clientele by which it is patronised and at which it is aiming its services, and the town of Phuket has its own character too.

There is no railway near Phuket. The nearest station is Surat Thani, from where it is a six hour bus ride. However, taking an overnight sleeper from Bangkok to Surat Thani, and then the bus, is quite a comfortable method of reaching the island if you need to undertake this long journey in a single leap. The bus from Surat Thani goes past the station (which is actually in an area known as Phun Phin), performing a loop round the divided road there and stopping right outside the station entrance.

By bus the journey from Bangkok takes fifteen hours, with most buses travelling overnight. The fare is Bt446 or Bt457 (two slightly different routes) by 1st class air-conditioned bus, Bt356 by 2nd class air-conditioned bus or Bt254 by ordinary bus.

Phuket has a quiet but modern international airport in the north-west. There are flights from Malaysia, Singapore, Taiwan, Hong Kong and Japan, as well as several flights every day from Bangkok and a few from other domestic locations.

When arriving by bus, as most visitors do, you would hardly notice that Phuket is an island, for it is reached by the 660 metre long Sarasin Bridge over the Pak Phra Channel which divides Phuket from the mainland. This channel is a mere 490 metres wide. The island is 48 kilometres long and 21 kilometres wide with a total area of 543 square kilometres, about the same size as Singapore. Phuket is surprisingly hilly, almost mountainous, and to reach most of the beaches on the west coast steep climbs have to be negotiated. Indeed, the name Phuket is probably derived from the Malaysian word 'Bukit', meaning hill.

Phuket used to be a trading centre for the Indians, Chinese, Portuguese, French, Dutch and English. Its main products in the past were tin, rubber and pearls.

The permanent population is 200,000, of whom only 65% are Buddhist. 27% are Muslim and 8% Christian. About 35% of the population is of Chinese descent.

Phuket Town, where you will first arrive, has no beach. If you want to go to a beach, come out of the bus station, turn right and walk for ten minutes. When you can go no further in a straight line, turn left for a few metres to a roundabout and on your right will be the market and, a little way down it, a row of *songtaew* waiting to go to the various beaches. Pick your beach and depart. The last *songtaew* leave at about 5:30 to 6:00. If you arrive too late, why not stay in town, for it is an interesting

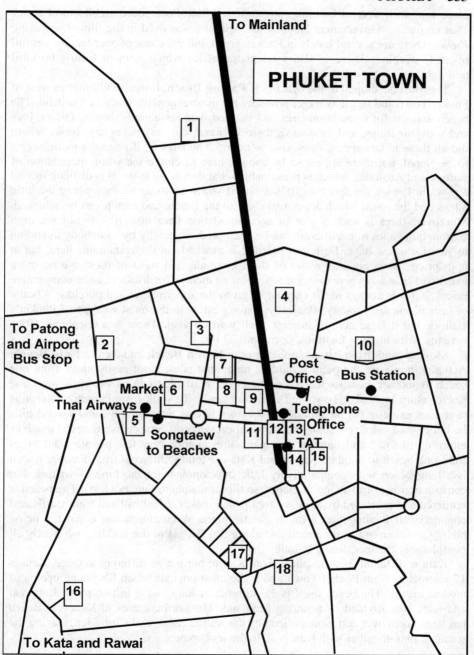

To Mainland

PHUKET TOWN

1

4

3

To Patong
and Airport
Bus Stop

2

10

7

Post
Office

Bus Station

Market

6

8

9

Thai Airways

Telephone
Office

5

11   12   13

Songtaew
to Beaches

TAT

14   15

17

18

16

To Kata and Rawai

place too, with several buildings in attractive Sino-Portuguese architectural style? That known as 'Government House', for example, was used in the film, *The Killing Fields*. There are several hotels in Phuket Town, but the cheaper ones tend to get full by early evening. There is also a telephone office which is open from 8:00 until midnight.

The most developed of the beaches is **Patong Beach**. It lies 15 kilometres west of Phuket Town and is, on average, probably the most expensive place in Thailand. The beach extends for three kilometres and is lined with restaurants, hotels, tailors, bars and souvenir shops, and, of course, the occasional, but very necessary, bank. Where did all these tailors spring from, one wonders? The answer, if one asks them, seems to be Nepal, but there appear to be enough here to clothe the whole population of Europe and Australia, which is presumably what they hope to do. It is difficult to find a room in Patong for less than Bt500, but, if you wish to do so, look along the little alleys and the roads which are not so close to the beach, and then it can be achieved. Moreover, there is such a glut of accommodation here that, if it is not the high season, quite a lot of negotiation can be attempted, especially by somebody intending to stay for a few days. Delicious seafood is available in the restaurants here, but at high prices. Bars abound, many of them open-air, and most of these are no more expensive than anywhere else. Indeed, some of them offer drinks at quite competitive prices, but it is always much cheaper to go to the supermarket and purchase a bottle of beer if one feels thirsty! Basically, Patong caters to the most wealthy of Phuket's visitors, but it is an area of interest, well worth a visit. There is a telephone office here too, with Internet facilities, open until 23:00.

Moving south from Patong, one comes to **Karon Beach** and then to **Kata Beach**. Actually, however, the point should be made that one cannot easily move from one beach to another, because there is no transport available to do so. Nearly always one has to return to Phuket Town and come out again. To walk from Patong to Karon is strenuous exercise (as the author knows from having attempted it), and several hills lie in between, while obtaining direct transport will cost four or five times as much as returning to town and coming out again. Presumably very few people want to go from one beach to another. Karon and Kata are totally different from Patong. Karon is a long beach with comparatively little development (at the time of writing, but construction is in full swing in places, so this atmosphere may not last). The beach is bordered and protected by a grassy area which makes it feel isolated from traffic and commerce. It is altogether a much quieter place. Accommodation is patchy, being mainly at either end of the beach and along Soi Bangla in the middle. It is nearly all considerably cheaper than at Patong.

Kata is different in atmosphere from Karon, but not so different in price. Kata is 17 kilometres from Phuket Town and is the most popular beach for young people of modest means. The beach itself is 3½ kilometres long and is in two parts, Kata Yai and Kata Noi, divided by a jutting headland. The northern area of Kata Yai Beach has been taken over and monopolized by the walled enclave of Club Med, leaving the southern half, together with Kata Noi, to the less opulent.

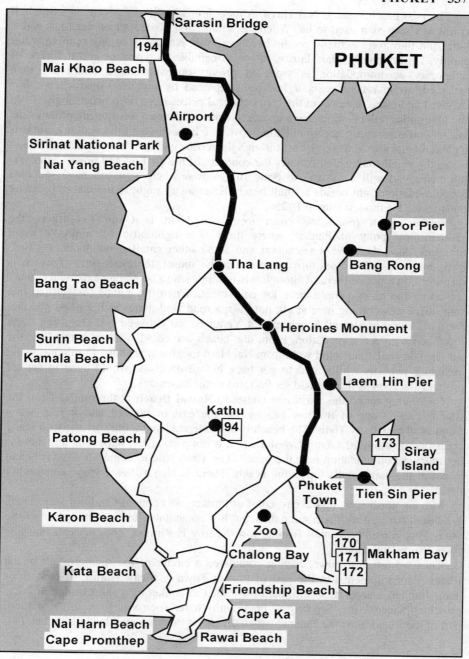

The next beach south is **Nai Harn**. Although this is still the poor man's beach, it is not as cheap as it used to be. When the author first visited, there were just a few huts, and they were actually on the beach, without electricity or any running water supply. Unfortunately, Nai Harn is rather susceptible to typhoons and this type of temporary accommodation is wont to prove somewhat more temporary than intended, so in recent years it has been replaced by bungalows which are less exposed and more resistant to the elements, and prices have risen accordingly. Even the ubiquitous tailors' shops have appeared here in this least developed corner of the isle. If you want cheap accommodation now, you have to do a little walking, but it is a pleasant and scenic walk. Set off through the territory of the Phuket Yacht Club and along the small road which follows the contours of the cliff up and down. After one kilometre you will come to Ao Sane Bungalows, where you can have secluded accommodation right beside a small beach, listening all night to the waves breaking outside, for the modest sum of Bt250.

Further south round the coast from Nai Harn is **Cape Promthep**, the southernmost point of Phuket, where there is a lighthouse containing a small museum. Also there are a restaurant and some other small monuments. Towards dusk, bus-loads of visitors turn up to watch the sunset, the exact time of which is displayed on a notice there. Although this is supposed to be a great experience, there are rather too many people there for enjoyment. When the author first visited this spot, there was nothing here at all, not even a road, and it was rather more pleasant for that. There is a small beach named Yanui Beach between Nai Harn and Cape Promthep with accommodation. From that beach one could walk up here to see the sunset if desired. One could walk from Nai Harn too, but it is about 45 minutes walk, including two steep hills, and to get back before dark one would need to set off promptly as soon as the sun had set (as most of the buses do).

Continuing round the coast, one comes to **Rawai Beach** at the south-east of the island. This is one of the few beaches on the east of Phuket, and it is a beach frequented mostly by Thais. The beach is of moderate length, but narrow, with many boats tied up along it. To most westerners it is not particularly appealing and there is not much accommodation near the beach. The Thais tend to come for day visits and to eat at the many stalls lining the beach. There is also a 'Sea Gypsy' community here.

Moving north now, up the east coast of Phuket, we come to **Chalong Bay**. There is a beach covered with coconut palms, but it is not suitable for swimming, so is little used. This is mainly a small fishing port. Nearby is **Phuket Zoo**, where admission costs a surprising Bt400.

Thus we return to town, having completed a circuit of the southern half of the island. Four kilometres to the east of Phuket Town is **Siray Island**, in fact, as its name implies, a separate island, but now joined to Phuket by a short bridge. It is the principal place for the 'Sea Gypsy' community here. Their village is in the southern part of the island, near the channel which divides it from the mainland of Phuket.

Moving now to the northern half of the island, there are more beaches in the north-west. North of Patong Beach are **Kamala Beach** and **Surin Beach** sharing a single bay, but divided by the Cape Sing headland with its interesting rock formations. Surin Beach is another very attractive area, although the beach is steep and the wind sometimes strong, so it is not always suitable for swimming. It is famous for its sunsets.

Bang Tao Beach comes next, a long beach dominated by expensive resort hotels and not easily accessible to those not staying there.

Further north still is the short **Nai Yang Beach** and then the **Sirinat National Park**, the main purpose of which is to protect the turtles which come here to lay their eggs. The airport is here too, in a very pretty setting.

There is one more beach and that is **Mai Khao Beach**. In fact, this beach, the most distant from the town, at 34 kilometres, is the longest beach on the island. It has an attractive tree-lined setting and is little used, a good venue for those who prefer to escape from the masses. As yet, few foreign visitors come here.

As you pass through the centre of the island, you will find a monument to two local heroines. In 1785, the governor had just died and the island was without a leader, while the Burmese were threatening to invade and the soldiers of Phuket were outnumbered. Thao Thepkasattri and Thao Srisunthorn persuaded all the women to dress up in men's clothes, in order that the Burmese would believe that defences were much stronger than they actually were, and the invasion never came.

Songtaew run from the market in town to most locations on the island and fares are fixed and generally adhered to. To get from one place on the island to another, however, it is often necessary to return to town. There are also *songtaew* around the town for Bt10. When services from beaches reach Phuket Town, they usually perform a loop round the town, but the official terminus is the market. If you get off there or at any prior place on the route, you will be charged the standard fare. If you go beyond that point, the driver will ask your destination in the town and deliver you there, but he will usually charge you the standard fare plus Bt10 for the ride within the city. Here is a list of *songtaew* routes from Phuket Town, with fares.

Destination	Fare (Bt)	Destination	Fare (Bt)
Bang Tao Beach	20	Makham Bay (Aquarium)	20
Bang Rong	20	Nai Harn Beach	25
Chalong Bay	15	Nai Yang Beach	30
Friendship Beach	20	Patong Beach	15
Cape Ka	20	Rawai Beach	20
Kamala Beach	25	Sarasin Bridge	20
Karon Beach	20	Surin Beach	20
Kata Beach	20	Tha Lang	15
Kathu	10		

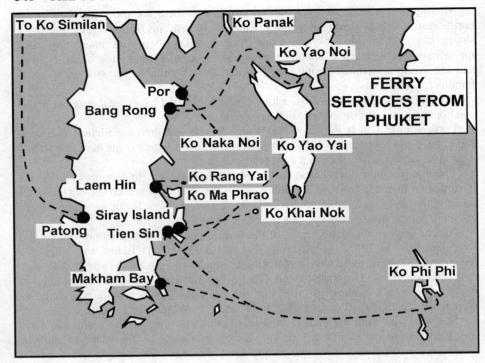

There are 32 small islands surrounding Phuket, to some of which there are regular boat services. Others can be reached by chartered boats. Here is a list of piers from which services leave, including those to rather more distant islands.

Pier	Destinations
Por	Panak, Naka Noi
Bang Rong	Yao Noi
Laem Hin	Rang Yai, Ma Phrao
Tien Sin	Phi Phi, Yao Yai
Siray Island	Khai Nok
Makham Bay	Phi Phi
Patong	Similan

Accommodation
Phuket Town

Name	No. on Map	Rooms	Cheapest Price (Bt)
Manora	1	72	600
Sub Siri	2	64	300
Siri	3	107	400
Suk Subai	4	53	200
Wasana Guest House	5	28	230
Down Town Inn	6	24	300
Thalang Guest House	7	8	250
On On	8	55	150
Sin Thawi	9	266	700

Name	No. on Map	Rooms	Cheapest Price (Bt)
Imperial 2	10	50	500
Thavorn	11	68	280
Imperial 1	12	39	750
Daeng Plaza	13	75	640
Crystal Guest House	14	26	250
Thanaporn G. H.	15	22	350
S. T.	16	200	900
Thai Inter	17	67	330
Arun Mansion	18	27	450

Patong Beach

Name	No. on Map	Rooms	Cheapest Price (Bt)
Sunset Mansion	19	13	550
Patong Penthouse	20	40	450
Nordic Bungalow	21	48	600
Shamrock Park Inn	22	28	450
Swiss Palm Beach	23	36	1,800
Patong Palace	24	28	800
Andaman Beach Suite	25	70	1,800
S.V. Phuket Andaman	26	30	900
Odin's Guest House	27	30	400
Sky Inn	28	36	900
New Tum Bungalow 1	29	17	450
Patong City	30	129	1,400
Jaranya Guest House	31	59	500
Living Place	32	12	700
Phuket Cabana Resort	33	75	5,000
Thara Beach Suite	34	128	3,000
K.S.R. Bungalows	35	23	450
Patong Bungalow	36	35	2,500
Patong Villa	37	52	1,200
Patong Bay Garden	38	61	2,500
Safari Beach	39	25	1,700
Patong Bay Inn	40	56	1,800
Jintana Patong	41	30	1,400
Neptuna	42	36	1,500
K-Hotel	43	40	900
Vises Patong	44	130	2,000
Royal Paradise	45	248	3,800
Royal Crown	46	102	1,500
Touch Villa	47	21	600
Expat	48	46	840
P.S. 1	49	36	1,450
Suksan Mansion	50	21	650

Name	No. on Map	Rooms	Cheapest Price (Bt)
San Sabai Bungalows	51	32	750
Sand Bungalow	52	34	750
Andaman Resortel	53	45	1,500
Summer Breeze	54	22	1,200
Sand Inn	55	29	800
Patong Inn	56	37	1,000
Tropica Bungalow	57	60	800
Patong Beach	58	247	3,500
Ban Sukhothai	59	86	2,900
Crystal Bungalow	60	29	1,800
Patong Resort	61	325	2,000
M.K. Tour	62	8	500
Sawasdee Apartment	63	10	350
Smile Inn	64	18	1,200
Hyton Marine	65	129	2,500
Royal Palm Resotel	66	43	2,000
Sea Sun Sand G. H.	67	25	700
Paradise Resort	68	11	700
Holiday Inn Resort	69	272	3,600
Nanai Residence	70	20	1,200
Pharin Hill	71	22	1,050
Le Jardin	72	23	700
Golden Land Plaza	73	206	3,000
Andaman Orchid	74	93	2,400
Patong Merlin	75	386	1,400
Holiday Resort	76	105	700
Sea Pearl Beach	77	63	2,600
Seagull China City	78	36	900
Pharin Beach	79	7	2,800
Patong Swiss Hotel	80	33	700
Nilly's Marina Inn	81	16	1,200
Sea View Patong	82	141	4,200

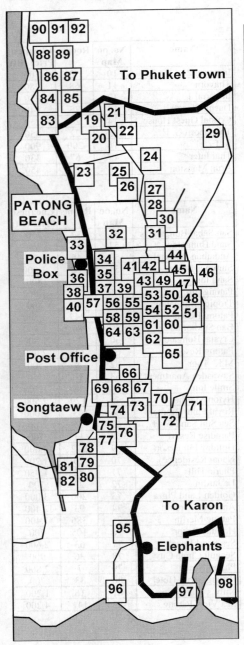

Kalim Beach

Name	No. on Map	Rooms	Cheapest Price (Bt)
Panorama Beach Club	83	60	900
Villa Atchara	84	14	2,500
Le Thong Beach	85	32	900
Novotel Phuket	86	210	4,000
Diamond Cliff Resort	87	207	5,000
Patong Lodge	88	129	800
Residence Kalim Bay	89	51	2,500
Orchid Kalim Bay	90	12	2,800
Malibu Island Club	91	30	1,700
Nerntong Resort	92	30	1,200

Nakalay Beach

Name	No. on Map	Rooms	Cheapest Price (Bt)
Thavorn Beach Village	93	199	3,200

Kathu

Name	No. on Map	Rooms	Cheapest Price (Bt)
Savary Delight	94	6	1,400

Karon Noi Beach

Name	No. on Map	Rooms	Cheapest Price (Bt)
Karon Hill	95	10	400
Meridien Phuket	96	470	5,000

Karon Beach

Name	No. on Map	Rooms	Cheapest Price (Bt)
Thepsomboon Inn	97	20	1,900
Felix Karon Swiss	98	121	4,000
Phuket Ocean Resort	99	150	1,300
Phuket Golden Sand	100	82	800
P.P. Villa	101	22	450
Islandia Travel Lodge	102	128	1,200
Melon Karon	103	27	400
Karon Guest House	104	33	450
Karon Corner Inn	105	14	400
Crystal Beach	106	120	350
My Friend Bungalow	107	45	300
South Sea Resort	108	100	3,500
Karon Villa	109	323	3,000
Sea View Bungalow	110	60	350

Karon Beach (continued)

Name	No. on Map	Rooms	Cheapest Price (Bt)
Karon Bungalow	111	24	450
Phuket Arcadia	112	468	4,500
Thavorn Palm Beach	113	210	5,700
Phuket Orchid Resort	114	100	1,800
Karon Southern	115	43	1,050
Karon View Resort	116	35	1,700
Oslo House	117	12	300
Robin House	118	10	300
Jor Guest House	119	9	300
Karon Silver Resort	120	33	600
Phuket Island View	121	81	1,800
Ruamthep Inn	122	14	700
Karon Beach Resort	123	81	4,300
Marina Cottage	124	104	2,200
Kata Tropicana	125	70	600

Kata Beach

Name	No. on Map	Rooms	Cheapest Price (Bt)
Kata Garden Resort	126	52	600
Fantasy Hill	127	22	250
Kata On Sea	128	25	300
Centre Inn	129	19	750
Peach Hill	130	126	600
Rose Inn	131	16	300
White House Inn	132	17	450
Smile Inn	133	26	600
Bougainvillaea	134	32	1,400
Club Méditerranée	135	300	3,600
Kata Beach Resort	136	267	3,500
Sea Bees Bungalow	137	10	300
Bell Bungalow	138	14	200
Sea Wind	139	32	900
Friendship Bungalow	140	23	350
Flamingo	141	11	400
Boat House Inn	142	36	4,700
Shady Bungalow	143	9	450
Kata Delight Villas	144	20	1,000
Pop Cottage	145	78	350
Cool Breeze	146	17	250

Kata Noi Beach

Name	No. on Map	Rooms	Cheapest Price (Bt)
Kata Thani	147	465	4,000
Kata Noi Riviera	148	27	350
Kata Noi Club	149	16	250

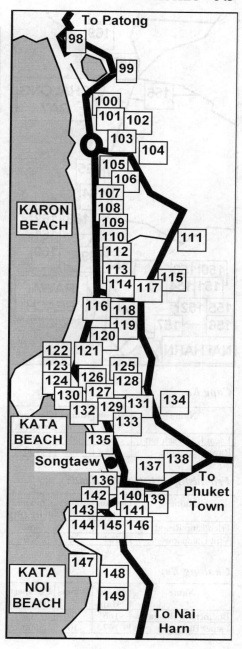

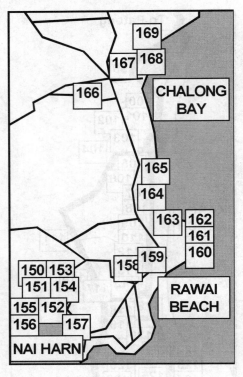

Nai Harn

Name	No. on Map	Rooms	Cheapest Price (Bt)
Nai Harn Beach Resort	150	20	600
Coconut Bungalows	151	25	600
Phuket Yacht Club	152	110	12,000
Romsai Bungalow	153	14	350
Nai Harn Villa	154	23	1,000

Ao Sane

Name	No. on Map	Rooms	Cheapest Price (Bt)
Ao Sane Bungalow	155	28	250
Jungle Beach Resort	156	44	500

Yanui Beach

Name	No. on Map	Rooms	Cheapest Price (Bt)
Yanui Bungalow	157	16	500

Rawai Beach

Name	No. on Map	Rooms	Cheapest Price (Bt)
Siam Phuket Resort	158	50	1,300
Porn Mae Bungalow	159	12	300

Cape Ka

Name	No. on Map	Rooms	Cheapest Price (Bt)
Laem Ka Beach Inn	160	20	500
Rawai Bayshore	161	40	400

Name	No. on Map	Rooms	Cheapest Price (Bt)
Phuket Island Resort	162	290	2,000

Friendship (Mittrapab) Beach

Name	No. on Map	Rooms	Cheapest Price (Bt)
Friendship Resort	163	9	450
Vijit Bungalow	164	36	500

Name	No. on Map	Rooms	Cheapest Price (Bt)
Atlas Resort	165	38	450

Chalong Bay

Name	No. on Map	Rooms	Cheapest Price (Bt)
Boomerang Bungalow	166	10	700
Father Bungalow	167	10	500

Name	No. on Map	Rooms	Cheapest Price (Bt)
Phuket Fishing Lodge	168	15	900
Bungalow Ao Chalong	169	15	250

Cape Panwa

Name	No. on Map	Rooms	Cheapest Price (Bt)
Cape Panwa	170	187	3,800
Panwa Bay Village	171	44	2,300
Siam Resort	172	24	350

Siray Island

Name	No. on Map	Rooms	Cheapest Price (Bt)
Siray Resort	173	6	400

Kamala Beach

Name	No. on Map	Rooms	Cheapest Price (Bt)
Kamala Bay Terrace	174	122	6,500
Kamala Beach Estate	175	21	6,500

Surin Beach

Name	No. on Map	Rooms	Cheapest Price (Bt)
Surin Suite Apartment	176	30	700
Pen Villa	177	19	1,700

Pansea Beach

Name	No. on Map	Rooms	Cheapest Price (Bt)
Amanburi Resort	178	40	18,000

Bang Tao Beach

Name	No. on Map	Rooms	Cheapest Price (Bt)
Bang Tao Lagoon	179	50	400
Royal Park	180	115	3,500
Laguna Beach Club	181	252	6,000
Dusit Lagoon Resort	182	226	7,000

Name	No. on Map	Rooms	Cheapest Price (Bt)
Sheraton Grande	183	322	10,000
Allamanda Phuket	184	260	6,200
Banyan Tree Phuket	185	110	14,000

Nai Ton Beach

Name	No. on Map	Rooms	Cheapest Price (Bt)
Nai Ton Villa	186	4	2,500
Nai Ton Beach Resort	187	14	14,500

Name	No. on Map	Rooms	Cheapest Price (Bt)
K.V. House	188	9	1,200

Nai Yang Beach

Name	No. on Map	Rooms	Cheapest Price (Bt)
Pearl Village	189	226	4,000
Nai Yang Ban Thai	190	8	700
Crown Nai Yang	191	96	2,800

Name	No. on Map	Rooms	Cheapest Price (Bt)
Garden Cottage	192	12	900
Sirinat National Park	193	9	350

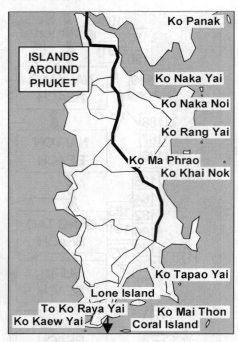

ISLANDS AROUND PHUKET

Ko Panak
Ko Naka Yai
Ko Naka Noi
Ko Rang Yai
Ko Ma Phrao
Ko Khai Nok
Ko Tapao Yai
Lone Island
To Ko Raya Yai
Ko Kaew Yai
Ko Mai Thon
Coral Island

Mai Khao Beach

Name	No. on Map	Rooms	Cheapest Price (Bt)
Phuket Camp Ground	194	10	250

Raya Yai Island

Name	Rooms	Cheapest Price (Bt)
Ban Raya	22	1,400
Jungle Bungalow	10	400
Raya Andaman Resort	7	800
Raya Executive	19	550
Raya Resort	17	800

Mai Thon Island

Name	Rooms	Cheapest Price (Bt)
Mai Thon Resort	75	8,000

Coral Island

Name	Rooms	Cheapest Price (Bt)
Coral Island Resort	63	2,200

Tapao Yai Island

Name	Rooms	Cheapest Price (Bt)
Phuket Paradise Resort	90	1,300

Kaew Yai Island

Name	Rooms	Cheapest Price (Bt)
Boat Lagoon Resort	82	2,400

Moving On

Buses operate from Phuket as follows.

Destination	Route No.	Price (Bt)				Journey Time (hrs)		Frequency	
		V.I.P.	A/C 1	A/C 2	Ord	A/C	Ord	A/C	Ord
Bangkok	63/949	690	446/457	356	254	15	17	12/day	5/day
Haad Yai	443		243		135	8	9	7/day	4/day
Krabi	438		101		56	3	4	30 mins	3/day
Nakhon Si Thammarat	440/739			155	115	7	8	2/day	Hourly
Pattalung	442		200		110	7	8	1/day	1/day
Phang-Nga	437				31		3		5/day
Ranong	430		170		91	5	6	2/day	2/day
Ko Samui	727		230			8		1/day	
Satun	734		247			8		2/day	
Sungai Golok	746		394	304		13		2/day	
Surat Thani	465		160		92	6	7	2/day	7/day
Takuapa	436				45		4		10/day
Trang	441		169	132	95	5.5	6.5	Hourly	6/day

There are also minibus services to Nakhon Si Thammarat (6 hours, Bt150, hourly) and Surat Thani (5 hours, Bt 160, hourly).

KRABI

กระบี่

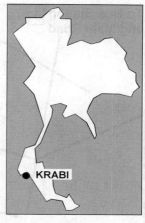

14 hrs by bus from Southern Bus Terminal
Krabi is most famous for its marine scenery and is one of the places which has become very popular over the last few years. The town of Krabi is pleasant enough, but it is the countryside nearby which is really beautiful, especially some of the islands in the proximity, and within the jurisdiction of Krabi Province.

There is no railway to Krabi. If you are travelling by train, the most convenient station to use is Trang, 131 kilometres to the south-east, from where it is a bus ride of 2½ hours. There are two overnight trains from Bangkok to Trang carrying sleeping accommodation. The express leaves Bangkok at 17:05, and terminates at Trang at 8:35. The rapid leaves Bangkok at 18:20 bound for Kantang, and arrives at Trang at 10:45. The railway station in Trang is three kilometres from the bus station. A *songtaew* is available for Bt5.

By bus, the journey from Bangkok to Krabi takes fourteen hours. The direct buses all run overnight and all except one are air-conditioned. They cost Bt655, Bt421 or Bt328, depending on the class of bus. The bus station in Krabi is on the edge of the town. *Songtaew* are available for Bt5 to the town centre.

The symbol of Krabi is the huge rock named **Khao Kanap Nam** which rises a hundred metres sheer from the water just in front of the town. Boats go there from Chao Fa Pier in just fifteen minutes and one can climb a stairway onto the rock to visit caves with stalagmites and stalactites. Human remains were found here, thought to be those of people stranded long ago by floods.

The **Hat Nopparat Thara - Ko Phi Phi National Park** includes much of the coastline here, as well as the Phi Phi Islands. Hat (Beach) Nopparat Thara is eighteen kilometres west of Krabi and is a beach several kilometres long lined with casuarina trees. There is plenty of accommodation available here. *Songtaew* run from the town to this and other nearby destinations for Bt20. **Ao Nang**, five kilometres further on (by road, although actually east of Hat Nopparat Thara), is a scenic bay with a sandy beach, and boats, canoes and diving equipment available for hire. Nearby islands can be visited from here. Accommodation is available here too.

Further east still round the coast is **Ban Laem Pho**, with its fossil beach, a 40 centimetre thick layer of pond snail fossils, an enormous number of such creatures since they are each only two centimetres long. The fossils are 40 million years old.

The **Than Bokkhorani National Park** is 45 kilometres west of Krabi on the border of Phang-Nga Province, just two kilometres from the main road (Highway 4). It contains a number of caves, some with prehistoric rock paintings. These caves, however, are not all easily accessible. Even though it is not difficult to get to the park headquarters, some of the caves can be reached only by boat.

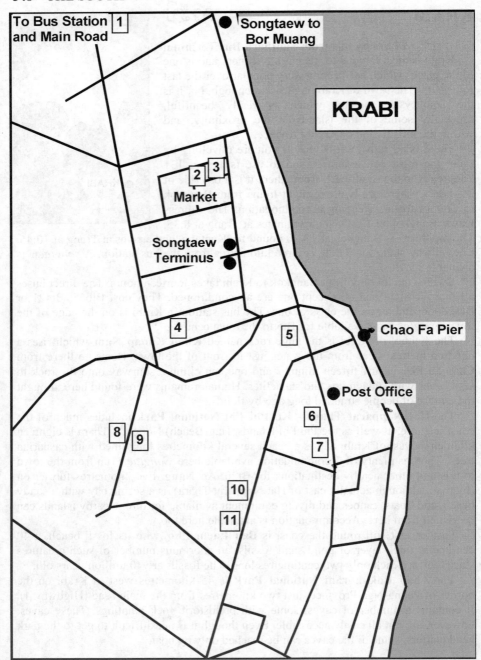

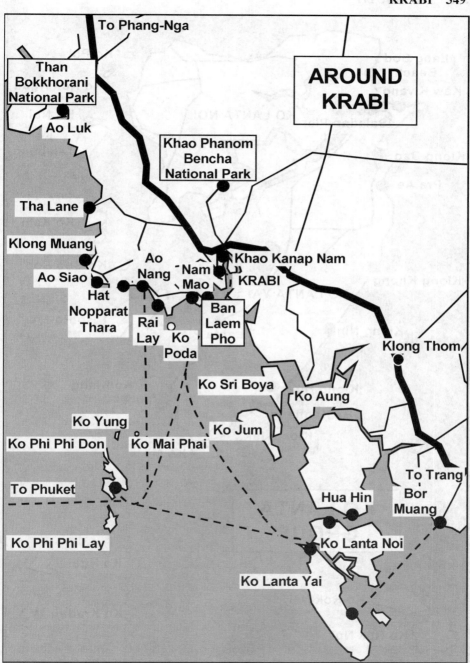

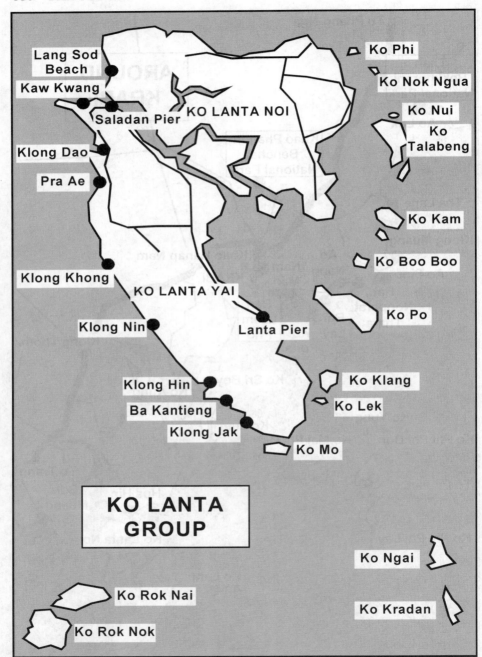

Lang Sod Beach
Kaw Kwang
Saladan Pier
KO LANTA NOI
Klong Dao
Pra Ae
Klong Khong
KO LANTA YAI
Klong Nin
Lanta Pier
Klong Hin
Ba Kantieng
Klong Jak

Ko Phi
Ko Nok Ngua
Ko Nui
Ko Talabeng
Ko Kam
Ko Boo Boo
Ko Po
Ko Klang
Ko Lek
Ko Mo

KO LANTA GROUP

Ko Ngai
Ko Rok Nai
Ko Kradan
Ko Rok Nok

The **Khao Phanom Bencha National Park** lies twenty kilometres north of Krabi. It contains forested mountains with waterfalls and caves.

East of Krabi, a distance of some 40 kilometres, is **Klong Thom** and the Wat Klong Thom Museum. The museum displays artefacts discovered during excavations here, including beads dating back 5,000 years.

Off the coast of Krabi are two groups of islands. The **Ko Lanta National Park** comprises, as one might expect, the Ko Lanta group. The two principal islands are Ko Lanta Yai and Ko Lanta Noi, rugged islands fringed with coves hiding little-used beaches. The smaller islands include several coral reef islands. Ko Lanta Yai also has 'Sea Gypsy' villages. There are two ways to reach these islands. A daily boat service leaves from Chao Fa Pier in Krabi and goes to Ko Lanta Yai, taking some 2½ hours for the voyage. Alternatively, one may take a *songtaew* to Bor Muang, 80 kilometres south-east of Krabi, for a much shorter crossing of about an hour. There is also a ferry for a very short crossing from Hua Hin to Ko Lanta Noi. Hua Hin can be reached by *songtaew* from Krabi.

However, the islands for which Krabi is most famed are the popular **Phi Phi Islands**, lying some 42 kilometres south of Krabi, and about the same

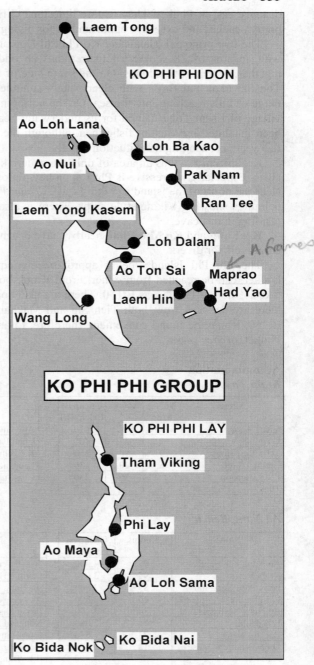

distance east of Phuket. They feature limestone cliffs rising sheer from the sea, with pretty beaches and excellent opportunities for diving among the coral reefs.

The two principal islands are Ko Phi Phi Don and Ko Phi Phi Lay. Phi Phi Don, with an area of 28 square kilometres, has an odd shape, like two islands joined together by a narrow isthmus. On the south side of this isthmus lies the beautiful Ao Ton Sai (Ton Sai Bay), with clear waters suitable for swimming and ending in a range of hills reaching into the sea. On the northern point of the island is the fishing village of Laem Tong, famed for its underwater beauty. Ko Phi Phi Don has mostly been inhabited by Muslim fishermen, although the influx of visitors during the last few years is changing that situation rapidly.

Ko Phi Phi Lay has an area of only 6.6 square kilometres. It is an island of steep cliffs. Especially impressive is Phi Lay, a bay almost totally enclosed by such cliffs. Near the north of the island is Viking Cave (*Tham Viking*), within which are old rock paintings showing Viking-style ships. There is also a large population of swallows residing in this cave.

Ko Yung and **Ko Mai Phai**, nearby, have beaches and, more especially, beautiful coral reefs for divers.

The Phi Phi Islands, being approximately equidistant from Krabi and from Phuket, can be reached from either. From Krabi, boats leave from Chao Fa Pier and take 2½ hours. The fare is Bt150. There are also boats from Ao Nang. From Phuket, there are services from both Tien Sin and Makham Bay. The fare from Phuket is Bt250. It may be found convenient, therefore, to arrive from Krabi and move on to Phuket, or *vice versa*.

Accommodation
Krabi Town

Name	No. on Map	Rooms	Cheapest Price (Bt)
Vieng Thong	3	145	470
City	2	25	400
Lek Guest House	9	10	250
Grand Tower	6	40	230
K.R. Mansion	11	36	230
Thai	5	151	230

Name	No. on Map	Rooms	Cheapest Price (Bt)
Ano Guest House	1	16	220
Chao Fa Valley	10	29	200
K.L. Guest House	4	43	120
Lee Guest House	8	12	120
Cha Guest House	7	8	100

Ao Nang Beach

Name	Rooms	Cheapest Price (Bt)
Ao Nang Pakasai Resort	77	4,000
Krabi Resort	95	3,000
Felix Phra Nang Inn	83	2,800
Lai Thai Resort	20	2,600
Ao Nang Seafront G. H.	34	2,200
B.B. Hotel	14	2,000
Ban Ao Nang	73	1,550
Dream Garden House	18	1,450
A.P. Resort	8	1,400

Name	Rooms	Cheapest Price (Bt)
Beach Terrace	40	1,200
Lavinia House	5	1,200
Ao Nang Royal Resort	16	1,000
Ao Nang Palm Hill	10	900
Peace Laguna	38	850
Nongeed House	9	800
Inter House	5	700
Ao Nang Villa	62	650
B.B. Bungalow	12	600

Ao Nang Beach (continued)

Name	Rooms	Cheapest Price (Bt)	Name	Rooms	Cheapest Price (Bt)
Krabi Sea View	20	600	Marine House	6	250
P.K. Mansion	37	600	Mountain View	7	250
Sea World	17	600	One Guest House	6	250
Cowboy Inn	12	450	Seabeer	6	250
Ao Nang Thara Lodge	40	430	Wanna's Place	17	250
Hillock Bungalow	8	400	Ya Ya Bungalow	10	250
Gift's Bungalow	19	350	Ao Nang Village	15	200
Penny's House	18	350	Green Park	20	200
Ao Nang Banlay	8	300	Jinda Guest House	6	120
Orchid Bungalow	10	300	Jungle Hut	20	120
Lotus Guest House	6	250			

Nopparat Thara Beach

Name	Rooms	Cheapest Price (Bt)	Name	Rooms	Cheapest Price (Bt)
National Park	3	350	Emerald	40	200
Blue Bayou	15	300	Bamboo	13	120
Sara Cove	10	300	Andaman Inn	37	100

Rai Lay Beach

Name	Rooms	Cheapest Price (Bt)	Name	Rooms	Cheapest Price (Bt)
Dusit Rai Avadee	100	16,000	Rai Lay Village Resort	49	350
Rai Lay Beach Club	17	3,500	Rai Lay Bay Bungalow	140	300
Sand Sea Resort	72	1,000			

Nam Mao Beach

Name	Rooms	Cheapest Price (Bt)	Name	Rooms	Cheapest Price (Bt)
Diamond Cave	20	900	Coco Bungalow	25	230
Dawn of Happiness	15	600	Ya Ya Resort	70	100
View Point Bungalow	43	350			

Poda Island

Name	Rooms	Cheapest Price (Bt)
Poda Bungalow	22	1,000

Klong Muang Beach

Name	Rooms	Cheapest Price (Bt)
Andaman Holiday Resort	79	3,900

Ao Siao Beach

Name	Rooms	Cheapest Price (Bt)
Pine Bungalow	30	200

Tha Lane Beach

Name	Rooms	Cheapest Price (Bt)
Coconut Home Group	19	500

Ao Luk

Name	Rooms	Cheapest Price (Bt)	Name	Rooms	Cheapest Price (Bt)
Bulan Anda Eco-Resort	20	700	Ao Luk Resort	20	300
A.P.	11	300	P.N. Mansion	40	300
Ao Luk Bungalow	9	300			

Laem Tong Beach (Phi Phi Don)

Name	Rooms	Cheapest Price (Bt)	Name	Rooms	Cheapest Price (Bt)
Palm Beach	80	6,500	Phi Phi Natural Resort	70	1,000
Phi Phi Coral Resort	51	1,900			

Loh Ba Kao Beach (Phi Phi Don)

Name	Rooms	Cheapest Price (Bt)
Phi Phi Island Village	83	2,000

Ran Tee Beach (Phi Phi Don)

Name	Rooms	Cheapest Price (Bt)
Liberty	7	120

Had Yao (Long Beach – Phi Phi Don)

Name	Rooms	Cheapest Price (Bt)
Phi Phi Paradise Pearl	70	350
Phi Phi Long Beach	70	120

Name	Rooms	Cheapest Price (Bt)
Viking Village	7	120

Maprao Beach (Phi Phi Don)

Name	Rooms	Cheapest Price (Bt)
Maprao Resort	24	300

Laem Hin Beach (Phi Phi Don)

Name	Rooms	Cheapest Price (Bt)	Name	Rooms	Cheapest Price (Bt)
Bay View Resort	50	1,600	Andaman Bungalow	25	400
Phi Phi Villa Resort	31	800	Andaman Beach Resort	33	350

Ton Sai Beach (Phi Phi Don)

Name	Rooms	Cheapest Price (Bt)	Name	Rooms	Cheapest Price (Bt)
Phi Phi Hotel	64	1,900	Phi Phi Don Resort	48	900
Phi Phi Cabana	203	1,600	Chao Ko Phi Phi Lodge	30	800
Ton Sai Village	50	1,400	Chong Khao Bungalow	47	350

Loh Dalam Beach (Phi Phi Don)

Name	Rooms	Cheapest Price (Bt)	Name	Rooms	Cheapest Price (Bt)
Phi Phi Princess Resort	79	1,600	Rim Khao	6	400
Phi Phi Pavilion Resort	20	1,400	Tara Inn	12	400
Phi Phi View Point	40	950	Gypsy Village 1	25	350
Home Pakklong Seaside	6	850	Phi Phi Charlie Beach	75	350
Banana House	6	700	Twin Palm Bungalow	40	350
Rimna Villa	27	500	Valentine	10	300
Mr. Jong House	4	450	Chan House	9	250
Sanya House	3	450	Gypsy Village 2	10	250
Lek's House	7	400	Orchid Guest House	15	200

Sri Boya Island

Name	Rooms	Cheapest Price (Bt)
Sri Boya Bungalow	24	200

Jum Island

Name	Rooms	Cheapest Price (Bt)
Joy Bungalow	25	200

Name	Rooms	Cheapest Price (Bt)
New Bungalow	15	200

Kaw Kwang Beach (Lanta Yai)

Name	Rooms	Cheapest Price (Bt)
Deer Neck Cabana	30	250

Name	Rooms	Cheapest Price (Bt)
Kaw Kwang Bungalow	41	100

Klong Dao Beach (Lanta Yai)

Name	Rooms	Cheapest Price (Bt)
Southern Resort	65	1,800
Lanta Sea House	28	700
Diamond Sand Inn	20	450
Lom Thalay	6	450
Ngao Mai	6	450
Lanta Island Resort	99	400

Name	Rooms	Cheapest Price (Bt)
Golden Bay Cottage	34	350
Lanta Bungalow	20	250
Lanta Villa	39	250
The Other Place	4	250
Lanta Garden Home	11	200

Pra Ae Beach (Lanta Yai)

Name	Rooms	Cheapest Price (Bt)
Lanta Long Beach	19	300
Rapala Long Beach	23	250
Lanta Coral Beach	21	200

Name	Rooms	Cheapest Price (Bt)
Lanta Marina	18	200
Lanta Palm Beach	21	200

Klong Khong Beach (Lanta Yai)

Name	Rooms	Cheapest Price (Bt)
Lanta Riviera	13	450
New Beach Bungalow	7	450
Emerald Bungalow	9	300

Name	Rooms	Cheapest Price (Bt)
Lanta's Lodge	15	250
Where Else	12	200

Klong Nin Beach (Lanta Yai)

Name	Rooms	Cheapest Price (Bt)
Lanta Nature Resort	12	350
Lanta Paradise	25	250

Name	Rooms	Cheapest Price (Bt)
Dream Team	27	150

Ba Kantieng Beach (Lanta Yai)

Name	Rooms	Cheapest Price (Bt)
Miami	22	120

Name	Rooms	Cheapest Price (Bt)
Sea Sun Bungalow	24	100

Klong Jak Beach (Lanta Yai)

Name	Rooms	Cheapest Price (Bt)
Waterfall Bay Resort	18	450

Name	Rooms	Cheapest Price (Bt)
Sun Moon Jungle Hut	10	350

Boo Boo Island

Name	Rooms	Cheapest Price (Bt)
Boo Boo Island Resort	12	400

Moving On

Principal bus services originating in Krabi are as follows.

Destination	Route No.	Price (Bt)				Journey Time (hrs)		Frequency	
		V.I.P.	A/C 1	A/C 2	Ord	A/C	Ord	A/C	Ord
Bangkok	950/983	655	421	328	234	14	16	5/day	1/day
Phuket	438		101		56	3	4	30 mins	3/day
Haad Yai	443		153			5		1/day	
Nakhon Si Thammarat	743				60		4.5		4/day
Surat Thani	482/710				70		5.5		4/day

TRANG   ตรัง

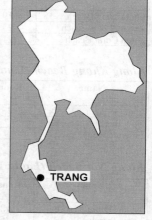

16 hrs by train from Bangkok
15 hrs by bus from Southern Bus Terminal

Trang is a much less touristed area than its neighbours to the west, but Trang too contains some attractive marine scenery and inviting beaches.

There are two overnight trains from Bangkok to Trang, both with sleeping accommodation. The express leaves Bangkok at 17:05, and terminates at Trang at 8:35. The rapid leaves Bangkok at 18:20 and arrives at Trang at 10:45. The final destination of the rapid is Kantang, a moderate sized port 21 kilometres (40 minutes) further down the line. Although it is understandable that a railway would run to a port, the strange thing is that it finishes one kilometre before the water with just a tiny station and no apparent connexion to the port area. Kantang is not a very large town. Trang is the better place to alight if travelling by train. An air-conditioned lower berth to Trang on the rapid train, as an example, would cost Bt621. If you wanted to sit up all night in a third class carriage, you could do the journey for Bt175. The railway station in Trang is three kilometres from the bus station. *Songtaew* are available anywhere in the town for Bt5.

Buses from Bangkok run directly to Trang, but only overnight and only air-conditioned buses. The cost is Bt443 for a 1st class air-conditioned bus. The journey takes approximately fifteen hours.

First there are beaches on the mainland around Kantang, stretching from **Hua Hin Beach** in the north through **Pak Meng Beach, Chang Lang Beach, San Beach, Yong Lin Beach** and **Yao Beach** to **Chao Mai Beach** in the south. On the other side of the Trang River estuary is **Sam Rarn Beach**, stretching for twenty kilometres. Accommodation is available at Pak Meng, Chang Lang, Yao and Sam Rarn, as well as in Trang and Kantang. These beaches are all accessible by *songtaew* from Trang.

Twenty kilometres east of Trang is the **Khao Chong Wildlife and Nature Education Station**, with attractive waterfalls and walking trails. Any bus going to Pattalung will take you there for Bt10.

There are 47 islands within Trang Province. Many are only barren rocks, but several are of interest to visitors. They are noted here in order from north to south.

Ko Ngai is actually part of the Ko Lanta group, which lies within the territory of Krabi. However, it is most easily reached from Trang via Pak Meng Pier, from where the journey takes one hour. The island is triangular, rising to a height of 198 metres. It has a long tranquil beach on the east side and coral reefs lying just below the surface of the sea.

Ko Rok Nai and **Ko Rok Nok** are also part of the Ko Lanta Group and lie much further out to sea. The voyage from Pak Meng takes three hours. Rok Nai has a hill rising to 208 metres and coral reefs which emerge from the sea at low tide. It has a short steep beach. Rok Nok has long white, sandy beaches and a hill 156 metres high. Talu Beach on Rok Nok, in particular, is long, wide and clean.

Ko Mah is uninhabited with a small peak rising to 40 metres. There is no regular boat service to this island, but the boats to Ko Ngai pass close.

Ko Chuak has strong currents in its vicinity, but is famed for its coral reefs, exotic fishes and deep-sea diving opportunities. It can be reached in 40 minutes from Pak Meng.

Ko Waen is another uninhabited island. It consists of a towering rock stack, impressive, but leaving no foothold for residence. However, there is a boat service from Pak Meng. It takes one hour.

Ko Mook has high cliffs inhabited by swallows, but is most famous for **Morakot Cave**. This cave can be entered only from the sea. Even then, it is accessible only by small boat at low tide. Otherwise, one must swim in. Once inside, one finds a totally enclosed cavern with steep high walls, open to the elements, with a sandy beach within. There is accommodation on the island and there are boats from both Kantang and Pak Meng. The journey takes 45 minutes.

Ko Kradan is a long thin island known for its diving opportunies to nearby coral reefs. It also has sandy beaches and suitable conditions for windsurfing.

Accommodation is available and boats operate to the island from Pak Meng taking an hour and a half.

Ko Libong is by far the largest of the islands in Trang Province. It is an island best known for bird watching. Many birds migrate here during the cool season and some almost extinct species are to be found. It is also a resort for dugong (sea cows), which feed on the abundant sea grass in the area. These harmless and defenceless creatures are fast becoming extinct, a situation which the Thai authorities will probably be unable to prevent. 40% of Libong is mountainous, with the highest peaks rising to over 300 metres. These elevated areas are the best vantage points for observing the last of the dugong. There is accommodation on the island and boat services from both Pak Meng and Yao Beach. From Pak Meng, services take two hours. From Yao Beach they take 30 to 45 minutes, depending on the landing point.

Ko Lao Liang is actually two islands close together. They are both mountainous and forested, but there is a small beach on the eastern shore. The only residents are those collecting edible birds' nests, so no accommodation is available. Boat services operate from other islands, including Ko Libong, but not from the mainland.

Ko Sugorn is a popular beach resort island, with beaches on both east and west. Boats operate from Laem (Cape) Long Star, further down the coast from Kantang, and take 45 minutes to cross.

Ko Petra is covered with dense forest and is occupied by collectors of edible birds' nests. No accommodation is available. Boat services are available from other islands, such as Sugorn, but not from the mainland.

There are two more well known diving sites at **Hin Muang** and **Hin Daeng** in this area. These two are underwater mountains covered in coral. Hin Muang is totally submerged, while Hin Daeng has just its tip protruding from the waters. They can be visited on diving expeditions arranged locally.

Here is a list of boat services available to and among the various islands.

From	To	Time Required
Pak Meng	Ko Ngai	1 hour
Pak Meng	Ko Rok	3 hours
Pak Meng	Ko Chuak	40 minutes
Pak Meng	Ko Waen	1 hour
Pak Meng	Ko Mook	45 minutes
Kantang	Ko Mook	45 minutes
Pak Meng	Ko Kradan	1 hour 30 minutes
Pak Meng	Ko Libong	2 hours
Had Yao	Ko Libong	30 – 45 minutes
Laem Yong Star	Ko Sugorn	45 minutes
Ko Ngai	Ko Mook	45 minutes
Ko Ngai	Ko Kradan	1 hour
Ko Mook	Ko Libong	1 hour 30 minutes
Ko Kradan	Ko Libong	1 hour 30 minutes
Ko Libong	Ko Lao Liang	1 hour
Ko Lao Liang	Ko Sugorn	40 minutes
Ko Lao Liang	Ko Petra	1 hour 30 minutes
Ko Sugorn	Ko Petra	1 hour

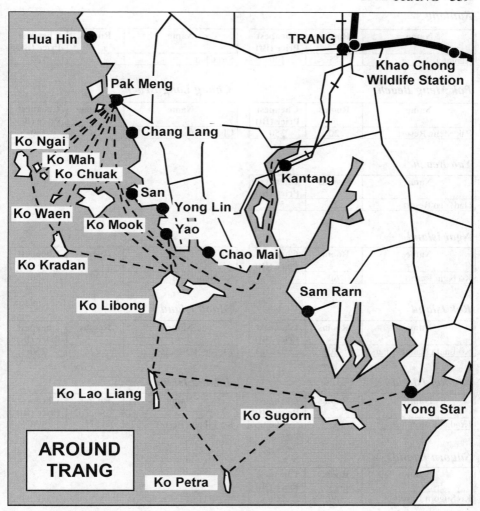

AROUND TRANG

Accommodation
Trang

Name	Rooms	Cheapest Price (Bt)
Trang	103	470
Chin Chon Iang	34	200
Plaza	28	200
Queens	148	200
Wattana	39	200
Caesar Bungalow	27	150

Name	Rooms	Cheapest Price (Bt)
Ko Teng	56	150
Thap Thiang	23	150
Nanthi	12	120
Saha Thai	30	120
Sri Trang	30	120

Kantang

Name	Rooms	Cheapest Price (Bt)
Kantang	15	120

Name	Rooms	Cheapest Price (Bt)
Siri Chai	23	120

Pak Meng Beach

Name	Rooms	Cheapest Price (Bt)
Pak Meng Resort	20	350

Chang Lang Beach

Name	Rooms	Cheapest Price (Bt)
Chang Lang Resort	20	450

Yao Beach

Name	Rooms	Cheapest Price (Bt)
Had Yao Resort	25	500

Ngai Island

Name	Rooms	Cheapest Price (Bt)
Ko Ngai Resort	60	700

Name	Rooms	Cheapest Price (Bt)
Ko Ngai Villa	38	450

Rok Island

Name	Rooms	Cheapest Price (Bt)
Ko Lanta National Park	30	250 (tent)

Mook Island

Name	Rooms	Cheapest Price (Bt)
Ko Mook Resort	22	250

Kradan Island

Name	Rooms	Cheapest Price (Bt)
Kradan Resort	43	700

Libong Island

Name	Rooms	Cheapest Price (Bt)
Ko Libong Resort	27	300

Sugorn Island

Name	Rooms	Cheapest Price (Bt)
Ko Sugorn Resort	50	700

Moving On

There are two trains back to Bangkok. The rapid departs from Kantang at 13:10, passes through Trang at 13:55 and reaches Bangkok at 7:15. The express starts from Trang at 17:10 and arrives in Bangkok at 9:05. For full details, see the timetable on page 369.

Principal bus services originating in Trang are as follows.

Destination	Route No.	Price (Bt)				Journey Time (hrs)		Frequency	
		V.I.P.	A/C 1	A/C 2	Ord	A/C	Ord	A/C	Ord
Bangkok	984	685	443	344		15	17	5/day	
Phuket	441		169	132	95	5.5	6.5	Hourly	6/day
Haad Yai	450/495				51/47		3.5 / 4		45 mins
Nakhon Si Thammarat	448				36		3		1/day
Satun					40		2.5		Hourly

SATUN

สตูล

SATUN

16 hrs by bus from Southern Bus Terminal

Satun follows on from Trang on our way down the south-western coast of Thailand. It is a relatively small province, but similar to its neighbour in having some beautiful marine scenery less familiar to visitors than that of Phuket and Krabi.

The nearest railway station is in Haad Yai, from where it takes two hours by bus. However, there are also direct buses from Bangkok. All four such buses are air-conditioned and travel by night, taking about sixteen hours over the journey. Cost ranges between Bt398 and Bt795, according to the type of bus.

Satun used to be part of the state of Kedah, now in Malaysia, and the majority of the people here are Muslims. In 1909, the British agreed to relinquish all claims to parts of Thailand, including Satun, in return for Thailand's acknowledgment that Kedah, Kelantan, Trengganu and Perlis were British territory, and so Satun became indisputably a part of Thailand.

The town of Satun is relatively small. It has some older buildings of interesting architectural style, such as Ku Den's Mansion, designed by a builder from Penang, and some of the houses on Buri Wanit Road.

Thale Ban National Park is some thirty kilometres away from Satun Town, on the Malaysian border. It contains pines and deciduous trees uncommon in this part of the country. Accommodation and a camp site (but no tents) are available. The National Park is reached by taking a bus towards Haad Yai (or a bus from Haad Yai to Satun) to a point nineteen kilometres from Satun called Khuan Satore and a *songtaew* from there. It is also possible to cross into Malaysia from here. There is a crossing point only two kilometres beyond the park.

To the west of Satun is **Pak Bara** with a four kilometre beach and a scenic view of the nearby and more distant islands. Accommodation is available. Pak Bara can be reached by *songtaew* from Satun in one hour. From Haad Yai it is not necessary to go

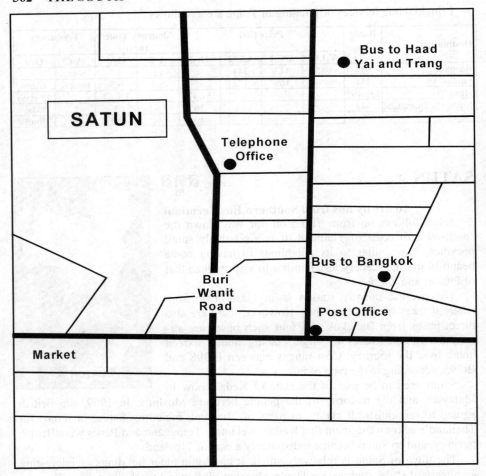

into Satun. The change from bus to *songtaew* can be made at Chalung, fifteen kilometres before Satun is reached. However, there is also a minibus running hourly from Haad Yai (Duang Chan Road) directly to Pak Bara. Travelling time for the 124 kilometre journey is two hours and cost Bt50. There is a bus service from Haad Yai to Pak Bara too, running hourly. The journey takes 2½ hours by bus and costs Bt40.

The prime attraction of Satun, though, is the **Tarutao National Park**. There are 105 islands within the territory of Satun Province and 51 of them are included in Tarutao National Park. The largest of these is Tarutao itself, 11 kilometres wide and 24 kilometres long, 40 kilometres west of Satun. It is a generally mountainous island, rising to a peak of 708 metres. Tarutao is only five kilometres from the island of Langkawi at its nearest point and obviously the two belong to the same group.

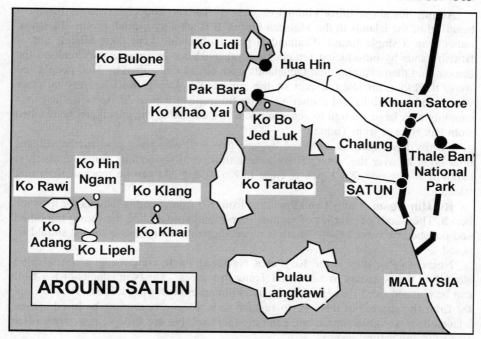

AROUND SATUN

However, due to the whims of politics, Langkawi is in Malaysia and Tarutao in Thailand. Tarutao has an interesting history, having been used previously as a maximum security detention centre for criminals and political prisoners. The remains of prison buildings, graves and roads are reminders of this former use. There are many other attractions on the island. Ao Son is a scenic bay with a long white beach. Talok Wau Beach claims to have the oldest rocks in Thailand, a type of red sandstone. Perhaps most interesting is Charakae Cave ('Crocodile Cave' – but not to worry; there are no crocodiles!). It can be entered by boat only with the rising tide, when the water flows into the cave. Within is a place where one may land, which is fortunate, because one cannot get out again until the tide turns and the water flows out once more with the ebbing tide. Tarutao is reached from Pak Bara (route mentioned above). There are two boats every day. The voyage takes three hours and costs Bt100.

Twenty kilometres west of Ko Tarutao lie **Ko Klang** and **Ko Khai**. They have sandy beaches and a multitude of wild animals, including wild boar, wild buffalo, monkeys and deer. Ko Khai has a natural stone arch which has been used as the logo for the Tarutao National Park. Turtles come here to lay their eggs. These two islands cannot be reached directly from the mainland, but boats travelling between Tarutao and Adang can usually be persuaded to drop off passengers (not too literally, one hopes).

Adang lies about thirty kilometres west of Tarutao and claims to be the most beautiful of the islands in the Malacca Straits. It is actually a small group of islands, rather than a single island. Thailand is proud of having kept these islands out of British hands by introducing settlers from other islands as soon as they realised the danger, and then claiming that the islands were already inhabited by Thai people and were, therefore, an integral part of the nation. Ko Adang itself has crystal clear waters and beautiful coral sheltering colourful tropical fishes. At Ao Son, there is a camping area large enough to accommodate 150 campers. The island can be reached from Pak Bara or from Tarutao.

Nearby **Ko Lipeh** is inhabited by 'sea gypsies', who have constructed villages built on stilts over the water. There is beautiful coral abounding, some of which is exposed at low tide. Ko Lipeh is close to Ko Adang and can be reached from that island.

Ko Hin Ngam is only two kilometres from Ko Adang and is famous for its stone beach. Thousands of pebbles of various shapes and colours line the shore, smoothed and polished by wave action. There is no accommodation on this island, it should be noted.

Nearer to Pak Bara is the **Ko Petra National Park**, comprising 22 islands and straddling the boundary of Satun and Trang Provinces. The twin islands of **Ko Lidi** can be reached from Hua Hin Beach, five kilometres west of Pak Bara. They are not far from the shore, but there is no regular service, so a boat must be hired. These islands have accommodation and camping facilities, but are little visited. They offer seclusion and natural beauty.

Another group of islands in the Ko Petra National Park is **Ko Bulone**, 22 kilometres from Pak Bara. The principal island in this group is Ko Bulone Lae. It has sandy beaches lined with casuarina trees and offers good diving, with colourful coral and exotic fishes. There is a daily boat from Pak Bara taking two hours and costing Bt100.

Ko Khao Yai ('Big Hill Island') is another in the Ko Petra National Park. From a distance, it looks like a stone castle. There is a natural stone gate, through which boats can pass. There is also a coral reef visible at low tide. Because the water is calm, pearls are cultured here and the pearl farms are open to visitors. Boats are available from Pak Bara.

Ko Bo Jed Luk ('Seven Wells Island') is just two kilometres offshore from Pak Bara. It has several attractive beaches, of which the best is probably Ka Sing Beach, a quiet beach with fine sand.

Accommodation
Satun

Name	Rooms	Cheapest Price (Bt)	Name	Rooms	Cheapest Price (Bt)
Sinkiat Thani	50	800	Satun Thani	50	250
Wang Mai	108	700	Rian Thong	20	150
Bubble	25	330	Udomsuk	38	150

Pak Bara

Name	Rooms	Cheapest Price (Bt)
Marina	8	500
Ban Suan Son	11	350

Name	Rooms	Cheapest Price (Bt)
Krajomsai	10	350
Saeng Tian	8	350

Thale Ban National Park

Name	Rooms	Cheapest Price (Bt)
National Park	13	600

Adang Island

Name	Rooms	Cheapest Price (Bt)
Adang National Park	20	150

Tarutao Island

Name	Rooms	Cheapest Price (Bt)
Tarutao National Park	5	150

Bulone Island

Name	Rooms	Cheapest Price (Bt)
Pan Sand Resort	33	750
Pangga Bay	26	600

Name	Rooms	Cheapest Price (Bt)
Ko Bulone	20	500

Bo Jed Luk Island

Name	Rooms	Cheapest Price (Bt)
Ko Bo Jed Luk	20	350

Name	Rooms	Cheapest Price (Bt)
Paknam Resort	15	230

Moving On

Principal bus services from Satun.

Destination	Route No.	Price (Bt)				Journey Time (hrs)		Frequency	
		V.I.P.	A/C 1	A/C 2	Ord	A/C	Ord	A/C	Ord
Bangkok	988	795	511/517	398		16		4/day	
Haad Yai	494			45	32	2	2	20 mins	20 mins
Haad Yai	452				32		2		Hourly
Trang					40		2.5		Hourly

POSTCARD HOME—Trang, 26th June 1980

Dear Folks,

Trang is a bigger place than I had expected and, like many Thai towns, not least Bangkok, dreadfully noisy because of the small three-wheeled, two-stroke vehicles which serve as taxis-cum-buses. Somebody should invent silencers for them. They sound like a hundred lawnmowers all going at once. The one place which I wanted to see, a public garden, I cannot get to easily. It is too far to walk twice, and too expensive to go by lawnmower.

HAAD YAI

หาดใหญ่

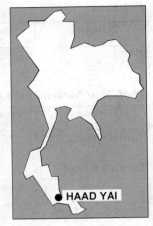

18 hrs by train from Bangkok
16 hrs by bus from Southern Bus Terminal

Haad Yai is the largest city in the south of Thailand, and yet, for historical reasons, it comes under the jurisdiction of the much smaller town of Songkhla. The city has expanded and prospered greatly in recent years due to its proximity to the Malaysian border. It is the weekend resort of Malaysians with time and energy to spare and much of its expansion has been for that reason.

There are four overnight trains from Bangkok to Haad Yai carrying sleeping accommodation, and a fifth which is a railcar with air-conditioned second class carriages, but no sleepers. The price for an air-conditioned lower berth on a rapid train is Bt655. The price for the air-conditioned railcar is Bt545 and this service covers the distance of 945 kilometres in only 13½ hours, which is faster than the quickest buses. The price for sitting up all night in a third class carriage on a rapid train is Bt189. For a little less, you can do the journey by ordinary trains in two days, stopping overnight in Chumphon (or Lang Suan). Train times are convenient for this division of the journey into two parts.

By bus it takes about sixteen hours from Bangkok to Haad Yai. Most services depart in the early evening or early morning and nearly all are air-conditioned. Fares range between Bt272 (for an ordinary bus, of which there are only three per day) and Bt760, according to the type of bus and the route followed. A typical fare is Bt520 for a 1st class air-conditioned bus.

Haad Yai is a city that one almost inevitably passes through on the way to somewhere, but which does not have many specific attractions. If you are arriving in Thailand from Malaysia, it will probably be the first Thai city encountered and will offer a good introduction to the feel of the country.

There are many hotels, but the most popular amongst budget travellers is Cathay Guest House, straight down the road from the station and at the third main corner on the right. Rooms cost Bt200 and there is a dormitory for Bt90. However, this guest house is popular enough to be full by mid-afternoon on many days, so try to arrive early if you want to stay here. There are other guest houses between the station and Cathay, but they are more expensive. There are also several noisy and dirty, but cheap, hotels of dubious repute in nearby streets, so budget accommodation can be found, but Cathay probably offers the best combination of low price and acceptable quality, which is why it is so popular.

West of Haad Yai, on the way to the airport, is a huge Reclining Buddha statue, 35 metres long. It is at **Wat Haad Yai Nai.**

To the east of the city is the **Municipal Park** which has a huge modern standing Bodhisattva statue. It can be seen from the bus on the way to Songkhla or to Nakhon Si Thammarat. The park is pleasant but a little far out of the town.

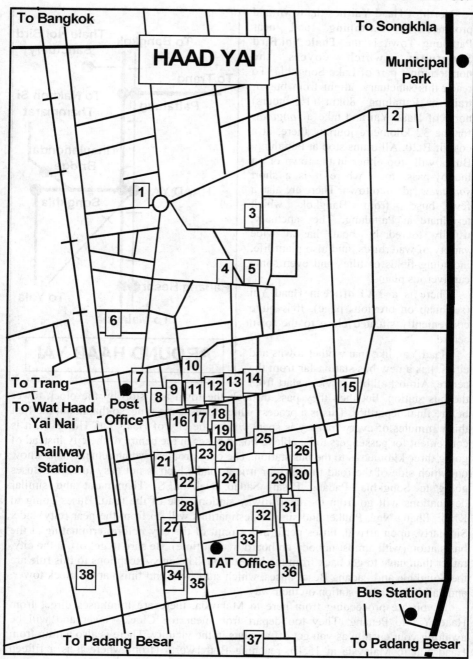

To Bangkok

To Songkhla

HAAD YAI

Municipal Park

2

To Trang

To Wat Haad Yai Nai

Post Office

1

3

4 5

6

7

8 9 10 11 12 13 14

15

16 17 18

19

20 25

21 23 26

22 24 29 30

28 31

27 32

33

34 35 36

Railway Station

TAT Office

Bus Station

38 37

To Padang Besar

To Padang Besar

North of Haad Yai lies the town and province of **Pattalung**, and near Pattalung Town is the **Thale Noi Bird Sanctuary**, which covers the northernmost part of Lake Songkhla. To reach this sanctuary, alight from bus or train in Pattalung, 80km (1½ hours) north of Haad Yai and take a *songtaew* for the 32 kilometre journey there, at a cost of Bt20. All trains stop at Pattalung. Buses will stop either in the town or on the by-pass, from where it is a short *songtaew* ride into town. There are also a few buses from Bangkok which terminate at Pattalung. The sanctuary, usually toured by boat, has a wide variety of waterbirds, and also plant life, including fields of lilies and even some carniverous plants.

There is a **TAT office** in Haad Yai (see map on previous page). It is quite conveniently situated close to the town centre.

Haad Yai, like many other towns and cities, has a new bus station far from the centre. Almost all bus services start from the bus station, but then they pass through the town and stop by the clock tower before final departure. This is a process which takes some time, so that about the first thirty minutes of every journey is spent within the city of Haad Yai. However, it is convenient for passengers to be able to board buses in the centre of the city instead of going three kilometres to the bus station. The only problem which remains is to know on which side of the road to wait, for it is a road which is not easy to cross. Buses going to Songkhla, Padang Pasar, Sadao, Nakhon Si Thammarat and similar destinations will go from the far (railway station) side of the road. Buses going to Krabi, Phang-Nga, Phuket and similar destinations will go from the near (city) side. Similarly, upon arrival, buses perform a circuit of the city before terminating at the bus station (with almost nobody on board by that time). Be sure to get off in the city, rather than have to get back from the bus station. The only exceptions to this rule are the Songkhla and Padang Besar buses, which start from and finish at the clock tower, and call in at the bus station on their way.

If you are proceeding from here to Malaysia, there are minibuses direct from Haad Yai to Penang. They too depart from near the Clock Tower and will be awaiting your custom as you get off any bus in the vicinity. There is also a train from Haad Yai to Malaysia at 15:10, reaching Butterworth (from where it is a fifteen

AROUND HAAD YAI

minute ferry ride to Penang) at 20:59 and Kuala Lumpur at 6:05, although this is an expensive option, since there is no third class accommodation on the train, which is an air-conditioned express.

Accommodation
Haad Yai

Name	No. on Map	Rooms	Cheapest Price (Bt)
Central Sukhontha	17	238	3,500
J.B.	3	430	2,000
B.P. Grand Tower	24	247	1,800
Regency	12	190	1,500
Lee Gardens Plaza	18	405	1,500
Sakura Grand View	28	230	1,100
Haad Yai Rama	35	152	1,100
Diamond Plaza	11	280	1,050
L.K. Sheraton	13	195	1,000
Siam City	8	143	950
Grand Plaza	19	216	950
Lee Gardens	34	192	850
V.L.	7	104	800
Royal	14	136	800
Kosit	27	182	800
New World	22	148	750
President	1	110	700
Haad Yai Merridian	36	50	700
Indra	20	118	655

Name	No. on Map	Rooms	Cheapest Price (Bt)
Emperor	32	108	655
Asian	9	104	650
My House	2	104	600
S.C. Heritage	4	60	600
Inter	10	210	600
Dai-ichi	30	175	600
Ambassador	31	170	600
S.K. Stardust	37	100	600
Haad Yai Merlin	26	104	550
Garden Home	29	103	500
Sakol	23	104	450
Cholatarn	25	60	450
Yee Fah Grand City	15	81	420
New Holiday	6	99	400
Maenam	33	38	400
Yong Dee	16	107	380
Lanna Inn	38	72	350
Haad Yai Green View	5	164	300
Cathay Guest House	21	28	90

Moving On

Here are the train timetables for trains back to Bangkok and for services on to Yala, Sungai Golok and Malaysia.

Type of Train	Ord	Exp *†	Exp *	Rap *†	Exp *†	Rap *†	Rap *†	Rap *†	Exp *	Exp *†	S.E. *†	S.E. *†	Ord
Classes	3	1, 2	2	1,2,3	1,2,3	1,2,3	1,2,3	1,2,3	2	1,2,3	3	1, 2	3
Sungai Golok							1100				1405		
Yala							1247	1310	1445		1550		
Kuala Lumpur ‡		2100											
Butterworth ‡		0602										1340	
Padang Besar		0835										1700	
Haad Yai	0615	0950					1445	1515	1620		1740	1810	
Nakhon Si Thammarat				1220	1400								
Kantang						1310							
Trang						1355				1710			
Surat Thani	1340		1025	1620	1737	1830	1952	2117	2030	2057	2238	2308	
Lang Suan	1539		1149	1806	1921	2009	2138	2309					0530
Chumphon	1700		1253	1927	2040	2130	2313	0047	2330	0016	0145	0220	0700
Prachuap Kiri Khan			1506	2249	0016	0118	0257	0406	0155		0443		1020
Hua Hin			1605	0033	0147	0310	0429	0531	0301	0457	0608	0645	1157
Cha-Am							0555						1224
Nakhon Pathom			1835	0320	0425	0539	0703	0812	0508	0729	0846	0920	1531
Thonburi													1650
Bangkok			2000	0505	0625	0715	0835	0945	0635	0905	1035	1100	

Type of Train	Rap *	Ord	S.E.	S.E.	Ord	Ord	Rap *	Ord	Exp *	Ord	Ord	Exp *†
Classes	1,2,3	3	1,2	1,2,3	3	3	1,2,3	3	2	3	3	1,2
Haad Yai	0630	0645	0705	0725	0802	0930	0945	1022	1217	1240	1433	1510
Pattani	0743	0808		0838	0936	1035	1100	1145	1319	1418	1620	
Yala	0815	0844		0913	1017	1103	1130	1248	1350	1505	1705	
Sungai Golok	1000	1037		1055	1235	1250		1505		1730		
Padang Besar ‡			0850									1700
Butterworth ‡			1255									2059
Kuala Lumpur ‡												0605

*Air-conditioned 2nd class available   †2nd class sleepers available
‡Malaysian Time (one hour ahead of Thai time).

Bus services from Haad Yai are as follows.

Destination	Route No.	Price (Bt)				Journey Time (hrs)		Frequency	
		V.I.P.	A/C 1	A/C 2	Ord	A/C	Ord	A/C	Ord
Bangkok	982		520		289	16	18	5/day	2/day
Bangkok	992	760	490	381	272	16	18	9/day	1/day
Chumphon	721		265	209	147	9	10	3/day	2/day
Surat Thani	490		185		103	5.5	6.5	5/day	5/day
Phuket	443		243		135	8	9	7/day	4/day
Phang-Nga	443		196			7		1/day	
Krabi	443		153			5		1/day	
Ko Samui	729		240			7		1/day	
Nakhon Si Thammarat	477/740			90	64/63	4	4.5	Hourly	Hourly
Pattalung	496/451			41/48	30/34	1.5/2	2/2.5	30 mins	30 mins
Trang	450/495				51/47		3.5/4		30 mins
Satun	494/452			45	32	2	2	20 mins	20 mins
Pak Bara	732				40		2.5		Hourly
Pattani	454/491				43/35		3/2		45 mins
Yala	470/459				49/45		2.5		40 mins
Yala	454				55		3		4/day
Narathiwat	456				71		4		3/day
Sungai Golok	714	148				5		4/day	
Padang Besar	1872			30	21	1.5	2	Hourly	10 mins
Songkhla	1871				12		1.5		7 mins
Songkhla	8296				12		1.5		40 mins
Ranote	8286				35		3		90 mins
Pak Payoon	716				23		1.5		30 mins
Ko Yai	8294				49		4		5/day

There are also minibus services to Surat Thani, Nakhon Si Thammarat and places *en route,* Pattani, Yala, Betong, Narathiwat, Sungai Golok, Pak Bara, Padang Besar, Sadao, Penang and Kuala Lumpur.

SONGKHLA   สงขลา

16 hrs by bus from Southern Bus Terminal
Songkhla is a seaside and fishing town thirty
kilometres to the east of Haad Yai, a much quieter town
than its larger neighbour. Buses run there every seven
minutes from Haad Yai, the trip taking an hour and a half,
or a little less. These buses, service number 1871, are
mostly conspicuous by their green colour and start from
the clock tower in Haad Yai.

You may well notice on many maps that there is also
a railway line running to Songkhla. Do not be deceived
by this. You can, in fact, still see remnants of the line
here and there, but there have been no trains on this line
at least since the author first visited Thailand, in 1975,
and probably for many years before that.

There are direct buses from Bangkok to Songkhla. They take sixteen hours over
the journey and run mostly at night. Cost varies between Bt514 and Bt286, according
to the type of bus.

Songkhla has a three kilometre long beach named **Samila Beach**. It has a pleasant
look with its pine trees and strategic rest pavilions, but, in fact, it is little used, and
visitors from overseas usually find this beach less appealing than those on the
southern coast of Thailand, not so far away. At the end of the beach is a copy of the
Little Mermaid statue. Out to sea are two islands known, in translation, as Cat and
Rat Islands. Round the corner is a market selling everything from fish to carpets and
beyond that **Sonn Onn Beach**, and then the colourful **fishing boat harbour**. Also
from near the Little Mermaid, one may climb to the top of **Khao Noi** and obtain a
view of the town.

There is a **National Museum** (admission Bt30, closed on Mondays and
Tuesdays), near the bus station. The building itself is of some interest. It dates from
the 1870s, built for a local merchant, and is a mixture of Southern Thai and Chinese
styles. Near the museum are the remains of the ancient **city walls**. The central market
is adjacent.

Songkhla Town is on a promontory sandwiched between the sea and the
extensive **Songkhla Lake**. The lake stretches for eighty kilometres and is twenty
kilometres across at its widest point. It is Thailand's largest body of inland water.

Recently a new highway has been constructed across this lake, connecting Haad
Yai with Ranote and using the island of Ko Yo as a stepping stone. This involved
building the **Tinsulanonda Bridge**, the longest bridge in the country (see
diagrammatic map on page 368). The total length of this concrete bridge is 2.6
kilometres, divided into two sections either side of the island.

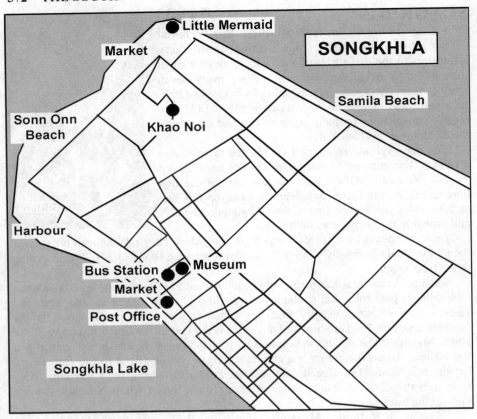

Accommodation
Songkhla

Name	Rooms	Cheapest Price (Bt)
B.P. Samila Beach	208	1,500
Pavilion Songkhla	179	800
Green World Palace	102	700
Viva	80	700
Songkhla Palace	40	600
Royal Crown	52	450
Lake Inn	79	440
Queen	22	350
Uma Guest House	15	300
Abritus Guest House	4	250
Charn	24	250
Chok Dee Inn	18	250

Name	Rooms	Cheapest Price (Bt)
Saen Sabai	20	250
Amsterdam G. H.	7	230
Suksomboon 1	28	230
Top Club	48	210
Orchid	55	210
Suksomboon 2	53	210
Narai	13	200
S.P.	6	200
Songkhla	17	200
City	67	160
Wieng Sawan	51	120

Moving On

The following principal bus services operate from Songkhla.

Destination	Route No.	Price (Bt)				Journey Time (hrs)		Frequency	
		V.I.P.	A/C 1	A/C 2	Ord	A/C	Ord	A/C	Ord
Bangkok	973		514	400	286	16	18	5/day	1/day
Haad Yai	1871				12		1.5		7 mins
Haad Yai	8296				12		1.5		40 mins
Nakhon Si Thammarat	477			85	60	3.5	4	3/day	Hourly
Surat Thani				139		6		2/day	

There are also minibus services to Pattani and Yala.

PADANG BESAR　　ปาดังเบซาร์

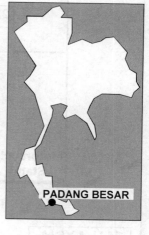

PADANG BESAR

18 hrs by train from Bangkok
17 hrs by bus from Southern Bus Terminal

Padang Besar, 66 kilometres south of Haad Yai, is the border town for the rail crossing to Malaysia. There are actually two towns, one each side of the border. Neither is very big, but, although the name is Malaysian, the Thai settlement is the larger of the two. The main road does not pass through this point, instead going via **Sadao**, a little to the east. If you catch a through road service, that is the way which you will travel. By local bus, however, the Padang Besar route is better. The Thai Padang Besar is quite a pleasant little town in which to spend a night before crossing, but the Malaysian town has little to offer in the way of accommodation, so do not make the mistake of crossing late in the day and then looking for somewhere to stay.

If you are travelling by rail, you will find that the train makes two stops. The first is at a platform in Thailand to the right of the train. Alight here if you want to stay in Thailand. It then proceeds another 500 metres to a larger station in Malaysia. Everybody gets off the train, goes through immigration and customs formalities, and gets back on board (or sometimes onto a Malaysian train waiting on the opposite platform) if continuing. About an hour is allowed in the schedule for this purpose. Remember that Malaysian time is an hour ahead of Thai time.

If you are travelling by bus, you will see the immigration checkpoint on the left of the bus immediately before entering the town of Padang Besar. Get off here if you want to proceed immediately to Malaysia. Otherwise continue into the town.

Since this is another town used by Malaysians for weekend jaunts, there is plenty of accommodation available in the Thai Padang Besar. One of the cheapest hotels is M.K. Guest House, which has the border fence as the edge of its back yard. Look out

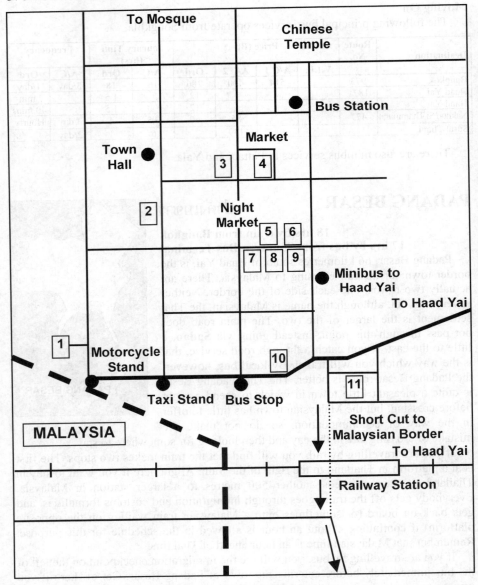

To Mosque

Chinese Temple

Bus Station

Market

Town Hall

3 4

2

Night Market

5 6

7 8 9

Minibus to Haad Yai

To Haad Yai

1 Motorcycle Stand

10

11

Taxi Stand Bus Stop

Short Cut to Malaysian Border

To Haad Yai

MALAYSIA

Railway Station

PADANG BESAR

of the window and you will be looking at Malaysia, although it does not look much different. Padang Besar also has a good night food market, and a Chinese temple which is worth a quick visit.

There used to be a border crossing point here, in this corner of the town. Unfortunately, however, it was closed a few years ago and now you must go back to the crossing which you saw as you entered the town. However, you can take a short cut to the border by going to the Thai station, crossing the railway and walking along the road which you will find on the other side (see map). It is about one kilometre to the border, and then you have to walk back another one kilometre between the Thai and Malaysian border posts, or you can accept one of the many offers of a motor-cycle taxi for Bt10. The walk is not a strenuous one, though, and, moreover, downhill in this direction. Upon entering Malaysia, most nationalities are given two months' stay, without any visa necessities. There is nothing to prevent you from turning round immediately and walking back into Thailand, if that is your intention. You will be given another month's stay in Thailand without any questions asked, unless you have done the same thing many times before, or irritated the Immigration Officer in some other way.

If you are going on to Malaysia, though, walk past the roundabout and straight ahead down the main road for about 400 metres and there will be a small bus station at the end of a short road to your right. From here express buses run to Butterworth and on to Kuala Lumpur at 9:00, 11:00 and 18:00. The fare is $M10.20 to Butterworth and $M29.90 to Kuala Lumpur. ($M1 is approximately Bt10.) If you arrive at the wrong times for the express, there is a local bus from the other side of the road (the left) every hour to Kangar for $M2.50 and from there you can easily find an express bus to take you further.

Accommodation
Padang Besar (Thailand)

Name	No. on Map	Rooms	Cheapest Price (Bt)	Name	No. on Map	Rooms	Cheapest Price (Bt)
Sathit	8	36	450	Merdeka Guest House	4	30	300
Padang Central	11	75	450	Light House	7	83	270
Berlin Guest House	9	30	390	Thai Malaysia	10	40	220
Royal Inn	5	36	350	M.K. Guest House	1	48	200
First	2	34	300	J.J.	6	54	200
Border	3	25	300				

Moving On
Trains leave Padang Besar (Thailand) for Haad Yai and Bangkok at 17:00 and for Haad Yai only at 9:00 (Thai time). Trains leave Padang Besar (Thailand) for Butterworth and Kuala Lumpur at 16:00 and for Butterworth only at 7:50 (Thai time). From Padang Besar (Malaysia), the same trains south leave at 18:00 and 9:50 (Malaysian time).

The following bus services operate from Padang Besar.

Destination	Route No.	Price (Bt)				Journey Time (hrs)		Frequency	
		V.I.P.	A/C 1	A/C 2	Ord	A/C	Ord	A/C	Ord
Bangkok	992		530			17		1/day	
Haad Yai	1872			30	21	1.5	2	Hourly	10 mins
Butterworth			$M10.20			4		3/day	
Kuala Lumpur			$M29.90			9.5		3/day	
Kangar					$M2.50		1.5		Hourly

There are also frequent minibuses and less frequent taxis to Haad Yai for Bt30.

PATTANI   ปัตตานี

18 hrs by train from Bangkok
17 hrs by bus from Southern Bus Terminal

Pattani is a medium-sized town historically famous for having had a female ruler for a long period. It still has a different feeling from most of Thailand and is, to some extent, a town of enigmas. For a start, like the remaining locations to be mentioned in this book, it is a predominantly Islamic community in a Buddhist country.

There is a railway, and a station named Pattani, but it is not really in Pattani. A *songtaew* ride of twenty kilometres is required to reach the town. For the timetable, see pages 74, 370 and 391. There are four direct services from Bangkok, three of which carry sleeping accommodation. As a guide, an air-conditioned lower berth on a rapid train costs Bt680. The journey takes eighteen hours. Sitting up all night in a third class carriage on the same train costs Bt200. The fourth train is an express air-conditioned railcar. The fare to Pattani is Bt570 and the journey is completed in fifteen hours on this train.

There are not many buses terminating in Pattani, the only services being to Haad Yai, Yala and Narathiwat. However, there is also an overnight service from Bangkok which passes through and continues to Sungai Golok. From Bangkok, the bus ride takes seventeen hours and costs Bt563 for a 1st class air-conditioned bus. Services to other towns are by minibus, which has become popular in this southern part of Thailand, or by taxi. The taxis are old, wide vehicles which cram in seven passengers and cost about the same as a minibus or air-conditioned bus.

Probably the most beautiful building in Pattani is the mosque. This is a modern construction following the town's enigmatic tradition by being named **Pattani Central Mosque** when it is anything but central. However, it is worth seeing, so try to make the expedition.

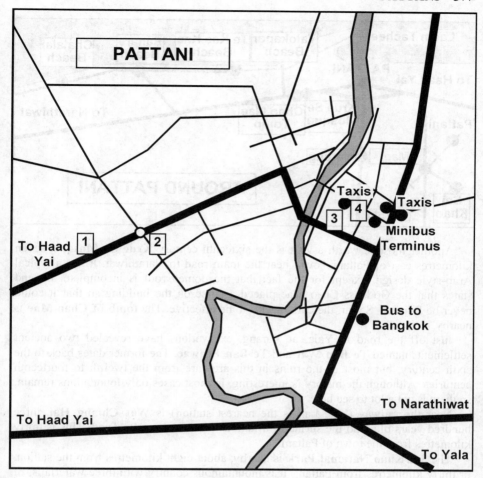

Pattani is also known for its beaches, but again they are not in the town itself. **Talokapor Beach** is 19 kilometres to the east of Pattani and is a palm-lined beach also known for its brightly painted *korlae* boats of particular local design. **Laem (Cape) Tachee** curves round from the east to the north of Pattani Town from Talokapor Beach, so that its tip is thirty kilometres from the town by road, but only five kilometres by boat.

Other beaches lie a little further east. **Te Kae Kae Beach** is about thirty kilometres east of the town and is followed by **Panare Beach** and then **Chalalai Beach**, the latter being some 45 kilometres from town. All of these beaches can be reached by *songtaew*. **Te Wasuri Beach** is further east still, at a distance of about eighty kilometres.

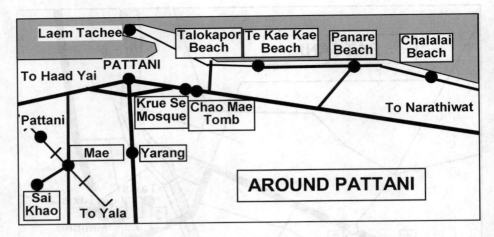

Laem Tachee

PATTANI

To Haad Yai

Talokapor Beach Te Kae Kae Beach Panare Beach Chalalai Beach

Krue Se Mosque Chao Mae Tomb

To Narathiwat

Pattani

Mae Yarang

Sai Khao To Yala

AROUND PATTANI

Another mosque worth a visit is the sixteenth century **Krue Se Mosque**, seven kilometres east of Pattani Town, near the main road to Narathiwat. It has a typical Arab-style design, except for the fact that the domed roof is incomplete. Legend states that the Goddess Chao Mae placed a curse on the building so that it could never be finished. So far, the curse seems to be effective. The **tomb of Chao Mae** is nearby.

Just off the road to Yala, at Yarang, excavations have revealed two ancient settlements named **Te Ban Wat** and **Te Ban Prawae**. The former dates back to the sixth century, but most of the ruins in this area are from the twelfth to fourteenth centuries. Although the history is interesting, in most cases only foundations remain, so there is not a lot to see here.

Near the railway (Mae Lan is the nearest station) is **Wat Chiang Hai**, three hundred years old, and the shrine of a famous monk, Luang Po Tuad. This is thirty kilometres from the town of Pattani.

The **Sai Khao National Park** is nearby, about eight kilometres from the station, or thirty kilometres from Pattani. It is mountainous country with three waterfalls, of which Sai Khao Falls is the prettiest.

Accommodation
Pattani

Name	No. on Map	Rooms	Cheapest Price (Bt)	Name	No. on Map	Rooms	Cheapest Price (Bt)
C.S. Pattani	1	50	450	Santisuk	3	28	200
My Garden	2	135	350	Palace	4	45	200

Moving On
The train timetable south is shown on page 370 and that north on page 391.

The following bus services operate.

Destination	Route No.	Price (Bt)				Journey Time (hrs)		Frequency	
		V.I.P.	A/C 1	A/C 2	Ord	A/C	Ord	A/C	Ord
Bangkok	986	875	563			17		4/day	
Sungai Golok	986		100			3		3/day	
Haad Yai	454/491				43/35		3/2		45 mins
Yala					15		1		30 mins
Narathiwat	457				35		2		30 mins

There are also minibuses to Haad Yai, Songkhla and Sungai Golok and taxis to Haad Yai, Songkhla, Yala, Narathiwat and Sungai Golok.

YALA   ยะลา

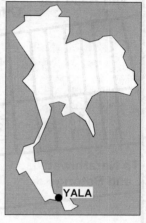

18 hrs 30 mins by train from Bangkok
17 hrs by bus from Southern Bus Terminal
The author's first experience of Yala was when the heavens suddenly opened, the rivers flooded, including the Pattani River, which flows past Yala, and, after three hours of waiting, the rumour began to circulate that my train to Sungai Golok might be able to continue no further. I paddled my way through the rising waters from Yala Station to one of the nearby hotels and was pleased that my allocated room was on the top floor. By nightfall, the water level in the lobby was up to my knees and searching for dinner was quite an adventure. This accidental experience of staying in Yala, however, created an agreeable impression of the town. It is a pleasant, wide-streeted town of a reasonable size, not too big and not too small. It is not touristy, because only the stranded traveller usually stays here, but it is not a bad place to stay if one wants to break a journey.

There is a railway station right in the town with four direct services to and from Bangkok, three of which carry sleeping accommodation. Two of the four services originate from and terminate in Yala. An air-conditioned lower berth on a rapid train from Bangkok to here costs Bt692. The journey takes 18½ hours. There is also the express air-conditioned railcar which terminates here. From Bangkok this train costs Bt582 and takes fifteen hours. If you are willing to sit up all night in a third class carriage, you can do the journey for Bt205 on one of the two rapid trains.

There are three buses a day, all air-conditioned, directly from Bangkok. One is a 'V.I.P.' bus costing Bt865. The others are 1st class buses costing Bt558.

Probably the most interesting of the features of Yala is **Wat Na Tham** (or, more officially, Wat Khuka Phimuk), which is seven kilometres away on the road to Haad

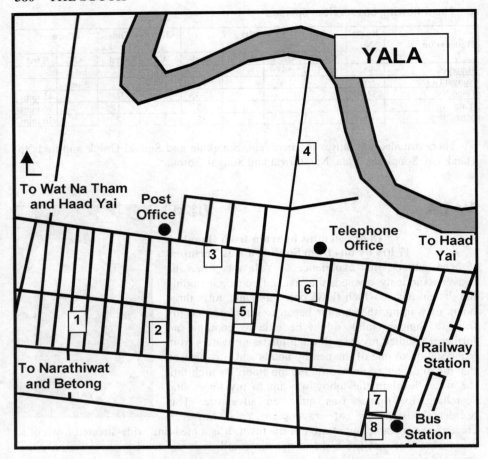

Yai. It is a cave temple with a large Reclining Buddha within. The Buddha is of
Srivichaya style and it is claimed that it dates from as long ago as 757.

Travelling south from Yala towards Betong, there are several attractions well out
of the city. First is the **Bang Lang Dam**, 58 kilometres from Yala, but twelve
kilometres off the main highway. It is in attractive scenery and popular as a picnic
spot. Accommodation is available.

A little further down the road is the **Ku Long Waterfall**, but this too is off the
main road, eight kilometres this time.

Than To Forest Park is only one kilometre off the main road, near the 57km
post, and offers mountain scenery and the pretty Than To Falls.

80 kilometres from Yala, and four kilometres off the main road, is **Ban Sakai**
('The Sakai Village'). The Sakai are an aboriginal people with a darker skin and

distinct physiological features who have somehow managed to survive into modern times. There are only about 25 households of these people who continue an existence of small-scale vegetable cultivation combined with hunting and scavanging. Their village is here and can be visited.

Buses, minibuses and taxis all run along this road to Betong. A few *songtaew* operate to the attractions on side roads, but it is best to start early in the day if you wish to reach the locations which are not on the main road.

Accommodation
Yala

Name	No. on Map	Rooms	Cheapest Price (Bt)
Yala Grand Palace	4	50	450
Park View	2	106	410
Yala Chang Lee	3	109	400
Yala Rama	7	133	315
Yala My House	1	60	310
Cola	5	42	220
Sri Yala	6	93	210
Thep Wimarn	8	87	200

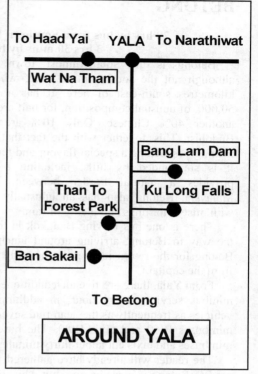

To Haad Yai YALA To Narathiwat

Wat Na Tham

Bang Lam Dam

Than To Forest Park

Ku Long Falls

Ban Sakai

To Betong

AROUND YALA

Moving On

The train timetable north is shown on page 391 and that south on page 370.
The following bus services operate.

Destination	Route No.	Price (Bt)				Journey Time (hrs)		Frequency	
		V.I.P.	A/C 1	A/C 2	Ord	A/C	Ord	A/C	Ord
Bangkok	987	865	558			17		3/day	
Haad Yai	470/459				49/45		2.5		40 mins
Pattani					15		1		30 mins
Betong	1191			50		3.5		5/day	

There are also minibuses and taxis to Haad Yai, Songkhla, Narathiwat, Sungai Golok and Betong.

POSTCARD HOME—Songkhla, 24th June 1980

Dear Folks,
    Today, I had a fruit binge. A pineapple cost me 1 baht, a fifth of the cost of posting this card. A bunch of sixteen bananas cost 3 baht and a durian cost 7 baht. Durian is the most sought-after of Asian fruits. It smells rather like public lavatories, so does not need such a lot of seeking after, in actual fact.

BETONG   เบตง

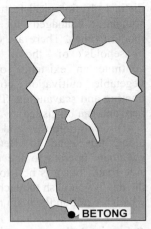

BETONG

**20 hrs by bus from Southern Bus Terminal
3 hrs 30 mins by bus from Yala**

Betong is the southernmost town in Thailand, although not the southernmost point, which is several kilometres south-east of here. It has a population of 50,000, of unusual composition, for half are Muslims and another 40% Chinese. Only 10% are typical Thai Buddhist. This, together with the fact that it is a border town, gives Betong a special flavour and feeling. Because it is surrounded by hills, including a range which provides a natural border between Thailand and Malaysia, Betong also has an unusually cool climate, with misty mornings and plenty of rain.

There is one bus leaving Bangkok in the late afternoon each day which runs all the way to Betong, arriving around lunch time of the following day and leaving Betong for the return journey in the early afternoon. This is the only direct service from the capital.

From Yala, there are five air-conditioned buses a day. These are supplemented by minibus services every hour, in addition to which two taxi companies operate vehicles as frequently as they can find seven passengers to fill them. Buses cost Bt50, minibuses Bt60 and taxis Bt80. The buses take 3½ hours for the journey, while minibuses and taxis cut about thirty minutes from that time.

The reader will already have gathered from the previous entry, on Yala, that the road to Betong is a scenic one, but why should anyone want to come to this remote southern corner of the country? For most visitors, the answer is that there is a border crossing point here. Even so, it is not a popular place at which to leave or enter Thailand. That is a pity really, for it is rather a pretty checkpoint, even if not entirely convenient. Moreover, it is actually the nearest entry point to Penang, which is the first Malaysian destination for many visitors. If you want to do something a little different, why not try crossing here?

Betong's claim to fame is that it has the **largest postbox** in the world. It was constructed in 1923, by a postman who had risen to be Postmaster of Betong and then Mayor of the town. It was used first for public announcements, but was then converted into an actual postbox, for which purpose it remains in service today. Why not send your postcards home from here? The box itself is 2.4 metres tall. With its base, it stands 3.2 metres, so the post slot is somewhat lower down than on a conventional box.

On a hill in the town is a pleasant park giving a good view. It claims to be the southernmost park in Thailand.

Thirteen kilometres away, five kilometres along the Yala road and then eight kilometres off to the left, is the **Ban Bo Nam Ron Hot Spring** where bathing is possible, but at the rather high price of Bt40 per hour.

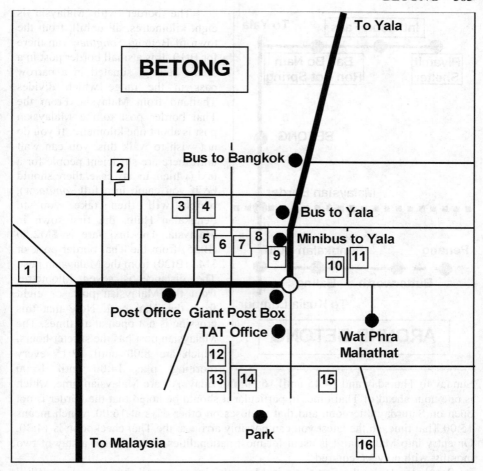

Two kilometres beyond the hot spring is **Inthason Waterfall**, and three kilometres beyond that is the interesting **Piyamit Underground Shelter**. This was constructed by members of the Communist Party of Malaya in 1976 and was for the purpose of escaping from air attacks and to store provisions. There are tunnels about one kilometre in length with a shelter large enough for 200 people. It took fifty members three months to dig it. The underground shelter can be entered.

Also in the town of Betong is a beautiful modern temple with a long name, so **Wat Phra Mahathat** will do. It is 40 metres tall, and is the largest temple in the south of Thailand, as well as claiming to be the most beautiful.

There is a small **TAT office**, with information only about Betong, right in the centre of the town, about thirty metres uphill from the post box, which, in this town, is a landmark hardly to be missed.

AROUND BETONG

The border with Malaysia is eight kilometres, all uphill, from the town of Betong. *Songtaew* run there for Bt10. It is a small border post in a scenic setting, situated in a narrow pass in the range which divides Thailand from Malaysia. From the Thai border post to the Malaysian post is about one kilometre. If you do not wish to walk this, you can wait until there are sufficient people for a taxi (which, in any case, there should be if you came in a full *songtaew*), which will then take you to Pengkalan Hulu, the first town in Malaysia. The taxi fare is $M2.50 (Bt25) from the Thai border post, or $M2 (Bt20) from the Malaysian post. The distance is seven kilometres from the Malaysian post, or eight from the Thai post. Note that this crossing is not open at all times. The Malaysian post has the stricter hours, which are 8:00 until 12:15 every morning, plus 14:00 until 16:00 Sunday to Thursday and 14:45 until 16:00 on Friday. All are Malaysian time, which is one hour ahead of Thai time. In particular it should be noted that the border is not open on Saturday afternoon and that it closes on other days at 16:00, which means 15:00 Thai time, so the latest you can possibly arrive at the Thai checkpoint is 14:30. On entry into Malaysia, it is usual for most nationalities to be granted a stay of two months, with no visa required.

Pengkalan Hulu, the first town in Malaysia, is very small, but in a pleasant hill setting. It has three hotels, so accommodation is not a problem. In fact, it is rather an attractive place to stay. If you want to go further, however, there are two buses direct to Kuala Lumpur – one in the morning and one in the evening – and there is a local bus service to Baling, which takes half an hour, from where there are buses to Butterworth taking a further hour and 45 minutes. There are also some buses direct from Pengkalan Hulu to Butterworth. Butterworth is the town on the mainland opposite the island of Penang. The ferry across to Penang takes fifteen minutes. The whole journey from the border to Penang takes about four hours.

Accommodation
Betong

Name	No. on Map	Rooms	Cheapest Price (Bt)	Name	No. on Map	Rooms	Cheapest Price (Bt)
Betong Merlin	14	190	1,000	Jacky Chan	9	16	300
Nice Resort	1	44	900	Thai	10	78	300
Grand View	16	80	700	My House	11	64	300
Penthouse Resort	4	36	700	Sri Betong	12	120	250
Cathay	7	99	650	Fa An Rung	6	38	230
Sometime Resort	2	30	600	Sri Charoen	8	40	210
Betong City Plaza	13	120	520	Sang Fa	3	38	200
Fortuna	15	72	520	Betong	5	40	150

Moving On
The following bus services operate.

Destination	Route No.	Price (Bt)				Journey Time (hrs)		Frequency	
		V.I.P.	A/C 1	A/C 2	Ord	A/C	Ord	A/C	Ord
Bangkok	987		632			20		1/day	
Yala	1191			50		3.5		5/day	

There are also the following minibus services.

Destination	Route No.	Price (Bt)				Journey Time (hrs)		Frequency	
		V.I.P.	A/C 1	A/C 2	Ord	A/C	Ord	A/C	Ord
Yala	1191		60			3		Hourly	
Haad Yai			120			5		4/day	

In addition, there are taxis to Yala for Bt80.

NARATHIWAT   นราธิวาส

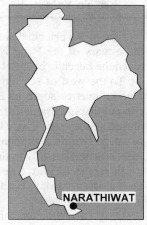

19 hrs by bus from Southern Bus Terminal
Narathiwat is another hundred kilometres east of Yala and is something of a backwater. The railway does not pass through, although there is a station only twenty kilometres away, at Ra-Ngae (Tanjung Mas is the name of the station), from where a green *songtaew* can be taken to the town at a cost of Bt10.

There are three direct buses every day from Bangkok to Narathiwat. All travel overnight and take approximately nineteen hours to cover the journey of exactly 1,200 kilometres. Cost ranges from Bt477 for the 2nd class air-conditioned bus to Bt950 for the V.I.P. bus. These services continue to Sungai Golok.

NARATHIWAT

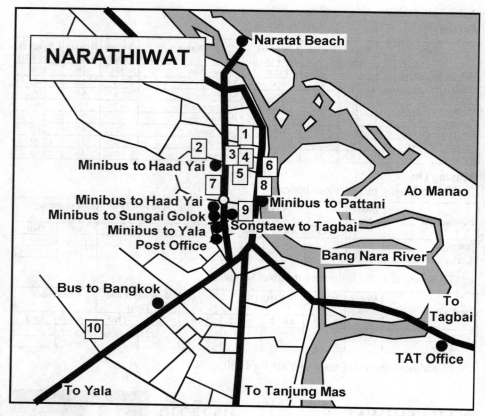

One of the principal attractions of Narathiwat is its **Naratat Beach** on an island in the estuary of the Bang Nara River. It is close to the town, but the easiest way to reach the beach is by a Bt10 *songtaew* ride.

To the west of Narathiwat, on the road from Pattani, is the village of Talomano, four kilometres south of Bacho, or about twenty kilometres from Narathiwat. This community is famous for the **Masjid Talomano** (or Masjid Vadial Hussein). The mosque combines Thai, Malay and Chinese architectural styles and is an impressive wooden building thought to have been constructed originally in 1769 (but reconstructed recently in the same style).

In Bacho is **Wat Chernkhao**, where the body of the former abbot, Luang Pho Daeng, is on display. He died in 1979, but his body has not decayed and is an object of local pilgrimage.

Only two kilometres from Bacho is the entrance to the **Budo - Sungai Padi National Park**. This park includes the most famous waterfall in the province, the Bacho Waterfall, and also the Chatwarin Waterfall, much further south.

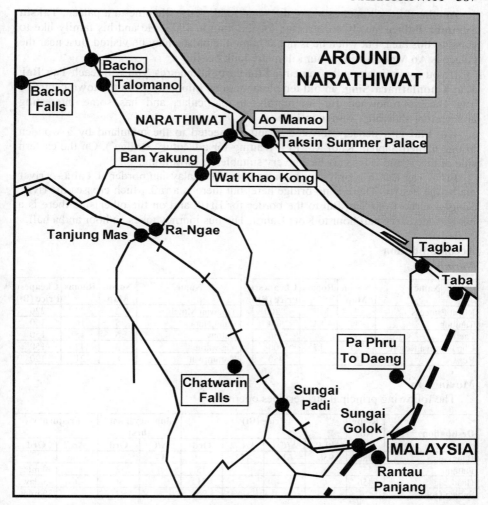

Near Narathiwat is a famous Buddha statue. This is the gold glazed **Phra Buddha Taksin Mingmongkol** at Wat Khao Kong, six kilometres out of Narathiwat, on the road to Ra-Ngae, another Bt10 *songtaew* ride. The statue is of a Sitting Buddha and is 24 metres high.

On the same road, only four kilometres from Narathiwat, is the village of **Ban Yakung**, known for its batik products.

There is a **TAT office** in Narathiwat, but in a particularly inconvenient location. It is four kilometres from the town centre, on the road to Tag Bai. It is a long way to walk, so take a Tag Bai bus or *songtaew* (both green) at a cost of Bt10.

Another four kilometres along the same road, you will come to a palace, **Taksin Summer Palace**, newly constructed for the king in 1973. He and his family like to come to this area, but when he is not at home the palace may be visited. Just near the palace is **Ao Manao** with a four kilometre long beach.

If you continue along the same road for thirty kilometres, you will reach **Tag Bai**. **Wat Chonlathara Sing**, an old temple about one kilometre from the town centre of Tag Bai, is renowned for its murals, in particular, and has some interesting architecture showing Chinese influence.

Ko Yao is a densely forested island connected to the mainland by a wooden bridge named Saphan Khoi Roi Pi ('Waiting for a Century Bridge'). On the eastern side of this island is a sandy beach very suitable for swimming.

From Tag Bai, it is only five kilometres to the Malaysian border at **Taba**. A river marks the border. There is no bridge here, but there is a raft which crosses the river. *Songtaew* run from Tag Bai to the border for Bt10, and on the other side there is a bus service every half hour to Kota Bahru. The bus journey takes an hour and a half.

Accommodation
Narathiwat

Name	No. on Map	Rooms	Cheapest Price (Bt)
Royal Princess	7	17	2,200
Tanjung	1	84	800
Pacific	9	21	350
Chao Phraya Resort	10	17	300
Rex	4	38	250

Name	No. on Map	Rooms	Cheapest Price (Bt)
Tipawan Motel	2	27	220
Bang Nara	5	16	160
Cathay	6	15	150
Yaowarat	3	42	150
Narathiwat	8	21	120

Moving On
The following principal bus services operate.

Destination	Route No.	Price (Bt)				Journey Time (hrs)		Frequency	
		V.I.P.	A/C 1	A/C 2	Ord	A/C	Ord	A/C	Ord
Bangkok	986	950	614	477		19		3/day	
Pattani	457				35		2		30 mins
Haad Yai	456				71		4		3/day
Sungai Golok					25		2		30 mins

There are also minibuses to Haad Yai, Pattani, Yala and Sungai Golok, and taxis to Haad Yai, Pattani and Yala.

POSTCARD HOME— Surat Thani, 4th July 2000

Dear Folks,

I made a mistake in my choice of bus from Nakhon Si Thammarat to here. The driver decided to have lunch after we had travelled one mile. That took him forty minutes. We drove for a while and then got passed by the next bus, so the driver slowed down and drove at a snail's pace, in the hope of getting some passengers. Then he took a fifteen minute cigarette break, and got passed by the bus after next, so more dawdling before a final mad dash to our destination.

SUNGAI GOLOK สุไหงโกลก

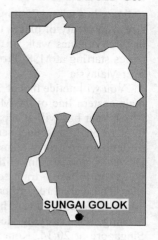

SUNGAI GOLOK

21 hrs by train from Bangkok
20 hrs by bus from Southern Bus Terminal

Sungai Golok is the end of the line for the railway and also for this book. It is the usual crossing point from south-eastern Thailand to Malaysia.

There are two trains every day from Bangkok which run this far, an express and a rapid. The express is scheduled to take 20 hours 10 mins for the 1,159 kilometre journey, and the rapid to take 21 hours 25 minutes. This is the longest single train journey wholly within Thailand. An air-conditioned lower berth on the rapid costs Bt727. Sitting in a third class carriage for the whole journey costs Bt220, which is very good value if you have the necessary endurance.

There are three buses from Bangkok which come all the way to Sungai Golok. By bus it is a journey of 1,266 kilometres, a hundred kilometres more than by train, taking approximately twenty hours. The buses are of three different types. The V.I.P. bus costs Bt1,005. The 1st class air-conditioned bus costs Bt646 and the 2nd class air-conditioned bus costs Bt503. There is also a bus service from Phuket, via Krabi and Haad Yai. This service runs twice a day, once by day and once by night, and takes thirteen hours. There are four additional buses from Haad Yai.

Sungai Golok has the interest of a border town, with markets aimed at Malaysian visitors, and, of course, a number of hotels. It is a town which continues to expand year by year, but it does not have many attractions for the visitor, seeming too busy with its commercial potential.

Nineteen kilometres out of the town, **Pa Phru To Daeng** is a huge peat swamp forest located between Sungai Golok and Tag Bai. There are *songtaew* which go there for Bt10. Pa Phru To Deng covers 80,000 acres and is the largest such forest in Thailand. It contains many rare species of fauna as well as of flora.

Crossing to Malaysia from Sungai Golok is simply a matter of walking across the bridge there. It is about one kilometre from the town. If you want to, once stamped into Malaysia you can turn round and return to Thailand immediately, but most people who simply want more time in Thailand do not come all the way to Sungai Golok when they can cross at a more convenient location, such as Padang Besar. On entry into Malaysia, most nationalities are granted a stay of two months without any necessity for a visa.

The town on the other side of the river is called Rantau Panjang. It is not a big town, seemingly consisting mostly of market areas where Thai visitors can buy things to take home. Another short walk of less than a kilometre will bring you to the bus station, from where there are services to Kota Bahru. Bus no. 29 or 29B is an air-conditioned service taking an hour and costing $M3.50 (Bt35). Bus no. 36 is an ordinary bus taking 75 minutes and costing $M3 (Bt30). Kota Bahru is a city of some size with plenty of places to stay to fit all pockets, and many such places within two or three minutes walk of the bus station, including three backpackers' hostels with prices starting at M$8. From Kota Bahru there are express bus services to places all over Malaysia.

You will notice that at Sungai Golok the railway also crosses the river. It joins the main eastern line of the Malaysian rail system (KTM) at Pasir Mas, a town through which your bus will also pass on the way to Kota Bahru. Many years ago, there used to be through passenger services on this line, but the customs authorities found it too difficult to control the smuggling of certain goods and the services were stopped. However, goods trains still use this line to travel between Thailand and Malaysia. If you want to take a train south immediately, you should alight from the bus at Pasir Mas. There are three ordinary trains: at 4:03 to Gua Musang, at 6:30 to Gemas and at 14:06 to Gua Musang. Then, probably more useful, there are two expresses in the evening, both carrying sleeping accommodation: to Kuala Lumpur at 19:09 and to Singapore at 20:14. Kota Bahru does not have a station, since there is no railway bridge to cross the river there. The nearest station to Kota Bahru is Wakaf Bahru, about twenty minutes away by bus. The northern terminus for the KTM rail system is the small station of Tumpat, one hour from Kota Bahru by bus no. 19 or 43 ($M2). Bus no. 43 goes right past the railway station, whereas no. 19 terminates at the bus station, a short walk away. A rail pass is available for the KTM rail system. It costs U.S.$55 for ten days first class or U.S.$80 for thirty days first class. These amounts are converted to and payable in Malaysian currency at the exchange rate for that week. Sleeping berths require supplements.

Accommodation
Sungai Golok

Name	No. on Map	Rooms	Cheapest Price (Bt)	Name	No. on Map	Rooms	Cheapest Price (Bt)
Grand Garden	24	118	750	Thai Eak	19	37	270
Marina	13	50	750	Amarin	16	34	250
Genting	1	234	650	Hawaii	6	26	250
Riviera	22	33	550	Marry	23	25	250
Merlin	11	96	460	My House	20	24	250
Inter Tower	17	80	450	Impress	14	29	250
Plaza	2	94	450	Valentine	5	40	230
Venice Palace	7	132	450	Taksin 2	21	49	230
City	8	40	440	Savoy	3	27	200
Parkson	15	40	430	Stellar	18	28	200
Tara Regent	12	119	400	Thani	9	52	170
Bang Kalo Kolok	4	16	380	Thai Liang	10	14	100

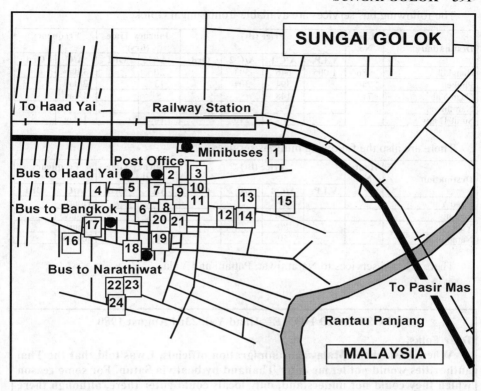

Moving On

Here is the train timetable for services from Sungai Golok, including trains which originate in Yala.

Type of Train	Ord	Ord	Ord	Rap *†	Rap *†	Ord	Exp *	Ord	Ord	S.E. *†	Ord
Classes	3	3	3	1,2,3	1,2,3	3	2	3	3	1,2,3	3
Sungai Golok		0630	0855	1100		1135		1315	1350	1405	1530
Yala	0630	0847	1132	1247	1310	1353	1445	1607	1528	1550	1740
Pattani	0705	0937	1210	1318	1341	1437	1511	1645	1555	1618	
Haad Yai	0845	1130	1345	1445	1515	1640	1620	1805	1700	1740	
Pattalung	1033	1327	1518	1600	1650	1825	1722			1857	
Nakhon Si Thammarat	1315		1740								
Surat Thani		1830		1952	2117		2030			2238	
Lang Suan				2138	2309						
Chumphon				2313	0047		2330			0145	
Prachuap Kiri Khan				0257	0406		0155			0443	
Hua Hin				0429	0531		0301			0608	
Cha-Am					0555						
Nakhon Pathom				0703	0812		0508			0846	
Bangkok				0835	0945		0635			1035	

*Air-conditioned 2nd class available   †2nd class sleepers available

The following bus services are available from Sungai Golok.

Destination	Route No.	Price (Bt)				Journey Time (hrs)		Frequency	
		V.I.P.	A/C 1	A/C 2	Ord	A/C	Ord	A/C	Ord
Bangkok	986	1,005	646	503		20		3/day	
Phuket	746		394	304		13		2/day	
Haad Yai	714		148			5		4/day	
Narathiwat					25		2		30 mins
Surat Thani				240		10		1/day	

There are also the following minibus services.

Destination	Route No.	Price (Bt)				Journey Time (hrs)		Frequency	
		V.I.P.	A/C 1	A/C 2	Ord	A/C	Ord	A/C	Ord
Haad Yai			150			4		Hourly	
Pattani			100			3.5		5/day	
Yala			80			3		Hourly	
Narathiwat			50			1		30 mins	

There are taxi services to Narathiwat, Pattani and Yala.

POSTCARD HOME—Haad Yai, 23rd August 1980

Dear Folks,

When I asked the Malaysian immigration officials, I was told that the Thai authorities would not let me enter Thailand by boat via Satun. For some reason which they could not understand, only locals could enter there, although there was no objection to people leaving Thailand and entering Malaysia by that route. I was told that I could try if I wanted to and, if sent back, should have no problem re-entering Malaysia, but I realised that it was likely to be a waste of a considerable amount of time and a certain amount of money too. I was also told that four Frenchmen had gone on the boat four days earlier and been refused entry. So, although it would have been interesting to try, on the whole I considered that the expense was not justified by the experiment. Much less excitingly, therefore, I took a bus to Kangar and then another to the border at Padang Besar. There I found the through train from Butterworth to Haad Yai waiting and got on it. The train was subject to a lot of careful scrutiny *en route,* as locals like to bring back certain goods from Malaysia. Finally, in Haad Yai, the detection experts did discover some contraband hidden under the carriage - not jewels or watches or anything so exotic, but apples and tinned fruit. How amazing! Can it really be worth smuggling such items?

INDEX

BY THE SAME AUTHOR

JAPAN FOR THE IMPOVERISHED

A travel guide to Japan designed principally for those who think that the country is just too expensive to visit. This book tells you where to find accommodation for the equivalent of U.S. $11 and how to go from Tokyo to Kyoto and back for less than $50. The book contains 800 maps, including individual maps for each of the over 300 youth hostels in Japan.

Published by Borgnan Corporation
U.S.$24.95, £14.95, ¥2,200
Available by mail from Jim Rickman
(address and e-mail at start of this book)

JAPAN FOR BUSINESSMAN
AND JOB-HUNTER

Do you want to do business in Japan? Are you looking for a job there? This guide contains over 3000 names and addresses to consult and offers a wealth of practical advice.

Published by Borgnan Corporation
U.S.$19.95, £9.95, ¥2,000
Available by mail from Jim Rickman
(address and e-mail at start of this book)